DENMARK
IN WORLD HISTORY

DENMARK
IN WORLD HISTORY

The external History of Denmark
from the Stone Age to the Middle Ages
with special reference to the Danish influence
on the English-speaking nations

VIGGO STARCKE

Former Cabinet Minister
and Member of the Danish Parliament

PHILADELPHIA
UNIVERSITY OF PENNSYLVANIA PRESS

University of Pennsylvania Press, 3933 Walnut St., Philadelphia, Pennsylvania 19104. Original title: Danmark i Verdenshistorien. Translated by Commander Frank Noel Stagg and Dr. Ingeborg Nixon, Lecturer at The University of Copenhagen and Mrs. Elmer Harp, Hanover, New Hampshire. First Danish Edition: 1946. (Ejnar Munksgaard.) Second Danish Edition: 1948. (Ejnar Munksgaard.) Published with the help of The Danish Ministry of Education, The Count Hjelmstjerne-Rosencrone Foundation, The Tuborg Foundation and A. P. Möller, Esq. © 1962 by Viggo Starcke, Copenhagen, Denmark. This work is protected by copyright; no part of it may be reproduced without written permission from the publisher.

Second Printing, 1968

8122-7374-5

Printed in the United States of America

CONTENTS

PREFACE

In early days, Denmark influenced other nations, especially the English-speaking peoples. However, since 1743, when the Danish Bishop Erik Pontoppidan wrote "Gesta et vestigia Danorum extra Daniam," no comprehensive account of this limited but important chapter of history has been published.

*

I am indebted to the following for assistance in the preparation and translation of this book:

The Danish Ministry of Education, The Count Hjelmstjerne-Rosencrone Foundation, A. P. Møller Esq., and The Tuborg Foundation;

Professor Dr. Francis P. Magoun, Jr., Cambridge, Massachusetts; Professor Dr. Arthur P. Dudden, Bryn Mawr, Pennsylvania; Rigsantikvar Professor Dr. Johannes Brøndsted, State-Antiquarian of The National Museum in Copenhagen; Rigsarkivar Dr. Svend Aakjær, Keeper of the Danish Public Records; Dr. C. O. Bøggild-Andersen, Professor of History at The University of Aarhus; Mr. Howard Trivers, Mr. Robert W. Caldwell, and Mr. Ward P. Allen of The American Embassy in Copenhagen—all of whom have helped in criticizing the manuscript.

The late Commander Frank Noel Stagg, R.N., London; Dr. Ingeborg Nixon, Lecturer at The University of Copenhagen; and Mrs. Elmer Harp, Jr., Hanover, New Hampshire—who translated the work into English.

To avoid distracting notes in the text, a bibliography and a special system of references to other authors have been placed at the end of the book.

VIGGO STARCKE

DENMARK IN WORLD HISTORY

Fifteen hundred years ago there were no Englishmen in England. There were Britons in Britain, but the westward movement that gave rise to the English-speaking nations originated in Denmark in the year 449 A.D.

Englishmen may still remember their close connection with the North, from which area came most of their language and many of their democratic ideals and institutions. Americans may still remember their close connection with England, from which they inherited most of their language and many of their democratic ideals and institutions. Most Americans, however, are unaware of the first chapter of their own history.

Three thousand years ago the Teutonic nations were living in the old realm of Denmark. The Teutonic or Germanic or Gothonic nations included such peoples as the Scandinavians, English, Franks, Frisians, Germans, Bohemians and many tribes of the turbulent Migration Period. Early Danish history, therefore, is of some importance if you wish to understand the subsequent history of the western world.

If a nerve and its functions are to be examined, its origin and ramifications are dissected and isolated, and a picture of the nerve is drawn. This, however, does not exclude the fact that other and more important nerves may exist. The same method of isolated investigation is necessary in a description of Denmark's contribution to world history. What other and more important nations have accomplished is outside the scope of such an analysis.

*

It is sometimes said of Denmark that it is only a small country and that small countries do not weigh in the scales of history as do the great countries. It is sometimes said of the Danes that they are only a small nation and that small nations do not have the same rights as large ones. Of course this is true. Denmark's share of the surface of the globe is small and the population of Denmark, compared to that of larger nations, is insignificant. But even though the Danes' numbers may be limited and their country small, in some respects they are worth noticing.

The Danes are the only Europeans who live in a land where no people other than their own ancestors have ever lived. All other nations have migrated and intermingled. The Danes, therefore, have a well-founded right to the soil of their forefathers, in which they are deeply rooted.

Map of Denmark and the surrounding parts of Scandinavia.

The Danes are the only people in Europe who have never been sub-jected to foreign rule as part of another realm. The waves have often risen high with foreign armies surging across the frontiers, threatening submersion and subjection, but when the waters ebbed and the surf retreated, the Danes were still there. Even during the German occupation, the independence and integrity of the country were formally guaranteed by the Germans. The King, the flag, the name Denmark and the inter-nal administration remained Danish despite all other encroachments.

The Danes are the only people with an unbroken line of kings throughout their history. Far back in the grey twilight of prehistoric times, kingship was the symbol of unity and continuance, bearing the luck, the honor and dignity of the nation above the struggle of conflict-ing interests, ranks and classes.

The Danish flag, called *Danebrog,* is the oldest of all existing national flags.

These traditions may belong to the past and history certainly can be a little dusty. The most important part of history is the future, and it has the great advantage over the past that we can influence it if we will. Among the forces responsible for the mighty events being enacted on the stage of world history, Denmark occupied a position not fully recognized by all. Hence, this book.

*

Most Danish historians have dealt with the story of their country in times of peace and war, and with internal conditions, influences from abroad, and the way in which these factors were transformed and ab-sorbed into the character of the people. Comparatively little has been written concerning Denmark's contribution to the evolution and fate of other nations. Its influence on other countries is also part of Denmark's history. Therefore, this attempt to write an introduction to that part of Danish history which lies outside its borders; the external, creative history.

In reading the works of foreign historians one is frequently struck by the fact that they often set a higher value on Denmark's contribution to the course of world history than do Danish historians themselves. A cer-ain caution and modesty make it difficult for most Danes to vaunt the claims of their country. Consequently, it is natural for a Dane to let others pass judgment on what his countrymen are and what they have

13

done. Therefore, this book is largely based upon the investigations of foreign scholars. As Bergthora said to her sons in Njála, "Few choose themselves the words that others say about them."

DENMARK

No race has ever shown a greater power of absorbing all the nobler charateristics of the peoples with whom they came in contact, or of infusing their own energy into them.

JOHN RICHARD GREEN.

Great events in early history, traces of which remain to this day, emanated from this low-lying land. In the ancient Danish lands the Gothonic or Teutonic tribes were born. The Gothonic peoples, whom the English call Teutons and the Germans Germanen, are closely related in race, language, law and character. They still bear traces of their origin.

In the later Stone Age, Denmark achieved the finest craftmanship in the arts of flint-chipping and pottery-making of any European peoples, and during this period the colonization of the southern Scandinavian peninsula and North Germany began.

During the Bronze Age, the ancient Danish lands reached a culture unsurpassed by any country north of the Alps, and the colonization of the middle of the Scandinavian peninsula and the Baltic lands spread along the coasts.

Throughout the Iron Age, migration after migration swept down over Europe from the countries in the North, to culminate in an imposing expansion of power during the Viking Period which led to the creation of kingdoms and the foundation of empires. Gradually, a sturdy national character developed, probably the result of two elements: the racial mixture of which the Danes were formed and the geographical nature and atmosphere of the country.

*

Ancient Denmark is one of the strangest of the European countries in shape, consisting of the peninsula of Jutland, north of the river Eider to the Skaw; the southern part of the Scandinavian peninsula with the provinces Skaane, Halland and Blekinge, and the 500 small and large islands between them. Geographically, it resembles Greece, composed as

14

it is of a peninsula and an archipelago. The cities occupy but a small part of the landscape, as Denmark is primarily farmland. The soil is fertile except for the sandy stretches of moorland in western Jutland, and the climate is one of constant change. There is a special flavor about Denmark, a smell of sea and soil, of corn and herbs, and busy hands have made things grow. No other country has such a large proportion of its surface under cultivation. She was, by the hand of Providence, destined to be a farming country.

The Swedish historian Curt Weibull says, "The stretches of land around the Sound, the Belts and the Kattegat, with their long and often deeply indented coastlines, their calm waters rich in fish, their fertile and easily cultivated fields and good grazing, provided the best conditions for a people at the Stone Age level of civilization."

The soil is the eternal bedrock of the people. In the very word 'fatherland' lies the fundamental truth that the country of one's fathers is the soil of one's fathers. The earth from which the Danes come, was cleared of stones and stumps by their ancestors who erected dwellings, farms and villages, and linked them together with roads and waterways between the harbors.

Denmark existed before the Danes, just as America existed before the Americans. Land can exist without man, but man cannot exist without land. The relationship between the living people, generation upon generation, and the inert but enduring soil is the most important element in history. In this relationship is revealed most of Denmark's national history. Strife between classes and groups of people has always been fundamentally a fight for the right to possess the soil.

In all those periods of Danish history wherein the people had access to the soil of the country, homes were built and work flourished, so that the people became strong and contented. But when the climate deteriorated or methods of agriculture failed, then men of importance, such as the King, the Church prelates, or the great landlords, seized the land and proclaimed, "You may work upon it, but we shall have the fruits of your labors!" Then it was as though the soil were washed away from beneath the people so that it did not thrive and bore but poor fruit. Then the people were in danger of sinking into serfdom and villeinage, bondage and socage, under pressure of mortgages, taxes and debt.

The sea, grey and restless, cuts deeply into the flanks of Denmark, dividing the country by sounds and belts, fjords and creeks, into islands, peninsulas and headlands. And yet the sea unites more than it divides.

Curt Weibull says, "The Sound, the Belts and Kattegat did not separate the various parts of Denmark. On the contrary, they served as great connecting highroads. These waters and the ease of communications they offered, created a means by which the Danish lands could coalesce into political unity in early historic times."

As soon as man could assemble a raft or hollow out the trunk of a tree he could cross the fjord and the sound to other islands. There he discovered something new: a fresh method of chipping an arrowhead or of tanning a deer skin, and exchanged goods and experiences. This developed initiative, a spirit of daring awakened, and with it a desire to explore new parts of the world. Trade and communications grew and flourished with the evolution of shipping.

Providence intended that Denmark should be not alone a farming country but also one of shipping and trade. Few countries in the world have as long a coastline in proportion to their land area. A coastline of 4,660 miles (7,500 km) encloses the 16,000 sq. miles (44,000 sq. km) of the Denmark of today. This is ten times longer than the circumference of a circle that would contain all of Denmark. It is equivalent to the perimeter of European Russia.

Steenstrup says: "However divided geographically, the Kingdom of Denmark, throughout history, has regarded itself as a united whole, and in respect to age, no kingdom can vie with it."

In Sweden and Germany a shaggy pelt of forest divided the various provinces until recent historic times. In Denmark there was no impenetrable division, for not until one crossed the Eider River to the south did one come to Isarnho—the Iron Forest—which formed a natural frontier between Danish Slesvig and German Holstein.

In Denmark, town after town and harbor after harbor lie along the coasts; few other lands have as many harbors in proportion to their population. Few countries have as large an import and export per capita. This testifies to the importance of the sea and of the trade upon it. The seas linked Denmark with other countries, provided trading possibilities, created a high standard of living and introduced fresh streams of culture, making existence vivid and varied.

In all the periods of history when the seas were open and trade was

16

free, the goods and riches of the world could flow in across the borders like an irrigating stream. This brought prosperity, so goods were to be found on the counter of every merchant and on the table of every housewife. But when the waters froze in severe winters, or hostile fleets blockaded the seas, there was a shortage of commodities, prices rose and poverty resulted. Exactly the same conditions occurred when the country isolated herself by means of customs barriers, tariff booms and restrictions. The level of culture dropped and the natural unity of the people dissolved.

In the affinity between the people and the open sea lies the other great fundamental component of Denmark's history. The sea united the kingdom and opened communications with other countries. In this element lies most of Denmark's external history, the history of trade and shipping, the history of colonization and war.

*

Human beings were consumers long before they learned to produce. The purpose behind the development of labor, of production, and of the creative faculty of man is to serve the consumer and raise the standard of livning. The development of trade and commerce and the exchange of goods have the task of serving both production and consumption. Trade carries the raw materials from where they are found to where they are to be used, and it transports the finished products from where they are produced to where they are to be consumed. The struggle between individuals and the wars between nations constitute a strife for consumption, production and trade, a struggle for the very basis and background of human existence: land, raw materials, and the rich resources of nature. A peaceable spirit of co-operation unites and ennobles men. A belligerent spirit divides and destroys but also strengthens the character of man. These are the main forces that run through history.

The oldest cross-bow in the world. Holmegaard. Zealand.

THE STONE AGE

Through thousands of years, from the very earliest Stone Age, the ancient Danish lands have played a completely dominating role in the north.

CURT WEIBULL.

Danish flint was an article much sought after during the many thousands of years that the Stone Age lasted and before the use of metal began. The importance of flint corresponded to that of metals today.

"Flint was the finest material for weapons and tools that Stone Age man possessed in Europe north of the Alps. The districts around the Sound, the Belts and Kattegat, are the only places in the north where flint suitable for weapons and tools is found and it enabled the people

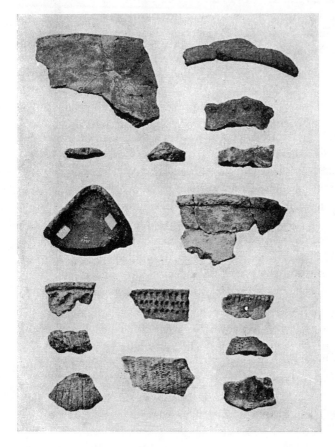

*The oldest dated
pottery
in the world.
Øgaarde.
Aamosen.
Zealand.*

18

to exploit their fertile lands, so favored by nature. Without flint it would not have been possible. Flint discoveries in the ancient Danish lands are beyond all comparison the richest, and in respect to quality, the finest, in Northern Europe, and its export was an inexhaustible source of wealth and prosperity" (Curt Weibull).

This wealth of raw material, which would today be comparable to supplies of iron, manganese and nickel in importance, was, together with the soil and the sea, the chief reason for Denmark's prominence in the Stone Age, that era during which the people and the ethnic group originated. The forces of nature to some extent assisted in forming their soul and character. A fertile soil stimulated growth and procreative power, the land became densely inhabited and there was a population surplus for migration. The keen wind and freshness of the sea induced restlessness and a desire to wander, developed energy, a faculty for organization, and the spirit of cooperation which is more easily learned at sea than ashore. The sea and salt streams formed the coastline and shaped the nation. The sharp, hard flint gave the Danes pleasure in their work and skill with their hands. Perhaps it also gave them that keen little edge of flint under their tongues.

THE HUNTING PEOPLES

Of old was the age
when Ymir lived.
No sand, no sea,
no waves there were,
no fields to be found,
no heaven high,
no grass was green:
nothingness.

(VÖLUSPÁ).

Pursuing mammoths and reindeer the first hunters came, crossing the tundra and the rivers swollen by thaw, trudging with slush oozing between their toes through thickets of bearberry and dwarf birch, while showers drifted in from the sea and heavy snow-clouds hung over the melting glaciers of the Ice Age. Denmark was in that era connected by land with England, Germany and Scandinavia, the areas which 15,000 years later would be inhabited by Teutonic tribes from Denmark.

Later, the forest crept slowly forward with new fauna, new types of game. Other tribes followed in the tracks of the earlier ones; hunters, fishermen and food-gatherers who settled by streams and lakes with fresh water where fish and fowl were to be found, where there was game in the forest, wood for the fire and flint. They fashioned their weapons and implements of reindeer antlers, of bones and flint. We find the early settlements of the Maglemosean culture (7,000–5,000 B.C.) in the marshes, along the streams and lakes. They stretch back into the early Stone Age, ten thousand or more years ago. The kitchen middens from the Ertebølle culture are found by the fjords and along the sea-shore. They are ancient rubbish heaps, and may be seven thousand years old. The Finnish scholar Nordmann says, without malice: "Denmark is the promised land of kitchen-midden culture." Love of food has indeed ever been a natural thing to the men of the north but this has not been irreconcilable with other and nobler achievements.

This Stone Age culture was a primitive one, poor perhaps, and without adornment. It has, however, left behind it something of archaeological interest, for the most ancient evidence of shipping found anywhere–a paddle–was discovered in Holmegaard Marsh. The oldest recorded boat was excavated in Aamosen on Zealand, a site which also yielded the earliest dated pottery. The oldest finds of domestic dogs have been made in Denmark, and in Holmegaard Marsh the world's most ancient cross-bow was unearthed.

Wherever these people may have come from they were partly long-headed and partly round-headed. The primitive population of Europe was long-headed, or dolichocephalic, and probably originated in the great steppes of Asia and migrated into Europe. The Nordic race is assumed to be an early variety of the Mediterranean race or a variant of the common original species, and it is closely related to Cro-Magnon and Aurignacian man. The round-headed, or brachycephalic, race came from Asia at the close of the early Stone Age.

These first hunting-people: hunters, fishermen and food-gatherers, represent in the main, mankind's original economic function. They were consumers, i e., those who take from their natural surroundings what they require.

THE MEGALITHIC PEOPLE

It is not too much to say that Europe's Stone Age reached a pinnacle in the lands around the Belts, Sound and Kattegat.

CURT WEIBULL.

The people who founded Danish agriculture came into the country about 5,000 years ago. "Suddenly and strikingly they arrive in the Danish districts, from Jutland to Skaane, bringing with them rich and magnificent forms of expression; Megalithic graves, an advanced technique of flint chipping, and pottery rich in form and ornamentation. A high degree of culture existed; its quality and degree seem almost incredible within the limits of a pure Stone Age. It is far less marked in the districts outside this area, i. e., the greater part of Norway end Sweden." This is the opinion of the Norwegian scholar Brøgger.

The new people introduced agriculture and cattle-breeding into Denmark and they built the Megalithic barrows and dolmens which form one of the most characteristic features of the Danish landscape. There are many of them. More than 23,000 barrows, dolmens and stone-passage-graves are protected by law in Denmark of today.

"Archaeological research has now brought to light the culture of the Stone Age in all the European countries, from the Mediterranean up to Northern Scandinavia and Russia. No other countries possess as many Megalithic barrows as do the ancient Danish lands. In none are stone implements found in such numbers. In none did their manufacture reach such a high stage of development, sometimes evincing considerable artistic merit. Many of the Neolithic axes and daggers found in the ancient Danish districts have been chipped to the ultimate perfection attainable in this material. At the same time early Danish pottery shows a richness of form and a dignity of ornamentation equalling or even surpassing the best European Stone Age pottery north of the Mediterranean countries.

The oldest oar in the world. Holmegaard. Zealand.

21

It is not too much to say that Europe's Stone Age reached a pinnacle in the lands around the Belts, Sound and Kattegat" (C. Weibull)

"It is difficult to understand how the magnificent flint implements on display at the National Museum in Copenhagen could have been made. The skill that has produced them is surprising when one compares them with Solutrean and Magdalenian techniques." (Klaatsch)

Weibull says, "The great number of Megalithic barrows and the richness and advanced culture of the Stone Age in the ancient Danish lands has been a source of far-reaching and fantastic conclusions on the part of German archaeologists. According to them, the Stone Age culture in Europe had its origin in the ancient Danish lands. Here was the primeval home of Europe's Aryan peoples, including the Germans. Horde after horde, during the Stone Age and the period immediately following, must have poured out of these lands. They are supposed to have subdued and civilized Europe right down to the Black Sea and the Mediterranean."

Penka, in his time, attached particular importance to the fact that the farther one travels from the ancient Danish lands, the less often does one encounter tall, fair, blue-eyed people. In Asia, which is supposed to be the original home of the Aryans, they are very rare. M. Much maintains, "The home of the primitive Indo-Germanic peoples does not lie in Asia but in northwestern Europe, and embraces the coastlands and islands in the western part of the Baltic." Erik Arup puts it thus, "Whenever that change took place, that leap in the process of development from which the Nordic white-skinned blond race with its peculiar characteristics arose, a study of its language shows its original home to have been in the districts around the Baltic and in central Europe."

Kossinna expresses himself thus, "We have now minutely considered the substantial and repeated waves of migration of Nordic hordes, more than a dozen of which, from the Megalithic Period to the end of the Stone Age and the transition to the Bronze Age, spread over the whole of Central Europe. Their paths led from Denmark to northern Germany, thence to central and southern Germany and Switzerland. From this point they moved on to the Sudeten lands, the eastern Alps, and to some extent to west and south Russia, the Balkan Peninsula and Greece, northern Italy, eastern France and southern England. Almost all these migrations of peoples originated ultimately in the densely populated, but comparatively small, native Indo-Germanic area."

Scholars are not in agreement as to the home of the Indo-Europeans

22

*Megalithic dolmen from Raklev on Refsnæs, Zealand.
Painting by Johan Thomas Lundbye 1839. Thorvaldsen's Museum.*

or Aryans and there are several indications that the German theories are exaggerated and incorrect. The general opinion is that they came from Turkestan, around the Caspian and Aral Seas, or from southern Russia. Oscar Montelius observes, "Here, in the Scandinavian north, we have the home of the Teutons (the Gothonic peoples) but not of the Indo-Germans." Yet, in his later years, Montelius was less in accordance with this theory.

Dolmens scarcely exist in Norway and Sweden. Weibull comments that within ancient Swedish territory the oldest form of Megalithic barrow, the dolmen, is non-existent. The considerable group of Megalithic graves which is located in Väster Götland in Sweden, appears to date from a later migration of Jutish Megalithic people. The greater part of Uppland, the central part of the later Sweden, was submerged during the Stone Age.

Weibull has demonstrated forcibly the enormous difference in density of population and development of culture between the ancient Swedish and ancient Danish lands. In Sweden, scattered, outlying settlements are

23

most common, and whereas stone weapons and implements have been discovered there by the hundreds, they are found in cart-loads in corresponding areas in Denmark. Among the shell-heaps of Meilgaard alone, Sehested reckoned there were about 103,400 manufactured articles. Noach maintains that in Skaane alone, three times as many flint implements have been found as in all the rest of present-day Sweden. Many of the best agricultural areas in Sweden lay at that time under water, especially along the east coast and in the districts round Lake Mälar. When one recalls that it was not until the 17th century that Skaane, Halland and Blekinge were transferred from Denmark to Sweden, it is, as Weibull says, wrong to describe the early history of those provinces as a part of Sweden's history. "It must appear the more remarkable then that this fact is almost completely ignored in the account of Sweden's earliest history." (Weibull)

The Megalithic farmers were capable people. Their pottery, as for example the bowls from Skarpsalling, Hvilshøjgaard or Hagebrogaard, is hardly surpassed in north or central Europe. They are presumably the work of the women. "No higher level, technically or artistically, was reached by the potter at any time throughout antiquity." (Brøndsted). A partial explanation lies in the fact that the Stone Age lasted longer in northern than in southern Europe, but nevertheless the results are remarkable.

Jankuhn stresses especially the geometrical designs of the ornamentations and regards these as an indication of aptitude in mathematics. He also describes the extensive Nordic colonization from the north, where the homeland of culture was Zealand and other Danish islands. There are scarcely any Megalithic graves in West Jutland; not so much because the soil there is sandy, for the Megalithic farmers with their primitive agricultural technique actually preferred light soil to heavy, but because West Jutland lacks flint, the principal requirement for the production of the stone axe.

The physical mixture of long- and round-heads was about the same as in our own time: 30 % long-heads, 23 % round-heads and 47 % medium, or mesocephalic, heads. These figures prove that there was no question of any form of racial purity (Coon).

The Megalithic people were, as noted, capable farmers and excellent craftsmen. In Barkær in Jutland there was recently excavated the oldest village known in Europe, dating from the early part of this period. The

24

Danish Stone Age pottery and mace of flint.

flintsmiths appear already to have formed a separate branch of artisans. "Denmark's flint industry raised the manufacture of flint axes to a technical and quantitative height which was probably unequalled elsewhere." (Brøgger). Danish commerce and shipping began to develop, and large quantities of raw and half-manufactured flint and finely made weapons were exported to adjacent Sweden, Norway, Holland and Germany.

"During the development of these new branches of industry, Stone Age culture in the ancient Danish lands reached its greatest heights, distinguished primarily by the independently developed, often excellent and artistically manufactured pottery, weapons and tools, as well as by the mighty chambered barrows. Everything indicates that the population of the ancient Danish lands was even then both numerous and economically prosperous and, for that period, at a high level of culture" (C. Weibull)

The agricultural people appear to have come to Denmark from the southeast, but their Megalithic burial customs, and the religion of which they must have been an expression, came as a cultural movement from

25

The Skarpsalling vessel. A most beautiful earthenware vessel from Europe's Stone Age. Himmerland. Jutland.

the west, whence it can be traced along Europe's coastal regions all the way from the Iberian Peninsula and the Mediterranean, and still farther east, to Egypt and India.

They were a people united by strong family ties, as evidenced by the dolmens and passage-graves which are family graves, graves of the kin, an expression of ancestor-worship. It is believed that a definite family resemblance can be clearly detected between the many people who have been buried in the same barrow. Their form of society appears to have been democratic and patriarchal.

"The Megalithic graves are in reality large cemeteries where the village families were buried in a common grave. They present a picture of small communities with a communal sharing of food, property and work which not even death could separate. As a fragment of the early history of communities and society, it is symbolic of what has been the strongest element in Danish history right down to our own time" (Brøgger).

The culture of the Megalithic peasants and craftsmen represents in the main the second basic element in the economic life of society, production. The creative faculty causes Nature to yield something better and more useful than that which she offers voluntarily. Production serves and increases consumption.

THE BATTLE-AXE PEOPLE

"Besonders kennzeichnend sind die schöne Waffen, nach denen man er auch das Volk der Streitaxtleute nennt."
HERBERT JANKUHN.

"The beautiful weapons, characteristic of this tribe, have led to the term Battle-Axe People."

Up through western Jutland a third people penetrated. They were the Battle-Axe People, or the Single-Grave People, one of the tribes of the so-called Corded-People. They probably came as hunters and shepherds from districts in south Russia, not from Thuringia, as German researchers have tended to believe. They came into an almost unpopulated West Jutland about 4,000 years ago. Perhaps they sought the ambercoast, perhaps they were caught in Jutland as in a seine-net. They soon dispersed and settled down, for nomadic life is not suited to islands and limited areas.

It took several centuries, however, before the new people, who were not accustomed to the open salt-water, gained a firm footing on the Danish islands where the Megalithic people remained intact for a long time. The belts and salt sea had long held back the Battle-Axe people who were afraid of wide expanses of water, and some part of the difference in character between the peoples of the islands and the Jutes is due to the fact that the Megalithic people predominated in the eastern Danish districts, while the Battle-Axe people left their imprint in the western area of Denmark.

The latter buried their dead in single graves, the body lying on its side in a squatting position, perhaps symbolizing its accustomed pos-

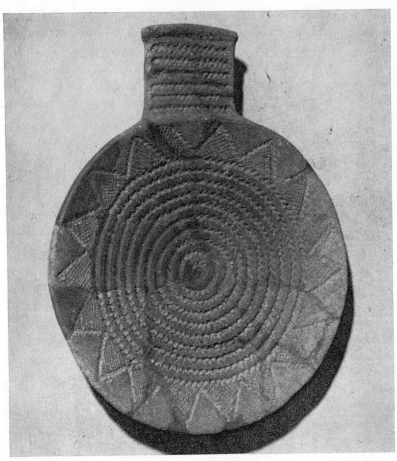

Sacrificial ladle of pottery from a dolmen in Jutland.
Grønhøj near Horsens.

ture in sleep or at meals. In the custom of using a single-grave, one is tempted to discern an individualistic feature, an expression of greater freedom of movement within the boundaries of the crowd. These were a people who travelled rapidly, and it was probably they who introduced the domestic horse to Denmark. They had organizing ability, and appear to have extended the contacts which the Megalithic people had already opened up for the trading of flint. They created a network of daring trade routes overland along the rivers which later provided the foun-

28

dation for the amber trade, the chief cause of the greatness of the Bronze Age. A passion for commerce is not unknown even in our time in west Jutland.

These people appear to have been warlike. In their finely shaped axes one can visualize the pride of the warrior in beautiful weapons. They had a sense of form, but otherwise were inept in the arts of flint-chipping and pottery.

The oldest types of battle-axes are found only in west and central Jutland, north of the Eider frontier, but in the course of the following centuries new arrivals pushed forward among the agricultural Megalithic people, intermingled with them, and became the leading force in the population, knitting the various roots together to form an entity. From the East another wave of the same people came to Skaane and south Sweden.

The Battle-Axe people represent in the main the third important element in the economic life: the trade that serves and facilitates production and brings the result to the consumer.

*

The problem as to when the Aryan, Indo-European people, or their language reached Denmark, is still unsolved. Judging by the finds in Europe, the Battle-Axe people were mainly long-headed, partly of Nordic type. Such evidence as there is, however, goes to show that there was no great physical difference between the Battle-Axe people and the Megalithic people.

The fusion of the three roots into one stem: the hunting tribes, the

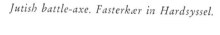

Jutish battle-axe. Fasterkær in Hardsyssel.

29

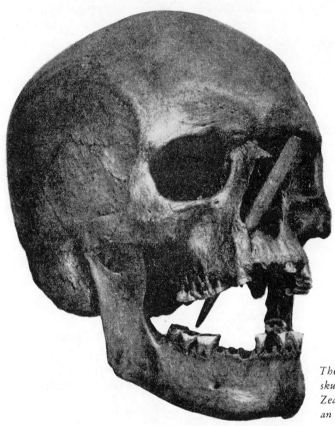

*The Stone Age
skull from Porsmose,
Zealand, pierced by
an arrow-head of bone.*

Megalithic people and the Battle-Axe people into the Danish people, is of importance in the history of Europe and of the world, for this was not only the genesis of the Danish race, but the origin of what later developed into the Teutonic peoples who were to play such a considerable role in Europe, America and other parts of the world. The type of the Danish people had been established, and since then no great immigration of ethnical importance has taken place.

The combining of races is a difficult art, but this mixture proved to possess a certain dynamic and germinative force. The interaction between

formed the core of this culture. From here the Teutons spread in the course of their later history, says Jankuhn.

The Teutonic tribes, the racial family which the Germans call Germanen, spread out from here in all directions, but as has already been said, the word Germanen has the disadvantage that at one moment it is applied to the Teutonic tribes as a whole and at another signifies only the German tribes. This may give rise to misunderstandings, intentional or unintentional.

The Teutons, or Gothonic tribes, play a special role among the Indo-Germanic peoples, for they can trace their genealogical tree furthest back. Only the Greeks and the Baltic peoples can be proved to have existed at as early a period as can the Teutons, according to Jankuhn.

The various formative tribes were neither Teutonic nor Danish until they met and intermingled. Where the tribes came from we do not know; their tracks are lost in the sands of time. But we do know where they met. It was here, in the ancient Danish lands, that the race was created. A green and gnarly tree with a short but sturdy stem grew from the entangled roots.

THE BRONZE AGE

No country in Europe north of the Alps possesses such a rich Bronze Age culture as do the ancient Danish lands. Complete agreement exists among archaeologists on this matter.

CURT WEIBULL.

Eumaeus, the herdsman of Odysseus, tells how as a boy, he was stolen from his father's palace by Phoenician merchants while they distracted the attention of the body-guard by displaying a costly necklace of gold set with amber.

That amber came from Denmark, from the land of the Hyperboreans. For thousands of years the sea had washed up amber on the coasts where it lay, shining like gold, in the sand; and as gold the ancient civilized peoples of the Mediterranean lands valued it. Schliemann found amber when he excavated the ruins of Troy, the royal graves at Mycenae and the Palace of Tyre. In the Mycenaean period it appears to have been the most costly of all adornments. Its value may have lain in its rarity, its bright color, its warmth against the skin, or in the mystical electrical forces which dwelt in its being. The Greeks called amber 'elektron'. Electricity derived its name from this source.

It can be stated with certainty that this amber came from Denmark, for it contains the same percentage of succinic acid as does Danish amber. It was fossil resin from submerged forests washed up onto the Danish coasts and there polished by the restless surf on the beaches.

But why did the Danes export golden amber? In order to import golden bronze! Denmark lacks metals, and bronze has properties which wood and bone and flint do not possess. Metallurgy came to Denmark in the form of copper and bronze. The alloy of copper and tin which we call bronze was probably discovered in Asia Minor, but it got its name from Brundisium, the Italian city now called Brindisi. There are only a few places in the world where copper and tin occur together; two of these are China and Cornwall, England. The discovery, however, was not made in either of these places. It was not from England that Denmark got her bronze, for England's copper is not contaminated with nickel as is the case with the copper in the Danish bronze, which con-

The Chariot of the Sun. Gilded bronze. Trundholm in Odsherred. Zealand.

34

tains the same percentage of nickel as the copper of Austria. Therefore, it was in that direction that trade was conducted.

In Egypt, which like Denmark is a land deficient in metals, the pure Bronze Age was in existence 3,000 years before Christ. In the north, however, evidence of bronze first appears at the end of the Stone Age, but the actual Bronze Age commences at about 1,500 B.C. Flint, however, continued to be the raw material available to the ordinary man and was used for crude work throughout the whole of the Bronze Age. Bronze was used for finer articles by the more selective portion of the population.

*

The Danish archaeologist C. J. Thomsen was the first to describe the Bronze Age. To him we also owe the celebrated division of prehistoric eras into three sections: Stone Age, Bronze Age and Iron Age—on the basis of which he founded Danish archaeology. It was the Danish archaeologist J. T. A. Worsaae who first divided the Bronze Age into Early and Late periods, the division between them being the introduction of cremation, and it was he also who described the kitchen-midden culture. Finally, it was the Danish archaeologist Sophus Müller who first described the Battle-Axe people. It is only natural that Danish scholars should have solved these important problems, for these cultures are particularly well represented in Denmark.

C. Weibull says, "The Bronze Age is a period of greatness in the history of the ancient Danish lands. A leading expert has stated that the Bronze Age in these lands attained a unique perfection such as had never before been seen nor will be again. Along with the Creto-Mycenaean era, it is one of those remarkable periods in the history of mankind when culture rose to a pinnacle and in which were established values which will endure for all time."

Denmark, then, had a material culture of such quality and extent that the southern Scandinavian lands are everywhere recognized as the seat of a central force of the first magnitude in Europe.

In the north, with the ancient Danish lands as its center, the Bronze Age flourished at its height, and it was here that it lasted longest. Denmark's 100,000 tumuli, together with the thousands of bronze articles and gold ornaments which the museums possess, are abundant proof of this. (Brøgger). "Denmark was the main center in the Bronze Age, and

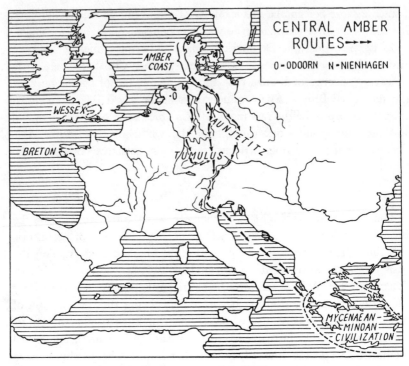

CENTRAL AMBER
ROUTES➝➝
O = ODOORN N = NIENHAGEN

AMBER
COAST

WESSEX

BRETON

AUNJETITZ

TUMULUS

MYCENAEAN =
MINOAN =
CIVILIZATION =

Central Amber Routes between Denmark and the Mediterranean.
(J. G. D. Clark)

no one who has visited the National Museum in Copenhagen needs to be reminded of the huge collection of beautiful gold and bronze objects of this period which attest by their richness and variety to the splendour of the Danish Bronze Age," says Kendrick.

The tremendous wealth of gold and bronze in a country which is itself so poor in metals, gives a strong impression of the foreign trade which was its prerequisite. "The necessary surplus which was required in order that upper class society in the Bronze Age could maintain the level which the finds demonstrate, was procured through wholesale trade. That such a trade existed is beyond all doubt. Denmark's main export was amber and furs. In return for these commodities it received the necessary metals, bronze and gold, in such quantities that Denmark, though entirely lacking in metals, could boast of a home industry in bronze and gold

36

of considerable size and of high artistic value. And these conditions continued, not for a limited period, but for the best part of a thousand years. This remarkable state of affairs calls for admiration. Their maritime trade must have been extensive, and their connections along the great rivers with central and southern Europe, stable and well organized. The people must surely have possessed initiative and energy, or they would not have succeeded in maintaining their cultural and trading connections throughout such a lengthy period, over the long distances in question and with such primitive resources at their disposal." (Brøndsted).

To this may be added the following observations. A large or small part of the price of commodities is due to transportation conditions. Denmark imported heavy goods—metals and raw materials—and as they could be brought down the rivers, transport was cheap. The exported goods, on the other hand, which had to go the expensive way up–river, were lighter goods—amber and furs. Denmark enjoyed the advantage of rivers running in a northerly direction—the Elbe, the Oder, the Vistula—which permitted low-priced imports. These factors were concurrent causes for the prosperous conditions in the Bronze Age.

When trade and transport are unrestricted, culture and material well-being are furthered. "The Bronze Age was a golden era for international trade and intercourse," says Sune Lindqvist. One gets an impression of the importance of shipping and trade by examining the petroglyphs, the 'helleristninger', the ancient rock-carvings of the Bronze Age, mainly found in Bohuslen, Østfold and Öster Götland. They are utilitarian religious documents, but give a picture of the significance of shipping, trade, and the conveyance of goods, which no doubt in winter-time was by means of sledge—a fact which the ancient rock engravings seem to prove.

In the early Bronze Age it was Jutland that was richest in gold. The center of trade lay in the harbors of the west coast such as Esbjerg, along the ancient Jutish military way, 'Hær-Vejen', and in the districts of the Limfjord, the long narrow fiord and trading route which breaks right through Jutland and connects the North Sea with the Kattegat. In the later Bronze Age the center shifted to the islands and Skaane, in conformity with a change of river trade from the Elbe to the Oder and Vistula. It was only eight miles from the Elbe's tributary to the Danube, whence the route went over the Brenner Pass and St. Gothard into northern Italy. It is unlikely that Denmark had direct communications with the Creto-Grecian lands.

River trading along European waterways was almost certainly conducted in the same manner as obtains on the present-day Congo River. The transport of goods in the well organized period during the peaceful and stable conditions of the Bronze Age was effected more rapidly than is generally believed. Diodorus tells us that tin from Britain, in Caesar's time, was carried in skin boats across the English Channel and thence on horseback along the river valleys to the Mediterranean. This transport took one month. Montelius therefore considers that in the Bronze Age we must count in months instead of years and centuries.

*

The structure of society itself was, insofar as one can judge, based on a farming and commercial aristocracy. The descendants of the Battle-Axe people probably formed the upper class, while the farmers, artisans and sailors of the Megalithic people accounted for the lower classes. It is scarcely likely, however, that there were great social distinctions among the people. Brøndsted considers that the obvious vigor and initiative of the upper class derives from that race of European immigrants known as the Battle-Axe people. He attributes the industry of the lower classes, their sense of form and line, and their familiarity with the sea and vessels, to the qualities they inherited from the Megalithic folk of the Stone Age. Concerning the actual culture, he says, "Everywhere there was an independent Nordic taste and style, and an independent Nordic craftsmanship in bronze. This partook of foreign influences, but was selective in reproduction and was applied along definite and purposeful lines. There is much in this that is worthy of admiration, and Nordic culture in these respects takes a high place among European countries, not merely in this first period of greatness, but throughout the whole of the Bronze Age. It was most certainly an upper class culture. This also applies to British culture today, and with all the natural reservations which are essential when that type of comparison is made, it can be pointed out that England's present material culture and wealth are in the main also based on trade, whereas agriculture has retreated into the background."

Apropos of England, it is strange that the culture of the Bronze Age, in a country rich in copper and tin deposits, did not attain a comparable

38

*The bronze helmets from Viksø. Zealand. In the background a bronze
statuette from Grevensvænge, Zealand, with a similar helmet.*

degree of development. There appear, however, to have been special reasons for this. According to Professor Brøgger, it was because the metal trade was controlled by a monopoly, a theory supported by the fact that tin and copper were never found together in the large depots where metals were collected. From this it is deduced that the mine owners released only small quantities of tin for the home market and thus prevented the development of a richer bronze industry.

In Jutland, the oak coffin finds from the early Bronze Age are, as Brøgger says, some of the most remarkable relics of ancient times that have ever been discovered in Europe. The tannic acid of the oak coffins, together with the hardpan of the heath soil, have preserved the skin and hair of the dead. Their clothing, the graceful, fringed skirts of the women, and the cloaks and skirts of the men, make these people seem almost to emerge from the 3,000-year-old tumuli in the full vigor of life. These Danish Bronze Age garments are the oldest everyday clothing preserved in the world. Incidentally, Brøgger considers that the Danish male clothing of the Bronze Age resembles the Scottish national dress.

The beautiful spiral ornamentation,—whatever it may have symbolized—the fine swords, the strange lur-horns and magnificent ornaments all speak of happiness, greatness and wealth. The curve of the celebrated lur-horns is music in itself. They can still be blown, and Strasser says that the tones themselves are of a purity and richness, harmony and majesty that have never been surpassed. They must signify that Nordic religious poetry and music already existed in the Bronze Age, and perhaps it was polyphonous, because the lurs are found in pairs, symmetrical in shape, and tuned together.

At all events, the first trace of musical harmony in the history of music is found among the Danes in Northumberland, according to Giraldus Cambrensis, who describes their part-songs about 1180 A.D. It is not certain that the song mentioned by Widsith was polyphonous, but it was a duet. Widsith says of his song in Eadgils' hall, "When Scilling and I with clear voices raised the song before our noble lord, loud to the harp the words made melody—then many cunning and great of mind said they had never heard a better song."

The spiral in ornamentation, undulating and resurgent, as though portraying the transmigration of the soul, is one of the most characteristic features of Danish Bronze Age art. "Early in the Bronze Age such

40

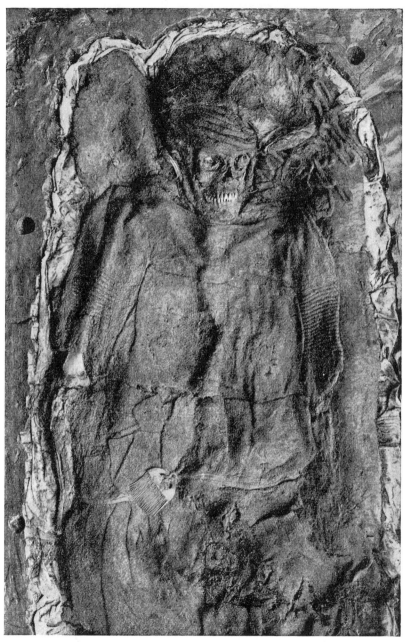

*The 3000 year old Bronze Age girl from Skrydstrup
in her oak coffin. Jutland.*

ornaments as the spiral motif came from northern Italian culture groups of late Mycenaean character, and after this the Danish Bronze Age developed quite independently to a level without parallel in any other European Bronze Age culture" (Brøgger).

Brøndsted says, "The Nordic sphere of culture produced at this time its own decorative art, an harmonious ornamental style with the spiral as its main motif. There is occasionally something severely academic about it, and one realizes that such a disciplined style must have had as its prerequisite, strong inner sources of strength within the people who created it.

"Now arose the first independent Nordic art in metal, which, after having gone through a period of apprenticeship in foreign schools, equipped the noble warrior with weapons so characteristic and pure in design, so strong and yet so varied that they were almost unequalled anywhere else in contemporary Europe. The Nordic swords, with their blades swelling lightly like a long narrow leaf around a strong midrib, and with their heavily cast hilts, are unique productions so stamped with the style of their homeland that they cannot be confused with articles manufactured in any other European sphere of culture" (Brøndsted).

According to Weibull, the rich culture which flourished in the ancient Danish lands has never been paralleled in the ancient Swedish districts. The Bronze Age—which lasted approximately 1,200 years—has left behind it in Sweden about 1,200 small bronze axes, spearheads, and other objects. The total quantity there corresponds to the yield of only three or four finds in Denmark.

From Jutland alone we have, at a low estimate, more than 20,000 bronzes, while according to Brøgger and Gjessing, we have from the whole of the vast area of Norway only 458, many of which were imported from Denmark.

*

From the middle of the Bronze Age period, colonists wandered up along the coasts and over the sea to Scandinavia and north Germany. Their shipping and trade probably opened the way for them. In busy periods their ships must have lain as close together as one sees the masses of ships depicted in the ancient rock engravings. Brøgger goes as far as to term the Bronze Age 'the great millennium of shipping'.

In northern Scandinavia the advancing settlers and trappers met the

42

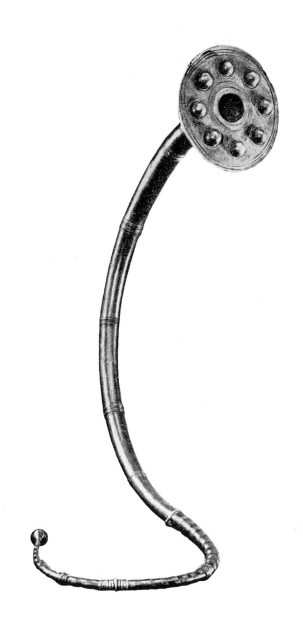

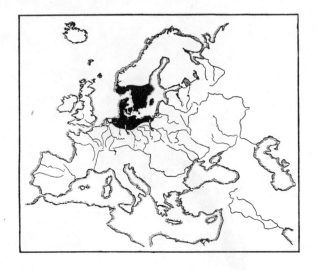

Territory of the Teutonic peoples in the later Bronze Age. (Herbert Jankuhn & Ernst Sprockhoff).

hunting people of the ancient Komsa-Culture, probably Lapps and Finns. Brøndsted says, "During the early Bronze Age the Nordic sphere of culture recognizable by the common form and type of ancient articles, embraces Denmark with Holstein, south Norway, south and central Sweden, together with those areas of the German North Sea and Baltic lands which, owing to the great rivers, had a constant and thriving trade connection with the north, viz., particularly the districts around the mouths of the Elbe and Oder. From the beginning of the later Bronze Age strong Nordic expansion and activity can be observed in those parts of the German Baltic lands which lie to the east of Denmark. In this and the succeeding period Nordic colonists seem to have made considerable advances to the south and east, from the districts around the mouth of the Oder. This is reflected in the archaeological material of Upper Pomerania, by the quantities of Nordic grave finds, ancient implements, pottery, etc. The central period of the Bronze Age shows the culmination of Nordic expansion and colonization southward. If the districts of north Germany are included, wherein the finds both from graves and from field and marsh are preponderantly, if not entirely, Nordic in content and composition, a great Nordic sphere of culture can be drawn embracing the main portions of the provinces of Oldenburg, Hannover, Schwerin, and Mecklenburg, together with Lower and Upper Pomerania as far as Danzig with its hinterland. Nordic culture reaches as far south

44

Danish bronze sword.

as this toward the close of the Bronze Age. It was a sphere of culture in which the ancient Danish lands formed the principal area and the center of gravity."

When one examines Professor Jankuhn's maps, it is obvious that, even in the early Bronze Age, the territory of the Teutonic peoples corresponded approximately to the old Danish kingdom as it was right down to the time of King Frederik III, 300 years ago. From here on archaeologists can follow the Teutonic tribes with great certainty, because their weapons and implements, their burial customs and ornaments, their decorations and pottery, and later the place-names which they left behind them, are so characteristic.

Perhaps the most interesting thing is not so much the fact that the relics of the Teutonic peoples from the early Bronze Age are found in the Danish lands as that, for all practical purposes, they are not found elsewhere.

Bronze ornament from Faardal near Viborg. Jutland.

THE IRON AGE

Argentum et aurum propitii an irati dii negaverint dubito.

TACITUS

The Gods have denied them silver and gold, whether out of sheer pity or in wrath.

Iron is a Celtic word. The Celts were tribes which spread out from the area around the Danube at the close of the Bronze Age. They appear to have been a mixture of the Nordic and Alpine races. Their noble cavalry, which bore the new sharp metal in their swordblades, extended Celtic rule like a belt right across the continent. Like a tempest the Celtic Hallstatt warriors swept eastward to Galatia in Asia Minor and westward to Spain. In several different waves they invaded the British Isles from the early part of the fifth century B.C. They conquered Rome in 388 B.C. and a hundred years later plundered Delphi in Greece. They were an Indo-European people, tall, energetic, long-headed, reddish-blond, outstanding in many respects, imaginative, but without real political gifts for colonization. They did not create a united kingdom, but were a confusion of tribes often waging active war against each other. By overrunning the peoples then living in Central Europe they prepared the way for the world empire of the Romans.

Carthage seized Spain from them as early as the 3rd Century B.C., and in the next century the Romans took cisalpine Gaul in northern Italy and, a hundred years later still, transalpine Gaul in southern France. Caesar conquered the whole of Gaul, and reached Britain almost as the Teutonic peoples from the north advanced down into Central Europe. Thus, in the first century before Christ, only Ireland remained as independent Celtic territory.

The boat from Hjortespring on Als. Celtic Iron Age. Reconstruction.

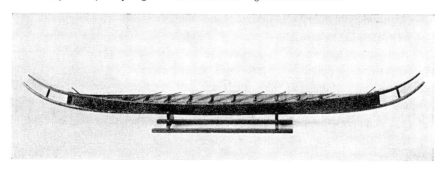

47

*Wooden shield from the
Hjortespring boat on Als.*

But before these events took place the Celts had managed to cut the old trading routes through Europe from north to south. They were not interested in trade. As always happens when commerce lines are severed, this led to a considerable drop in wealth and culture. The routes for imports were throttled, and this resulted in Denmark's suffering a severe commercial crisis. This, however, Becker recently disputed.

At the same time weather conditions changed, the climate deteriorated in the north, becoming rainy and cold, and this resulted in Denmark's suffering a severe agricultural crisis.

The introduction of a new metal, iron, jeopardized and nearly brought to a standstill the handcraft and export of bronze, and Denmark experienced a severe industrial crisis.

In times of hardship man shows what he is worth. The farmer took up the fight and tried to stand firm. He had a good foundation to build upon, a many-thousand-year-old culture in stone and bronze. He transformed agriculture and cattle-breeding, built up the fields in ridges so that they did not become so easily flooded, learned to stall-feed cattle, and thus somehow survived the difficult times. According to Hatt, the knowledge of cultivated plants possessed by the north Jutland farmer in the Roman Iron Age was very little less than that obtained around 1800 A.D. The wide prehistoric fields in Jutland are believed to have been worked with the primitive type of plough, the ard, and the long, narrow prehistoric fields can be ascribed to the use of the later wheeled plough, of which the oldest known example in the world was found at Tømmerby near Silkeborg. In time the farmer learned to recover iron from the bog-ore of the swamps, and he also tightened his belt. Waist belts had, in fact, been introduced. Between them, the Celts and increasingly cold weather had taught the Danes the use of trousers.

THE TEUTONIC PEOPLES

Von hier aus haben sich die Germanen im Verlaufe ihrer weiteren Geschichte ausgedehnt, und hier liegen ihre Wurzeln, die tief in die Vorzeit zurückgreifen. HERBERT JANKUHN.

From here the Teutonic peoples expanded during the following historic periods, and here their roots are to be found, running deeply down in the past.

The Nordic Stone and Bronze Ages have left behind them no traces in the written history of the world. From our standpoint this is regrettable, but it does not in itself affect the measure and importance of their cultures. It is not until the Iron Age that the Teutonic peoples make their appearance in literature.

"All of a sudden they stand before us in history", says Grønbech. "They arrive at the very moment when Rome was about to extract the result of its long and active life, and to crystallize the endeavors of the classic world and their achievements into that form in which the ancient civilizations were to be transmitted to posterity. We, the descendants of these Teutonic peoples, first see them from outside. From the south we

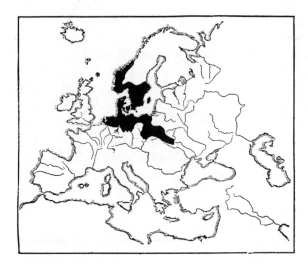

Territory of the Teutonic peoples in the Celtic Iron Age. (Herbert Jankuhn).

gaze into their midst as though we were looking at a foreign land. At first the eye lights on a heavy sea of men, a wave of warriors who, with the elemental violence of the ocean–or so it appears–hurl themselves into Eastern Gaul, break against Caesar's legions, and are obliterated in a tremendous backwash. And behind this surf we look into a dark, barren, comfortless land, bristling with relentless forests and full of swamps. There we see groups of men who, in their leisure moments between plundering and wild raids, sprawl at ease on deerskins, pass the day in brawls and drunken feasting, and from sheer idleness gamble away their few possessions, ranging from horses and women and even their own lives and liberty, to the fur pelts on their backs. And among them move tall, stalwart women with hard eyes and aloof manners."

The Teutonic tribes which advanced southward from the Baltic lands through north Germany to the warmer districts of Europe were followed by fresh tribes which passed down from Scandinavia through Jutland, or southward through the Sound and across the Baltic to the river systems of central Europe. In the Celtic Iron Age, which lasted from 400 B.C. to the birth of Christ, and in the Roman Iron Age between the years 1 A.D. and 400 A.D., we meet a succession of tribes on their wanderings southward through Europe.

Tribes began to take shape in Denmark as early as the transition between the Stone Age and Bronze Age. These tribes formed themselves

50

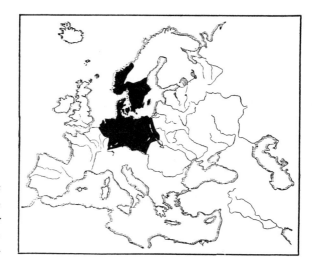

Territory of the Teutonic peoples in the later Roman Iron Age. (Herbert Jankuhn).

into regional societies for which we use the old Nordic word for a people: 'Tjod'. A 'Tjod' is a small group of people which has grown up within the natural limitation of a district. We can distinguish them in the grouping of the finds, in the situation of the graves and ancient roads, and in the old name of the province. North of the Limfjord we find the Teutons in Thy-syssel and the Vandals in Vendsyssel. South of the Limfjord we find the Cimbri in Himmersyssel and the Hardi in Hardsyssel, and farther down in Jutland we find the Jutes around Hjerting Bay and the Angles in Anglia, etc. These Tjod-lands were often separated from each other by unpopulated areas. Roman historians give us our first knowledge of these peoples in their references to the Cimbri, Teutones, Ambrones and Hardi.

THE CIMBRI

Wir besitzen eine Reihe einwandfreier Zeugnisse für die Herkunft der Kimbern aus dem nördlichen Jütland –

R. Much.

We have incontestable evidence of the Cimbri's originating in northeastern Jutland.

It was wet and cold in Jutland. The fields were flooded and the cattle did not thrive. Therefore, one cannot be surprised that the Cimbri and

Teutons moved southward circa 120 B.C. They marched with their chariots and cavalry, these warriors with keen grey swords and sharp, pointed spears. Images of wild animals gaped ferociously atop their helmets. So Plutarch describes them, and so they appear in the silver moulding of the Gundestrup cauldron. They were accompanied by their tall, blonde women with blue, steady eyes, and by a swarm of fair, almost white-haired youngsters whom the Romans described as 'children with old men's hair'. One can picture them: wild village children, as you still se them in Denmark peeping out of the flowered edge of the ditches along the roadside.

Down they surged into Europe, through Bohemia and Silesia to the valley of the Danube, where they forced the Helvetians into Switzerland and pushed on to France and Spain. Time after time they came up against strong Roman forces and defeated them. The consul Cneius Papirius Carbo, along with his army, was completely crushed by them at Noreia in Carinthia in 113 B.C., after he had treacherously attacked the Cimbri during peace negotiations. In southern France, Consul Marcus Junius Silanus was defeated by them in 109 B.C., and four years later they first overcame the Legate Marcus Aurelius Scaurus and then, under the command of the Cimbrian King Boiorix, vanquished a large army under Consul Gnaius Mallius Maximus and Proconsul Quintus Servilius Caepio. These events amounted almost to a catastrophe for the Romans, but instead of advancing directly into Italy, the Cimbri pushed farther west over the Pyrenees into Spain. Thus the Romans were spared in this round of combat.

Some years later the Cimbri returned to southern France and advanced toward Italy through the Brenner Pass while the Teutons and Ambrones marched through the valley of the Rhone. Only two hundred years after Pytheas of Marseilles had visited the Teutons in Thy, they stood before the gates of his native city. Here Caesar's uncle, Gaius Marius, succeeded in defeating them in two battles at Aquae Sextiae, now called Aix-en-Provence. He first overcame the Ambrones, and then the Teutons, whose King Teutobod was taken captive to Rome in the year 102 B.C.

In the meantime the Cimbri crossed the Alps where, yelling like boys on toboggans, they slid on their shields down the snow-covered slopes until they arrived in the sweltering valley of the Po. In the roasting heat of July, while the sweat ran down their foreheads, and a stench of leather, blood, and iron made their nostrils quiver, they fought the Battle

52

of Vercellae the 30th of July in 101 B.C. Here Marius completely routed them despite the amazing bravery with which they fought. When the clouds of defeat began to overshadow them in the dust-laden air, even their women took up arms, and when a debacle was certain they returned to the camp, killed their children and then took their own lives so that they should not be enslaved or become mothers of slaves. The Cimbri died as magnificently as they fought, comments Plutarch. So great had been the terror they inspired in the short, hardy Romans, that mothers for a long time thereafter threatened their children with the name of the Cimbri if they did not behave.

In the district around Marseilles the peasants are said to have used the long sun-bleached thigh-bones of the tall fallen Scandinavians as

The Cimbri and Teutons. (J. Wulff).

props in their vineyards, and so great was the joy at the victory that to this day seemingly every other boy in Marseilles is christened Marius.

In the districts near the Tyrol, around Verona and Vicenza, there dwells a tribe called Zimbri. At one time it was believed that they were descended from the remnants of the Cimbri, but this is not the case. When King Frederik IV of Denmark visited them during his Italian journey in 1709, they greeted him with the cry: "Long live our King!" A regrettable misunderstanding.

*

The Cimbri came from Himmerland in Jutland and the Teutons from Thy; the Harudi were Hardi from Hardsyssel, all adjacent to the Limfjord. The Ambrones probably came from the coastal districts in the region around what is now the island of Amrum. The tribes joined forces in the campaign and are mentioned together by the Roman historians. Their ancient tribal districts in Jutland lie not far from each other and are full of barrows that bear witness to the strength of the tribes in former days. The names of the tribes and those of the provinces match each other well from a linguistic point of view. As is well known, Frenchmen cannot pronounce the letter 'h'. The 'h' of Himbri was pronounced 'ch' by the Celts, and this was pronounced 'k' (c) by the Romans; it is the same consonant inutation as in the Danish horn–cornu. Originally they were called Himbri, but we call them Cimbri after the classical authors. The name Himbri is perhaps derived from a word meaning a forest glade.

*

In the year 5 A.D. the Emperor Augustus undertook a naval expedition to the districts of the Rhine and Elbe, and this reached as far as Danish coasts and waters. In an inscription on a marble slab at Ankyra–Ankara, the present capital of Turkey–the Emperor writes, "My fleet sailed across the Ocean from the mouth of the Rhine toward the lands of the rising sun as far as the territory of the Cimbri, whither no Roman had ever before come either by land or by sea. The Cimbri, Charudi, Semnones, and other Germanic peoples in this district sent missions to beg for the friendship of myself and of the Roman people."

This naval expedition is also described by Strabo, who speaks of the

Cimbri as dwelling on a peninsula, but appears to place them west of the Elbe. He says that the Cimbri begged the Roman's pardon for what had happened, which probably refers to their attack on Roman territories 100 years previously. He also says that they sent the Emperor "their most sacred cauldron as a gift."

Pliny says, "The fleet sailed to Germany, to the promontory of the Cimbri–to districts which are quagmires through excess of moisture." He mentions "the huge bay–Codanus–which extends all the way to the Cimbrian promontory and is filled with islands, of which the most famous is Scadinauia."

With the arrogance of a cultivated Roman, Pliny declares, "Here lives a small and miserable people. With their hands they collect slime, which they dry up by wind more than by sun. With this they heat up their food and their entrails, frozen by the northwind. The people assert that if they were conquered by the Romans they would be enslaved. Indeed, providence spares some peoples, but to their own undoing."

Mela places the habitat of both the Cimbri and Teutons in Sinus Codanus, by which he means either the Baltic, Kattegat or Limfjord. Ptolemy, on his celebrated map of Europe, places the Cimbri and Harudi alongside each other in the north of Jutland, on the Cimbrian peninsula.

The fact that Strabo and Velleius Patercullus place the Cimbrians west of the Elbe is regarded by some historians as a proof that they did not originate from Himmerland, but had their habitat in the Elbe districts. But Strabo and Velleius are actually the only authorities to support such a theory. All other sources and finds definitely point to Himmerland. The explanation of the difference is probably that there was confusion, or that in the time of Augustus, Cimbrian tribes may actually have lived in the Elbe districts. Similarly, evidence of their presence in the Rhineland has been preserved, such as the votive inscriptions at Main to 'the Cimbrian Mercury' and the celebrated Teuton Stone, which seems also to bear traces of the simultaneous presence of the Cimbrians, Ambrones and Harudi. Feist considers that the tribes of the Cimbrian expedition were Celtic people, but the probability is that the Cimbrian expedition was in fact originally directed against the Celts.

In 1891, in Rævemose at Gundestrup in Himmerland, the celebrated Gundestrup silver cauldron was found, "certainly the most magnificient piece of its kind that has ever been discovered." One recalls Strabo's statement that the Cimbri used such cauldrons when they sacrificed their prisoners and that they presented 'their most sacred cauldron' to the Emperor. This one may be a facsimile, and the styling of the cauldron points to its connection with the very districts through which the Cimbrian expedition passed.

In Borremose in Himmerland, an ancient Cimbrian fortress has been discovered which dates from that period. Concerning the waste fields of olden days, Gudmund Hatt says, "It is tempting to link up the prehistoric waste fields with the migrations from Jutland in pre-Roman times, especially with the celebrated expedition of the Cimbrians."

Finally, we have in Himmerland clear proof of bull-worship, which is known to have been part of the cult of the Cimbri, and is not known to have been practised by other Teutonic tribes.

That Ptolemy clearly located the Cimbrians on "the Cimbrian peninsula" is a strong argument. The whole description by Pliny of their native districts on "the Cimbrian promontory" points in the same direction. Himmerland's position as a province (syssel): Himmersyssel, and archaeological finds in the districts, indicate that the area between the

Interior plate of the silver cauldron from Gundestrup. Himmerland. Jutland.

56

Limfjord, Hvalpsund and Mariagerfjord was the home of the Cimbrians. The probability that this is correct is so great that it is recognized nowadays by most investigators.

THE TEUTONS

This explanation leads us to conclude that both the Cimbri and the Teutoni really lived in what we now call the north of Jutland.   H. MUNRO CHADWICK.

Vilssund and Næssund, the narrow sounds which flow between Thy and the island of Mors in the Limfjord, are two of the most beautiful waterways in Denmark. No one who has sailed through them will ever forget the magnificent sight of the land of Thy to the westward, where rows of dark, solemn barrows bear witness to ancient families of mighty chiefs, sea-farers and merchants from the Bronze Age. In ancient days Thy was rich in amber. Both Thy and Himmerland were provinces which, like Hardsyssel and Vendsyssel, bestrode the important east-west trade route, the Limfjord.

The name Teuton can without difficulty be traced linguistically to that of the district Thy. The old name of the province, Thiuth is the same word as Tjoð, an old Danish word denoting 'a people', as is the root of the name Teuton. We find the same root in the Danish word 'Tysk', meaning German. If we use the name of the district Thy adjectivally we have the word 'Tysk', and the adjective of 'Teut' forms the 'Teutsch'. The word Deutsch was spelled this way as recently as the time of Martin Luther, and it was still more recently that the T in 'Teutsch' was softend to a D in 'Deutsch'. The word 'Tysk' is currently used in Danish in its old meaning of 'people'. In Danish an 'Utyske' is someone beyond the pale, and remote from honest folk. It must, however, be observed that there are no sure indications that the present Germany, 'Deutschland', (in Danish: 'Tyskland') derived its name from the ancient Teutons of Thy. The word 'Tjod' could have been used by many other tribes.

About the year 325 B.C. the Greek merchant, mathematician and geographer Pytheas of Marseilles, sailed to Britain and the north, probably to see the places where the tin and amber in which he dealt were produced. A number of the place-names he writes about can be deci-

57

phered as Jutish trading points on the west coast of Jutland, either in the Ringkøbing and Limfjord districts or those of Hjerting and Fanø.

In Roman tradition and literature the name of the Teutons is closely linked with those of the Cimbri, Hardi and Ambrones. They appear to have been tribes which were neighbors and closely related (most of them surrounded the Limfjord) and it is highly probable that in Thy we find the native land of the Teutons.

Among the tribes which Pytheas mentions are the Teutones and Inguiones. In 'Inguiones' we have the oldest common designation for those tribes which were later to become the Danish people. Among the Inguiones Pliny includes the Cimbri, Teutons and Chauci. In the Beowulf poem the Danish King is called 'Lord of the Ingviones' and the Anglo-Saxon runic poem says, 'Ing wæs ærest mid Eeast Denum', 'Ing was first among East Danes'.

THE HARDI

In the area between Harboøre on the Limfjord and the Skjern River to the south, there lies a well-defined ancient tribal district which was the home of the Hardi. The Romans called them Harudi, and the ancient, still surviving name of the area is Hardsyssel. Since Ptolemy places them on his map of Denmark to the south of the Cimbri and east of the Jutes (Eudusii) it is possible that they originally dwelt farther east toward the Randers district in the Hundred of Harz.

The name 'Hardi' is related to a word meaning forest. These people probably enjoyed their greatest prosperity in the days of the amber trade, prehistoric roads leading to the district round Nissum Fjord. In this ancient tribal district are some of the oldest place-names in Denmark which, in the course of thousands of years, have been shortened until they are all but unrecognizable:–Hee, No, Naur, Tim, Lem, etc. On the other hand, the peculiarly east Danish village termination '-lev', is practically unknown in Hardsyssel.

The Hardi have given their name to Hordaland in Norway, probably after a migration there during the 3rd or 4th century A.D. Harz, in Germany, is also believed to bear the name of the Hardi. Caesar encountered them in Gaul in the year 58 B.C., in company with Jutes in the army of Ariovistus. Caesar, who for propaganda purposes always exaggerated numbers when it was a question of hostile armies, says that there were 24,000 of them. On the Ankyra monument Augustus mentions them along with the Cimbri.

Ancient sources connect the names of kings of the Jelling dynasty –Hardeknud and Hardegon–with Hardsyssel, and Dr. Lis Jacobsen considers this to be correct.

The 2000 year old man from the bog in Tollund. Jutland.

End-board of the Dejbjerg chariot. Hardsyssel. Jutland.

THE AMBRONES

It is uncertain where the native land of the Ambrones lay. The name has probably been preserved in that of the island of Amrum, west of Slesvig. There, in the flooded area called 'Vadehavet', the North Sea has swallowed up large stretches of land since the days of the Cimbrian expedition, the North Frisian islands being the remnants of them. Some people are of the opinion that the name is hidden in the ancient one of the island Fehmern–Imbre. The tribe which the Widsith poem calls Ymbre is probably the Ambrones.

*

The expedition of the Cimbri was the first of the great migrations from the north to be recorded in history. It antedates the actual migration period, but there is no principal difference between these migrations. This was the first of the violent blows which ultimately were to cause the destruction of the Roman Empire.

THE MIGRATIONS

> *Ex hac igitur Scandza insula quasi officina gentium aut certe velut vagina nationum – egressi.* JORDANES.
>
> They came from this island of Scandza, the workshop or womb of nations –.

Myths are like moonlight, obscure and filled with deceptive shadows. They must not be confounded with the clear light of reality. Legends are often a compound of poetic tales and living tradition. Sometimes they contain a historical kernel which cannot always be found, but in some instances we are able to reconstruct the outlines of the kernel from the fragments of the shell.

In days when there were no written records, people lived perhaps even more directly and intensely than they do today, when books, newspapers and television often come between them and reality. A book can easily become a substitute for life. In ancient times memory and oral tradition were more exact and more firmly bound to reality than they are now. There exist occasional proofs that a local popular tradition has survived from the days of the Bronze Age. For example, there is the legend concerning Dronninghøj (Queen's Barrow), near the ancient city of Hedeby. In it there was said to lie buried a man who had been decapitated by a queen. When the barrow was opened a male skeleton was found within, the skull lying between the thighbones.

Tradition concerning the large royal graves at Seddin maintained that there a King lay in three coffins—the first of stone, the second of clay, and the third of gold. The barrow had, of course, been ransacked by tomb robbers, but they had not dug down as far as the grave which lay beneath the ancient surface level. When it was opened a stone chamber was discovered in which stood a large, lidded earthenware vessel, and within that was a beautiful bronze urn which had at one time had the golden hue of bronze, and in which lay the charred bones of a man. This tradition is 3,000 years old.

Nerman's identification of King Ottar's barrow in Vendel seems to confirm a 1,400-year-old tradition. It must, however, be admitted that in

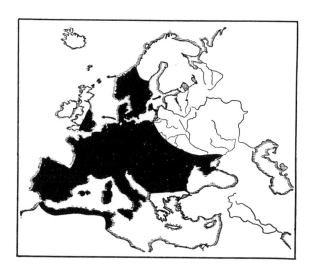

Territory of the Teutonic peoples in the Migration Period. (Herbert Jankuhn).

61

the case of countless traditions it has not been possible to confirm them by investigation.

Sagas, traditions and lays are undependable historical sources, yet they often tell a part of the truth. For example, insofar as Denmark is concerned, if the only source obtainable were 'Højskolesangbogen' (the songbook of the Folk High Schools), then history would be inexact, but nonetheless we should have a picture of that part of history which the people themselves treasured. When one considers the many traditions of Teutonic origin which have later been substantiated by modern archaeological facts, one must take care not to reject anything without weighing it carefully.

Arup says, "It is undeniably strange that so many of the so-called 'peoples' who worked their way up the Elbe or Oder to the final conflict with the Romans should have preserved in their institutions, and to some extent in their language, relics which appear to have a Nordic rather than a common Germanic origin, and names which can easily be explained as those of Nordic, including Danish, localities; and many of them also preserve a tradition that in very early times they had migrated from the north."

Actually, there are few of the Teutonic tribes which do not possess in their lore reference to a migration from Scandinavia. What kept alive the people's interest in these traditions if they were not true? In ancient and mediaeval times the north was not a famous land, and tribes usually venerate and cherish traditions which trace their descent from the great civilized lands of antiquity.

*

A number of different forces are decisive in migrations. There are the driving forces of overpopulation and lack of food in the country of origin. These causes we find in the northern countries in the period preceding the migrations. Due to climatic deterioration the fertility of the soil failed, while this was not the case with the fertility of the tribes.

Forces of attraction in the land of destination are the enticements of richer soil, better climate and higher culture. The Roman and Byzantine Empires were mighty magnets of attraction.

The controlling forces determine the direction. These are mainly geographic and traffic conditions, and the strength and resistance of other peoples.

If periods of decadence are followed by a decline and fall of defensive

62

power, a weak nation may well be a temptation to more robust and aggressive neighbors. Like liquids, migrations often follow the line of least resistance.

Sometimes there are forces pushing from behind, which was the case when the hordes of the Huns pressed the Goths westwards into the Roman Empire.

In freedom-loving peoples a sense of liberty and independence may be decisive as a motivating force. This was the case in the Exodus of Israel from Egypt, the colonization of Iceland, the trek of the Boers in the Transvaal, the North Atlantic crossing of the Pilgrims and the drift of North Americans to the untamed West.

During the Migration Period, wave after wave of tribes from the north advanced up the rivers and down through Europe: the Goths, Gepidi, Eruli, Burgundians, Vandals, Silesians, Rugians, Swabians, Langobardi, Franks, Saxons, Angles and Jutes and others, besides. The European countries of today spring from the most important of these tribes.

THE OSTROGOTHS AND VISIGOTHS

The powerful Gothic peoples came from the north. They probably belong to Sweden's history and have therefore only an indirect connection with that of Denmark. Probably they were the Göter from Öster Götland, and perhaps especially from Väster Götland. It is possible that they were Guter from Gotland, and although it is by no means probable– they might also have had connections with Jutland and the rest of Denmark which, in the ancient Icelandic sources, is called Gotland or Hreidgoteland. Hreidgoteland is, however, probably the valley of the Vistula. The Gutones, whom Pytheas refers to 300 years before Christ as dwelling 'a day's journey' from the supposedly Jutish amber coast were, in the opinion of Nerman, a Jutish tribe which can scarcely have had any connection with the Goths of later times. According to the researches of Eric Oxenstierna, the Goths appear to have come from the district around the Göta River, moving down through the Sound to the Baltic Coast, just as did the Vandals before them.

The Goths had ancient tribal lore concerning bitter fights with the Vandals when they moved from the north to new dwelling places south

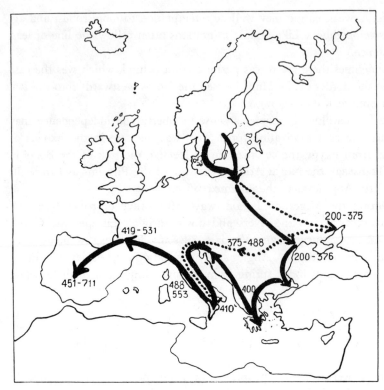

The Ostrogoths .... and the Visigoths _____

of the Baltic. In the centuries before the birth of Christ they kept to the eastward of the lower Vistula until, in the years 150-200 A.D., they advanced to the Black Sea districts of South Russia, where they are last encountered in 214 A.D.

The Visigoths were driven westward by the Huns. In the Battle of Adrianople they inflicted a major defeat on the Romans, Emperor Valens himself falling in this conflict in 379 A.D. At the close of the century they broke into Italy, where Alaric conquered Rome in 410 A.D. Farther westward they set up kingdoms in southern France and Spain that lasted 300 years until the Franks, under Clovis, defeated them in France and the Arabs overcame them in Spain. In far off Britain, the effects of the sacking of Rome were to be seen in the departure of the last of the Roman legions.

64

The Ostrogoths, whose mighty kingdom under Ermanaric is said to have stretched from the Baltic to the Black Sea, and who still maintained connection with the north, were overcome by the Huns, fierce Mongol horsemen, in about 370 A.D. Eighty years later they threw off the yoke of the Huns. Under Theodoric the Great they attained their zenith with the assumption of sovereignty over the West Roman Empire and the western Mediterranean. In 493 A.D. Theodoric defeated Odoaker the Erulian, who in 476 had made himself master of Italy. Odoaker had carried out great land reforms in Italy whereby one-third of its soil was parcelled out and subjected to taxation. Theodoric died in 526 and the kingdom of the Ostrogoths lasted until the middle of that century. Theodoric's name endured for a long time in Edda song and ballads as 'Didrik of Berne', warriors returning home no doubt bringing them to the north. Incidentally, the term Ostrogotae (East Goths) originally had nothing to do with the word 'east', but meant something like 'splendid Goths'. According to Askeberg, some evidence indicates that it was the Goths in the Vistula area who created the runic script influenced by the Roman alphabet. Von Friesen's theory that the runes came into existence among the Goths by the Black Sea under the influence of the Greek alphabet, has proved to be untenable. Nor have Hammarstrøm's and Marstander's hypotheses that the runes had their origin from Etruscan alphabets in Alpine districts proved correct. Fantasies on the part of German scholars that German tribes had invented the runes are characterized by Askeberg as "baseless fabrications and tendentious hypotheses." As a result of the latest investigations, Erik Moltke is of the opinion that the Runic script came into existence in Denmark.

THE ERULI

His glaucis Herulus genis vagatur imos Oceani colens resessus
algoso profundo. SIDONIUS APOLLINARIS.

"Here the Erulian roams, who lives at the sea-weed filled corners at the farthest ends of the Ocean — the Erulian with blue eyes almost the same color as that of the ice-cold sea."

Thus, in 476 A.D., the Roman poet Sidonius Apollinaris beheld the ambassadors of the Eruli at the Court of the Visigothic King Euric at Bordeaux. One can picture them with their blue eyes–or, as some trans-

The silver helmet from Thorsbjerg. Angel. South Jutland.

late it, their blue cheeks, which could be a poetic description of their helmets of corrugated silver with visors similar to the famous silver helmet found in the bog-finds at Thorsbjerg in Angel.

They are forerunners of the Vikings, sturdy sailors, hardy business men, intrepid warriors. At the beginning of the 3rd century A.D. we meet them by the Black Sea, in the Crimea, and on the Taman Peninsula, where they had wandered and sailed from the north, along the Rivers Vistula and Dnieper. They turn up in company with Goths, Jutes, Skiri and Bastarni, raiding the coasts of the Black Sea, their forays like these of the Vikings. They preferred to fight completely naked, like the Athenians in the battle of Marathon, literally like Berserks. In the year 267 A.D. they sailed with 500 ships from the Sea of Azov through the Dardanelles, conquered Byzantium and plundered the coasts of Greece, Syria and the Balkans.

In the north the Eruli had been companions of the Rugians from the island of Rügen who, in about 350 A.D. settled in Rogaland in Norway. They founded a kingdom on the Danube, in Hungary and Czechoslovakia, and through the entire period had their own kings. In the year 350 A.D. the East Eruli were defeated by Ermanaric, King of the

Ostrogoths, and 20 years later they were subjugated by the Huns. In 437 A.D. they joined with the Huns in conquering Gundahar, King of the Burgundians, but after Attila's death took part in overthrowing the powerful Huns.

The closing date of this period of antiquity is generally regarded as being August the 23rd in the year 476 A.D. when Odoaker the Erulian, by a coup d'état, overthrew the last of the West Roman Emperors, Romulus Augustulus. No other Teutonic tribe appears so frequently as mercenaries in the Roman armies, and it was as the leader of such mercenaries in Rome that Odoaker came to power. He ruled Rome until 493, when Theodoric in Ravenna, despite solemn assurances of friendship, cut Odoaker down with his own hand. While in power, Odoaker had succeeded in carrying through great land reforms in Italy whereby no less than one–third of the soil was parcelled out. These 'agri Herulorum' were of considerable importance in future times. Right down to the middle of the 6th century Erulian mercenaries fought in the Roman armies over large areas of the world against Persians, Caucasians, Slavs, Vandals and Goths. They were considered the crack troops of the Roman armies. They were crushed by Narses in 556 after a revolt. Thereafter they abruptly disappear from the scene of history.

In the west the Eruli turn up at about the same time that we meet them in the east. Together with Rugians, Saxons and Chauchi they are encountered on Viking raids along the coasts of Friesland, Gaul, Spain and Britain in the 4th and 5th centuries. In 286 A.D. Mamertinus refers to them in Gaul in a panegyric upon the Emperor Maximianus on the occasion of his defeating a host of the Eruli, 'viribus primo barbarorum locis ultimi', and in later times they are mentioned by several classical authors. In 459 they penetrated right down to the Straits of Gibraltar and threatened both Cadiz and Bordeaux.

We meet with the Eruli in both eastern and western branches, similar to a widespread pincer movement. The eastern branch of the Eruli formed a connection between the north and the East Roman Empire along the Vistula and Dnieper, while a western branch put the north in communication with the West Roman Empire along the Frisian Coast, the Rhine and West Europe. Both these branches issued from Denmark. The Eruli are said to be the only one of the Migration Period tribes that persistently retained a home in the north at the same time that they embarked on their far-reaching expeditions.

Who they were and where they dwelt is not known for certain, but scholars agree that they had their home in the ancient Danish lands. The Norwegian scholar Sophus Bugge realized this, and it was also he who directed attention to their importance in spreading Runic script. He also suggests that the considerable Danish bog finds may be connected with the Eruli. The Swedish scholar von Friesen's research appears to have established that as late as the year 500 A.D. the Eruli had their ancestral seat on Fyn or in Jutland in the district around Kongeaa and the Little Belt. It was here that in Roman times a very important trade route ran from Friesland and the Rhine-trade via Ribe and the waterways of the Kongeaa, to the Little Belt. There the trade route divided, one branch going north around Fyn and Zealand to the districts of the river Göta and Viken in the Kattegat district—and the other south around the islands and Skaane in the Baltic area. In the days of the Cimbri, Teutons and Vandals, the Limfjord seems to have been the most important transverse trade route. In the period of the Eruli, however, it was the Ribe–Kongeaa route. Later, the trade moved south to the Sli–Eider line. Neergaard has pointed out that the Kongeaa district at that time had a peculiar culture with ribbon motifs in its pottery and cremation in urn graves under flat fields, whereas the districts north and south of it were characterized by meander ornamentation and skeleton burial, as on Zealand. Most of the remarkable ornaments known as gold bracteates are found along this artery, and it is also here that the oldest Runic writings have been discovered. The gold finds of this period have been made particularly in the Kongeaa area, along the military way, on South Fyn and in the southeast of Zealand.

Like the Vikings, the Eruli were a sea-faring, trading and fighting people who negotiated the exchange of goods between large parts of the north and western Europe's commercial artery the Rhine. They were the people who brought the arts of runes and minstrelsy to the north. According to von Friesen, they became teachers of the art of writing to the Danes, Norwegians, Swedes, Thuringians, Alemanni, Bavarians, Burgundians, Frisians, Angles and Saxons.

In the 3rd, 4th and 5th centuries the Eruli showed great strength and power of expansion, and as late as circa 500 they were of such importance in European politics that Theodoric the Great sent ambassadors, and letters which have been preserved, to King Hrodulf of the Eruli. In these letters he proposed an alliance against Clovis, King of the Franks,

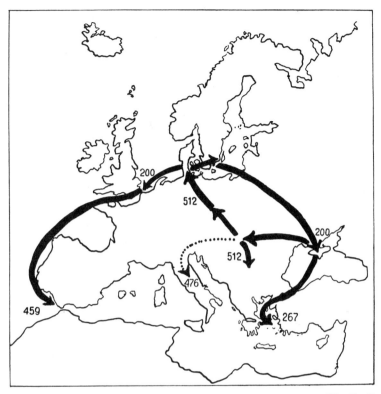

The Eruli.

who threatened the kingdom, of the Visi- and Ostrogoths, similar missives being sent to the Thuringians and Varni. These letters are preserved in the 'Variae' of Cassiodorus, Chancellor to Theodoric. At that time the Kingdom of Thuringia alone lay between Denmark and Theodoric's kingdom, so that if Theodoric's plans had materialized, a direct connection would have been established between the Scandinavian north and the east Germanic, Arian culture.

It is known that Theodoric was visited in Ravenna by a king called Hrodulf. He is said to have come from Norway, but Wessén thinks that the king was none other than the Danish King Hrolf Krake from Hlejre, and that the visit was a link in the negotiations concerning the great plans for an alliance against Clovis, designed to embrace the Empire of the Franks in a gigantic pincer movement. The King of the Franks forestalled them and the alliance seems never to have formed. It is not known whether or not King Hugleik's attack on Merovingian Franconia a decade later had any connection with these events.

In about 550 A.D. Jordanes, the Gothic historian, says of the Eruli that they had been driven out of their home by the Danes. It is uncertain when this is supposed to have happened and from whence they were driven—Skaane, Zealand or the districts of the Little Belt? Wessén thinks that this event must have been quite recent at the time of Jordanes, and that it may have occurred shortly before 500. Others consider that if the account is based on fact it took place far back in time, perhaps before the year 200, or during the 3rd century. If the famous bog-finds have any bearing on the battles between Danes and Eruli, then the dating of these finds points in that direction and the appearance of the Eruli in Europe in the 3rd century may well be a consequence of these events. It can however, as Chambers maintains, have been just as well a question of spontaneous Viking expeditions and migrations, so that the home-dwelling tribes were thereby weakened and consequently exposed to attack.

In about 550 the Byzantine historian Prokopios, secretary to the celebrated army leader Belisarius, says of the Danubian Eruli that in the reign of the Emperor Anastasius (491-518), they were conquered by the Langobardi who had wandered down along the Elbe and through Bohemia. A part of the Eruli pressed into Serbia, but another part wandered under the leadership of their chiefs northward to Denmark. In 512 they advanced through the territories of the Slavonic tribes and the depopulated districts which had been abandoned by the Germani. When they arrived on the other side of the settlements of the Varni they roamed through the tribes of the Danes without suffering from the barbarians, and after they had reached the Ocean (the Baltic?) they sailed over to the island of Thule, where they settled down near the Göter people. Prokopios also states that the Danubian Eruli committed regicide, being curious to see what it was like to live without kings. They soon regretted the experiment and in 545 they sent 200 Eruli emissaries to the north to fetch a descendant of their ancient royal house. The royal prince, however, died on his way down through Denmark, and then the emissaries returned and fetched a new one, under whose leadership they deposed the Byzantine Erulian King whom the East Roman Emperor had meanwhile installed.

It is not known where these repatriated Erulians really settled down, but various signs point in the direction of Värend and Blekinge. Here is to be found in the local dialect the word 'Järul' which denotes a 'companion-in-arms' and which appears to have a connection with the word 'Eruli', the meaning of which was originally a man, a warrior of noble parentage. It has been related of the Eruli that they cared for their old people by the simple method of killing them. A similar tradition exists in Värend and Blekinge and also at Endrupskov in south Jutland.

Fahlbeck, in his time, drew attention to the fact that in Värend and Blekinge there exists a peculiar law of marriage and inheritance which is radically different from that of other parts of the north. Women have equal rights of inheritance with men and also equal rights to the ownership of land. Out of all the Teutonic tribes, the only parallel is to be found among the Visigoths, and it was not until as recently as 1845 that Swedish women obtained the same rights. In Denmark, women have from the time of Svend Forkbeard had half-inheritance rights with men. It was therefore not a Teutonic custom, but is thought to be a result of the influence of Roman law.

It is known that the Eruli and Goths in the Black Sea and Danubian districts were in close touch with Roman civilization. It is also known that no other Teutonic tribes appeared so frequently and so numerously as mercenaries in the Roman armies as did the Eruli who, in their exile, persistently maintained relations with their native land in the north. Von Friesen construes these circumstances as strongly supporting the supposition that Värend and Blekinge were the districts in which the repatriated Eruli settled down in 512 A.D. These provinces lie in close proximity to the Göter people, Östergötland, and it is possible that they acted as reinforcements for the East Göter in their battles with the Danes. Since the repatriated Eruli had their kings with them it is natural that Roman legal procedure should accompany them. It is not known whether remnants of original Eruli tribes existed in these districts, but it was a customary rule among the Teutonic people that tribes which had migrated preserved a certain right to return home to their native land. Since lastly, the district around Blekinge was, after the year 500, a center of Runic learning, there are quite a number of indications which point in the same direction.

In the earlier Runic inscriptions throughout the north, those which are supposed to originate from Eruli travelling as traders, we often

71

find the word 'Erilar', which is closely related to 'Erul'. Until now it has not been found on Zealand. Whether it is the name of a people or a word for a magician or a warrior is undecided. In the opinion of some scholars it is the same name we have preserved in Earl or Jarl, but von Friesen disputes this. Chadwick draws attention to the fact that the name 'Eruli' or 'Heruli' is often mentioned in Roman, Gothic, and Langobardic sources but hardly ever in Frankish, Saxon or English. From this he concludes that the Eruli must have used more than one name, which make their identification a difficult matter, and as they have not left their name behind in that of any province, Bugge thinks that Eruli can scarcely have been their ancient tribal name. Perhaps this name first came into existence on the Continent. Possibly the name 'Eruli' originally signified simply 'host of warriors'.

Perhaps the Eruli are mentioned in *Widsith*–the Herelingas according to Grimm. Probably they are mentioned in *Beowulf*. Based on a suggestion of Sewell, Wrenn in his 1953 edition of the poem has reconstructed the scribal error in the 6th line of the first page of the manuscript. In the magnificent opening about the Danish King Skjold (Scyld Scefing) the manuscript has the two words "egsode eorl", where the last part of the word is missing. Since the days of Kemble it has been reconstructed, 'egsode eorlas', meaning, 'he terrified the earls'. Wrenn proposes the reading, 'egsode Eorle', meaning, 'he terrified the Eruli'. The last reconstruction gives a historical meaning of political importance and it is more likely that the hero was remembered for having subdued the most ferocious and warlike tribe, the Eruli, than for having merely terrified some petty earls. If Wrenn is right in this attractive conjecture, the poem fits in well with what is related by Jordanes and Procopios at the same time. The Eruli disappear from the scene of European history and the Danes suddenly appear in all their fame and glory around 500 A.D. The King is then praised for the heroic political deed of overcoming the feared Eruli and, by doing so, laying the foundation for the hegemony of the Danes and the Scyldings in Denmark and uniting the kingdom. The royal Danish house is still called Scyldings and the name of the realm, 'Denmark', is derived from the Danes.

The three important trade-routes across Jutland uniting the North Sea with the Kattegat and the Baltic are first the Limfjord in the north, where we in *Beowulf* find Wulfgar, the Prince of the Vandals, mentioned as a vassal at the court of the Danish King Hrodgar. Vendsyssel, the homeland of the Vandals, controls the entrance to the Limfjord. Secondly the middle waterway of the river Kongeaa and Kolding Fjord, where the homeland of the Eruli is supposed to be and thirdly, the southern waterway of the fjord Sli and the river Eider, where we find the Danes after the emigration of the Angles. In the control of these trade-routes we have perhaps an outline of the political idea behind the conflict between the Danes and the Eruli.

In the years 100-500, South Jutland and the islands were the homelands of the Runes to an extent far greater than any other place in the north, but these inscriptions in the early, long Runic alphabet disappear, together with the name 'Eruli', in the 6th century. Not until about the year 800 does the later series of short Runes turn up. These too appear to have come into existence in Denmark and travelled from there over to Sweden along with the custom of erecting Runestones in memory of important personages.

The Eruli are the oldest Viking people from the north. They are the predecessors of the Danes, and their descendants in all probability constitute a considerable portion of the Danish people to this day.

THE VANDALS

"Le fait essentiel qui détermina cet effondrement de la puissance impériale en Gaule, avait été le passage des Vandales en Afrique sous Genséric ... On a considéré Genséric comme un homme de génie." HENRI PIRENNE.

"The cause of this collapse of the Imperial power in Gaul was the fact that the Vandals, under Geiseric, had crossed over into Africa. – Geiseric has been regarded as a man of genius."

The name Vandals has become a far from flattering term in most languages. This is a result of their conquest of Rome in 445, but in actual fact they were no worse than other conquering peoples. Indeed, the Romans themselves had not been exactly humane.

Linguistic and archaeological evidence points to their original home as being in Vendsyssel, north of the Limfjord. An ancient legend of the Goths and Langobardi tells of their battles with the Vandals when they moved out of Scandinavia, while in old English sources both the Vandals and the dwellers in Vendsyssel are called Wendlas. Some hold that the

73

name has the same root as Vand (Water) and Væde (moisture), i.e., the country by the water. Others have connected it with the verb 'vende' (to turn) because the sea and land bend at the Skaw, while still others have linked it up with 'Handel og Vandel' (trade and commerce). Aakjær has made it appear overwhelmingly probable that it has the same root as 'Vaand' (wand, branch or rod), and that the name is related to the peninsula 'Grenen' (branch of land) at the Skaw.

Vendsyssel, north of the Limfjord, is a province to which the Battle-Axe people did not come during the Stone Age. It is a part of the country which in many respects has its own character which the local inhabitants, the Vendelbo (dweller in Vendsyssel), retain to this day. Judging from the types of the ancient implements, the cultural associations of this territory ran more toward the southeast over the Kattegat and Zealand than westward through the Limfjord and the North Sea. Vendsyssel has always turned its face to the east and its barren, forbidding back to the North Sea. It was a kingdom of the Limfjord and the Kattegat.

The finds in Vendsyssel of pottery, burial customs and house-building show close conformity with those along the Oder and in Silesia, and point to a close relationship between these districts. Jahn, as a result of Schultz's researches, thinks that the Vandals departed from Vendsyssel about the year 100 B.C., and that they followed the Cimbri and Teutons. He postulates that they sailed over Zealand through the Sound to the Oder. In opposition to most other scholars, he holds that the Cimbrian expedition did not go overland in its first stages but sailed directly to the Oder and some distance up the river and only later went farther south. This is probably true of the Vandals, but scarcely of the Cimbri and Teutons.

In the period following the birth of Christ the Vandals are found east and west of the Oder, especially in Silesia around Breslau. Here for centuries they had a mighty kingdom from which they later wandered to Siebenbürgen, where the Ostrogoths defeated them in the 3rd century. Then for a while they lived under the Romans in Pannonia but, in the beginning of the 5th century, marched through Gaul into Spain. This westward movement of the Vandals broke the Roman front in west Germany and thus opened a way for the Alemanni and Bavarians down to the Alps. In Spain the rich province of Andalusia (Vandalusia) still bears the name of the Vandals, and there is said to be some resemblance

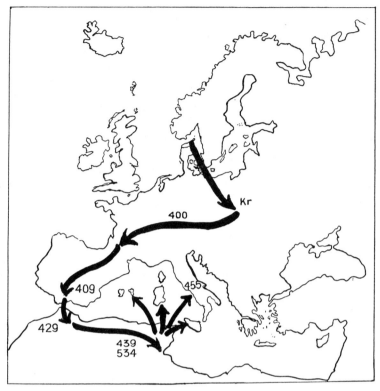

The Vandals.

between the timber-work houses in northern Jutland and those in Andalusia.

Their King Geiseric, who was a genius, led the Vandals on board the ships of Cartagena in 429 across the Straits of Gibraltar to North Africa, the granary of Rome. There they conquered a kingdom for themselves that embraced Tunis, Algiers, Tangier and later Tripoli. This occurred when Augustine was Bishop of Hippo. In 439 they conquered the important naval base Carthage and created a navy with which they overcame Sicily, Sardinia, Corsica and the Balearics. When they had thus become rulers of the sea they were able to cut off Italy from getting supplies of corn, and the country and its army became so weakened that the Vandals were able to conquer Rome June the 2nd in 445. Geiseric had promised Pope Leo that Rome would be plundered, but that the population would not be massacred, that he would not burn the city nor destroy works of art. These promises he kept, as contemporary witnesses have confirmed. How many conquering peoples have behaved as well? One may say that people should not conquer at all, and that is undoubtedly true, though somewhat unrealistic where history is concerned. As Renan says, "Seen from a moral standpoint, history is one continuous scandal." In considering conquering peoples it is therefore unjust to use the word 'vandalism' as a stigma and taunt, especially when one remembers how Rome itself had treated other cities, as witness Jerusalem and Carthage. The word 'vandalism' was coined by nervous Frenchmen as late as the 18th century.

The historian Procopios, who was also Belisarius' secretary, states that when the Vandals had created their kingdom in the hot and luxuriant surroundings of North Africa, "they began to take warm baths every day and load their tables with the finest dishes. They adorned themselves with gold jewelry and silks, and spent their days playgoing, at races, games and hunting. They threw themselves as keenly into the pleasures of wine and women." As a consequence, their kingdom quickly fell to pieces, and was crushed in 533 by the East Roman Emperor Justinian's renowned army leader, Belisarius.

THE BURGUNDIANS

In the days of antiquity the island of Bornholm in the Baltic was an important stepping-stone for the trade between the north and the Continent, and it is still a strategically important point. The Burgundians used the old east Danish term for an inhabitant, ending in –far: Burgundafar. The ancient name of the island was Burgund or Burgundarholm, a name which still exists in Burgundians, Burgundy, and the name of the dark red wine, Bourgogne. The emigration of the Burgundians from Scandinavia is referred to in the Vita St. Sigismundi Regis, which was written circa 600 A.D.

Bornholm is rich in archaeological finds, but in the two centuries preceding the birth of Christ there is a drop in their quantity. This was the period in which the Burgundian culture manifested itself south of the Baltic between the Vistula and Oder. The Burgundians broke away from these areas in the 3rd century and moved southward, so the quantity of finds in the Polish districts dwindles and ceases entirely in the 7th century, after which the Slavonic tribes occupied the areas.

The Burgundians moved westward through the districts around Main and into Gaul, where the Romans repulsed them in 278. The celebrated Burgundian Kingdom of the Niebelungen Saga at Worms, under King Gundahar, was destroyed in 437 by the Romans, with the assistance of Huns and Erulian mercenaries. The remnants of the people settled down on the Rhine, where they had a kingdom as late as 534, when it was absorbed by the Franks. Traces of the Burgundian population survive in the districts around Besanzon and Belfort. The legends about Helge Hundingsbane and his father Sigmund, the son of Volsung, tell of the Danish sea king's connection with the Gjukunger and Gunnar, who is King Gundahar of the Burgundians.

In King Alfred's translation of Orosius' geography, dated circa 900 A.D., Wulfstan states that at this time the island of Bornholm had its own king, who may have been grandfather to the jomsviking Bue hin digre (Bue the Big). We do not know how long this kingdom existed; it may have been a transient phase, a forerunner of the disorganized conditions during the Swedish rule in Hedeby. Wulfstan's emphasis on Bornholm's special sovereign position seems indirectly to hint that, except for this island, Denmark was at that time a united kingdom.

THE LANGOBARDI

Saxo writes of the Langobardi that they sallied forth from Scandinavia under the leadership of Ebbe and Agge. These two chiefs are called Ibor and Agjo by the historian of the Langobardi, Paul Diaconus, who states that they originated in Scandinavia. In his chapter about King Snjo, Saxo connects the emigration of the Langobardi with the fact that some ancient cultivated areas of Denmark had become wasteland and overgrown. It is uncertain if the Langobardi came from the Danish islands or Skaane (Scania), but that they came from eastern Denmark is indicated by the local termination '-fara' which exists among the Langobardi and Burgundians as family names in the administrative divisions. It corresponds to our 'Sjællandsfar' (fellow from Zealand), etc. In the time of

77

the Emperor Augustus they inhabited the district of Lüneburg on the Lower Elbe where in Bardovic and Bardengau their names are preserved. In the time of the Skjoldunger (Scyldings) they ruled over the coasts near Lübeck and Wismar and were thus able to threaten the passage of shipping through the Baltic. The Hadbardi, whom the Skjoldung tradition describes, were probably an offshoot from them. In Widsith, a Langobardian King Sceafa is mentioned, the same name as the father of King Skjold in the myths.

After migrations along the Elbe, they are encountered in the 5th century in Austria and Hungary at war with the Eruli, Gepidi, Vandals and Rugians. Under Albuin, in 568, after having received reinforcements from 'their brothers' the Saxons, they crossed the Alps into Italy where they conquered most of the peninsula, with the exception of Rome and the larger cities. Albuin established his capital in Pavia and was killed in 573 by his Queen, Rosamund, because, as tradition has it, he had forced her to drink from the skull of her father, King Kunimund, of the Gepidi, whom Albuin had killed. The machinery of state built up by Odoaker and Theodoric fell into disorder after Albuin's death until Authari took over the reins of government in 584. He regulated the laws and once again parcelled out one-third of the soil of Italy, with duty of military service based as a tax on the land.

The Langobardian kingdom existed for 200 years until it fell before the might of Charlemagne of the Franks in 774. After the victory, Charlemagne placed the Langobardian Iron Crown on his own head, that Crown which is still preserved in the Cathedral of Monza, in northern Italy. The name of the Langobardians still lives in the north Italian Province of Lombardy, where hundreds of place-names with the old Nordic termination '-inge' commemorate them: e.g., Marengo. Certain Italian masculine names such as Garibaldi are also of Langobardian origin.

The Langobardi possessed the legal talents of the dwellers in the north and their Code of Laws is more reminiscent of Nordic jurisprudence than of German. The grave-finds also show a resemblance to Nordic finds, and like the Eruli, Danes and Goths, they built up their administration and military regulations on the parcelling out of land.

In the course of time, foreign elements were added to the population of northern Italy through the immigration of Celts, Cimbri, Eruli, Rugians, Goths and Langobardi. These have perhaps contributed to the character of the inhabitants today. At all events, the northern Italians

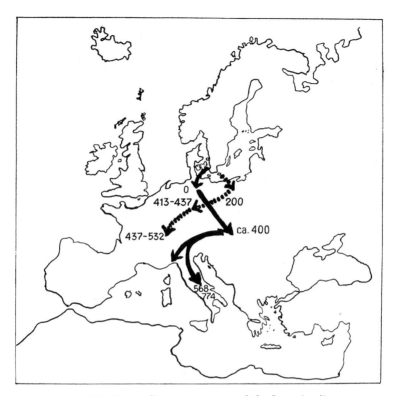

The Burgundians .... and the Langobardi——

have a stronger sense of independence and more initiative than the Italians of the south. It was in these northern districts that the Renaissance attained its richest forms of expression, and perhaps this was to some extent due to the mixture of races. Karl Madsen observes, incidentally, that "Strangely enough, the Italian madonnas are always blonde." Penka believes he can prove that in the northern Italian portraiture of the 15th and 16th centuries there is an overwhelming majority of blonde types, but that these become less frequent the nearer we approach the present day. To this day, blonde types are more common in northern Italy than in the south.

Southern Italy was conquered in the 10th century by Normans, but these contributed a ruling class rather than a new element in the people.

THE SILINGI

The pottery found in the rich chieftain graves at Sachrau in Silesia shows a close correlation with the pottery in Vendsyssel, as well as with that of Zealand, Fyn and south Norway. The name Silesia is certainly a Slavonic transformation of Silingia—the land of the Silingi. The Silingi were a branch of the Vandals on Zealand, and bore the ancient name of the island of Zealand (Sjælland, Silund, Selund). The Sachrau finds, dating from the 3rd century, form a culture group which can be followed northward through Pomerania to the Danish islands and Vendsyssel, with Zealand as a focal point. The artifacts show a continuous cultural harmony which seems to have passed from south to north; doubts have therefore been raised as to which direction the migration took. But a migration southward can easily be reconciled with a cultural influence from the opposite direction, i.e., from the richer southern districts to the more northern ones. It is like the sea currents in that Sound through which the Vandals must have sailed; the deep salt-water currents run southward from the Kattegat along the sea-bed, while the more fresh-water surface currents run from the Baltic northward. The finds at Kraghede in Vendsyssel in any case provide a sure proof that an affinity existed between the Vandal cultures in the north and Silesia in the south.

THE INGVAEONI

"Ing was first amongst East-Danes."
THE RUNIC LAY.

Mythical lore states that Mannus had three sons—Ingve, Ermin and Isto. From Ingve are descended the Ingvaeoni, who were coastal-dwellers in the western part of the Baltic; from Ermin come the Hermioni—the Swabians, or High-Germans; and from Isto come the Istvaeoni—the Franks.

This ancient ancestral tradition, which reflects exactly the development of the Teutonic peoples, is related by Tacitus in his book *Germania* which was published in the year 98 A.D. Ingvaeoni is the oldest designation for the Danish people and their nearest relatives. They are mentioned by Pytheas as far back as 2,200 years ago. He considers the Teutons and the peoples on Jutland's west coast as being a section of them, while Pliny assigns the Cimbri, Teutons and Charudes to them and calls the Ingvaeoni "the first in Germania." Mela also mentions the Ingvaeoni.

Schmidt thinks that the classical authors are on firm ground and that these groups of tribes were bound together partly by blood ties, partly by political necessity, and to some extent by a common religious cult–the Ingvaeoni were worshippers of Nerthus. Some German scholars have unreasonably averred that the Ingvaeoni consisted only of Angles, Saxons and Frisians, to the exclusion of the Scandinavians. This is undoubtedly incorrect, since the northmen appear to have been the central tribes in the league. In old English verse, 'Ingvini' is used as the designation for the Danes themselves. In Beowulf, the terms 'Dene' and 'Ingwine' are apparently synonymous, though the latter seems to be obsolescent. Chadwick maintains that the Ingwine of the sixth century were the descendants of the Ingvaeones of the first century, and that we probably may equate the Danes of the Middle Ages with the Ingvaeones of the 1st century. Ing is called their ancestor. The Anglo-Saxon Runic lay states, "Ing was first amongst East-Danes."

THE FRISIANS

God made the sea, but the Frisians made the coast.
ANCIENT FRISIAN PROVERB.

The Frisians, like the Saxons, probably came from the north. They were essentially coastal-dwellers and settled down between the rivers Ems and Weser, as far as Bruges. They had a rare faculty for reclaiming the sea and for protecting the land with dykes. They were peaceful and capable traders on the rivers and along the shores and the development of their trade in the Netherlands is compared by Pirenne to that of Venice. Their trade flourished especially in the years 500-900 and played a great part in the commercial life of Northern Europe after the Mohammedan destruction of shipping and trade in the Mediterranean. As Pirenne says: The sea was closed and trade disappeared. Askeberg thinks, however, that Wadstein and Arup have exaggerated the significance of Frisian trade at the expense of that of the Scandinavians.

Prior to the invasion of Britain, the Jutes, Angles and Saxons seem to have had auxiliary outposts in Friesland. Prokopios, who obtained his information from certain Angles who accompanied a Frankish emissary to Byzantium in about 550, described the Frisians, rather than the Saxons, as one of the conquerors of Britain. The story of the Jutish King Hengest's fight in Friesland with the Frisian King Finn is perhaps a picture on a miniature scale of the Jutes' battles to acquire auxiliary outposts in Friesland, and Beowulf's and Gregor's account of King Hugleik's expeditions in about 516 witnesses to Nordic interests on the Frisian coast. The Vikings were involved later, for King Gudfred's attack on Friesland in 810 was the introduction to a long series of Viking expeditions whose objectives were the creation of Nordic kingdoms at the mouths of the Weser, Scheldt and Rhine. Both historical and archaeological sources reveal close trading practices between the Frisians and Northmen.

In the 7th and 8th centuries the free Frisians succumbed to the might of the Franks. In 689 their King Radbod was beaten by Pepin, who acquired West-Friesland, the Holland of today. The next year Willibrord, the Anglo-Saxon missionary, arrived and laid the foundation for cooperation between the Anglo-Saxon and Frisian churches. Frisia was converted and Willibrord also visited Denmark in about the year 710. The Danish King Ongendus (probably Angantyr) was not disposed to conversion, so Willibrord calls him: 'Harder than stone and wilder than an animal'. That is, however, purely the judgment of a theologian, since the Danish king received him well and honored him greatly, even granting permission to take 30 boys with him to be instructed in Christianity. Arup suggests that it may have been these boys who brought to England the Danish lore to be found in Widsith and the Beowulf Poem. After further struggles for emancipation, the whole of Friesland was subdued by Charlemagne in 785, and the towns and harbors became Frankish custom-houses. (Pirenne.) The larger part of the country later came under German rule and the west-Frisian countries around the mouth of the Rhine were compelled to adopt Frankish folkways, and became Holland.

In the 11th and 12th centuries the Frisians colonized parts of the Wendish lands of Vagria and Mecklenburg, while the so-called North-Frisians settled down on the coast and islands of Slesvig, where they still exist today as far north as the Danish town of Tønder. Under William the Silent of Orange they played an important part in the development of modern democracy, and they have stubbornly preserved their character and their love of law, justice and personal independence right down to the present day, almost as it runs in an ancient Frisian legal formula: "as long as the wind whistles, grass grows, trees are leafing, the sun rises and the world stands."

THE FRANKS

Hi populi porro veteri cognomine Deni
Ante vocabantur et vocitantur adhuc ...
Pulcher adest facie, vultuque statuque decorus,
Unde genus Francis adfore fama refert.
ERMOLDUS NIGELLUS.

These people, whose name of old was the Danes, are still called so ... Their complexion is fair, and noble their stature and poise, the Frankish people is sprung from them, so the legend relates.

It was the Franks who gave France its name. They also had the mythical, ancestral tradition of Mannus and his three sons, wherein they traced their origin from Isto. Nigellus refers to this lore in his poem written in 826 about the Danish King Harald Klak's christening at Mainz. He writes about "a people whose name of old was the Danes. The Frankish people is sprung from them, so the legend relates."

The Franks came from the north across Belgium to Gaul, where the Merovingians created their powerful kingdoms. King Clovis, who ruled from 481 to 511, from small beginnings united the whole of France, drove out the Romans, fought the Visigoths, and overcame numerous other Frankish and Celtic tribes. The Merovingian kingdom lasted nearly 300 years and was replaced by that of the Carolingians which at length, under Charlemagne, embraced France, Germany, Friesland and Italy, i.e., more than half of Europe.

The Franks gradually allowed themselves to become denationalized by the Celto-Latin majority of the population—even as the Normans did later—but in return the people allowed themselves to be rechristened Franks, or French. The empire of the Franks was based on a land-owning aristocracy. Particularly in the west of Europe this landed aristocracy grew very powerful, small farms were absorbed and the free peasantry disappeared. However, in the eastern districts which were more Teutonic, the soil was always mainly in the hands of a free peasant class and the valuable qualities which resulted from this order of society were preserved longer here than in the romanized districts. It was principally on the foundation of this compact peasant population that the Carolingians were again able to build a mighty Empire.

Of special interest to Denmark was Charlemagne's progress to the north, where the Saxons were suppressed and converted with bloody violence. Schütte writes of Charlemagne's policy here, "In 782 he put to death 4,500 Saxon prisoners of war, in 793 he carried off a third part of the inhabitants of Bardengau in East Hannover, in 796 a considerable number of people from the Weser districts, in 797 a third part of the inhabitants in the three northeastern Hannoverian provinces, in 798 all land was laid waste from the Weser to Bardengau and 1,600 hostages were carried off, and in 804 he led away captive a further 10,000 from northeastern Hannover and Holstein."

THE SUEBI

Merce gemærde wid Myrgingum bi Fifeldore; heoldon ford siþþan Engle Svæfe, swea hit Offa geslog.   Widsith.

He drew the boundary against the Myrgingas at Fifeldor. Engle and Svæfe held it afterwards as Offa established it.

The mythical sons of Ermin, the Hermioni, who virtually comprise the High-German tribes, are the Suebi or Schwabians or Alemani, the Hermunduri or Thuringians, the Chatteri or Hessians, the Cheruski, the Marcomanni or Bavarians, etc.

Ancient Suebian legends tell of their having originally sailed to Slesvig from an island toward the north called Swevia—which is probably the same as Scandinavia. In the southwestern part of Slesvig there is an ancient, well-defined tribal district lying westward of the territory of the Angles and to the north of the Eider around its tributary the Treiaa (Trene). Here the town of Svavsted retains the name of the Suebi.

The old English Widsith Lay—which Gudmund Schütte calls the "Who is Who?" of that age—twice mentions the Angli and the Suebi side by side, 'Engle and Swaefe' (44) and, "mid Englum ond mid Swaefum" (61). It tells of Offa, King of the Angles, and of his fighting at the mouth of the Eider against the Myrgings, who were probably the most northerly of the Saxons in Holstein, and says, "He drew the bound-

84

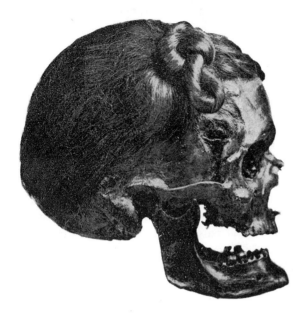

The 2000 year old skull with the Suebian plaited hair-knot from Østerby in Angel. South Jutland.

ary against the Myrgingas at Fifeldor. Engle and Swæfe held it afterwards as Offa established it." Offa is 'Uffe hin Spage' in Danish folklore, and it is his battles on the frontier to which reference is made, corroborating the theory that at that period the Suebi were allies of the Angles.

Among the Suebi the men wore their hair in a plaited knot. It is depicted on Trajan's Column in Rome and described by Tacitus as typical of the Suebi. In 1948, in a bog at Østerby in Southern Slesvig, the skull of a man with such an extremely well-preserved hairknot was found. It is about 2000 years old.

From South Slesvig the Suebi moved to Thuringia where Swebengau bears their name. Caesar tells of his encounter with them and their King Ariovist in 59 B.C., when the Suebi, together with the Hardi and Jutes, endeavored to advance into Gaul, "The Suebi are by far the largest and the most warlike nation among the Germans. It is said that they have a hundred cantons, from each of which they draw one thousand armed men yearly for the purpose of war outside their borders. The remainder, who have stayed at home, support themselves and the absent warriors; and again, in turn, are under arms the following year, while the others remain at home. By this means neither husbandry nor the theory and

85

practice of war is interrupted. They have no private or separate holding of land, nor are they allowed to abide longer than a year in one place for their habitation. They make not much use of corn for food, but chiefly of milk and of cattle, and are much engaged in hunting; and this, owing to the nature of the food, the regular exercise, and the freedom of life —for from boyhood up they are not schooled in a sense of duty or discipline, and do nothing whatever against their wish—nurses their strength and makes men of immense bodily stature."

The easterly tribes of the Suebi created the celebrated kingdom of the Marcomanni in Bohemia which had its period of glory about the time of the birth of Christ. They later called themselves Bavarians. The southwesterly tribes were originally called Semnones, but they were reinforced by various other tribes—Teutons, Cimbri, Jutes and Hardi. They became known as Alemanni, the actual meaning of which is a confederation of tribes—a mixed people. They settled down in Schwabia in southwestern Germany. At a later date some of them wandered to Spain where they were forced westward by the Visigoths and laid the foundation of Portugal.

THE SAXONS

From the Saxon, that is,
from the region that now is
called that of the old Saxons,
came the East Saxons, the South
Saxons and the West Saxons.
BEDE. HISTORIA ECCLESIASTICA
I. 15.

The monk Widukind, who wrote the history of the Saxons in 967, says that some are of the opinion that the Saxons are descended from the Greeks, others that they come from the Danes and Northmen. Possibly Widukind believed in the learned theory that the Danes descended from the Greek Danai. The Saxons' native home was in western Holstein but later they settled farther south, on both banks af the Elbe. Strasser says that the Saxons, apparently gradually and without opposition, moved southward from Jutland across the Elbe.

In the 3rd century the Saxons and Eruli raided in the English Channel, in Gaul and Britain, and appear to have forced the Franks westward.

In the 4th century the Saxon coastlands were densely populated and there were numerous small colonies along the coast of the English Channel. Together with the Jutes and Angles, they invaded Britian. At the close of the 5th century they conquered southern England, where the termination 'sex' in Essex, Wessex, Sussex and Middlesex reminds us of the Saxons. However, it was not the name of the Saxons that was taken by the English people, but rather that of the Angles. The Celtic inhabitants of Britain called all the new Teutonic tribes by one name—Saxon—perhaps because it was they who had been the first to undertake Viking raids on their coasts. But the new tribes called themselves Anglian, Engle, English, and never used the term 'Anglo-Saxons'. Since the Scots and the Welsh object to being called Englishmen, the term Anglo-Saxons later came into use, but the use of the word 'Saxon' did not appear until the 19th century. It looks as though the Saxons were of less importance in England than were the Angles, although there were more of them, possibly because the Saxons lacked kings, and were thus more loosely organized than the Angles, and because they were not interested in commerce.

Concerning the religious beliefs of the period, there seems to be no evidence that the Saxons and Frisians worshipped Nerthus, whose main territory was Denmark and Sweden.

At the close of the 8th century the Saxons were subjugated by the Franks under Charlemagne. This was one of the reasons for the conflict between the Franks and the Danes which led to the inception of the Viking period.

THE GERMANS

It would lead us too far afield if we were to follow all the migrations, battles and histories of the numerous Teutonic tribes.

The concept of Germans, or Deutsche, arose very late. Alexander Bugge writes, "Charlemagne had united the Germanic tribes in Germany, but it was long after his time that the German nation came into existence during the conflicts with the Magyars and Normans and the great expeditions into Italy. Then, for the first time, the Saxons, Franks, Alemanni and Bavarians learned to regard themselves as a unit."

The actual 'Deutsche' are first mentioned 300 years after the Danes are named in the sources. Despite this, there are still Germans who have tried to assert that, for example, Jutland was originally German. Concerning this, Schütte says, "The term German is not used in antiquity in references to the tribes in Jutland, and for the very good reason that it did not then exist. It appeared for the first time in the 9th and 10th centuries and never gained a foothold as far north as the North-Frisians, nor among the other inhabitants of Jutland. The Cimbri, Angles and Jutes have never been called German except by German intellectuals who misinterpreted Germanic = German. Not even the Saxons called themselves Germans until they became Germanized by bloody compulsion, while their feeling for the Germans is shown by the fact that after the 6th century they were in almost incessant conflict with them.

"After the German nationality had advanced right up to the Danish frontier over the corpse of the Saxon nation, the memory of their original relationship was gradually obliterated. The name of the denationalized people was adopted by the victors, just as occurred in northeast Germany, where the German colonists took their name from a denationalized Lithuanian tribe–the Prussians".

The Empire of Charlemagne never reached farther than the Eider frontier of Denmark, where King Gudfred repelled further advance. At no time was the Emperor himself present in the country between the Elbe and Eider, and never had a Frankish emperor or king set foot on the northern bank of the Elbe.

THE JUTES

It is with the landing of Hengest and his warband at Ebbsfleet on the shores of the Isle of Thanet that English history begins. No spot in Britain can be so sacred to Englishmen as that which first felt the tread of English feet.

JOHN RICHARD GREEN.

Long before England aspired to rule the waves she was herself their subject, for her destiny was continually being decided by the boat-crews which they floated to her shore. Since the distant past, when England was connected by land to Denmark and to France, the prehistoric population of the Stone Age had become mixed with infiltrations of Iberian tribes related to the Basques in Spain. Some centuries before Cæsar came to Britain, that country had been invaded and conquered by Celtic tribes –Gaeli, Cymbri and Britons. The Iberians were dark-haired people, but the Celts were tall and reddish-blond. They set themselves up as rulers of the country, blended with the Iberians and waged constant internecine warfare.

Pytheas, the merchant and geographer from Marseilles came to Britain in the time of Alexander the Great. Perhaps he wished to have a look at the production of tin, in which the Mediterranean lands had considerable interest. He also visited Norway and the amber coast of Jutland in about 325 B.C. This must be considered as proof that even at this early period trade was carried on between the north and Britain.

The dominion of the Romans, which commenced with Cæsar's expedition in 55 B.C., endured four and a half centuries until 410 A.D., when the last Roman soldiers were withdrawn to defend Rome against Alaric and his Visigoths. This event is called 'the departure of the Eagles'. In the Roman period Northmen had sailed to and traded with Britain, and had enrolled as mercenaries in the Roman armies. The Romans had completely depopulated many areas in Britain, selling their captives as slaves in Italy.

The Jutes, Angles and Saxons arrived shortly after the Romans had left the country. They had visited the shores before. The Roman, Frankish and British sources mention Saxon raids since 287 A.D. The Gallic chronicle mentions in 441 that the Britons, abandoned by the Romans, fell into the power of the Saxons. This suggests that severe attacks were made, but not that the Saxons had definitely conquered Britian, inasmuch as Bishop Germanus of Auxerre visited Britain in the year 447, and there were then no foreigners in the southern part of the country. The Gallic chronicle was prepared at a distance and ill-informed, and the word 'Saxon', found in Roman, Frankish and British sources, is used in a way that must comprise collectively all the sea-faring Teutonic tribes. They were closely related and it was difficult to distinguish between them. It was like the word 'Normans', used by the Frankish sources later on, which comprised Danes, Norwegians and Swedes.

Trevelyan says, "The settlement of the Nordic peoples is the governing event of the British history. The various irruptions of Anglo-Saxons and Jutes, of Danes and Norsemen form a single chapter; it has its prelude in the first plundering raids of Saxon pirates on the coast of Roman Britain well before 300 A.D., and it ends about 1020 when Canute completed the Scandinavian conquest of England by reconciling on equal terms the kindred races of Saxon and Dane. The racial basis was fixed by the time of Canute.

"The Nordic invasions are more important than the Roman interlude, more important even than the Norman Conquest.–The distinctive character of modern English is Nordic tempered by Welsh, not Welsh tempered by Nordic.

"The 'Nordic' race, then, had certain distinctive features which gave a family likeness to the innumerable and widely scattered tribes of Scandinavians, Anglo-Saxons, Franks and Teutons, who ranged, conquering and colonizing, from Ireland to Constantinople, from Greenland to the Desert of Sahara."

　　　　　*

The storm that burst upon Celtic-Christian Britain began, according to the Anglo-Saxon Chronicle, in 449 A.D., when, under their Kings Hengest and Horsa, the Jutes landed on the isle of Thanet at the mouth of the Thames. It is said that they had been invited by Vortigern, King of the Britons, to act as auxiliary troops against the invasion of the Scots from Ireland and the Picts from Scotland. Their position on the Isle of Thanet indicates that they had been mainly used to repel sea-raids. Dissension soon arose between them and the Britons, and six years later the Jutes marched into Kent and won a victory at Aylesford. Horsa fell in this battle, and was buried under a heap of stones which is to be seen near the town that still bears his name–Horsted. The name Horsa has been preserved also in the Danish village Horsted which lies northeast of Husum in the Jutes' homeland, and in Horserød and Hostrup as well. Hengest's name does not appear to have survived in any Danish place-name, but perhaps exists in the English place-names Hinxhill, Hinksey, Hengist-Head and Hingston Down. Strangely enough, the Historia Brittonum, which seems to have dipped into the same sources as Bede, states that Hengest and Horsa came from the island Oghul, which can scarcely be other than Bede's Angulus or Angel.

There has been some question as to whether the names of Hengest and Horsa are genuine names. The word Hengest means a stallion. In those days horses were sacred animals, so that there is nothing depre-

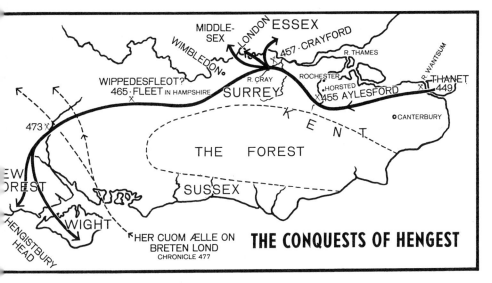

The conquests of Hengest. (Gordon Ward).

ciatory in it. The word Horsa does not mean a mare. If so, it would have been disparaging. Horsa is the general name for a horse without distinction of sex. Both Hengest and Horsa are names with the initial letter 'H', the sacred royal runic letter. The names, of course, may have been nicknames, but animal-names among prominent men of the Migration Period were not uncommon, possibly in connection with clannish totemic representations. Their names may derive from the crest on the apex of their helmets, because we know animal representations of boars, birds and wolves on helmets depicted on one of the plates of the silver-cauldron from Gundestrup and in famous Swedish finds. We have helmets preserved with pictures of mounted men along the brim of the helmet, but none with a horse on the crest. On many of the gold brachteates horses are seen in central places, and we know golden vanes from Viking ships adorned with horses. They are supposed to have been used as royal signs, such signs which *Beowulf* calls 'segen gyllene' in the description of the ship of King Skjold.

At all events Horsa's name is definitely verified as a man's name by Swedish runic inscriptions. The famous runic inscription, now nearly illegible, which Swedish Varangs from the imperial bodyguard in Mikla-

91

gaard (Byzans) carved centuries later, in the flanks of the marble lion at Piraeus–the same lion that now stands guard in front of the arsenal at Venice–is, according to Brate, supposed to be in memory of a man called Horsa. No less than four runic inscriptions in Sweden itself–the stones in Skillinge, Skokloster, Åkersby and Broby–are carved in memory of men by the name Horsa.

Hengest crossed the Wantsum from Thanet and marched in the coming years through Kent over Canterbury, Aylesford, Dartford, Crayford and London. From there he led his forces in a southerly direction over the chalk hills, down to the Hampshire coast around Southampton Water and the Isle of Wight. When he reached the culminating point of his career, before the invasion of Ælle and his Saxons in 477, Hengest is said to have ruled Kent, Essex, Middlesex, London, Sussex, Surrey and the Isle of Wight.

There is no recorded instance of the new invaders having dwelt in Roman villas. This curious fact must have an explanation. Perhaps it is to be found in Bede's statement that just before the invasion, Britain suffered from a great plague. If the superstitious invaders had seen several villas with corpses within, they would naturally have drawn the conclusion that Roman villas were haunted and evil.

Kent was the central area for trade across the English Channel between Britain and the Continent. With the commercial instinct of a Jute, Hengest selected this district. It was a well-defined area, easy to defend, a bridgehead controlling important trade routes. From here the Jutes traded with Frisians and Franks, learned much from them, and later gradually created for themselves a particular culture which surpassed those of the other invading tribes. Nowhere, says Shetelig,–he said it before the excavation of the ship-burial at Sutton Hoo–has the goldsmith's art of the period left behind it more beautiful work than that of the Kentish ornaments of gold filigree with mosaics of enamel, polished stones and inlaid ivory. Judging by the famous gold horns of Gallehus in Jutland, they were far from inferior goldsmiths in their native land. Oxenstierna calls the gold horns the most important religious documents between the Bronze Age petroglyphs and the Elder Edda. They were found in 1639 and 1734 respectively in Gallehus in western Slesvig, and date from between 400 and 450 A.D., i.e. during the generations immediately preceding the invasion of Britain. Gallehus is not far from Horsted and Hollingsted. According to the runic inscription on the horn

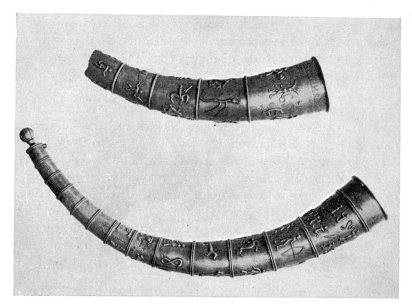

The golden horns from Gallehus. South Jutland.

found in 1734, Hlewagastir the Holting had the horn made. This man
has the same sacred initial letter 'H' as have Hengest and Horsa. We
find the same custom obtaining in the Skjoldung Dynasty–Halfdan,
Helge, Hrodgar, Hjargar, Hrodulf, Hrodrik, Hrodmund, Hjarvard, Hoc,
Hnæf–and in the Kings of the Geati–Hredel, Hugleik, Hardred, etc.
One can surmise a connection here, for Hengest and Horsa were, according to Beowulf, of princely birth, and Hlewagastir the Holting must
also have been a man of importance. The horns were used for both secular and religious purposes, princely and priestly dignity being closely
allied. Bede states that the ancestors of Hengest and Horsa were named
Victgisl, Vitta and Vecta, but Scheel thinks that these names can hardly
have had any original connection with Hengest and Horsa, but that they
are eponyms, hero-names, which are variants of the name of the Isle of
Wight. The fact that Hengest's son was called Eric or Oisc or Aesc
weakens the hypothesis. It is only supposition, but nonetheless a possibility, that Hlewagastir belonged to the same dynasty as the Jutish kings
or the Geat princes, and that the deposition of the gold horns may have
been a sacrifice previous to the important emigration to Britain with its

93

uncertain future. Gold horns were deposited in the earth only on very special occasions—either when hostile invasions threatened, or when great undertakings dictated the need of intervention by supernatural powers. When should they sacrifice the ancestral gold horns if not on setting out to conquer England?

Jutish trading was responsible for the development of the high level of Kentish culture. The resemblance between the finds in Kent and those of the Rhineland coast may be due to the fact that the Jutes stayed for a while in Friesland and used it as a springboard or steppingstone on their way to England. Another contributory cause would have been the reciprocal influence of commercial intercourse, shown in burial customs and language. Chadwick thinks it unlikely that the Frisian dialect forms which exist in the Kentish language are older than the 9th century and therefore must be later than the invasion. There is much to suggest that relations were maintained between the Jutes in Kent and the Jutes in Jutland.

*

Based on Gildas, Nennius, Bede, The Anglo-Saxon Chronicle and the geographical conditions of that time, Gordon Ward has attempted to reconstruct the march and battles of Hengest. In outline he draws a sketch of Hengest's interesting personality, which inspired the minstrels to famous poems and the audiences to be all attention. "They show him as competent and, if anything, rather less ruthless and less blind to humanitarian motives than most leaders of his age.—He even left intact the taxation system, the land tax, which was the basis of political economy. This was collected from the units set up before the Romans left. In due course these units fell into the hands of Jutes, but no other basis for taxation was needed or devised.—Alongside this official tolerance there was, no doubt, much of the brutality, the murder and rapine, of the Dark Ages; but the persistence of Kentish custom speaks so loudly, we know that Hengest must have adopted a deliberate policy of making himself a ruler acceptable to the tillers of the land. It has, of course, been argued that the Jutes brought these Kentish customs from Jutland, that they are not Kentish customs at all but Jutish. This view needs no further discussion until someone sees fit to offer some evidence in support of it, and, for choice, the evidence should show that such customs were previously known in Jutland or at least in Teutonic lands. No such evidence has yet been discovered."

94

An entry in the Chronicle belonging to the year 488 reads as follows, "Here Aesc began to reign and for 24 winters he was king of the men of Kent." We can hardly do otherwise than conclude that Hengest died in 488. The Royal line of Hengest comprises 18 kings of Kent. They lived long, and as Hengest arrived in 449, he must have ruled in 41 years. Gordon Ward says of him, "He had the gifts, the touch of genius, the understanding of management and of men, which are essential in the pioneer who sets out to found a kingdom.–Only in Kent was the miracle achieved of combining invader and invaded so that much of the best of each could survive. And this miracle was carried through by Hengest."

*

Where did they come from, these sturdy Jutes?

From Jutland. In the districts round Hjerting Bay, Esbjerg, Varde and Ribe, the Jutes had their tribal area. This was situated between the areas inhabited by the Angles and the Hardi. The old trade route from Ribe over the river Kongeaa to the Little Belt was of importance to them, while Olmer's Dyke, the ancient earthworks at Tinglev, was their southern defensive position.

Tacitus, Cæsar and Ptolemy mention them under the name Eutii, Eudoses, Edusii, Eudusioi? They got their name, as did so many other Danish tribes, from the water surrounding them–'eut' means 'wet'. Venantius Fortunatus puts the dwelling-place of the Jutes between those of the Saxons and Danes. Bede, the venerable historian of the English Church who was born in 672, calls the Jutes 'Jutae' or 'Jutarum natio', tells us that the homeland of the Angles lay between the Jutes and the Saxons, and refers to the Kentish royal family as 'oiscingas', a name derived from Oisc, the son of Hengest. The Beowulf poem and the Finnsbury Lay mention a young Prince Hengest–referred to as a Dane or a leader of the Half-Danes who, in King Halfdan's time, ravaged in Friesland and fought with Finn, probably a reference to battles in the Jutish colonies in Friesland prior to the invasion of England. In Friesland we find perhaps Jutes (Eote) as a band of retainers in the service of King Finn. Chronologically, the events in Friesland synchronize with the conquest of Kent, and Chadwick is of the opinion that it is the same Hengest we meet in both instances. Modern Dutch excavations of cemeteries in Friesland have shown–'with almost startling clarity'–as Blair puts it–that in the years between 400 and 450 a strong new so-called

Saxon element intruded itself upon the native civilization, thus giving the literary tradition in Finnsbury Lay and Beowulf, archaeological support.

Gudmund Schütte says that it would be as foolish to imagine that there were two contemporary famous chiefs called Hengest as to imagine that there were two contemporary conquerors by the name Julius Cæsar. The name is rare, both men had the same social and military status, were of the same nationality, lived at the same time and in the same district beside the English Channel. And why should the English heroic poems have so great an interest in the songs about Hengest—the Finnsbury Lay calls him: 'Hengest sylf'—if he had not been a man connected with great historical events in Britain? Hengest was presumably a *condottiere* who collected his hordes along the whole of the North Sea coast from Jutland to the Rhineland.

Archaeological finds make it probable that the emigration to Britain did not take place directly from Jutland, but with Friesland as an intermediate link and springboard. As early as 200 A.D. a diminution occurs in the number of graves in western Jutland, and this may perhaps have some connection with an emigration to Friesland. At all events Jolliffe, basing his opinion on legal and agrarian historical conditions, considers that the majority of the Jutes who colonized Kent were Ripuarian Franks from the Rhineland, even though it is possible that in a more remote past they had set out from Jutland. But Hodgkin makes the following objection, "It asks us to believe that a branch of the Franks ceased to be proud of their descent from that all-conquering race, and forgot their Frankish language so completely that there remain not even traces of it in the Kentish dialect. The difference between the agricultural systems in Kent and the Anglo-Saxon part of England can be compared with the differences which exist between the field systems in west- and north-Jutland and those of the Elbe countries."

The language and traditions of Kent contradict the theories of Leeds and Jolliffe. Bede's positive statement that the Jutes came from Jutland is important. Hodgkin says, "Bede's statement needs to be qualified, but it should not be wholly set aside unless the argument against it becomes overwhelming."

Bede was a learned scholar and a sober historian in constant contact with traditions living in the Kentish clergy and royal family. Sir Frank Stenton says, "In view of Bede's relations with the Northumbrian court,

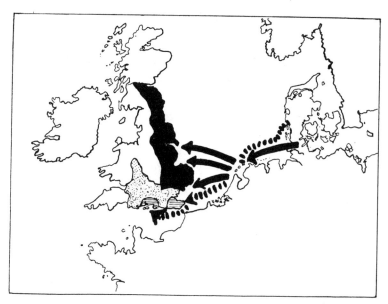

The Jutes . . . . and the Angles _____

it is highly dangerous to reject anything that he offers as a statement of historical fact.–Most of this information probably came to Bede from learned friends in Kent, and there is no reason to doubt its accuracy.– It satisfied a king of the Northumbrians in an age when kings were accustomed to listen to heroic verse covering all the nations of the Germanic world. It was the work of a cautious scholar, who had known eminent persons and was in communication with friends in many different parts of England. Its precision in regard to the obscure race of the Jutes, who had not given their name to any English kingdom, proves the care with which it was written. But it is not a mere piece of scholarly reconstruction. Titles of kings and bishops, recorded before the date of Bede's work, show that different English peoples actually regarded themselves as Angles or Saxons. It was not as a result of any deliberate theory that two adjacent peoples came to be known respectively as East Saxons and East Angles. Names like these stood for a real, if faded, memory of origins. In representing the *gens Anglorum* as a composite people drawn from three distinct Germanic nations, Bede was reflecting the common opinion of his time, and the vitality of tradition makes it very unlikely that this opinion was fundamentally mistaken."

Hengest's forceful personality and the tragic conflicts of honor and loyalty in which he had been involved must have formed the nucleus of the tradition preserved to the time of Bede. The best explanation of the contradictions in facts and theories lies in the supposition that the forces of Hengest were composed of a mixture of Jutes, Danes, Frisians, Angles, Saxons and Franks, and that the Jutes themselves had sojourned in Friesland before coming to Kent. This supposition explains the variations in Kentish graves and archaeology and the contradictory theories based upon them.

We know but little concerning the ancient history of Jutland itself, unless the Geatas in the poem of Beowulf belong to Jutland. A large section of the Jutes must have remained behind in their native districts, for after the emigration of the Angles they were in a position to bestow their name upon the population of the whole peninsula. This was no doubt due partly to their being a dominant tribe, and partly because, after the migration of the Angles, they were the most southerly tribe on the peninsula and therefore their neighbors to the south, the Danish newcomers, used the name of the Jutes collectively for all the remaining tribes in that part of the country. Many comprehensive tribal names have arisen in a similar manner. Jutland must have been united with the Danish island kingdom of Hlejre before the days of King Gudfred, about 800 A.D.

Saxo Grammaticus says that Hamlet was a king of the Jutes who fell in a battle with Viglek, King of the Angles and grandfather to Offa, who must have lived in the beginning of the 4th century. Saxo says, "His grave can be seen in Jutland on a heath which bears his name." This is probably Ammel Hede, east of Randers.

Shakespeare's immortal tragedy Hamlet, Prince of Denmark, has appeared on stages all over the world sprinkling his glittering words over men's minds. In some ways the Danish patriotic resistance movement during World War II was compelled to play the role of Hamlet, waiting patiently until the proper time, misleading an all-powerful opponent under imminent threat of death.

THE GEATAS

His ita gestis, Dani cum rege suo Chlochilaichum
evectu navale per mare Gallias appetunt.
After these events, the Danes and their King Hugleik
crossed the seas with their fleet and came to Gaul.

GREGORY OF TOURS.

Nobody knows for certain who the Geatas were. Therefore they have been assigned a chapter of their own. Were they Gautar from Sweden, or Jutes from Denmark? The unification of the Gautar and the Swedes is an event of great importance in the history of Sweden, just as important as is the unification of Jutland and the island Kingdom of the Danes in the history of Denmark. The problem is of more than philological importance.

Linguistically, the word 'Geatas' corresponds to Old Norse 'Gautar', which seems to indicate that the home of the Geatas was either in East Gautland or in West Gautland in what is Sweden today. This linguistic identification is the cornerstone of the Gautar theory.

In *Beowulf*, the finest Old English epic, the Geatas are mentioned about fifty times, but in such a problematic way that it has given rise to difference of opinion.

The Beowulf manuscript is preserved in only one manuscript which dates from the 10th century, but the poem is thought to have been composed by a gifted bard at one of the English courts in the 8th century, presumably that of King Offa of Mercia or King Aldfrith of Northumbria. The events celebrated in the song are from the 6th century. Since the poem extols the Danes and does not contain even a hint of ill-will toward them, it must have been composed before the Viking expeditions fomented bitterness. It cannot be derived from one of the Nordic courts in England because it would then have been written in the Danish tongue instead of Old English.

In *Widsith*, which is an older poem than *Beowulf*, the word 'Geatas' is mentioned once, the scald telling us that, among others, he visited the Swedes, the Geatas, and the South Danes, information which does not help us.

Finally the Geatas are mentioned in King Alfred's translation of Bede's *Historia Ecclesiastica*, where Bede's Latin word for Jutes in the forms 'Jutis' and 'Jutarum' is translated into Alfred's Old English 'Geatas' and 'Geatum'.

Alfred's translation is the only place where we find an identification. The identification of the 'Jutes' with the 'Geatas' cannot be a scribal error, as it is repeated three times. The word 'Geatas' is never mentioned in Scandinavian or Continental sources. Nowhere in the Old English literature are the 'Geatas' identified with the 'Gautar'. Nowhere do we find an identification of the 'Geatas' with any other tribe than the 'Jutes'. This shows that the linguistic cornerstone is not the philosophers' stone.

When in 449 Hengest and the Jutes came to England they arrived after an interlude in Friesland. If the word 'Jute' also came to England via Friesland, the transition from 'Jutar', through 'Jatar', to 'Geatas' is linguistically feasible. Unfortunately there was no standardized spelling in those days.

Beowulf is the hero of the Geatas, but in the poem is mentioned another Beowulf, son of the Danish King Skjold, which shows that the name has a connection not only with the Geatas but also with the Danes.

In *Beowulf* the Geatas are sometimes called Weder-Geatas and their country Weder-mearc, Weder meaning wind or weather. Knut Stjerna has connected this name with the Wäder Fjord and the Wäder Islands off the coast of Halland in the western part of present Sweden. But from days of old Halland was part of the Danish realm and the West Gautar were an inland tribe of whom no activity at sea is known. Near Samsö, the Danish island, is another Wäder Island now called Vejrö, and West Jutland is full of place names veritably whistling with wind and weather. The name 'Weder' is appropriate for windswept weatherbeaten Jutland and not for Halland.

The poem describes the coast of the Geatas as being rocky with 'brim-clifu' and 'beorgas steape', which might hint at Halland and would not be applicable to Jutland, but as the Danish coasts are also described as being rocky, most scholars agree that the description was drawn from the poet's homemade experience and that he himself had never seen the Scandinavian countries. One recalls Shakespeare when in *Hamlet, Prince of Denmark* he describes the shore at Elsinore as 'the dreadful summit of the cliff'. In *Beowulf* the Jutes are only mentioned as living in Friesland, never in Jutland, which is strange if the Geatas were not the Jutes.

The enemies of the Geatas were on one side the Swedes, and on the other the Franks, and since the expeditions against both enemies took place by ship, Jutland, with sea on either side fits best.

In ancient times, West Gautland was separated from Sweden and

East Gautland by miles and miles of impenetrable forest. The West Gautar were for the most part an inland people, without much coastline except around the Göta river. It would have been difficult for them to wage war against Sweden, unless the operations were carried on with small ships across the lakes of Central Sweden, or across the ice in winter. If the Kingdom of the West Gautar had ceased to exist after Beowulf's death in the sixth century, one would have expected to have heard in the Norwegian Sagas of wars between Norwegian and Swedish Kings. Such wars are never mentioned, but wars between Norwegians and West Gautar are often mentioned in the Viking period. Weibull maintains that it was not until after the trade route along the Russian rivers had been closed to the Swedes that they acquired a vital interest in expanding toward the West. We know nothing about Swedish rule in West Gautland until the year 1000, after the battle of Svolder. The Swedish suzerainty in West Gautland was presumably the price the Danish King Svend Forkbeard had to pay to the Swedish King Olof Skotkonung for his support in the decisive battle against the Norwegian King Olav Trygvason.

At different times the Danes in *Beowulf* are called East Danes, North Danes, West Danes, or South Danes, the words perhaps being chosen for alliteration or meter. But such names may originally have had a political significance, if the Danes were pressing for access to trade and shipping on the North Sea, the East Danes being the Danes of Zealand and in Skaane, the North Danes being settlers in Vendsyssel and along the Limfjord, the West Danes being Danish settlers along the shores, inlets, and rivers in Eastern Jutland, and the South Danes being the Danes succeeding the Angles in Slesvig along the Sli-Eider route.

This supposition gets a certain support from what Procopios relates ca. 550. He tells us that when in the year 512 the Eruli returned from Hungary to Scandinavia, they had to pass through the settlements of the Varni and the tribes of the Danes before sailing across 'the Ocean', settling down near the Gautar. The plural form 'tribes' indicates that they had to pass through Slesvig to the Limfjord in north from where they embarked for the vicinity of the West Gautar who at that time were still an independent tribe. If the chronology is reliable, it would have been in the days of Hrodgar, Hugleik, and Beowulf.

If we study the English colonization of North America, we see that the colonists settled down along the coast and penetrated along the inlets and rivers. If we study the Danish colonization of East England, we see how the newcomers settled down along the coast and from there penetrated along the inlets and rivers. If we study the map of Denmark we see in East Jutland a similar distribution of the place names with the ending –lev along the coast and from there penetrating along the inlets and rivers, maybe being traces of an old Danish administrative division of land. The word –lev is related to the English word leave. They are clustered along the Limfjord, the Mariager Fjord, the Gudenaa river, and the Aarhus river. There are many in Vendsyssel, which controls the entrance to the Limfjord. On the small peninsula of Salling, central in the Limfjord, we find Roslev with the name of Hrodgar in the prefix. It is interesting that in *Beowulf* as a vassal to the court of Hrodgar, we meet Wulfgar, the Prince of the Vandals, 'Wendla leod'. Adam of Bremen mentions a town at the Limfjord, called Vendila. It might have been near Lindholm Höje with the many graves in the shape of stone ships. This might have been Wulfgar's capital.

In Central and West Jutland there are no –lev towns, excepting a few on the strategically important exits of rivers and inlets—Villerslev, Hillerslev, and Uglev in the western part of the Limfjord—Hyllerslev and Alslev at the Varde river near the important natural harbor, Hjerting Bay—Vilslev at the Kongeaa river—and in Slesvig Emmerslev, and two Sejerslevs at the Vidaa river.

In those parts of Jutland where we have the –lev towns, we find in the language the definite article as a suffix—hus*et*, mand*en*—while in Central and West Jutland the article is put in front of the noun as in English, *the* house, *the* man—æ hus, æ man. Central and West Jutland, with its windy weather and sturdy population may have been the territory of the Geatas.

The Danish royal names begin with the holy letter 'H'. The same habit is found among the Geatas. The names Hlewagastir, Hengest, and Horsa, of famous Jutish chieftains, follow the same tradition. Most of the Swedish royal names, however, begin with a vowel.

The hostilities between the Geatas and the Swedes are supposed to have brought the Gautar under Swedish rule shortly after the death of Beowulf, but the later Norwegian sagas still refer to strife between Norwegians and Gautar, which indicates that the West Gautar were not under Swedish rule. The East Gautar could easily have waged war with the Swedes in Uppland, but neither the West Gautar nor the East Gautar could have the slightest reason for fearing the Franks and the Frisians. (L. 2910 f.) The Jutes, on the other hand, had reason to fear the closing of rivers to shipping and trade.

The poem's description of the treasures loaded in King Skjold's funeral ship (L. 28 f.) has met with distrust. The munificence of King Hrodgar's gifts to Beowulf (L. 1020-1049) was looked upon as exaggerated. Now the rich equipment in the East Anglian burial ship from Sutton Hoo has confirmed the reliability of the poem. What was believed to be poetical fiction has turned out to be historical fact.

The manifest traces of Vendel-styling on the sword, the shield, and the helmet found in the ship have strengthened the Gautar theory, and so Nerman draws the conclusion that the boat-grave contains a Swedish King or Chieftain. It is possible, but the two silver spoons with the inscription 'Saulos' and 'Paulos' does not prove that the Apostle is enshrined there. The great silver dish with the stamps of the Byzantine Emperor Anastasius (491-518) does not prove that the Emperor is buried there.

We happen to know from the poem and from many other sources that magnificent weapons would change hands as tokens of friendship, from family to family as dowries, or from tribe to tribe as spoils of war. Hrodgar's sister was married to Onela, King of the Swedes (L. 62), and Hrodgar's daughter was married to Ingeld, King of the Hadbards (L. 2020 f.). Goldsmiths and artisans were, like scops and minstrels, often peripatetic figures. It is therefore too early to draw conclusions as to the nationality of the Geatas from the international collection of objects in the Sutton Hoo ship.

It is also too early to draw into the discussion the bog-hoards of weapons sacrificed to the Gods which are found in East Jutland, because several explanations are possible as to who were fighting whom. Yet Sir Mortimer Wheeler says, "The astonishing bog-hoards of the third and fourth centuries are presumably, however, the product of victories and successful forays on the fringes of the Empire, and again emphasize the dominance of the Danish lands."

The study in the geographical mythology of the Geatas which Dr. Jane Acomb Leake has published shows that the information given by the classical historians and patristics are based on universal misunderstandings of what Herodotus and Ovid relate about the Getes and the Goths. She believes that respect for the Church Fathers was so great in the English Monasteries that nobody dared contradict them, and therefore constructed a fictional concept of the Geatas. The explanation is interesting but hardly a solution.

Stjerna advances the theory that the Danish islands were the wealthiest and most important parts of Scandinavia, rich in gold exacted from the

Romans. The Northern lands were poor though populous, which led to Conquests from Uppland resulting in the wealth of gold found in the Swedish graves. Weibull maintains that Uppland's wealth of gold throughout several centuries cannot be explained by one single plundering expedition. Only the continuous wholesale trade through Russia can explain it. He rejects Stjerna's hypothesis as an intelligent but over-imaginative conjecture.

Our sources do not permit any decision as to whom the Geatas were. American scholar Francis Magoun has shown how great is the oral-formulaic part of Anglo-Saxon poetry. Danish scholar Axel Olrik maintains that with our present knowledge the riddle cannot be solved. English scholar R. W. Chambers dismisses all reservations and declares that the Geatas were Gautar. Swedish scholar Elis Wadstein suggests that the traditional material of which the poet has made use was preponderantly Dano-Jutish, containing Gautic reminiscences. Swedish scholar Pontus Fahlbeck declared, "Beowulf's Geatas are not our Gautar." Swedish scholar Curt Weibull adds, "Beowulf's Geatas are the Jutes."

*

What is wrong in the previous attempts in solving the problem of the identity of the Geatas is that many scholars primarily begin with the poem, and secondarily look for additional information elsewhere. This must be methodically wrong. If we look at the problem from another angle, an interesting aspect is opened.

There is one person, and one person only, among the Geatas of *Beowulf* who is known from other sources. That is King Hugleik (Hygelac, Chlochilaichus). He was killed in action against the Franks, the Frisians, and the Hetware in the battle of the Rhine estuary about 520. In 1817 Grundtvig laid the foundation for the study of *Beowulf* by pointing out that Hugleik's battle of the Rhine is described by Gregory of Tours in *Historia Francorum*. Let us follow Grundtvig and begin with Gregory. He is our oldest source. Moreover, almost contemporary. Topographically, he is nearest to the events. He is well informed from the Merovingian court circle, and, with all his short-comings, he is an honest historian. His testimony must be preferred to that of a bard with poetical predisposition singing before an English audience about events that took place in France several centuries before. Gregory says, "His ita gestis, Dani cum rege suo Chlochilaichum evectu navale per mare Gallias appetunt." (After these events, the Danes and their King Hugleik crossed the seas with their fleet and came to Gaul.)

The identification of Hugleik as a King of the Danes is confirmed by another local Frankish source, the anonymous *Liber Historiae Francorum* from 727. It amends Gregory's information about the victory of the Merovingian King Theuderic by adding that the battle took place in the land of the Attoari which is the Hetware mentioned in *Beowulf* 2363 and 2916, and in *Widsith* 33. The *Liber Monstrorum*, possibly written in England in the eighth century, reports that the gigantic bones of Hugleik, 'Rex Hugilaicus qui imperavit Getis', were on display on an island in the Rhine mouth. In Denmark Saxo Grammaticus in the twelfth century states that 'Huglecus' was a Danish King.

If the problem of the Geatas is to be solved, it is necessary to start from historical facts and not from poetical conjectures. Hugleik was a Dane and a Geat, the way Hengest is alternately called a Jute, a Dane, and a Halfdane. Even today a man can be both a Dane and a Jute.

From the Baltic it was possible to sail through the narrow inlet of Sli to the middle of Jutland. The town of Hedeby was later built here. At the entrance of the Sli lies Arnæs, the possible site for Beowulf's death 'under Earna-næs'. (L. 3031.)

Sophus Bugge and Axel Olrik have discussed the old legend from Slesvig about 'The Robber from Graasten' and its connection with 'The Elegy of the last Survivor' in *Beowulf* (L. 2230.2553.2744.). The town of Graasten lies near Arnæs. Its name means 'the grey stone' which could be the 'harne stan' of the poem.

From the North Sea it was possible to sail through the Eider and its tributary to the middle of Jutland, where we find Hollingsted, which in olden days was connected with Hedeby. As in 1285 Hollingsted was spelt 'Huglæstath', Clausen believes that Hugleik's name is contained in it. His name is still used in Slesvig in the forms Hugle, Haule, Hoglek, Hollesen.

Why did Hugleik attack the Rhine mouth? The Frisians living there usually followed the policy of the open river and open port; but shortly before 520 the Franks had suppressed the Frisians and the Hetware. If the Franks—as they have often done—followed the policy of closing harbors and blocking up rivers, it might have started a war with the Jutes.

Sir Mortimer Wheeler described the amazing amount of Roman wares from the workshops in the Rhineland found in Danish soil. He says, "Attention has been drawn to the early prominence of the islands of Denmark in this traffic, and it has been suspected that their prominence reflects some measure of political cohesion, probably with Zealand as its focus." As a young warrior Beowulf took part in Hugleik's battle of the Rhine. He later became King of the Geatas. His heroic deed in killing the monster, Grendel, in Hrodgar's hall was performed before Hugleik's death in 520. Hrodgar gave a banquet in honor of Beowulf, described in L. 1063-1159 of the poem. The culmination of the feast was when the Danish court scald took his harp to sing. Presumably, the harp was like the one found in the Sutton Hoo ship. Placed on a tabletop it gives out a sonorous sound. Beowulf later told King Hugleik how the old King Hrodgar, relating old tales, sometimes played the harp, called 'wood of joy'. (L. 2107.)

The scald recited a well-known song, 'gid oft wrecen', the song about Hengest, at the time of current interest because Hengest died in 488, a few decades before Hrodgar's feast. Hengest fought in Friesland like Hugleik and Beowulf, and he was the first to conquer part of England. Like Hamlet he was a figure caught between two conflicting duties, loyalty towards his lord, Hnæf, and loyalty towards his host, Finn.

If Beowulf had been a Gaut it would have been an insult to celebrate a Gautish hero by extolling a Jutish hero. If, on the other hand, Beowulf had been a Jute, the famous song about the famous Jute would have been just the thing to please Beowulf and rouse the interest of an English aristocratic audience.

In the 9th century Nennius, drawing up the genealogical table of Hengest, places a King by name of Geat as the first link in the royal pedigree. He must have been an eponym of the Jutish people, the Geatas.

*

Most important of all are the geographical, political, and economic facts about the shipping and trade of the Geatas. Trade routes and sea lanes are often constant factors.

In the Stone Age, the custom of constructing Megalithic graves came to Denmark from the West, and Danish export of flint reached as far as Friesland. In the Bronze Age part of the amber and bronze trade went in the same direction. In the Roman Age close connection in trade existed between the rivers of Northern Europe and the harbors of Western Jutland. The West Eruli, between 200 and 500, directed their expeditions in the same direction; and when the Eruli disappeared, the Danes appeared instead. Hnæf and Hengest fought in Friesland, and the Jutes and Angles sailed to Britain via Friesland. The feud between the Danes and the Hadbards might have been due to conflicting interests on the rivers Elbe and Trave. About 520 Hugleik and Theuderic's son, Theudebert, fought in Frisian Gelderland at the Rhine. In 565 Duke Lupus defeated a Danish fleet at Groningen near the river Ems. We know of Danish shipping along the coast in the centuries preceding the clash between King Gudfred I and Charlemagne, in which the rivers Eider, Elbe, and Rhine were involved. The Viking Period teems with Danish activity in Friesland and at the estuaries of the rivers, resulting in the forays of Lodbrog—in the creation of the smaller Kingdoms of Harald Klak, Hroric, and Gudfred III near the rivers Weser, Ems, Rhine, and Scheldt—the greater Duchy of Rollo's around the Seine—and in the North Sea Empire of Canute the Great.

This is a chain of events, connected by geopolitical facts and continued for economic reasons. On no occasion do we hear about Gautic activity along the coastal route from Jutland to the Rhine, unless Hugleik and his Geatas were Gautar. Danes and Jutes were then about to unite into one nation. In fact, Beowulf recommended that peace should remain between the Geatas and the Danes, 'sib gemæne ond sacu restan', and Hrodgar agreed. (L. 1857.) As Hugleik in the earliest and most reliable sources is called King of the Danes, the probability of the Geatas being the Jutes is so great that it approximates certainty.

THE ANGLES

If we seek out the original England of the continental Angles, we must go to the districts of Angel, in the Cimbric, that is the Danish, peninsula. R. H. HODGKIN.

Between Flensborg Fjord and the Sli there lies an ancient tribal land: Angel in Slesvig.

"In this old England," says Professor Hodgkin, "there is still much to make those of us who belong to the new England of Britain feel at home. Not only do the faces of the men and women constantly remind us of types to be seen in the Anglian districts of our island, but by some chance the appearance of the land itself, with its irregular fields and hedgerows and the undulating well-timbered country, is also what we should call typically English."

"The point to notice is that the Angles, though hemmed in on a narrow peninsula and forced to take to the sea, had an excellent position with one good harbour facing east to the Baltic and another facing west toward the North Sea and Britain. The Eider, which lay between them and the Saxons, being a navigable river, must have brought the two folk into close connection. They were bound to be either great enemies or allies."

The venerable Bede, the English Father of the Church, who wrote in about 700 A.D. states, "The newcomers came from three very powerful Germanic nations, namely the Saxons, the Angles and the Jutes. From the stock of the Jutes are the people of Kent and the people of Wight, that is, the race which holds the Isle of Wight, and that which in the province of the West Saxons is to this day called the nation of the Jutes, situated opposite that same Isle of Wight. From the Saxons, that is, from the region that now is called that of the old Saxons, came the East Saxons, the South Saxons and the West Saxons. Further, from the Angles, that is, from the country which is called *Angulus,* and which from that time until today is said to have remained deserted between the provinces of the Jutes and Saxons, are sprung the East Angles, the Middle Angles, the Mercians, the whole race of the Northumbrians, that is, of those people who dwell north of the river Humber, and the other peoples of the Angles.—In a short time, as bands of the aforesaid nations eagerly flocked into the island, the people of the newcomers began to increase so much that they became a source of terror to the very natives who had invited them." Bede's statement of the Angles coming from that country which is called Angel and lies between the lands of the Jutes and Saxons: —"de illa patria quae Angulus dicitur—inter prouincias Jutarum et Saxonum"—is a very definite statement. It must have originated in an English tradition among princely or ecclesiastical circles, since it cannot have come from Gildas. Gildas, the old Briton who wrote about the invasion in the years around 560, and who refers to the Saxons as 'the fierce Saxons, hateful alike to God and man', however, makes no reference to the native home of the Angles.

Many things suggest that the Angles may have come from Thuringia, since the ancient Alexandrian geographer Ptolemy, on his 1900–year–old map, placed the Angles to the south of the Elbe. It so happens that in that exact location in Thuringia, at Unstruth, there is a district called Engelin, and also numerous place names ending in -'engeln', even as

108

The Nydam boat.
Sundeved. North Slesvig.

there also exist in that region place names with the termination -'leben' (-lev), and personal names which resemble those of Danish place names.

To these two pieces of evidence can be added a third, a legal historical one, since Thuringia's ancient Book of Laws, dating from the beginning of the 9th century, has the superscription '*Lex Angliorum et Werinorum hoc est Thuringorum*'. So Angles and Warni were then regarded as being Thuringians. The Book of Laws is admittedly of later date than the emigration to Britain, but nonetheless it is a piece of evidence which, in conjunction with the other two, favors the theory that the Angles came from Thuringia. Finally, there are some references among Roman authors which may point in the same direction.

The Danish historians Steenstrup and Erslev were, in their time, also inclined to deny a Danish origin to the Angles. Some German historians think the same. Otto Scheel of Kiel in particular worked hard to prove a German origin for the Angles; indeed, he went so far as to entirely set aside the ancient English sources and relied solely on Ptolemy and the Romans. Scheel argues something like this: The number 3 is typical of folk-legends and fairytales–there are always three princes, three daughters of a king or three tests to be undergone–and, since in this case Gildas and Bede state that Hengest and Horsa came sailing in three ships, it is obvious that there must originally have been one more king besides Hengest and Horsa, and since there were three kings the account is a fairytale, and thus these sources can be entirely disregarded.

Now legendary history should not be taken so literally that the number three can never occur in the world of reality, but since only two kings are actually mentioned, Scheel's argument is not convincing. Herbert Jankuhn also rejects Scheel's method of approach, and concludes that from the historical sources alone it is impossible to come to any decision, owing to their conflicting contents and statements.

Scheel also advances the argument that Angel, between Flensborg Fjord and Sli, is such a small province that it could not have been the starting-point for the great conquest and colonization of England–the Anglian counties in England being seventy-six times larger than the Angel of Slesvig. But in this connection it must be noted that the tribes which, in their day, colonized Germany, came mainly from the ancient Danish lands which are small in comparison, and also that relatively small England, in a later era, colonized a couple of continents. Finally, the Thuringian Province is not much larger than Angel, and, judging by archaeological finds, was extremely thinly populated before the migration, whereas Angel had a very dense population. There is, moreover, some evidence that Fyn and the islands around it belonged to the kingdom of the Angles, which would have increased both the numbers of the peoples and the strength of its fleet.

Tacitus, the Roman, wrote in 98 A.D. that the Angles and Jutes belonged to a confederation of tribes which worshipped Nerthus, the Goddess of Fertility. The other five tribes in the confederation cannot be definitely identified, though Chambers thinks that the Aviones must have lived on Fyn. The Goddess Nerthus had her sacred grove on an island in the Ocean, perhaps Zealand or Als. The Nerthus-worshipping tribes had their native home at the western end of the Baltic, to the north of the Eider.

The Thuringians were an inland people, and Chambers does not think it probable that the men who sailed across the sea to conquer Britain came from a district 200 miles inland. However, they could conceivably have wandered to the Frisian coast, where it is also believed that Jutes, Saxons and Angles tarried a while before the invasion of Britain.

In King Alfred of England's translation of Orosius' geography, there is an account of a Norwegian trader named Ottar, who relates that the commercial city of Hedeby lies between the Wends, Saxons and Angles and belongs to Denmark. He adds, "The Angles lived in this country before they went to England." Several other English sources–Ethelwerd, Nennius and William of Malmesbury–give the same information, as does a German source, Annales Quedlinburgenses, dating from the 11th century, and stating that in 445 A.D. the Angles, led by their King Angling, 'went to England from Angel which the Danes now occupy'. It is an ethnic tradition which thus refers to the same eponym that Saxo mentions in his legend about the foundation of the Danish Kingdom by Dan and Angul. Saxo says that Uffe was succeeded by Dan and Hugleik. The latter is perhaps the King of Geatas mentioned in Beowulf. From Bede we actually have a statement that the native land of the Angles became depopulated after their emigration to Britain and that the Danes then took possession of it. Thus the foundation was laid for the later united Kingdom of Denmark.

It is possible that Danes from Zealand may have advanced into Thuringia after the migration, since there are place names there ending in 'leben' or 'lev' which point to Danish occupation, and the graves bear a strong resemblance to those of the Danes.

The legend of the three generations: Viglek, Vermund and Uffe, and their fight with the Saxons at the Eider frontier, is found in Saxo and Svend Aggesen. Saxo regards Uffe as a Danish King, though he was in fact a King of the Angles, and the legend reflects an ancient political conflict between Angles and Saxons concerning the dominion over the river Eider and its mouth, 'Ægir's Door'. This was the approach and sally-port to the North Sea and the connecting trade link between it and the Baltic. The duel, according to the accounts, took place on the island where the brother of King Erik Ejegod later built the town of Rendsborg.

In an ancient royal pedigree of the Anglian Kings of Mercia in England, the same kings are named in sequence:–Offa, Vermund and Withlaeg. Almost all authorities agree that these kings ruled in Angel before the invasion of England, and a calculation of dates from the genealogical table bears this out. Historians believe that Offa is a historical character who is identical with Uffe, and that he must have been born about 360 A.D. Widsith says, concerning himself, that he dwelt at the Court of Ermanaric, King of the Goths. Ermanaric died about 370, so this dating of the lifetime of Offa equates well with the former calculation.

The West Saxon Kings of Wessex have a genealogical table in which the names Freawine and Wig occur at the same period around 350 A.D. The same names appear in Saxo, Frøvin and his son Wiggo; they were King Vermund's earls in South Jutland. This earl family was at war with a king whom Saxo calls Adils, King of the Svear.

Now Widsith, the old English Lay, which is the oldest surviving poem from the territories of the Teutonic peoples, and although probably dating from the close of the 7th century, reflects traditions from the

5th and 6th, says that there was a King of the Myrgingi named Eadgils who was a contemporary of Offa in Angel. The Myrgingi were Widsith's own people and were probably a Saxon or Suebian tribe, and Widsith states that he was in the service of Eadgils. The scald seems to be principally interested in continental Angel and in the Danish kings.

Widsith says of Offa, "He drew the boundary against the Myrgingas at Fifeldor (the Eider). Engle and Swæfe held it afterwards as Offa established it." So it seems probable that Saxo has confused the names Eadgils and Adils and the words Suebes and Swedes.

Widsith admires Offa and says of him, "Offa ruled Angle, Alewih the Danes." It is important that here one finds the Angles and Danes closely connected. Chadwick has supposed that this Danish King Alewih is the king whom Saxo and Svend Aggesen call King Dan. The ancient Beowulf Poem calls Offa 'the best of all mankind betwixt the seas'. Beowulf also entertains a lively interest in the Danish kings, just as almost all ancient epic Anglian literature extols the Danes, but almost ignores the Saxons. This is an important clue, because psychologically it fits in very poorly with any suggested German origin for the Angles.

The legends thus give the picture that the Angles came from Angel in Slesvig, that they were the leading tribe in South Jutland, that the Kingdom of the Danes did not at that time include Angel, and that the Angles were victorious in the struggle for the River Eider—that important sea-gate to the North Sea and to Britain. At the same time, this ancient conflict perhaps explains why the Angles became the leading tribe in Britain, and gave their name to the whole of England. Trevelyan says of the conflict between Offa and the Saxons that "it was the last great battle between English and Germans until a day more dark and drear, and a more memorable year."

This close relationship between Angles and Danes, which the English and Danish sources mutually supplement and confirm so neatly, points strongly to the probability that the Angles came from Angel and not from Thuringia. The old English sources point in the same direction and in them one might reasonably expect to find preserved a recollection of the emigration and original native home of the Angles, as no lengthy period had elapsed since these great events transpired. The very name of the province—Angel—and its ancient tribal historical boundaries are also valuable indications. In addition, economic and geopolitical considerations bear this out.

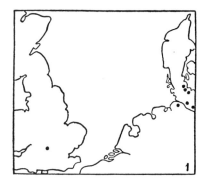
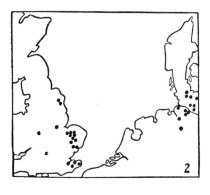

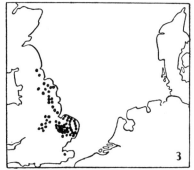

The distribution of cruciform brooches before and after the emigration of the Angles. (Ohlhaver & Jankuhn).

None of these reasons is quite decisive. But archaeological investigations in Germany have now shown that the district where Ptolemy's map places the Angles is extremely meager in artifacts from the centuries before the emigration to Britain, whereas the quantity of finds shows a considerable increase in the periods during and after the emigration. These discoveries show a close affinity with Danish antiquities of the same period, and therefore it is reasonable to conclude that an immigration has taken place here from the north, from Angel or Zealand. This may also explain that group of place names with the termination 'by' and 'leben' (lev) which implies a Danish settlement. On the other hand, in Angel itself there is a tremendous wealth of cultural residue which indicates first a dense population, and secondly a close tie between Angel and the districts lying north, as well as Fyn.

In Angel itself the burial places from the 3rd, 4th and 5th centuries show a great increase in the population but from the 5th and 6th centuries the finds practically disappear. Jankuhn describes how the urns and other archaeological finds typical for Angel suddenly appear in East-Anglia in England. It seems, he say, that the cemeteries of Angel are continued in East-Anglia. The pollen analysis of the moors in Torsbjerg and Satrupholm in Slesvig show clearly a well developed agriculture in the first centuries after Christ, and then a sharp decline is seen—a fine confirmation of Bede's statement.

The urn pottery, with its vigorously modelled vessels, shows great resemblance between the artifacts found in Angel and the Anglian counties north of the Thames. The little bow-shaped brooch which is called a fibula, is a leading artifact of great archaeological interest because its form and ornamentations are so characteristically disparate for different areas and periods. There is a little cruciform brooch which, in its oldest form, is particularly representative of Angel in Slesvig, and surrounding districts. Only one specimen of this type has been found in England. In the next phase of its design it is found distributed in both continental Angel and eastern England, especially East Anglia. Finally, in the last phase of its development, it is found in England in considerable numbers, but appears no more in Slesvig. This cogent archaeological proof, in conjunction with the historical traditions, decides beyond all question that the English came from Angel, and to this day England bears an ancient Danish name for its country, people and language. This confirmation, as far as the Angles are concerned, indirectly supports the theory of the Jutish origin of the Jutes. It is an obvious solution that the Angles came from Angel and the Jutes came from Jutland.

Recently, Bjerrum has tried to dismiss the historical sources and archaeological results and build his argument mainly on linguistic theories, but he disregards the following important passages from Procopios and the monk of Fulda.

Stenton has stressed the importance of a passage in *De Bello Gotthico* written about 550 A.D. by Procopios of Caesarea. This brilliant Byzantine historian, who wrote shortly after the events and nearly 200 years before Bede, relates that a great number of the Angles (Angiloi) in the beginning of the sixth century crossed the channel from Britain to the Frankish territory on the Continent and planted themselves in the less densely populated lands of the Frankish king. This reverse migration is supposed by Stenton to be an effect of the Britons' victory over the Anglian invaders at Mons Badonius, the location of which is unknown.

On the continent the Angles were involved in a war with a tribe of the Warni.

Through this migration and settlement in Frankish territory, the king of the Franks had come to assert a claim to Britain itself, and in order to impress the Byzantine emperor, he sent to Constantinople emissaries, among whom were some Angles. It must have been these Angles from whom Procopios received his information about Britain.

It is important that we thus have an almost contemporary authority relating that Angles in great numbers were crossing *from* Britain *to* the Frankish territory on the continent. This statement is confirmed by an independent tradition of a migration of English people from Britain to the continent in the first half of the sixth century, and this version was described by a monk of Fulda in his *Translatio Sancti Alexandri* a little before 865, at which time it was already regarded as an ancient story. It asserted that the ancestors of the continental Saxons sprang from the Angli of Britain. Being compelled to find new land for settlement, they had crossed the ocean at the time when Theuderic, king of the Franks, was at war with the Thuringians. When the king learned that the immigrants were eager to settle in Germany, Theuderic invited them to join him in the Thuringian war and, after his victory, circa 531, he gave them land to the north of the river Unstruth in the Thuringian territory which he had conquered. Centuries later, Master Adam of Bremen relates a similar story.

In this way the strongest support for the theory of the inland origin of the Angles from Thuringia is removed. The conclusion is that the Angles did not come to Britain from Thuringia, but from Angel to Britain and, some decades later, a part of the Angles re-crossed the channel and came to Thuringia. In this way we have a well-authenticated explanation of the fact that Anglian place-names are to be found near Unstruth in Thuringia, and of the title of the Thuringian law: *Lex Angliorum et Werinorum hoc est Thuringorum.*

Ptolemy's geographical statement must consequently have been based upon a misconception—not the only one to be found in Ptolemy. He places the Langobardians down near the Rhine, instead of in Bardengau by the Elbe, where they belong. If the Langobardians are transferred to their proper place, then logically, the Anglians should be moved parallel with them, so that they would automatically assume their proper location in Angel.

*

In England itself the course of the invasion is obfuscated. Presumably, the Roman roads simplified the invasion and directed its course, and the rapid success of the invasion is partly explained by the depopulation of vast areas in Britain as a result of the Roman hunt for slaves. The Celts were driven to Ireland, Brittany, Wales and the hilly districts of Scotland. Many of those remaining behind became slaves.

Trevelyan says that no matter whether the two Jutish kings Hengest and Horsa are mythical or real persons (Myres thinks they are real) they stand as types of those great forgotten makers of history who 'unwittingly founded England and all that has since come of England in the tide of time'.

We know ancient British churches went up in flames and smoke, that Roman villas were destroyed, that the populace was evicted, exterminated or enslaved so thoroughly that scarcely any Celtic place-names remain in England, with the exception of those of rivers and a few cities, such as London. Otherwise, 'The most important page in our national annals is a blank'.

The Angles constituted the principal element among the conquerors of England, but they received considerable reinforcement from other tribes. Bede states that the Jutes, who were the first to undertake the conquest around 449, settled in Kent, on the Isle of Wight and the coast of Hampshire. The Saxons settled in south England—the South-Saxons under Aella, in the present Sussex, in about 477 and the West-Saxons under Cerdic and Cynric in about 491. The termination 'sex' in the counties of southern England derives from the ancient name for Saxon. Myres considers Bede's account of the departure point and the native lands of the emigrants to be correct, but regards the settlement itself in Britain as being more mixed and confused than Bede would have us believe, "Increase of knowledge has led to a growth of ignorance."

The Angles must have come to England in the latter half of the 5th century. As in the case of the Jutes, they spent some time in Friesland, and would hardly have arrived in England in one united horde, but rather as waves of conquerors streaming in through those two great portals—the Thames and the Wash. The conquest of the rest of England probably started, as did the colonization of America, with small bands camping on the eastern seaboard and gradually spreading west up the river valleys into the rest of the country. Myres considers the main causes for the emigration of the Angles and Saxons to have been three sets of

116

The helmet from the Sutton Hoo Ship-burial. Suffolk. East Angel.

forces: a rise in sea-level, which reduced the amount of land, the attacks of the Goths on Rome which compelled the Romans to abandon Britain, and the invasion of Europe by the Huns from the east which created pressure on the west-European tribes. The ancient British tribes, whom the Jutes, Angles and Saxons conquered and rolled westward like a carpet, called all the foreign conquerors Saxons, which perhaps was a holdover from the earlier Saxon raids on their coasts, in which no doubt Erules, Frisians, Jutes and Angles also took part. But these raids occurred long before England's conquest. During the 200 years before the time of Bede we do not hear of the Saxons as a seafaring people.

But the new people in England never took the name of Saxons or

Anglo-Saxons. They called themselves 'Angli', 'Engle' or 'Angelcyn'. Freeman says that he does not know of a single instance where one of the new inhabitants of England before the Norman Conquest in 1066 has used the word Saxon as a designation for the entire nation. Therefore, he continues, one should always call a nation by the name it calls itself in this case, English. The hyphenated name Anglo-Saxon was coined later on the continent, by Alcuin.

That the Angles gave their name to the country is evidence that they were the leading tribe. Perhaps the reason for this lies in the fact that the Angles had kings long before the emigration, and consequently had a more firmly organized social structure. The continental Saxons had no kings, while the later West-Saxon kings were descended from men of good family who had been earls under Vermund.

A hundred years ago, Grundtvig wrote that we know from the history of the north "that in heathen times, while an impenetrable darkness brooded over vast Germany, there ruled in little Denmark and in all the north a comparatively light and noble outlook on the whole of human life, loud in song, fruitful in great achievement and of praise-worthy renown. And we know, moreover, that it was our near relatives, the Angles from Jutland and Slesvig, who gave England its name and became the great spiritual mediators between the south and the north, between antiquity and more modern times, between Christianity and the Nordic paganism. Yes, the Englishman has been from time immemorial the nearest relative of the Dane."

The Angles were also skilful merchants and navigators. To sail many thousand families across the North Sea from South Denmark via Fries-land to England in craft such as the Nydam boat, was unique in the age of migrations. They had with them their families. "We cannot withhold our admiration from these gallant women," says Trevelyan.

The counties which the Angles colonized were East-Anglia, which included Norfolk and Suffolk, Mercia in central England, and North-umbria with Deira and Bernicia, in the north. They were the same districts as those which, during the later Danish invasions, became the 'Danelaw'. The names for the inhabitants of Norfolk and Suffolk–'North Folk' and 'South Folk'–are designations which have their parallels only in the north, not in Germany.

The Angles also appear to have been one of the leading tribes within the Amphiktyons of the Nerthus-worshipping tribes, whereas there are

118

no traces to show that the Saxons worshipped Nerthus. This Goddess was Mother Earth herself, the source of life, growth and blessing. Tacitus states that she dwelt on an island in the Sea, in a sacred grove, and at festivals she drove over the fields, scattering blessings on people, plants and animals, while every weapon was laid aside. After the procession, the sacred chariot, which no doubt resembled one of the magnificent chariots found in the marsh at Dejbjerg, was washed in the forest-lake, and afterward the serving slaves who had gazed upon the sacred objects were drowned.

We do not know what dim ancestry Nerthus-worship has in the north, but the soil and fertility have surely been worshipped for as long as there was need of it, i.e., since the inception of agriculture. The Trundholm chariot from the Bronze Age shows the cult-picture of the Sun driving in his chariot, and the ritual pictures in the rock-engravings of ploughs, ships, sleighs, chariots and love scenes are certainly allied with a similar cult. We know that plough-rites and ritual-ships have been closely associated with fertility worship right down to our time. On Als, for example, the plough-rites of Spring were celebrated up to the present day with songs redolent of soil and fertility:

The earth with tall ripe rye,
and fair foals thereby,
with fishes in our nets,
and lovely girls in beds,
that many children fair
be rocked in cradles there.

On Als, this lovely and fertile island, there is an unusual number of the so-called 'Cup-stones' (Skaal Sten), from the Stone and Bronze Ages. They were associated with the cult of fertility. When one considers how much ancient lore still exists today in old customs preserved by the peasantry, despite the inquisitorial eye of the Church, it is natural to suppose that the cults of the Stone and Bronze Ages showed a similar stubborn persistence into the days of the Iron Age. The worship of Nerthus survived to a later time in the worship of Njord, in that of their children Frey and Freja, and in the worship of Gefjon and Skjold on Zealand and in Skaane.

Some think that Als may have been the sacred island in the ocean, while others believe that Zealand was the main seat of the Nerthus cult,

119

and that the Amphiktyon had its wealth, power and ritualistic center at Hlejre. Alexander Bugge writes, 'From the most ancient times, all life in Denmark one might say, had had its focus on Zealand, from the days when people from the Danish islands and from the southern shores of the Baltic—all the tribes of the Ingvaeoni—assembled here in a sacred grove in order to worship Nerthus, the female Njord, the Mother of the Earth.' The cult of Nerthus seems to have been bound up with the tribes of the Ingvaeoni along the Baltic all the way up to Uppsala in Sweden, where Frey later had his capital. Chadwick, Chambers, Olrik and Elle-kilde all think it most probable that the principal seat was on Zealand. The worship of Gefjon on Zealand is certainly a continuation of Nerthus worship, and in the district around the little river of Lejre there remain a number of place-names containing the word 'Gefn', i.e., the giving, or bounteous. The old memories of Gefjon and her spouse, Skjold, and their close affiliation with plough-rites and ship ritual, are linked to Zealand, to the circles of the Danes and the Skjoldungs. The tie that bound Angles and Danes was knitted closely and firmly. The Anglian and English legends and traditions profess only warmth and sympathy. It is therefore reasonable to suppose that the advance of the Danes into Angel, after the emigration of the Angles westward, took place in mutual agreement and in the peaceful spirit of the amphiktyon, even though the great marsh finds may hint that battles had occurred at an earlier date.

THE DANES

Lo! We have heard the fame of the Kings of the Spear-Danes!
BEOWULF.

Denmark became united from its center.

Because of its location, Zealand, surrounded by Skaane on the east and Jutland on the west, naturally became the central connecting link in the realm. Something cautious yet open in the Zealander's character, his faculty for negotiation, his curiosity and joy in social contacts, equipped him to unite the kingdom. 'Let us chat together while we live; when we are dead we may find ourselves lying beside someone who says nothing.' That is an old Zealand phrase. The Zealander has never been a separatist.

Now the country is one thing, the people another, and the realm and its boundaries a third. The country has been there since the Ice Age, the people have lived there for thousands of years, but the process of internal coordination and organization, and the delineation of the frontiers of what was to become the Danish Kingdom, are not as old as the country and the people.

In the Bronze Age there seem to have been no noteworthy differences between the cultures of the provinces which lay within the area of Danish civilization, but in the Iron Age we see the tribes appearing as more distinctive types.

The question as to who the Danes originally were is disputable. But, while discussing the various possibilities, one must not forget the fact that in the oldest accounts extant they were localized on Zealand and perhaps Skaane. Norway's celebrated archaeologists Sophus and Alexander Bugge, father and son, state that even the linguistic character of the name Dane shows that its origin dates from a period long before the time when we first find it recorded in about 500 A.D.–certainly 1,000 years prior to that date–and that the Danes themselves are probably a very ancient tribe.

The legendary Kings of Hlejre–the Scyldings or the Skjoldungs–lived on Zealand. But of all the tribes of which the legends speak–Danes and Hadbardi, Skjoldungs, Eruli and Halfdanes, Vølsungs and Siklings–we cannot say with certainty what each was. The sources are scanty, entangled in verse and overgrown with legends, and even though scholars have wrung them hard, no clear wine has come forth.

Curt Weibull writes that 'Danes' is a common designation for the peoples who dwelt in South Scandinavia and who spoke the same language.

Mela and Pliny, in the first century after Christ, refer to a large bay–Sinus Codanus–which is probably the Baltic. Mela, who wrote in about 40 A.D., calls the large island in this bay 'Codanouia' and this is probably the same area which Pliny calls 'Scandinavia',–Skaane or Zealand. There are those who believe, probably in error, that the name of the Danes lies hidden in 'Codan'.

In the second century after Christ, Ptolemy refers to some south Scandinavian tribes: "East of the Cimbrian Peninsula are situated four islands called Skandiai, three of them small and one larger more to the East opposite the estuary of the Vistula ... It is in particular called Skandia, and on it live to the West the Chaidonoi, to the East the Fauonai and Firaisoi, to the North the Finnoi, to the South the Gutai and Daukiones, and in the Center the Leuonoi." The Gutes were previously mentioned by Pytheas in the neighborhood of the amber-coast of Jutland, and Nerman believes that this must have been a Jutish tribe and not the Götar. Schütte supposes that the word Daukiones may be a slip of the pen for Danniones or Daneiones, and draws attention to the fact that among the many hundreds of Teutonic tribes there is not a single one which begins with the letters 'Da-' excepting only the Danes. Since Ptolemy places the Daukiones in South Scandinavia and mentions them in proximity to the Gutes, then irrespective of whether these are a Jutish or Götic tribe, this geographical localization strongly supports the supposition that Ptolemy was referring to the Danes as being settled here. The word 'Daukiones' is verified in the Gothic language in the form 'Ga-Daukans', meaning housemates.

To this may be added that when Procopios refers to the return of the Eruli to the north, he mentions them actually in close connection with Danes and Götar. These are, however, only uncertain possibilities. The name of the Danes is first mentioned definitely by Jordanes the Goth and by Procopios the Greek in about 550 A.D. But the fact that the Danes had not with any certainty been mentioned earlier does not mean that they were not there, since Roman information concerning the Teutonic peoples was meager and obscure. Their acquaintance with the north stemmed mainly from their expeditions to the Elbe districts where they came to know a number of Jutish tribes, and partly through their trade with the Prussian amber-coast at the mouth of the Vistula where they were in contact with a number of East-Scandinavian tribes. In the center lay Zealand, which from both points of view was on the extreme edge of the field of vision, or as Askeberg says, in a vacuum.

Jordanes refers to a number of Scandinavian tribes, among whom he says "the Swedes were renowned for being tall; yet the Danes, who originated from their tribe and who drove the Eruli from their dwelling places, claim first rank in this respect among the tribes of all Scandia." This interesting passage in Jordanes, which has given rise to so many suppositions and hypotheses, reads in Latin as follows, "Sunt et his exteriores Ostrogothae, Raumarici, Aeragnarici, Finni mitissimi, Scandzae cultoribus omnibus mitiores; nec non et pares eorum Vinoveloth; Suetidi, cogniti in hac gente reliquis corpore eminentiores: Quamvis et Dani, ex ipsorum stirpe progressi, Herulos propriis sedibus expulerunt, qui inter omnes Scandiae nationes nomen sibi ob nimia proceritate affectant praecipium ..."

122

Alas, the exasperating thing about this quotation is that from the language used by Jordanes it is not clear whether he means that the Danes were descended from the tribe of the Swedes or that both the Danes and the Swedes descended from the tribes of Scandinavia. Both interpretations are possible. If Jordanes had written Latin as did Cicero, the first interpretation would have been most probable, but in the barbarous language of Jordanes the latter is not improbable.

We know that the Danes are connected with Denmark, but their connection with Sweden is only a hypothesis. Chambers maintains that the Jordanes quotation need not mean that the Danes are descended from the tribe of the Swedes and that an examination of the sense in which Jordanes elsewhere uses the word 'stirps'–tribe–allows only the conclusion that the Danes have issued from the same comprehensive tribe as the Swedes, i.e., that they were Scandinavians, which is something we already know. In addition, the word 'Scandinavia' itself usually means Scania, or Skaane, which in ancient times was considered to be an island, as the termination 'avia' implies, but it also appears to have been used for the Danish islands. Ptolemy's map, for example, designates the Danish islands west of Skaane: as 'Scandiae minores.'

Next, there is uncertainty due to the fact that Jordanes often uses the word 'propriis' in the sense of 'suus' so that one cannot see whether the meaning is that the Danes had expelled the Eruli from the original dwelling-places of the Eruli (which is something that we do not know), or whether the Danes had expelled Eruli, who had penetrated into the original dwelling-places of the Danes (which is something we do know). Procopios records that the Eruli, in about 512, invaded the dwelling-places of the Danes, so it is reasonable to take the latter possibility into account, especially as Jordanes' information seems to point to a contemporary incident and not one occurring several hundred years earlier, as would have been the case had the coming of the Danes been connected with the change in burial customs.

Von Friesen maintains that the text, in the Jordanes manuscripts gives a confusing impression, which perhaps is ascribable to Jordanes himself or to his source, Cassiodorus. But in spite of Jordanes' confusion and regrettably uncultivated style, von Friesen nevertheless believes that what Jordanes intends to imply is that the Danes originated in the tribe of the Swedes, while J. V. Svensson thinks that he merely states that the Danes originated from Scandinavia's tribes. That Jordanes' ideas about these tribes were both uncertain and vague is apparent in his reference to the Swedes under two distinct names—Suehans and Suetidi—and that he construes them as two separate tribes. If the Danes were a tribe which emigrated from Sweden, it is not easy to understand how they could have been taller than the Swedes themselves, as Jordanes tells us they were. Gutenbrunner translates Jordanes in such a way that the excessive height points to the Eruli and not to the Danes.

Wadstein maintains that it is not possible to conclude, either from Procopios or Jordanes, that the Danes had their original home on the mainland of Scandinavia. Lauritz Weibull of Lund says of the theory that the Danes descend from the Swedes, "This view is the outcome of a false methodical presentation which occurs far too frequently and is therefore fatal, since the very opposite of that assertion is the only standpoint possible. The first account is at best a tradition concerning something which must have occured several centuries earlier and it cannot be considered true until it has been proved to be so. There is every reason to doubt the second account, upon which diffuse theories have been built. What has been said above may perhaps open the eyes of some people to the false valuation of sources which characterize such a large part of modern research."

Schütte does not think either that one dare draw definite conclusions from Jordanes. The anonymous geographer from Ravenna in the seventh century calls the Danes an old tribe—'patria quae et Dania ab antiquis dicitur.'

If there is historical truth to the legend about the fall of the famous heroic King Hrolf Krake, it should be remembered that Hjarvard, Hrolf's subordinate king in Skaane who undertook the assault at Hlejre, was himself a Skjoldung, son of Hrolf's paternal uncle Hjargar, and that he came sailing with Swedish mercenaries on board. This event may possibly form the background of the narrative in Jordanes.

The Lejre Chronicle of the 12th century contains a legend about the Swedish king Ypper who had three sons: Nori, Østen and Dan. The latter was sent to the lands which are now called Denmark to rule over Zealand, Møn, Falster and Laaland, that kingdom which was called Witheslef or Withesleth. He later vanquished the Jutes and gave the united kingdom the name of Denmark. The persons mentioned are eponyms of the Nordic lands and Uppsala. Poul Johs. Jørgensen interprets the Lejre Chronicle's legend as an attempt on the part of the

124

people of Zealand to explain why the Thing-assembly in Viborg, despite Hlejre's historical priority as the royal seat, had secured the right to be the first to elect the king. The Viborg Thing-assembly possessed this right throughout the middle ages, and Jørgensen thinks that the reason for this was that the kingdom had been united on several occasions.

As recounted by Snorre, the ancient Gefjon myth, wherein Gefjon ploughs Zealand out of Lake Mälar in Sweden, has been thought to be a derivative legend which might support the theory of the Danes being of Swedish origin. But there is a geographical district near Mälar called Sjøland, and it is probable, thinks Erslev, that the myth about it was transferred to Sjælland (Zealand) because of the resemblance in names.

Snorre says of Odin in the Ynglinge Saga, that he came from the Black Sea districts to Zealand and Hlejre, and later set out for Sweden. This legend therefore directly contradicts the one concerning Ypper. There are other derivative legends about Fornjotr and Snjo which trace the descent from Finland.

It is to be expected that people as belligerent and restless as were the Nordic tribes in the Migration Period would have fought with one another, and the legends resound with such conflicts. The Beowulf Lay tells of battles between Swedes and Danes in the beginning of the 6th century, and Swedish chieftains later entrenched themselves firmly for a while at Hedeby, and on Laaland, in about 900. Thus there is a possibility that Swedish chieftains may also have come to Danish shores at an earlier period.

Jordanes mentions no date for the Danish eviction of the Eruli, nor does he give a geographical location. Some think that he must be referring to ancient events occurring about the year 200 since, in the 3rd century, the Eruli appear as Vikings in the southeast and in the west. Others, including Wessén, think that the events may have been recent—from about the year 500–and that the Eruli, Skjoldungs and Halfdanes are one and the same people, while the Danes equate with the Hadbardi, and that the legends of the Skjoldungs have, in retrospect, been attached to the Danes. Concerning Wessén's theory, Chambers remarks drily, "We must never base an argument on the assumption that all our authorities mean the reverse of what they say."

Müllenhoff thinks that the Hadbardi and Skjoldungs are the same; Kendrick that the Hadbardi are Jutes; Koegel that the Hadbardi are Danes; and Lukman has tried to show by a series of hypotheses and suppositions that the Skjoldungs and Skilfingi were originally Kings of the Huns and Eruli. These are such controversial viewpoints, rich in so-called philological legends, that for the present one can only accept the legends for what they are, ancient myths which express something of the people's own spirit, as they imagined themselves to be through the ages, and to establish the homeland of the Danes in the place where they are actually to be found, i.e., in Denmark.

*

In the early Roman Iron Age, after the birth of Christ, funerary customs in Denmark began to change from the cremation-grave to earth-burial. A variation in burial customs does not necessarily imply immigration, but could be a modification in religious ceremonies. This particular change gave us material for the measurement of skulls, which show that the proportion between long and round heads in the Stone Age was about the same as in modern times—namely, 30 % longheads. The Iron Age crania show 84 % longheads. This is a striking difference, and the change may be due to immigration. In his measurements of Swedish Iron Age skulls, Fürst has found nearly the same percentage as in the Danish of the same period.

In Denmark there are only about 100 measurable skulls, and that is very little material from which to draw conclusions, especially since the rich burial graves must have been those of the aristocracy. The long-headed people are believed to have been more warlike and dominant than were the round-headed. For example, a description of the crania of the Danish royal family in recent centuries would not give a representative picture of cranial proportions in Denmark; moreover, according to Frets' investigations, the laws of heredity applying to the cranial-index are both involved and complex.

The extraordinary difference between the 30 % of the Stone Age, the 84 % of the Iron Age, and the 30 % of the present day, may be due to immigration, or to preferred racial types prevailing in the upper class, and maintained through intermarriage, as was probably the case in the Viking Period. The difference between the Iron Age and the present day may occur because we now have all the strata of our population measured. Also, the more adventurous and warlike element migrated to some extent during the colossal emigrations in the Viking Age, and was severely decimated during campaigns and feuds. We

126

know this to have been true of the Danish noble families, and it is also to be seen in the racial change occurring in Greece following the wars of antiquity. Finally, it must be noted that this change in cranial-index from the Stone and Early Bronze Ages to the Roman Iron Age may have taken place at any time during the 1000 years under consideration. In the cranial material itself there is nothing which leads one to suppose that its changes occurred at the same time as the alterations in burial customs, and concerning the stature of the skeletons, the Swedish Stone Age population was much shorter than the Danish, which is supported by Jordanes' record. Interment was a widespread custom among the Teutonic peoples beginning in the Celtic Iron Age, and as the grave-finds in Vendsyssel show a connection with Silesia it is possible that religious influences may have evolved from there.

Treasure-troves, decrease in number of graves, remnants of burnt buildings and defensive constructions are a combination of archaeological finds typical for turbulent periods of strife and warfare. Such were the conditions in the Migration Period after the downfall of the Roman Imperial power, and such were the conditions on the Baltic islands and in Skaane, according to the investigations of Märta Strömberg. The succeeding Vendel Period, from about 600 to 800 A.D., looks less warlike. Her investigations indicates repeated piratical attacks and feuds between neighboring tribes, especially in the years from 500 to 550 A.D., but no greater organized invasions.

*

The Danes and their kings are mentioned and given prominence in the old English lays–Widsith, the Finnsburg Lay and Beowulf. The old English Runic Lay says, "Ing was first among East Danes," and Beowulf often refers to the Danes as Ingwini. Now Ingvaeoni, at the beginning of our era, was virtually a collective designation for the Danish tribes. Chadwick says that at the time when history is first recorded, the Teutonic peoples of the western Baltic are all included among Danes. In Beowulf, the terms Dane and Ingwine are apparently synonymous, although the latter seems to be obsolescent. Our discussion has led to the conclusion that the Ingwini of the sixth century were the descendants of the Inguaeones of the first century, whether or not the two words are identical.

The Widsith Lay from the 7th century says, "Offa ruled Angel,

Alewih the Danes." This Danish Alewih, a contemporary of Offa or Uffe hin Spage in Angel, is said by Widsith to have been the boldest of all men, yet he did not in his deeds of valor surpass Offa,–or could not claim lordship over him. Perhaps here lies hidden the echo of a conflict between Danes and Angles; the bog finds in Slesvig may contain relics of it. Chadwick thinks that King Alewih may be identical with King Dan in Saxo and Svend Aggesen, whose name is wrapped in a wealth of legend. Alewih's name appears in the genealogical table of the Kings of Mercia.

The kingdom which is called Videslet or Witheslef embraced the east Danish islands Zealand, Møn, Falster and Laaland. The very fact that in ancient times such a term existed indicates that it was at one time a kingdom. As far as one can judge it formed the nucleus of the union of Denmark.

If the Danes came from Uppland in Sweden, one would expect the place-names to show this. In ancient Sweden the typical village termination 'tuna' is encountered, as is also the 'hundred' for a district. In Denmark we have place-names with the termination 'lev' and 'herred' as the terms for a district instead of 'hundred'.

In eastern Denmark there is a characteristic national term: 'far' meaning people or family. Sjælandsfar, Laalandsfar, Langelandsfar, Hallandsfar and Blekingfar are thus the inhabitants of these districts. In western Denmark and in Sweden this term does not exist. In western Denmark we meet the termination–'bo'. The inhabitants in all Jutland's districts have this designation–Vendelbo, Tybo, Himmerbo, Sallingbo, Angelbo, etc.

No one knows how ancient the division 'Herred' is. It probably dates back to the Migration Period or earlier. The word means: army company (Hærfølge) and corresponded perhaps to an original division into districts from which soldiers were recruited. The Herred is essentially a Danish unit of administration which was also a jurisdictional area and a religious cultic center. The fact that ancient Danish lands as far as the Eider frontier were divided into Herreds may mean that the subdivision is later than the Skjoldung period, at which time the kingdom had still not been politically united. But the Herreds need not have been organized from above; moreover, the system of division of the Skjoldung kingdom may well have spread over the whole country when it was united for the first time. The old Swedish districts conquered by the

Swedes do not have the Herred, which is to be found only in east Göt-land, where it seems to have travelled north from Denmark.

Among ancient place-names in Denmark, towns with the termination 'lev' such as Sigerslev, Skuldelev and Frøslev have an interesting posi-tion. The first syllable generally consists of a man's name, or the title of a chieftain or his deputy (Jarl, Aar and Levmand). These lev-towns are always good-sized villages, usually possessing a church, and land of good quality. They never lie close to one another, but are separated by a distance similar to that between church towers in neighboring parishes.

The first syllables of personal names are almost always composed of names from the Migration Period, and many of them are old acquaint-ances from Saxo's History of Denmark. Gudmund Schütte says, "No other group of Danish place-names has anything even approximately similar; in no other do we breathe to such an extent the atmosphere of the Skjoldung period."

The word 'lev' is related to the English word 'leave', and presumably means: property given or handed over, a sort of official property, and this is thought to derive from ancient military or administrative organiza-tion, to have been the basis for recruitment of troops, or assessment of taxation and control of land. These lev-towns are found especially on Zealand, ordinarily in the interior of the island, located on good, rich soil. They are also encountered in Skaane and Halland, but there they usually lie along the coast and are grouped around harbors. On Fyn they are found especially in the northeast, while toward the southwest the old village names have the termination–'inge'. Finally, they are found in Jutland, notably in the east and along the Limfjord where, as in Skaane and Halland, they are generally located near the coast and harbors. In west Jutland and Sweden they are extremely rare, and they do not exist in Blekinge, nor do they appear in old Swedish districts conquered by the Swedes. There is, however, a strip which stretches from the Kattegat to Lakes Väner and Vetter which possibly indicates Danish influence.

Where we find the lev-towns in Jutland, we also come upon the old place-names reflecting the divinities Thor and Odin. It is also pecu-liar that about one-third of the names of the Herreds– the ancient legal and military districts–in Jutland and Halland begin with the holy letter H, which was so marked a magic name custom in the Skjoldung family.

The strange topographical distribution of the 'lev'-towns is advanced by H. V. Clausen as proof of the union of the Skjoldung kingdom, and thus it would appear that it was in Zealand that this conquest originated, and that it established itself firmly in Skaane and Jutland along the coasts and at the important points of ingress—the Harbors.

The celebrated sacrificial finds found in bogs and mosses were warlike offerings often comprising thousands of weapons dating from the second to the fifth centuries. Caesar gives a description of Celtic sacrifices about 52 B.C., "Before fighting a battle they usually vow the spoils to the war-god. After the battle they sacrifice the captured animals and collect the remainder of the booty in one place. In many parts heaps of such objects are seen in sacred places, and rarely does someone dare to defy religion by hiding away spoil once deposed—a crime, which is punished severely." In the fifth century Paulus Orosius tells about the Cimbri how they treated the Romans after their victory at Orange, "Their clothes were torn off and thrown away, gold and silver sunk into the river, the men's byrnies cut to pieces, harness dispersed, and the horses themselves precipitated in the abyss, the prisoners hanged in the trees with a noose round their necks, so that there was no more left of the booty than mercy for the vanquished."

The great finds are not found on Zealand, but in two groups, one on Fyn and in East-Jutland, another smaller group in Västra Götland, Skaane, Öland and Bornholm. The great masses of offered weapons point to warlike operations, the initiative for which came from Zealand. If this be true, it seems to indicate that the Danes did not come from Sweden. The wealth of grave-finds in the Zealand area, when compared with the relatively poor finds in Uppland in Sweden from the same period, point in the same direction.

In discussing the trade routes from the Roman Empire through Germany, Sir Mortimer Wheeler says, "Attention has been drawn to the early prominence of the islands and mainland of Denmark in this traffic, and it has been suspected that their prominence reflects some measure of political cohesion, probably with Zealand as its focus. The astonishing bog-hoards of the third and fourth centuries are presumably, however, the product of victories or successful forays on the fringes of the Empire, and again emphasize the dominance of the Danish lands."

Chadwick thinks that the political power of the Danish kings grew out of a priestly hegemony on Gefjon's island of Zealand, and that here was to be found the most important seat of political power in the western Baltic. We know from Thietmar that Hlejre was a great cult-center, and therefore it was presumably the central source of the Skjoldung's power. Finally, if the form Witheslef in the Lejre chronicle is the original designation of the island kingdom, we have here represented the typical 'lev' of Zealand in the very name of that island kingdom.

From all the data available, Denmark appears to have been united from its center, Zealand. It is possible that at one period or another partial immigrations occurred, the latest about 200 A.D. There are several alternatives for the interpretation of finds and traditions, and more or less well-grounded suppositions are all that can yet be advanced. Sture Bolin states the position thus: "That Denmark should have been founded from Sweden or Skaane is guesswork. How loosely founded are all such opinions is manifest from the fact that many have asserted the opposite to be the case, i.e., that it is Skaane which has been conquered by Zealand." And Birger Nerman writes, "One therefore cannot say that the theory of the Swedish origin of the Danes is solidly based or that it does not require further support to attain a desirable degree of certainty." He thinks that if there had been a Swedish invasion it could only have involved a small force of warriors. Chambers rejects the theory that the Danes came from Sweden. We know with certainty that the Danes are connected with Denmark. Their connection with Sweden is only an hypothesis founded on the ambiguous quotation from Jordanes. It is therefore natural to connect them with Denmark, where we in fact find them.

*

In the chapter on the Eruli it was mentioned that Wrenn, in his edition of *Beowulf,* says about Scyld Scefing (Skjold), King of the Spear-Danes, "His terrifying of the Heruli (1.6.) may, if the attractive conjecture which explains the passage is right, indicate that he was remenbered in tradition as a strong king who overcame the most terrible and warlike tribe then living in Denmark, and first consolidated the Danish state."

Taken in conjunction with what Jordanes and Procopios relate about the Danes and the Eruli, and what Saxo relates about King Skjold, Wrenn is right in stating that if it were the Eruli whom the king terrified and not only some petty earls, the sources confirm and complement each other. Such a victory would have secured for the Danes the hegemony in the country and therefore it is understandable that his political deed was remembered and later formed the nucleus of a heroic legend. At exactly the same time that Jordanes and Procopios wrote (around 550) the Eruli disappear from the historical sources and the Danes appear in glory.

Seen from the point of view of the Danish King in Hlejre on Zealand, the problem of conquering the Jutish peninsula entailed dominating shipping and trade through the three important waterways across Jutland, the Sli and Eider in the south, the Kongeaa in the middle, and the Limfjord in the north.

Procopios of Caesarea, in about 550, states that "a group of Eruli from the Danubian districts returned to the north, and after passing through the lands of the Varni they marched through the Danish tribes without suffering at the hands of the barbarians. When they reached the sea they sailed over to the island of Thule where they settled down near to the Götar." These words show that at that time Danish tribes were firmly established in southern Jutland (Beowulf's 'South-Danes'?). Chambers thinks that the Danish advance at the close of the fifth century into Angel in southern Jutland—which had been abandoned by the Angels emigrating to England—took place, for the most part, peacefully and in harmony with the Angles, for otherwise it is difficult to understand the sympathy and interest in the Danes and their kings which is expressed in the Widsith Lay and Beowulf. Widsith mentions four succeeding Danish kings, whereas most other European tribes had to be content with a single one.

After the emigration of the Angles to Britian, the Danes occupied their deserted dwelling-places. A large section of the Jutes living north of the Angles had also emigrated westward, and the Jutes who remained at home were thereby, perhaps to some extent, weakened. At all events, it looks as though it were not the Jutes who went down into Angel, but the Danes from Zealand. To this day the South Jutland dialect is more closely related to island-Danish than to Jutish. We thus see the Danes dominating the southern trade lane.

If the district around the Kongeaa was the dwelling place of the Eruli, we can understand the Danes' interest in subduing the Eruli and conquering the second water-way. In western Jutland, towns ending in 'lev' are extremely rare, but at the North Sea estuary of the Kongeaa we find a 'lev'-town, Vilslev, situated at an important strategic point.

To control the northern water-way, the Limfjord, it would be necessary

132

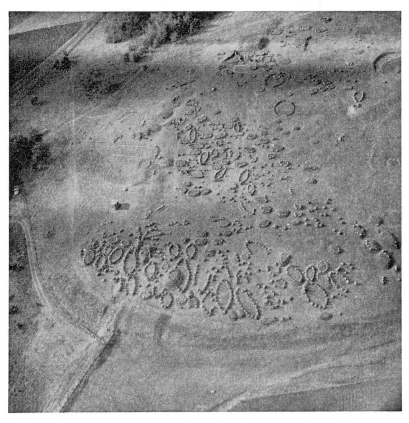

Viking graves in the shape of stone-ships. Lindholm Høje. Jutland.

to control Vendsyssel. This district appears to have been united to the Danish kingdom at an early date, inasmuch as Beowulf refers to Wulfgar, Prince of the Vendles (Wendla leod), as a vassal at King Hrodgar's Court. Archaeological finds appear to confirm such a connection, and along the Limfjord we find many 'lev'-towns, one of them in the center of the small peninsula, Salling, at a very important strategic position for control of this trade route. Its name is Roslev, and perhaps contains the name Hrodgar (Roar or Roir?).

Shipping and trade were all-important for the kingdom. In outline we can see a glimpse of the policy behind the uniting conquest of Denmark. To this day, the realm is named after the Danes, and the Danish royal

133

family is still poetically called Skjoldunger, descendants of Scyld. We do not know when Skaane and Zealand were united, but Beowulf refers to a kingdom which he calls: 'Scedelandum', which appears to have embraced Skaane and the island kingdom of Witheslef.

About the year 200 A.D. an abrupt change took place in the burial grounds, dwelling places and types of pottery in northern Jutland. "Great events of vital importance seem to have occurred at the close of the 2nd century A.D.–at the beginning of the Late Iron Age–for how else can one explain the break in tradition and the dissolution of civilized provinces which occurred in Jutland at that time? If one looks for the origin of the new Jutish pottery, which in comparison with the earlier was of a more uniform type, then one naturally turns to the Danish islands, where the prerequisites for some of both island–Danish and Jutish late Roman Iron Age pottery seem to be present. It is interesting that in the same eastern districts there are burial grounds which were constructed in the early Roman Age which continued to be used into the late Roman Iron Age. From this it would appear as though in the decades previous to 200 A.D., successful expeditions of conquest set out from east Denmark to Jutland, and thus the ground was actually prepared for the union of the Danish kingdom which was completed several hundred years later, during the Viking Period" (Norling-Christensen).

The emigrations of the Cimbri and Vandals from Himmerland and Vendsyssel in the north of Jutland must have led to debilitation of these districts, thus opening the gate for the invasion of the Limfjord kingdoms by the Danes. In Himmerland the legendary eponym King Dan is popular in folk-memory, and he 'lies buried' not merely in one, but in several places in Himmersyssel, while south of Himmerland there is a defensive earthwork called "Dan's Dyke"–Dandiget. According to the Lejre Chronicle, King Dan was proclaimed king on a large stone south of Viborg called Danærygh.

The date in which the whole of Jutland became united with eastern Denmark is unknown. However, this must have occurred so late that the name Jutes could be used as the common designation for all dwellers on the peninsula, as was the case with the Angles, in England. In King Gudfred's time, about 800, Denmark appears to have been an organized and united kingdom.

The name of the kingdom—Denmark—is first mentioned about 900 A.D., in King Alfred the Great's translation of Orosius' Geography. Its earliest appearance in Denmark itself is on King Gorm's runic stone in Jelling, dating from about 935.

What the word Denmark really means is not certain, but most probably it means 'the land of the Danes'. Dan is a word frequently found distributed throughout the north in the place-names of provinces characterized by damp, moist climates, without any direct connection with the people—the Danes. In Norway and Sweden it appears as the stem-syllable in names of islands and estates. On the Danish island Laaland, in Uppland in Sweden, and in Norway, it exists in the names of parishes. It is therefore possible that, like Jylland, and Sillende in Slesvig, it contains a reminder of the Danish dampness. This theory is reinforced by the remarkable fact that the ancient Irish name for Denmark is Lochland, and since Loch means 'sea' or 'wet district', this may therefore be an ancient literal translation. The Irish and Scots called the Danes Dubgalls —'the dark strangers'. Now Danes are not ordinarily dark, so either the word refers, for example, to the color of their shields or sails, or else it is a pun on, or a misunderstanding of, the word 'Loch-land', since the word 'loch' may mean both 'sea' and 'black'. The Scottish name Mac Dougall and the Irish name MacDowell therefore actually mean 'the son of a Dane'. There is, however, still no general agreement as to the meaning of the word Dane. Brøndal has discussed the many possible explanations which exist, and thinks that the word was originally connected with a word meaning: bue—bow.

Wadstein has drawn attention to the commercial importance which the frontier around the Eider used to possess, and thinks that Denmark got its name from the large and widespread marshes and watermeadows that exist in the district: The Sli-Eider area may have been not merely the cradle of the Danish name but also that of the Danish kingdom, he says. Saxo's old legend about Dan and Angul, the sons of Humble, from whom the Danes are said to be descended, suggests that the union of the kingdoms of the Danes and Angles was a decisive event for the genesis of the Kingdom of Denmark.

.

In his book *The Races of Europe,* Coon says. "Throughout the prehistoric period Denmark was the cultural center of Scandinavia, and likewise the center of greatest population. The profusion of Neolithic and Bronze Age monuments and graves shows that before the Iron Age invasions both the mainland and the islands were densely inhabited; in view of this crowding, it is not surprising that the newcomers found a greater room for expansion in Sweden and eastern Norway. From Ertebølle times onward the Danish Islands, and to a lesser extent the mainland, was the focal point in northern Europe for the settlement of the brachycephalic Borreby people. With them had mingled Megalithic seafarers in large numbers, while the Corded people had concentrated their activities on the mainland. It is not surprising, therefore, that a population so firmly attached to its milieu as that of pre-Iron Age Denmark should have survived the vicissitudes of centuries and eventually have reëmerged in considerable strength. That this is exactly what happened is the sense of the present section.

"During the Iron Age Denmark continued in its cultural leadership of Scandinavia, owing largely to its greater proximity to the source of civilized influences farther south, for Denmark was greatly affected by the repercussions of Roman civilization. In the Völkerwanderung period, Denmark, furthermore, contributed heavily to the stream of migration southward; the Cimbri, the first Germanic people to come under the eyes of Rome, were natives of Jutland; the Jutes and the Angles who settled England with the Saxons from Schleswig-Holstein again came from Denmark. The later inroads of Danes into Britain strengthened the earlier contingents. Hence, Denmark played an even greater part in the settlement of the British Isles than did Norway."

In the Roman Iron Age–the first four centuries of our era–the archaeological finds show that the center of gravity in the North still lay in Denmark. C. Weibull says, "The ancient Danish lands, first and foremost Sjælland (Zealand), were the centers whence the new Roman culture spread in the North. The ancient Swedish lands on the other hand, in Roman times do not appear to have played a prominent role." The Svea provinces in particular are very poor in finds from Roman times. Not till the early Migration Period does the ancient Swedish mainland gain really considerable importance. Dr. la Cour says, "In the 5th and 6th centuries Östra-Götland was one of the richest lands in gold in the North. Not until toward the beginning of the 7th century did this wealth of gold dry up, and from about 600 A.D. it is the Svea provinces–especially Uppland–which yield the greatest finds."

"There scarcely can be any doubt that Zealand in the Migration Period was the seat of the leading tribe in the country," says Brøndsted. It is especially toward the east and south of the island that we find these magnificently furnished tombs. While the number of finds in North and East Jutland decreases in the late Roman period, these on Zealand rise considerably, and the custom of cremation on Zealand and northeast Fyn, the area of the lev-towns, is displaced by earth-burial. Kendrick says that in the two first centuries of our era the Danes on Zealand must have been a powerful and advanced people.

The splendour and wealth which distinguish the Zealand area are described by Shetelig thus, "It has been mentioned that we have here a junction for North Sea and Baltic trade, as also connections southward overland.–Here a wealth was accumulated which is astounding, and we must believe that these islands acquired a corresponding position of power. If the Danish lands had possessed a written history from Roman times we should certainly have made the acquaintance of a powerful kingdom whose role in Northern Europe was perhaps just as important as that of the Marcomanni and the Goths further south. But this period is, however, still entirely prehistoric in the North, and only scattered features in the poetry of later ages may, it is believed, go back to legends from this forgotten period of greatness in Antiquity."

THE SKJOLDUNGS

"Highminded heroes,
hoping to die
in deeds of valour
which men will remember."

BIARKAMÁL.

Fame and achievement were the mighty driving forces behind these men, not stemming from a desire for public acclaim, but as an expression of abundant happiness and vitality. The poetic myths of the Skjoldung Lays were possibly not completed and written down until the Viking Age, but their central theme reaches back to the Migration Period. "The Skjoldung poetry is a Nordic product of the Migration Period, and is the only great heroic saga that has arisen independently in the north," says Wessén.

137

Dr. Lukman has made an attempt to show that the Skjoldung and Skilfing heroes came into existence from a mélange of legendary material which originated with the kings of the Huns and Eruli in the Danubian districts. His explanation suffers from a marked intrinsic improbability. It is possible, of course, as everything becomes possible in legend, but quite apart from the large number of hypotheses and coincidences which such an explanation makes necessary, it seems strange, de facto, that a people possessing a culture as remarkable as that revealed by Danish archaeology, and a legendary material as rich as that preserved by Saxo, should choose legends concerning Hunnish heroes for their most beloved and inspiring lays, in which their own ideals are recognized and reflected. Moreover, the Skjoldung legends are preserved in the Old English Widsith and Beowulf lays, and the place-names of Zealand contain the same names as those of the men mentioned in the Skjoldung myths.

Askeberg has asserted with force and clarity that Nordic culture and poetry are mainly independent and autochthonous, and that influences and borrowings from without are far less than was formerly supposed.

Axel Olrik, in his fine characterization of the Skjoldung legends, says, "A distinctive feature of the lays about the Skjoldung family is their social interest. The individual is present, not merely as an individual, but as a part of the whole. But, even stronger than the community feeling, there runs through the verses an awareness and appreciation of human spiritual values. The clarity and penetration with which the poets interpret their heroes, in relation to universally accepted spiritual values, appear to be the result of an early civilization within the people. It is remarkable that this interest in ideals is not accompanied by any religious movement, but it will be remembered that the Danes were also converted to Christianity with comparatively insignificant religious conflicts. In Hrolf Krake's Saga it is related of Hrolf and his men that they had never worshipped gods, but believed only in their own might and main. Ethics, not religion, were for them the enduring elements of life.

"In the heroic figures of the ancient Danish lays we become acquainted with powerfully developed personalities. Fate does not daunt them, nor do moral failings hamper them in the full flowering of their natures.

"There is a stylistic differentiation in the Skjoldung and Starkad legends as represented in the three Nordic lands. In Danish legends the he-

138

roes never exalt themselves above human values. This Danish caution in respect to what is noble in the heroic figure is the more remarkable because the Norwegian traditions never understood it; they always passed into the crude and ludicrous. Human life is the stuff of Danish poetry. Supernatural powers are seldom mentioned, still less do they play a part, for neither in a religious nor in a fabulous sense have they the slightest importance in the poetry" (Olrik).

"The matter of life is not a future goal, but a state to be maintained by striving and fighting. Human life exists during a ceaseless conflict between those who wish to destroy it and those who wish to defend it. *That* is the basic condition of life" (Olrik).

The Danish view of life is characterized by Olrik as a simple humanity, whereas the Norwegian has, as a rule, a division and contradiction in its nature; radiant strength and powers of darkness, happiness and despair, human being and ogre, originating from the Norwegian nature itself and from the environment of a fishing and hunting people. The Norwegian has a lively interest in supernatural creatures and finds a poetic form for the intervention of the divine powers. Giants and heroes easily grow to huge dimensions, and can pass into the grotesque. Olrik says, "Norway never produced an independent epic song-cycle of the memories of her past."

Of the Swedish attitude to life in the legendary period, Olrik says that our knowledge of it is too limited to enable us to draw as clear a picture as of the Danish and Norwegian. Their epic poetry does not stand out with the same force and clarity as does the Danish. Their poems are often clothed in a lyrical cloak, with an enthusiasm for the great, the remote, and the sweetness of love. In the rich royal legends of Uppsala, Sweden had excellent subjects for epic poetry, but it never attained enough importance to establish itself in Denmark and Norway. The Skjoldung legends are strangely alien to the celebrated Swedish royal family. Sweden's own Yngling legend perished without leaving the slightest trace behind it in the Chronicle. Among the Nordic countries, Sweden does not appear ever to have known the Hrolf legend. Since the Danish Skjoldung legends also contain very little of Swedish tradition, this does not suggest any originally close connection between Uppland and Zealand.

In the Skjoldung Legends, King Hrolf Krake and his heroic house carls Bjarke, Hjalte and Viggo stand as figures of unique plastic clarity

139

and lucidity. In the Viking Period the Biarkemál was still the living poetry of inspiration in the north, as indeed it is today. The short, laconic verses seem like the sharp glint of distant weapons.

Listen to Hjalte's song:

> Dawns the day,
> cocks' feathers flutter.
> Men who labor
> long for deeds.
>
> Wake, wake up!
> To weapons, friends!
> All the ablest
> athelings of Hrolf.
>
> Wake, not to wine
> nor the whisper of women.
> Rather I rouse you
> to singing swords.

Bjarke's awakening:

> Get up, boy!
> get fuel for fire!
> Brush off the ash
> and blow on the embers!
>
> Freezing fingers
> fumble at sword hilts.
> Weapons are weak
> in frozen fists.

Hjalte singing in the battle, when King Hrolf falls:

> Our byrnies are broken,
> sundered our shoulders,
> blows of the battle axe
> shake the shield.

The large-hearted Lord
has lifeless fallen.
Lost in the life
men will longest remember.

The dying Bjarke, singing in vain hope of revenge:

Well it were
if the vast battle-field
itself might see
the war-god vanish.

Here by my chieftain's
head I shall fall,
you by his feet
will find your rest.

High-minded heroes,
hoping to die
in deeds of valour
which men will remember.

*

Historical sources are scanty as far as the late Iron Age is concerned.
The period between 400 and 800 is poor archaeologically, especially the
two last centuries, because the burial customs are characterized by extreme plainnes and reflect a stark simplicity in their grave furnishings
and sacrificial gifts. Perhaps the trade routes ran outside Denmark at that
time as a result of the Slavic advance along the coast of the Baltic, river
trade in Germany being thus blockaded; and yet the finds show a regular
continuity and coherent culture.

The legends are difficult to date and evaluate as only brief glimpses
of the face of that age are revealed; the motley hordes of heroes of the
Migration Period appearing in Saxo's History of Denmark and in the
Elder Edda. The Edda legends were written down in Iceland by men
who were mainly of Norwegian origin, but, strangely enough, not one of
the heroes mentioned is Norwegian or Icelandic. Those whom we meet
are Danes, Swedes, Franks, Goths, Burgundians or Huns. We are shown

141

the princely courts of the Heroic Age, wherein war and strife, honor and sport are the substance of life. The heroic legends of the Edda depict the ancient thoughts and experiences of the race. Phillpotts says, "The ideas underlying them were the common heritage of the English and Scandinavian peoples."

*

King Ivar Vidfadme, son of Halfdan, is said by the legends to have created for himself a mighty kingdom with Skaane as its nucleus, embracing both Denmark and Sweden, extending its influence to the east Baltic countries – East Prussia and Esthonia. To what extent he is a historical personage is uncertain, but inasmuch as Sweden's List of Kings does not mention any other monarch in the period where Nerman places him (about 650–700) Nerman thinks that historical reality does lie behind his Dano-Swedish domain. If the sources are fundamentally correct in their presentation, it may be said that Ivar Vidfadme was the first king of a Dano-Swedish union. His empire also reached beyond Scandinavia.

King Harald Hildetand was the son of Ivar Vidfadme's daugther. He reconstructed the same empire, and ended his illustrious career in the celebrated Battle of Braavalla, near Braaviken in the district of Norrköping. Here, at an advanced age, he fell at the hands of Hring, who was his nephew and vice-king. The date of this event is uncertain; Nerman puts the Battle of Braavalla at about 750, but la Cour places it at about 600, as he thinks that the conflict must have hinged upon the wealth of gold in Östra-Götland, whose period of splendor was in the 5th and 6th centuries. The Svea provinces then commenced their period of wealth and greatness, after about 600.

King Helge Hundingsbane was the most magnificent among the family of the Ylfings. He appears to have ruled Zealand, with his center of power around Ringsted, Sigersted and Himlingøje. Others think that he belongs to Östra-Götland. He is believed to have lived in the 7th century, and was given the name Hunding's–slayer because of defeating Hunding, King of the Saxons, at Stade. Saxo says of him, "He promulgated the law in Saxony that the same fine should be paid for the manslaughter of a freed slave as for a free-born man. Strangely enough, we meet this same law in the Saxon parts of England, but not in the Anglian districts. It is said that Helge later fought in Östra-Götland and Södermanland and there defeated Høgne and the sons of Granmar. It is of Helge Hundingsbane that one of the most beautiful love-stories in the literature of the world is recorded—the love of Høgne's daughter Sigrun for the king.

*

The Migration Period was like a mighty avalanche of tribes beginning in the ancient Danish lands, Sweden and Norway, and pouring southward through Europe. It was as though a Noah's Ark had been opened to emit all kinds of animals, some of them good and useful, but all with sharp teeth bared. Nearly the whole of Europe was overrun, and the Roman Empire toppled and fell, occupied by armed forces. But it appears as though these conquerors could not endure the warmth and sunshine of southern latitudes. Their kingdoms lasted for only a few centuries, then were absorbed by the indigenous populations. It is as though the ability of races to thrive is linked with certain isotherms, for it was only in northerly latitudes that they established themselves permanently, in the north, in England, in the Kingdom of the Franks, and later on, in North America.

The migrations, however, did not destroy the culture of Antiquity. Pirenne has shown that the rupture of connections between the Orient and the Occident actually took place much later, when Islam had swept over North Africa and Spain and thus destroyed the old trade road of the Mediterranean with its shipping and exchange of ideas.

At the time of the birth of Christ, the whole of north Germany was Teutonic, while south Germany was still Celtic. At the close of the Migration Period these tribes had penetrated south and west, so that south Germany became Teutonic, while north Germany had become Slavic, owing to the Slav tribes' slow advance from the east into the depopulated districts; thus Germanic tribes were hardly any longer to be found east of the Elbe. The advance of the Slavs appears to have occurred without major conflicts.

Not until well into the Middle Ages were these districts again conquered and colonized by Germanic tribes from the west and south; thus the German language superseded the Slavic and the population types became mixed. The Germanic tribes became, on the whole, strongly mixed with Celtic people, Roman and Alpine tribes from the south, Hunnish and Baltic blood from the east, and a strong infusion of Slavic tribes from the east and northeast, while the numerous Germanic tribes roamed and intermingled. Askeberg says, "In all Ages, one wave of peoples after another has swept across Central Europe. They were drawn as by a magnetic force to the plains of the Danube and the Po, and perhaps ebbed out in Gaul or on the Iberian Peninsula. In no other place in Europe has the confusion of peoples been greater, or the displacements more violent, than here." Even Kossina, a pronounced nationalist, says, "From a racial point of view we Germans are strongly mixed. The present composition of Nordic blood in Germany is estimated to be 60 %, yet the proportion of pure Nordic people is only 6 % to 8 %." According to Penka, the Nordic race is no longer predominant in Germany, and is in fact an exception in many parts of the country.

When widely divergent races are mixed together the result is not always good. But where the races are related, the possibility of new combinations of the hereditary forces can produce outstanding personalities and characters. Too much racial purity seems to cause development to stop and the race to degenerate.

In north Germany there are many Slavic place-names right up to the old Danish frontier, but no farther. North of Danevirke there are none, but south of it the names of large and celebrated cities are completely Slavic—Berlin, Stettin, Leipzig, Dresden, Meissen, Danzig and Breslau.

Contemporaneously with the migrations in central Europe, the Angles and Saxons, those intermediate tribes between Danes and Germans, wandered westward to England. Anglia was occupied by the Danes, and east Holstein became Slavic. The combination of these circumstances between the German and Nordic peoples created a clearly defined ethnic boundary in language, mind and stock. For this reason, the south German was in a way closer to the peoples of the north than was the north German.

From the days of antiquity until the war between Germany and Denmark in 1864, the Eider river was the southern frontier of the north. With the exception of the southern part of Slesvig, which has become Germanized in language, and to some extent in outlook, even though it is still of Danish origin in race, customs, and place-names, the north today still possesses the same territory it had in the days of antiquity.

KING GUDFRED

Gedanke und Tat waren beide gross. Was er gewollt und was er durchzuführen begonnen hatte, sichert ihm für alle Zeiten einen Platz unter den grossen Gestalten des Nordens.

OTTO SCHEEL.

In thought and deed he was equally great. What he planned and what he tried to carry through place him for all time among the great figures in the north.

Running along the ridge of Jutland's backbone from north to south is an ancient highway, one of the oldest in Europe. It is the old military route, Hærvejen. People travelled along this track even in the Stone Age, because here, on the watershed, were encountered the fewest of such obstacles as rivers, marshes and lakes.

Footprints in the snow attract others and a path is gradually worn in the grass and heather. In the course of time it broadens and becomes a road. For the space of 10,000 years and more, Jutland has felt the footsteps on this road creeping along its backbone. Its wheel tracks can still be detected through the heather on the heaths. In some places it has been incorporated in modern highways.

In Slesvig the north-south road cuts across an ancient east-west trade route at Danevirke. The Sli is a long, narrow fjord, cutting inland from the Baltic to the center of Jutland, while the river Eider and its tributary, the Treiaa or Trene, were in ancient times navigable between the North Sea and the heart of the country at Hollingsted. There were only eight

The district round Hedeby, Sli and Ejder. Angel. South Jutland.

miles of solid terrain between these two waterways, so trade between the Baltic area and western Europe could easily be linked up. Westward there was contact with Friesland and the important Rhine trade, eastward with the shipping route south of the Danish islands and the route along the south coast of the Baltic, and also the trading centers at the mouths of the rivers. Merchandise could be transported overland on horseback, or a ship could be portaged across on rollers. As late as in King Svend Grathe's time, in the middle of the twelfth century, a whole fleet was thus transferred.

The ancient city of Hedeby was located at the junction where the old military way (Hærvejen) cuts across the trade route. It was ideally placed for transit trade at a time when merchants were reluctant to sail north around the stormy, dangerous Skaw. From ancient times this district had been the main base of the Angles, both politically and from a commercial point of view, as is reflected in the legends concerning Uffe and Vermund. South of the rampart of Danevirke and Kovirke there are traces of a still older dike, probably dating from the time of the Angles, and the Beowulf Lay states that Sceaf, the mythical father of King Skjold, ruled here in Hedeby.

Westward in Friesland, after the time of Beowulf, the Franks had been driven back from the coast in the 7th century, but in 689 Pepin had again conquered Friesland and the commercially important city of Dorestad. There are indications which suggest that the Danes had interests here and that emigration took place to Friesland and Franconia. The first Danish chieftain who is mentioned at the Court of Charlemagne was Holger Danske himself, 'Olger Daniae dux'. In 788 he rebuilt St. Martin's Abbey at Cologne.

Hedeby's importance as the main trading-center in northern Europe was developed by King Gudfred who, according to Wadstein, was one of the most remarkable figures in the early history of the north. He became king shortly before 800, succeeding his father, King Sigfred, who was a nephew of a King Harald who had formerly ruled over Denmark, but is otherwise unknown, unless he was King Harald Hildetand himself.

In 771 Charlemagne became sole ruler of the mighty Frankish Empire which consisted of France, Germany, the Netherlands and Italy. Charlemagne's advance to the north and west threatened the Saxons in Holstein, and in 777 Widukind, the Saxon chieftain, was obliged to seek refuge with his brother-in-law, the Danish King Sigfred. Charle-

146

magne speaks of 'the bumptious Sigfred' in a poem to Paul Diaconus, the Langobard, inviting him to undertake the mission in Denmark. Paul answered:

"I do not desire to see the ferocious face of King Sigfred,
and for yourself you would gain little advantage thereby;
unlearned is he and dull, and of Latin he knows almost nothing,
I will be unable then, to understand what he says."

In 782 there were diplomatic complications between Sigfred and Charlemagne concerning Danish support for the refugee Saxons, and Sigfred sent emissaries to the Diet at Lippsspringe. Both Sigfred and his son Gudfred would naturally have felt themselves threatened by Charlemagne's expansion, and his brutal, forced conversion of the Saxons to Christianity could not have been attractive to the heathens of the north.

By his conquest of the territory of the Saxons, Charlemagne had made himself master of the Elbe, with the double aim of insuring himself against a union of Saxons, Frisians and Danes that might threaten the Rhine, which was an important geopolitical line of the Frankish Empire and a most vulnerable point, and in addition giving control of the shipping and trade on the Elbe. We know that Charlemagne, after a quarrel with the English King Offa, who died in 796, banned all English merchants from the ports in Gaul, and it is most likely that a similar ban closed the harbors for Danish ships. Probably Charlemagne's policy had, as its final goal, the conquest and control of the Eider and Hedeby in order to push through to the Baltic, and the slave-trade in the Slavonic districts. Charlemagne had a great export of slaves and eunuchs to the Moslems.

In order to impair the strength of the Saxon people and to suppress any possibility of revolt, Charlemagne instigated a policy involving eviction of population, wholesale destruction of districts and a system of concentration camps. Thousands of Saxons were deported from their native land and other thousands were killed in bloody massacres. On one single day he ordered 4,500 Saxon hostages cut down at Verden. All Saxons were forced to become Christians on pain of death, and Charlemagne battered and baptized them with typical German thoroughness. In return, the Saxons were burdened with counts, bishops and taxes.

The situation must have appeared threatening to Denmark after

Charlemagne had gradually advanced the frontiers of his empire right up to the Eider River and encouraged Frankish colonists to move in from the west and Slavic Abodrits to emigrate from the east, in order to create a form of barrier against the Danes from the north. In his Frankish empire he was able to close his harbors with import restrictions and protective tariffs. A collision was unavoidable since the conflicts in interests were economical, political and religious. The war between Franks and Danes was partly a contest between German Catholicism and Nordic Paganism, but also a simple struggle for control of an important trade route.

Gudfred did not hesitate. He faced a great aggressive power, embracing more than half the continent of Europe, and he stopped it. The kingdom over which Gudfred ruled embraced both Denmark and the Province of Vestfold in Norway. It is not known for certain if it also included North Jutland, but it is difficult to conceive that it did not. A king of Gudfred's resolute character, with the support of an organized power which enabled him to take the offensive against Charlesmagne's mighty Empire with a fleet of 200 ships, a king who endeavored to extend his power over Friesland in the west and the Wendish lands in the east, must surely have ruled over a large and united kingdom possessing both organization and tradition. Since it is known that Gudfred ruled over South Jutland in the south and Vestfold in Norway in the north, it would seem that an independent North Jutland would scarcely have been a political possibility. Had it been independent, Charlemagne would have had the greatest interest in North Jutland in accordance with the political precept 'divide et impera', but the Frankish annals which refer to conditions in Denmark never refer to an independent Jutish kingdom, and it is certain that the existence of one would have been reflected in the sources. When Charlemagne's son, Louis the Pious, was at war in 815 with the sons of King Gudfred, he advanced up into Jutland without any mention being made that there was an independent kingdom; and as we know from Rimbert's biography of Ansgar that King Haarik, son of Gudfred, ruled as sole master in Denmark, everything suggests that this was also the state of affairs in Gudfred's time. We hear later of joint kings in Denmark, just as there were in France during the Merovingian and Carolingians periods, but this probably did not exclude the concept of the kingdom as a whole, since the joint kings were often brothers, or of the same family.

148

Coin from Hedeby about 800.

The fact that Danish kings ruled in Vestfold around Oslo Fjord has caused certain authors to advance the hypothesis that Gudfred belonged to the Norwegian Yngling family, and had conquered Denmark, and that he was identical with Gudrød Veide-king in Vestfold. But this does not appear to be possible, since Halvdan Koht has shown that Gudrød Veide-king must have been born at about the time that Gudfred was killed in 810. It would be more correct to assume intermarriage and namesakes, since many of the personalities of the Yngling family have Danish names. It seems that Denmark was the dominant power-factor, centered around the Kattegat, with an influence which extended as far as south Norway. This influence was probably as old as the Migration Period and existed, in any case, in the eighth and ninth centuries. Its purpose would have been to control the trade over the Kattegat through Skiringsal, which is believed to have been founded during the Danish rule, the kings of Vestfold being under Danish suzerainty until 900 A.D., when Norway became a united kingdom. The Danish overlordship was re-established by the Jelling Kings.

Gudfred's military and land statutes must have been one of the main reasons for the kingdom's cohesion and strength. Shetelig thinks that through its influence in Vestfold it became the model for the land-system employed by King Harald Fairhair a hundred years later to build up the kingdom of Norway. "Judging by Vestfold's relations with Denmark as a whole, it is quite probable that Denmark was the model for Harald's Government. At all events, one can say that a universal tax paid to the king was one of the important features in the union of the kingdom and was the first step toward making Norway into a state."

In the provinces east of Oslo Fjord (Østfold) there are clear traces of old Danish administration, such as division of land into 'skipæn' as the basis for military recruitment. Bull has shown that this division may go back to the Dansh kings' levy-statutes and suzerainty in the 9th and 10th centuries, or perhaps even a little farther, since the Danish overlordship

149

was particularly definite east of Oslo Fjord in Ranrike and Bohuslen. Poul Johs. Jørgensen writes, "There has been a tendency to place the system of summons-to-arms in the late Viking Period and to regard it as a consequence of the levy-statute of the Viking expeditions. It is more likely, however, that it belongs to an earlier period, some think possibly to the 10th century and perhaps to an even earlier time. Directives issued by the State or the King must have been necessary to give it the uniform, compulsory, and universal character which appears in the sources. Incidentally, it was not necessarily an entirely new regulation. If there had been an older organization much of it might have been transferred to the levy-statute."

Hedeby or Slesvig's exceptional location for transit trade was quite apparent to King Gudfred. He saw clearly the geographical value of Denmark, just as did the Danes 150 years ago when, they based their commercial policy on the fact that Denmark's position between the seas made it a logical choice for a Free Harbor and open mart for northern Europe. Hedeby must have served a purpose similar to that of Singapore in the days of Sir Stamford Raffles.

In 798 Danish Vikings harried the Frankish coasts. Charlemagne himself is said to have seen these Viking ships on the Garonne and been filled with fearful forebodings. He therefore issued orders for a fleet to be built, but a fleet does not spring into existence merely because an order has been given, and the Franks obtained no fleet of any consequence until the Normans became their teachers.

In the years 802-804 Charlemagne suppressed the last Saxon resistance in Holstein. Gudfred replied with a naval demonstration and military display at Hedeby. The Frankish annals say of Gudfred that he "with his fleet and all the cavalry of his Kingdom came to the place which is called Sliesthorp, on the frontier between his Kingdom and Saxony." Charlemagne initiated negotiations in the hope of dissuading Denmark from supporting the Saxons, but these led to no result. Charlemagne therefore retaliated by giving East-Holstein to the Slavic Abodrits. In this country lay the commercial city Reric which, in the light of recent excavations, was probably located at Altgartz in the Bay of Wismar. According to the Frankish annals, Reric (Rerwic) was a trading center for Danish Vikings and was under Danish suzerainty. It is related that the Danish king received a considerable income from the trade there. Transport of merchandise from the Baltic was carried on between Reric and the Elbe, but since Charlemagne had now blocked the Elbe, the value of Reric to Denmark had been greatly reduced. This was probably the reason why Gudfred, in 808, sailed to the country of the Abodrits, brought two-thirds of the land under tribute, and destroyed Reric, taking care, however, to transfer the merchants and artisans to Hedeby, which he developed. The destruction of Reric was a blow to the allies of Charlemagne, but not to trade, which was brought back under the protection of Gudfred to a place that was strategically safer and more favorable for purposes of commerce. In order to ensure his vital artery against attack from the south, Gudfred built the great earthwork Danevirke across the peninsula "from Baltic salt to Western Sea."

Müller and Neergaard think that it was the Danevirke rampart itself that Gudfred built. Others maintain that it was the straight dike Kovirke, to the south of the Danevirke. North of the earthwork the transport of goods could then be carried on in greater safety. The importance of this cross trade-route was particularly great at a time when the Slavs had partly blocked the river systems of north Germany. On the whole, everything seems to have dovetailed in Gudfred's farsighted policy; considerations of trade, administration, finance and strategy were united, and a European sphere of influence of the first rank was created. The erection of Danevirke was not primarily an expression of a national-Danish Eider policy of isolation, since Gudfred's political aims were much wider, contemplating as he did the incorporation of northern Germany into the north.

Einhard, who wrote Charlemagne's biography, states that Gudfred maintained that Saxony and Friesland were his possessions or spheres of interest and that he threatened to obtain by force the mastery of the whole of Germany, and in order to give the finishing touch, seek out the Emperor in his residence at Aachen and water his horses at the castle well. This was not mere idle boasting, for in 882 a later King Gudfred carried out this threat, conquered Aachen and used the Church of Mary as a stable.

Einhard's ridicule reveals the very greatness of Gudfred's plans. Einhard jeered, but Charlemagne recognized the danger of the situation threatening him. Despite his great age he hastened to the front, not daring to hand over the reins to his sons, counts or generals. Gudfred reckoned, not without reason, that the Saxons and Frisians would join with him in a decisive battle, and that this coalition would be very dangerous for Charlemagne since it would have gravely threatened his vital positions on the Lower Rhine.

Charlemagne was furious at the 'mad' King's behavior, just as he had previously been with that of Gudfred's father, Sigfred. A conference held at Beienfleth, near Stør, between the emissaries of Charlemagne and Gudfred, proved fruitless, and war became inevitable. Steenstrup says that in this way the thousand–year conflict between Germans and Danes was initiated. Charlemagne, threatening, built the castle of Itzehoe on the farther side of the Elbe just south of the Danish frontier in order to block the trade route from the north to the River Elbe, and collected troops for an attack on Denmark. But Gudfred, undaunted, struck back. As Hodgkin says, "Charlemagne had stirred up a wasp's nest."

By sea Gudfred could outflank Charlemagne's positions, so with a powerful fleet of 200 ships he descended on Friesland, and in three engagements defeated Charlemagne's local troops and made the country tributary.

Baker stresses the importance of the Nordic long-ship in warfare. "The nearest and most graphic parallel to the invention of the northern ship is the invention of the aeroplane. Both similarly cut right across all the accepted rules and accustomed methods of war. The seagoing ship was the military answer of the north to the empire of Charles; and it was destined to be a very terrible answer indeed."

Charlemagne, with all his great military strength, was defenceless against Gudfred's fleet. He assembled his army at Verden to meet Gudfred's advance, but the latter's forces circumnavigated his army and sailed home in order to prepare a direct blow at the heart of Frankish power. From the Frankish annals the ingenuity and greatness of Gudfred's policy clearly emerge. Everything appears to have been well considered and coordinated. His diplomacy and strategy seem to have been the equal of Charlemagne's. There was only one item with which he had not reckoned—the blow from the rear.

In 810 King Gudfred was murdered by a member of his bodyguard. Nothing in the Frankish or other sources contains material which suggests that the Franks had any connection with the murder, except for the fact that it was very much to their advantage. Saxo relates about the murder, "When Charlemagne heard the news he jumped up overjoyed and confessed that he had never experienced anything more pleasant." At a later time, in 885, when the second King Gudfred was murdered in Friesland, and again in 942 when William Longsword, the son of Rollo, was murdered on an island in the Somme, the initiative came from the Emperor of the Franks.

Otto Scheel of Kiel says, "In this manner the Viking world lost the man who had devised the greatest constructive plan in the north, and had begun to develop it." Even if Gudfred was not able to achieve all that he desired, that which he did effect was not without consequences. "The town of Hedeby is the greatest monument that we possess of Nordic antiquity." Those are the words of Herbert Jankuhn of Göttingen, a leader in the excavation of the extensive areas of the old commercial city inside the mighty crescent-shaped earthwork. Wadstein of Göteborg says that Hedeby is without parallel in the north. During the city's period of prosperity Frisian merchants came there, sailing in their broad-bowed sloops. Here the Danes were visited by At-Tartusi, an Arabian traveller, presumably an envoy from a Mohammedan ruler in Spain; in the Cosmography of Al-Qaswini is preserved his interesting description of the town from the tenth century. Norwegian Vikings moored their vessels with plaited ropes of walrus-skin along the wharves. Here came the tarred and painted merchant-ships of Danish and Swedish convoys, and here Icelandic chieftains such as Gunnar from Hlidarende visited Danish kings in Hedeby.

*

The Viking Period in Denmark commenced with Gudfred's war against Charlemagne. In his book *The Vikings* Brøndsted calls Gudfred "an impetuous and reckless ruler of Denmark." Perhaps he was, but then his impetuosity must be seen against the background of Charlemagne's reckless rule in the land of the Saxons south of the Danish border. Brøndsted calls Gudfred "an aggressive character". There is nothing aggressive in constructing a defensive and protective rampart against Charlemagne's aggression. Technically, Gudfred's attack in 810 was one of offence, but in reality it was a defence against a menacing threat against the Danish border. Brøndsted underestimates the policy and importance of Gudfred. Otto Scheel, Herbert Jankuhn, Elis Wadstein, Gudmund Schütte and Johs. Steenstrup appreciate him much more. Arnold Toynbee says, "When Charlemagne set out in A.D. 772 to bring Saxony within the fold of Roman Christendom by force of arms, he was making a disastrous breach with the policy of peaceful penetration – and it was inevitably and immediately followed by a counter–attack in

153

which the Scandinavians—awaking, full of vigour, from their 'heavy winter dreams'—avenged upon the exhausted Franks the wrongs of the prostrated Saxons."

The Viking Period in Denmark began with a war. Characteristically enough, one of the main features of Danish Viking expeditions was that they were regular military operations on a large scale. Denmark is the only Nordic country where the kings played a decisive part in the Viking campaigns. The Norwegian and Swedish Viking expeditions were more in the nature of private enterprise, the trade of merchant princes, the raids of individual chieftains. Gudfred's expedition to Friesland in 810 was a regular war between the Kingdom of Denmark and the Frankish Empire. It was followed by a conventional peace-treaty in 811, the year after Gudfred was murdered, by his nephew, King Hemming, who made peace with the Franks at a meeting on the Eider, where the Eider was recognized as the boundary between Denmark and the Empire.

For some years now Denmark experienced a series of successional troubles in which several branches of royal families fought one another. Frankish policy seems to have been successful in keeping alive disunity, particularly by providing support for King Harald Klak, whom King Haarik, son of Gudfred, had driven out of Denmark.

But we know from the Frankish annalist Einhard that prior to this, Harald Klak and his brother Reginfred in 813 sailed to Vestfold in Norway, the most remote part of their kingdom, in order to suppress an uprising there. The representative of the Yngling Dynasty in Vestfold, possibly Halfdan Eysteinssøn, the great-grandfather of Harald Fairhair, no doubt considered the disturbed conditions in Denmark auspicious for an attempt to throw off Danish supremacy. This does not seem to have succeeded until the time of Harald Fairhair, in about 900, following the defeat of the Danes at Dyle and the conquest of Hedeby by the Swedes. At all events, at the close of the 9th century Østfold, east of the Oslo Fjord, still belonged to Denmark, since Ottar the Norwegian told King Alfred the Great that when he sailed from Skiringsal to Hedeby he had 'Denmark' to port, and open sea to starboard during the first three days.

Gudfred's military and land statutes became the pattern for the Norwegian kings Halfdan Svarte and Harald Fairhair in their development of the power of the Yngling Kings in Norway. Bull says, "For their new military statutes they could take as models the districts on the

154

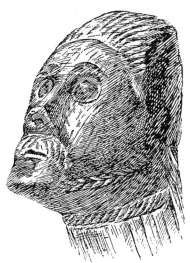

*Viking head from the Oseberg cart.
Viken. Norway.*

opposite side of the Oslo Fjord where the Danish kings had ruled or were still ruling, or possibly the actual kingdom of the Danish kings, where the levy-division of land in 'Skibsrede' (i.e., areas paying ship-money) and thus the whole military administration, certainly goes back to the 9th century or still farther."

We have certain details concerning Danish activity during these years. In 807 a Danish chieftain named Halfdan had received the Frisian island Walcheren in fee, thus securing influence in the important Frisian trade. His fief was inherited by his son, Hemming. We know that in the course of the 9th century Danish Viking kings created for themselves more or less independent kingdoms along the Frisian and Frankish coasts. In 826 Harald Klak was given Rüstringen at the mouth of the Weser in fee; from 850-875 his brother or son Hrorik reigned over the whole of Friesland, and his kinsman Gudfred ruled in Friesland from 882 until he was murdered in 885. Danish colonists are mentioned at Arnhem in 833, and one of Regner Lodbrog's sons, Ubbe the Frisian, was called 'Prince of the Frisians'. We know that in 838 King Haarik I laid claim to Danish supremacy over Friesland and east Holstein. There was thus an uninterrupted sequence in Danish activity and policy.

King Haarik I also came into conflict with the Frankish Empire and in 845 sent a fleet of 600 ships to Hamburg. In the same year he may have also supported Regner Lodbrog's expedition up the Seine, when Paris itself was plundered.

Hrorik of Friesland is an interesting figure. Arup describes him as unquestionably the greatest political figure of the Viking Period. With his fief in Friesland as a starting point, in 857 he secured for himself 'that part of the kingdom which lay between the Sea and the Eider.' This must have been either Eidersted, which controlled the western approach to Hedeby along the Eider, or the whole of the cross route, including Hedeby. Arup thinks that the semicircular earth-work at Hedeby dates from Hrorik's time, since it was probably erected at a period when Hedeby was not in the possession of the Danish King, and one discerns the outlines of a plan to bring under his control the entire trade route from Friesland and the Rhine through Hedeby. How long he retained his South Jutland possessions is not known.

Historians think that the great King Gudfred's plan was to separate the Saxons and Frisians from the Frankish Empire and to make them the plinth and base for the column of Jutland. Thus he hoped to extend and defend his commercial power. Wadstein says, "If Gudfred had lived and had succeeded in severing these peoples from the Frankish Empire to which they were still linked only by force, then this might have led to Denmark's becoming the dominating power, not merely in the eastern North Sea, but also, in the course of time, along the south coast of the Baltic. After Gudfred's death there was no one in Denmark qualified to take his place and execute his great plans."

And yet, at a later date and under other forms, it was mainly this policy which the Jelling Kings adopted and brought to a full state of development.

THE VIKINGS

For indeed he was, in his time, the most capable of mankind.
W. G. Collingwood.

"How is it that in every region of the globe the spread of the English-speaking peoples and their language far exceeds that of all the other European nations combined?"

This question was asked by Paul du Chaillu many years ago in the introduction to his book, *The Viking Age.* He continued,

"Why is it that, wherever the English-speaking people have settled, or are at this day found, even in small numbers, they are far more energetic, daring, adventurous, and understand the art of self-government and of ruling alien peoples far better than other colonizing nations?

"Whence do the English-speaking communities derive the remarkable energy they possess; for the people of Britain, when invaded by the Romans, did not show any such quality.

"What are the causes which have made the English such a preeminent seafaring people?—for without such a characteristic they could not have been the founders of so many states and colonies speaking the English tongue.

"In studying the history of the world we find that all the nations which have risen to high power and widespread dominion have been founded by men endowed with great, I may say terrible, energy; extreme bravery and the love of conquest being the most prominent traits of their character. The mighty sword, with all its evils, has thus far always proved a great engine of civilization.

"We find that a long stretch of coast is not sufficient, though necessary, to make the population of a country a seafaring nation. When the Romans invaded Britain the Britons had no fleet to oppose them. We

Viking head of bronze.
Found in 1961 in Anst. Seest, Jutland.

157

do not until a later period meet with that love of the sea which is so characteristically English:—not before the gradual absorption of the earlier inhabitants by a blue-eyed and yellow-haired seafaring people who succeeded in planting themselves and their language in the country.

"Britain, after a continuous immigration which lasted several hundred years, became the most powerful colony of the northern tribes, several of the chiefs of the latter claiming to own a great part of England. At last the time came when the land of the emigrants waxed more powerful, more populous than the mother-country; and today the people of England, as they look over the broad Atlantic, may discern a similar process which is taking place in the New World.

"They will look back with pride to the progenitors of their race who lived in the glorious and never-to-be-forgotten countries of the north, the birth place of a new epoch in the history of mankind."

*

Is this pompous overture of du Chaillu justified? The answer is for the most part, yes.

M. W. Williams writes that the Northmen were "a people who for a long period played a leading and unique part in European history, and who, to an extent seldom realized, made, directly and indirectly, a lasting contribution to the development of Europe and America."

What kind of contribution have the Vikings made that has endured until today? Many appear to agree with Kendrick when he refers to the Vikings as "Bloodthirsty and abominable barbarians, enemies of society, capable of infamous, indefensible outrages, of arson and slaughter." Brøndsted says in *The Vikings,* "To begin with they dealt out the *dona Danaorum:* destruction, rape, plunder, and murder; and later they expended their energy and blood on colonization. Otherwise the Vikings could teach Europe nothing." And Belloc, who does not seem to recognize values disassociated from the Roman Senate or the Catholic Church, calls them 'men quite barbarous who lived a dull sort of base, undeveloped life, with no institutions worthy of remark, and no distinctive religion or political ideas.' Even Sir Winston Churchill reflects upon 'the brutal vices of these salt-water bandits, pirates as shameful as any whom the sea has borne'. But yet he also remembers 'the discipline, the fortitude, the comradeship and martial virtues which made them at this period beyond all challenge the most formidable and daring race in

158

the world.' Were they, then, like this? Yes, they appear to be so if one looks at them from a particular angle, but it gives a one-sided and incomplete picture of their nature and significance. In the Viking Period it was a normal thing to be a Viking.

The most widely read of modern histories of England is that of Trevelyan, who says, "They were savage robbers in an age of universal savagery and they had what others had not—a noble joy in maritime adventure and exploration."

The English could not sail, trade or colonize before the Vikings came to England, whereas the history of England since the period of Canute the Great has dealt mainly with shipping, business and colonization.

The Danes took home from England what is called Parliamentarianism, but this was something which the northmen had in their time brought to England. It was an ancient custom in the north for the people to meet in their Thing-assemblies and make the laws dictated by circumstances and the people's own conviction of right. Originally, the king was not the lawgiver in Denmark, but rather the man who represented prosperity, honor and dignity, combined with noble birth. He was the leader of the cult of sacrifice, the chief of the army, and the man who backed the law with his sword to give it force. Parliamentarianism comes naturally to the Nordic lands because it epitomizes the spirit of their spirit and the blood of their blood.

The Danes took home from England what are called jury courts, but the northmen in their day had laid the foundation for such institutions in England. The old 'Næfn' and law-courts were ancient legal institutions in the north, but there, at a later period, they had to give way to other forms of jurisprudence. "The free country of England is, as is well-known, the only country which, despite all upheavals, has preserved juries down to our time," said Worsaae a hundred years ago.

Trevelyan says, "Thus far had the first Nordic settlers in Britain advanced on the path of civilization and national unity when the second wave of Nordic invasion broke upon them in their turn. The heathen Danes and Norsemen destroyed for a while the higher civilization of the island collected in its monasteries, and for a while increased its disunion by establishing the Danelaw over against the areas ruled by Saxon and Celt. Yet before a hundred years were out, the Scandinavian invasions were seen to have greatly strengthened the forces of progress. For the Vikings were of a stock kindred to the Saxon, but even more full of

159

energy, hardihood and independence of character, and with no less aptitude for poetry and learning. They brought back to the island those seafaring habits which the Saxons had lost in their sojourn on up-country farms, and it was due to them that a vigorous town life revived in England for the first time since the departure of the Romans. Had it not been for the Scandinavian blood infused into our race by the catastrophes of the ninth century, less would have been heard in days to come of British maritime and commercial enterprise."—The deficiencies of the Anglo-Saxons, prior to this stern process of reinvigoration, were indeed many and great. They had forgotten their sea-craft to such an extent that when Alfred sought men for a navy he had to call in Frisian mercenaries.

"More will be heard of Viking trade in the narrative that follows, for the northman was at heart always more of a chapman than a robber, and is deemed to have played no small part in the development of European commerce." says Kendrick, and Williams adds, "The old northmen were unusually shrewd and successful traders. In their interest in mercantile affairs, and in the part which they played in the distribution of commodities, they excelled all other contemporary peoples of Europe." Commercially, they were to their time what the Phoenicians were to the Eurasian lands a thousand years before.

They knew how to sail. Their spheres of activity embraced all Europe and the Arctic Ocean, as well as parts of Asia, Africa and North America. "The sea was their school of war and the storm their friend" (Green). They could stand long and strenuous voyages without scurvy and vitamin deficiency, owing to the quantities of herrings and onions they took with them. In open boats across the North Sea, across the Arctic Ocean, across the Atlantic and back again, "The courage and craft of sailors who could venture in such ships on such voyages has never been surpassed in maritime history," says Trevelyan, who continues:

"The Scandinavians had always been traders as well as pirates in their dealings with one another in home waters, and so they remained in the larger field of foreign enterprise now open to them. They combined the pride of the merchant with the very different pride of the warrior, as few people have done. In a tomb in the Hebrides a pair of scales has been found buried in a Viking chief's tomb, alongside his sword and battle-axe. Their first thought when they founded a colony in England or Ireland was to build fortified towns and to open markets. They carved their runes on the stone lion of the Piræus that now keeps guard before the Arsenal at Venice. They were known to avenge, in the streets of Constantinople, blood feuds begun among themselves in Dublin. Their far journeys brought them wealth, civilization and the knowledge of cities and men. The Saxon peasant, who regarded them as outer barbarians, was ignorant and provincial compared to them. Fur traders, whalers, fishermen, merchants, pirates, yet all the while assiduous tillers of the soil, the Scandinavians had always been an amphibious people."

With the crisp freshness of morning air, the Hávamál states:

> He must early get up
> who is living alone,
> and see to his work himself.
> Much remains undone
> for a slug-a-bed.
> Half-won is wealth for the swift.

*

At that time there was not a united England, and despite its civilization and Christianity it was far behind he northmen, in respect to political and military organization. (Collingwood).

The early Anglo-Saxons were not city dwellers. They had no mercantile instincts except for selling slaves overseas, and they lost their old sea habits when they had won themselves good lands in the interior. (Trevelyan).

England still did not constitute a political unit and was a typical peasant land with a somewhat undeveloped business life.–The Anglo-Saxons had no government machinery that could control distant provinces, nor had they any fortresses or standing armies. (Askeberg).

The Saxon farmers had no desire to colonize other Saxon kingdoms as conquerors, although they were still busy invading and settling new lands in Welsh territory beyond the Exe and Severn.–The desire to be united in one State only came into being as a later consequence of the Danish wars, after Northumbria and Mercia had been destroyed by the heathen flood. The Anglo-Saxon ploughman was not only an unskilled, but an unwilling soldier. He had forgotten the warlike desires of his ancestor who helped to sack the Roman villa hard by (Trevelyan).

Terrible as were the ravages of the Scandinavian invaders, it is generally admitted that on the whole the benefit which resulted therefrom was greater than the suffering. That benefit was the consolidation of Anglo-Saxon England into one kingdom (T. Hodgkin).

But as warriors, the Vikings had uncommon abilities and a natural genius for war. Green says that their strength did not lie in numbers but in superiority as warriors, and in their rare mixture of wariness and boldness. Their wars were regular campaigns of armies which marched to conquer and whose aim was to settle on the land they had won. They were, in fact, the first European warriors who realized the value of quick movement in war. The Danes were as superior to their opponents in tactics as in strategy. The Scandinavian warband was a force of drilled warriors tried in a hundred forays, knit together by discipline and mutual trust, grouped around a leader of their own choosing, and armed from head to foot.

At the siege of Paris in 885 they employed catapults, battering-rams, combustibles and several machines unknown to the Franks. They showed great ability in the science of military engineering and were masters in amphibian operations.

Sir Edmund Gosse says, "In their rules for battle, and for attack and defence, the northmen appear to have been guided by a natural sense of what was upright and just." To this very day the same rule applies in England and in Denmark that two do not fight against one.

Their ability as warriors, so Kendrick asserts, showed itself in a sense of strategy, camouflage, rapid movement, unusual tactics and an imperishable bravery.

"Of his courage not much needs to be told. Yet we cannot easily realize how all embracing that courage was," says Keary, in speaking of the Vikings. Their strategy of pretending during battle that their whole army was in flight, and then suddenly turning when the ranks of the pursuers were in disorder, was quite new. "I think any general would admit that there have been but few disciplined armies in the world's history which could be trusted to execute such a manoeuvre as this; that with the vast majority of troops the signal in the face of an enemy would be fatal to the hopes of the day, even though the reasons for the retreat were well understood. What makes the military achievements of the Vikings the more remarkable is that they were not organized by any despotic power above; they lived under a constitution which was more republican than monarchical" (Keary).

Hodgkin compares them to the English sea-dogs of the Elizabethan age, part pirates, part traders, part statesmen, while Keary likens them to Englishmen such as Drake and Hawkins. He says, "We understand how these lands came to be set apart for the cultivation of the art of boat-building and their children a destined race of explorers; and we are led to ask ourselves how much we may owe to the Scandinavian blood which runs in our veins."

In Collingwood's book *Scandinavian Britain*, there is the following characterization of the Nordic type, "It is of a type which we pride ourselves upon as essentially British–a sturdy, thrifty, hardworking, law-loving people, fond of good cheer and strong drink, of shrewd, blunt speech, and a stubborn reticence when speech would be useless or foolish; a people clean-living, faithful to friend and kinsman, truthful, hospitable, liking to make a fair show, but not vain or boastful; a people with perhaps little play of fancy or great range of thought, but cool-thinking, resolute, determined, able to realize the plainer facts of life clearly and even deeply. Of course some of these characteristics are those common to other nations in their rank of development, but taken together they show a character such as no other race of that day could probably claim, and enable us to understand how that quiet storage of force had gone on which, when released, was capable of such results, as the succeeding centuries witnessed with amazement."

Those men who lifted a whole continent off its hinges–those Danes who conquered England, northern France and the coasts of the Baltic–those Norwegians who conquered Scotland and Ireland, plundered western France, colonized the wastes of Iceland and frigid Greenland, and set foot on the coasts of America–those Swedes who founded the Russian Empire, and traded in the Caspian and across the Black Sea with Greeks, Arabs and Persians–were they barbarians?

No, says du Chaillu: "The people who were then spread over a great part of present Russia, who overran Germany, who knew the art of writing, who led their conquering hosts to Spain, into the Mediterranean, to Sicily, Greece, the Black Sea, Palestine, Africa and even crossed the broad Atlantic to America, who were undisputed masters of the sea for more than twelve centuries, were not barbarians. Let those who uphold the contrary view produce evidence from archaeology of an indigenous British or Gallic civilization which surpasses that of the north."

The American historian Laurence M. Larson says that by the standards of his own era the northman was no barbarian. Contemporary sources very seldom use the word 'barbarians' about the Vikings, whereas they almost always describe the Slavs and Magyars by that term.

The history of the Vikings has been written by their enemies. The writers of the English and Frankish chronicles were the worst enemies of the Northmen, ignorant and bigoted men when judged by the standard of our time. (du Chaillu).

There are many accounts of misdeeds and cruelties by Vikings, but, says Hodgkin, "there is no more reason to condemn the Norsemen wholesale for such tastes than to write down our own generation as criminal because it enjoys stories about crime. They made good stories."

It must be admitted that a study of the shameful deeds of the Vikings brings things to light which are not considered good taste in the best circles. The spirit of humanity and sympathy is indeed most often confined to more or less limited circles and scattered connections. The Vikings were scarcely more affected by what occurred than we are, for example, about what takes place in a slaughterhouse. The fate of distant peoples usually affects us very little. One can assert with some justification that it is not for us, in our era, to regard ourselves as in any respect raised above Viking morality. The Vikings would never have descended to the level of torture and cruelty to which our generation has borne witness. They would have called it 'Niddingsdaad' (infamous deeds), or as it is defined in the Hervarar Saga: "shame of shames and scabby lewdness."

The Vikings were cruel, and the destruction they wrought in England, France and Germany was terrific. Collingwood writes, "The Vikings were often beaten, and sometimes treated with greater cruelty than they had intended to inflict. There is no trace, in the earlier period, of needless cruelty on their part, except the fact, which seems needless to us, but was by no means so in that age, of their making such attacks at all. It was only later, through contact with the south, that they learned to torture; but we cannot say that they met easy deaths when they were captured. The Viking was only doing what the most civilized were doing; his fault was that he did it rather more skilfully." One need merely think of the impression that Charlemagne's propagation of Christianity must have made upon the Danes. It was the Franks who began it.

It must also be remembered that the Church and the Christian states used torture throughout the Middle Ages, right down to Voltaire's time, and it is not recorded that any spokesman for the Church arose in in-

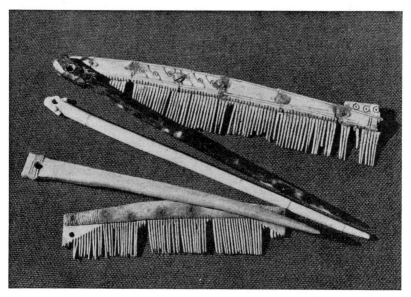

Combes and needles carved in bone.
From the Viking fortress Trelleborg. Zealand.

dignant protest; on the contrary, they employed torture as an effective theological argument in religious questions. And what is the state of affairs in some countries today? Nor must one forget that piracy was already flourishing actively among the British kingdoms themselves. Trevelyan says, "The English and Irish were already showing the example of the very deeds they lamented with such bitterness a little later." When in Christian Ireland monks fought with monks and kings made war on priests and women, it was the normal course of nature, but "that Gentiles should come in and poach upon the preserves of royal sportsmen was the unbearable shame."

Nevertheless, the Angles and Danes were so nearly related that it was not very long before a new unity grew out of the warring tribes. So long as the Viking battle-axe was crashing through the skulls of monks, and the Englich were nailing to their church doors skins flayed off their Danish enemies the hatred between Anglo-Saxon and Scandinavian was profound. (Trevelyan).

John of Wollingford, the old Anglo-Saxon, relates that one of the reasons why the Anglo-Saxons hated their enemies was, amusingly enough, because 'the Danes combed their hair every day, took baths every Saturday, and changed their underclothing frequently so that they were held in high favor by the ladies.' Of course they were hated! To this Shetelig adds the remark, "If this seemed surprising to their contemporaries, as it did, we may venture to draw the inference that the later English partiality for baths and washing is not an Anglo-Saxon characteristic, but a heritage from the Viking times."

On numerous English church doors the flayed skin of Danish Vikings has been found. The microscope shows that it is skin from blond, fair-haired and freckled men. It is sometimes preserved under the iron studs on oaken church doors. At Stillingfleet Church in Yorkshire the skin of a Dane was thus found under an iron strap forged like a Viking ship, and Pepys states in his Diary for April 10 1661, "Then to Rochester, and there saw the Cathedral, which is now fitting for use, and the organ then atuning. Then away thence, observing the great doors of the church, as they say, covered with the skins of the Danes." Small pieces of these Danish skins fetched large sums at English auctions. In his treatise: 'On Danes' Skins', St. George Gray says in his dry English manner, "The average mind generally regards flaying alive as extremely gruesome."

If we gaze at the smoke of the burning abbeys and plundered churches, at the fleeing crowds of Anglian peasants, we must not forget that the picture is not so very different from that which England experienced when, four or five centuries earlier, the Angles themselves broke in and evicted the Christian Celts and burned their churches. Earlier English historians often overlook this. And the Franks who knelt in their churches praying to God to save them from the wild Normans, it was not so very long since they themselves had come roaring into Roman Catholic Gaul rampaging wildly in what was then regarded as civilization. The internal conflicts of the Frankish and German kings, to say nothing of the destructive quarrels of the barons, were in no way more agreeable to the common people. If the French peasants attempted to collect together in organized opposition to the Vikings they were dispersed and struck down by their own lords, who had no desire whatsoever for popular opposition. Askeberg says, "The age that also experienced the ravages of the Magyars and Arabs, of Charlemagne's war of extermination against the Saxons, and the vicious Frankish civil wars, could scarcely have had reason to accuse the northmen of a more barbaric trespass into European events. The lamentations of the monks and

166

priests over smoking abbey ruins and violated saintly relics are easy to understand from their own point of view, since in religious matters the heathen northmen had not forsworn greater tolerance than had been meted out to them by the Christians. The evidence of their savagery and cruelty is, however, one–sided, partial and often bigoted, and in their condemnatory judgment there may sometimes be faintly discerned an involuntary recognition of their bravery, solidarity and trustworthiness,– virtues which the Christian world itself so sadly lacked."

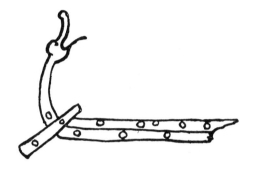

A Viking ship in iron work over a Dane's skin from the door of Stillingfleet Church, Yorkshire.

These northmen were a remarkable people, insatiable in many respects. But what the Vikings sought after was not merely the gold of the abbeys and the silver of the Danegeld, not only soil to plough, or trade routes to frequent. They delighted in beautiful and well–tried weapons which could win them victory, fame, and reputation. Egil Skallagrimson sings, "Now blood-stained swords bear flowers of gold." To the swords which could win them victory and honor they gave names such as Graaside (Grey-side), Kongsbane (King-slayer) and Ættetange (Kin-blade). They delighted in amassing gold and success. "Life seems brighter when seen through a gold ring," says Egil. But they were just as magnificent in generously scattering it again. "The ring is round. It can roll."

But it was not only gold and weapons they chose. Grønbech says, "The old idea of the Vikings as sweeping like a storm across the lands they touched, destroying the wealth they found, and leaving themselves as poor as ever has, in our time, had to give way to a breathless wonder at their craving for enrichment. The gold they found has disappeared. But we have learned now that there was gathered together in the north a treasure of knowledge and thought, poetry and dreams that must have

167

been brought home from abroad, despite the fact that such spiritual values are far more difficult to find and steal and carry safely home than precious stones or precious metals. The northmen seem to have been insatiable in the matter of such spiritual treasures."

In Hávamál is written,

> Better burden
> no one bears
> than wisdom won.

The civilization of the Vikings differed from that of Catholic Europe. In some respects it was poorer, in others richer. The Vikings were frank and truthful and they glorified their favorite heroes because they did not lie. Compare this with the pious, but alas, sometimes unreliable monks' legends of the saints. The honor of one's word, the sacredness of a promise, were to them a source of strength. For truthfulness gives spiritual health, and trust in one another is of practical importance for trade and prosperity. To break a promise or agreement was "Niddingsværk" (a work of infamy) which destroyed life and devoured happiness from within.

Trevelyan says, "The Danes had a word for acts of cowardice, desertion, or dishonorables of any kind–"Niddingsværk"–as distinct from the ordinary breaches of the law, and more terribly punished by public opinion. It was worse to be a "Nidding" than a man-slayer. The liar too, is rather despised than honored. The Nordic race would not have found its hero in Jacob or even in Odysseus of the many wiles, in spite of close similarities between the society described in Homer and in Beowulf respectively."

Monastic writings have given the Vikings a reputation for cunning and deceitfulness. But, says Mawer, that was because the Vikings overcame their enemies more by shrewdness than by deceit. Williams thinks that the breaches of agreement of which they were often accused were frequently founded on the fact that the "contributions" which had been promised them were not paid in time or in full, or that fresh hordes of Vikings appeared who were not bound by the agreements of their predecessors. Stefánsson admits that the northman also found a certain satisfaction in discovering shortcomings in the law and holes in the agreements, and in utilizing them to his own advantage. We must remember, he says, "that we rely upon the writings of their enemies for the story of their conquest. It is only when the monkish lies are too gross and palpable that we can certainly label them as the falsehoods they are."

Trevelyan says of the northmen, "The worship of Odin and Thor, the religion common to primitive Anglo-Saxon and Scandinavian, was pre-eminently a layman's religion, a religion of highhearted gentlemen not overburdened with brains or troubled about their own souls. Its grand old mythology inculcated or reflected the virtues of the race: manliness, generosity, loyalty in service and friendship, and a certain rough honesty. The social standards of the modern English schoolboy come nearest to it, as the most elementary expression of the racial character."

Catholicism did not always have a beneficial effect on the people of the north. It was often followed by a deterioration in their moral strength. It dissolved the Nordic kinship-feeling and personality, de-stroyed the direct approach of Man to God, setting up between them a rule of priests and cult of saints. Catholicism first brought the fear of life, death and sex to the North. Louis the Pious used it as a deliberate policy, in an attempt to paralyze the northmen with Catholicism. The northmen themselves had that feeling of personal responsibility which Christianity originally possessed, though it was limited to their own sur-roundings. The extension of human feelings toward all mankind was one of the most precious gifts of Christianity. But to come from the pure, invigorating air and fresh spontaneity of the Sagas to the melancholy medieval Church history is like entering cramped, narrow rooms, musty with the heavy odor of cats and candles beneath the arches.

There was no small element of hysteria in Catholicism at that time, and even a fine personage such as Ansgar is not without traces of it. Steenstrup portrays him thus, "In his relations with God and in his devotion, Ansgar felt that a contrite heart was the supreme good, and he thought that life ought to be lived in sorrow and tears. Therefore he was distressed when not in this state, or when the source of tears appear-ed to have dried up, even though the heart might be heavy. Only in his later years did he acquire the facility for crying which old age gives and which he so earnestly desired."

After this, one views almost with affection a couple of brine-pickled heathens such as Gaukathor and Afrafasti. Before the Battle of Stiklestad they went to King Olaf the Saint and offered their help in the fight.

169

The King asked them if they had been baptized. Gaukathor replied, "No. I am neither Christian nor heathen. We and our men have no Faith other than that we believe in ourselves, our strength and our luck in victory, and we are well served with these "But King Olaf insisted that they must be baptized before taking them into his service, and thereupon they left him in anger. Nevertheless, they returned later because, as Gaukathor said, "The King has greater need for help, and if I am to believe in some god it is no worse to have faith in the White Christ than in any other." They then allowed themselves to be baptized and took part in the battle. They were all slain. One may well ask, who showed the greater love and nobility of soul—the King or Gaukathor?

This account reminds one of the tale about King Hrolf and his men who never worshipped gods, but believed in their own might and main. This did not mean that they were without ethics or morals. Their relations with reality were, in fact, characterized by ideals: faithfulness, patience, hospitality, generosity and truthfulness. In 'The Gallic War' (VI. 21.) Caesar wrote about the Teutons of his time, "They have no Druids to regulate divine worship, no zeal for sacrifices. They reckon among the gods those only whom they see and by whose offices they are openly assisted—to wit, the Sun, the Fire-god, and the Moon; of the rest they have learnt not even by report."

Their religion was one of practical, sober utilitarianism. The Viking Helge the Meager was a cautious type. He believed in Christ when ashore, but worshipped Thor when at sea.

In other respects the attitude of the heathen northman to reality was upright and sturdy, sometimes arrogant, yet open and ready to learn from others. He was not humble, but he was fair. Within the limits of his own hard world he was just. Williams says, "Among themselves the Scandinavians were unusually honest and straightforward. They showed a special contempt for the backbiter, the thief, the liar, the traitor, and the breaker of oaths."

Their outlook is revealed, for example, in their attitude toward women. Sir Edmund Gosse says, "The position of women among the Scandinavian nations presents some very interesting peculiarities. It was one of the noblest sides of the Northern character that appeared when the fate of a woman was discussed. It was the Norseman's creed that there existed something sacred and divine in woman; and in consequence he treated his wife and daughters with gentleness and courtesy, and the rest of their

170

Dragon figure head from a Danish Viking ship
found in 1951 in the River Scheldt.
Nationaal Scheepvaart Museum. Antwerpen.

countrywomen with respect. In spite, however, of all excesses that local barbarity may have fallen into, without question the position of a Scandinavian woman was more honourable than of any of her sex in other parts of Europe in that age."

Hundreds of years before the Viking Age, Caesar said about the Teutons, "Their whole life is composed of hunting expeditions and military pursuits; from early boyhood they are zealous for toil and hardship. Those who remain longest in chastity win greatest praise among their kindred; some think that stature, some that strength and sinew are fortified thereby. Further, they deem it a most disgraceful thing to have had knowledge of a woman before the twentieth year; and there is no secrecy in the matter, for both sexes bathe in the rivers and wear small cloaks of deer skin, leaving great part of the body bare."

In their ancient worship of fertility, the northmen treated the virtue and blessing of procreation boldly and naturally, but without levity. The peculiar attitude of the Catholic monks to that phase of existence was foreign to them, and they never learned to think of sexuality as wicked. A certain aloof modesty was one of their peculiarities but they were not ashamed of their sex-life and bore their children with pride.

171

It is typical that Adam of Bremen, who was present at the sacrificial rites in the great temple at Uppsala, should purposely refrain from recording the ritual songs because he considered them indecent. No doubt they sounded shocking to the ears of a monk—something like the old poem Skirnismál, which must be a remnant of such a ritual cult-song, carved in rank runes. It is strange that this vigorous cult of fertility, which was a most natural thing to the northmen should, in the opinion of the Catholic Church, be the very epitome of sin. Nothing suggests that the northmen worshipped sexuality for its own sake. Their deepest passion and desire was not for sex but children. The procreative force was closely connected with fertility.

The northman did not love his enemies. The Catholic did so only rarely. The attitude is typically expressed in what is said about Gunnar from Hlidarende, 'He was faithful to friends but careful in his choice of them.' And Hávamál has these lines:

> "His friend's friend
> shall a man remain,
> and gifts with gifts requite.
>
> But never a man
> shall friendship make
> with the friends of his foe."

No humanitarian he belived in self-help and philanthropy was certainly not in his line, but there was nonetheless a certain balance in his limitations.

It was trade, long voyages, and subsequent exposure to other cultures which dissolved the spiritual and ethical isolation of the northman. The surrounding world became a part of his world, the boundary between Utgard and Midgard disappeared. Much the same thing had happened before the birth of Christ, when, at the time of the Greek and Roman empires, international trading by the Mediterranean peoples dissolved their national isolation and spiritual confines. Men began to be fellow-men.

They were not only men grave with the darkness of winter and the grey sea in their minds. The light summer nights brought a touch of humor to their lips and a twinkle to their eyes.

Keary says, "Along with the fierce qualities there went another, very

172

characteristic of the northmen, a vivid sense of humor. The Vikings and the Saga heroes had a schoolboy love of two things: nicknames and practical jokes. These nicknaming habits of the Scandinavian people were peculiar. All the early kings of Denmark, for instance, down to the fourteenth century, had their nicknames ... I do not know where we should find a modern parallel to such a character as I have described, unless it were in the Western states of America."

Loud gaiety rang through the hall when brown mead was drunk from the crooked horns of wild bulls, and a weather-beaten fore-finger drew sea-charts in the puddles on the rough table top. But they also mastered a keen, biting wit. Typical of this are Queen Gunhild's words to the guard when she had had Hrut, Dala-Koll's son, sleeping with her at night in the loft, 'It will not cost you anything at all—your life, of course, excepted—if you talk to anyone about Hrut and me'.

In the northmen's philosophy, body and soul were not divided into two parts of no concern to one another. According to their view, the body was an important part of the soul. They were a race of athletes whose strength and beauty of body complemented their resilience of mind. Later, during the Crusades, epidemic and endemic diseases undermined health and intellectual and moral fiber in Europe. Malaria took its toll south of the Alps as early as the decay of the civilization of antiquity, having, in the centuries previous to the birth of Christ, made its entry into Greece and Rome. The plague, carried by ships' rats, followed in the tracks of the crusaders and pilgrims. Smallpox spread far and wide, while the sailors of Christopher Columbus brought back syphilis from the North American Indians. Deep scars were left on the moral and intellectual face of Europe by this series of afflictions.

In his book *Rats, Lice and History,* Zinsser makes this remark on the influence of epidemic diseases on political and military history, "Soldiers have rarely won wars. They more often mop up after the barrage of epidemics and Typhus, with its brothers and sisters—plague, cholera, typhoid, and dysentery—have decided more campaigns than Cæsar, Hannibal, Napoleon, and all the inspectors—general of history. The epidemics get the blame for defeat, the generals the credit for victory."

Sir Edmund Gosse thought that the northmen were perhaps the most elevated people of heathen antiquity. He continues, in his rich Victorian style, "Never, probably, since the world began, save during one short century on the plains of Nemæa and Olympia, have men so perfect in vigour and shapeliness been seen on the surface of the globe as those who shot over the ice or galloped in frantic races over the hillsides in the palmy days of pagan Scandinavia ... The careful elimination of all elements of physical weakness, the unwearied and unsparing system of muscular training, the absence of those epidemic diseases which afterward sapped the health of all northern Europe, combined to produce a nation whose magnificent virility and well-balanced bodily perfection have hardly found a rival in the world's history ... Its inhabitants were a race of aristocrats–the nobility of the whole of Scandinavia–and in the splendor of their manhood and the pride of their birth they regarded neighbouring nations with much the same scorn as the Hellenes regarded Persians or Sicilians.

"The art of poetry flourished in Iceland when it was dumb elsewhere in Europe, and the luxurious products of the south, introduced by the Vinkingar, gradually led to the adaption of such a highly cultivated life among the pagan Norsemen that it was possible for Iceland to produce, during the darkest midnight of the middle ages, a brilliant school of poets, historians, and critics.–The introduction of Christianity was the ruin of all this intellectual splendour.–It is, doubtless, an instructive question to ask ourselves–why has the spread of Christian truth been in so many parts of the world a death blow to the fine arts?"

Askeberg says, "The spiritual culture in the north retained its peculiar stamp, particularly in two fields, even after the final break-through of Christianity. For centuries it had possessed a system of writing, and it preserved a living literature in verbal tradition."

In Denmark the destructive intolerance of Catholicism eliminated almost all the ancient literature and poetry which corresponded to the Edda and Sagas of the Icelanders. This had most certainly existed, according to what one can judge from its traces in Icelandic literature. Jan de Vries writes, "It is of no importance that we do not know of a single copy of such sagas from Denmark, since the Norwegian sagas also have only been transmitted to us in Icelandic recension. On the contrary, there are several indications that such a saga-tradition also flourished in Denmark, but it was hampered in its further development by other cross-influences. The mere fact that there is so much Danish material in the Fornaldar-saga makes it probable that a living native tradition has existed which has left its traces in the later Icelandic tradition."

174

The destruction of the Old Danish literature was so thorough that it may quite likely counter-balance the devastation by the Vikings of several abbeys. That Iceland's resplendent literature was saved is partly due to the fact that Catholicism was introduced there in a peaceful and parliamentary manner. There were no despotic monarchs in Iceland with whom the Church could ally itself. Icelandic literature later became a great inspiration to European romanticism. In Denmark in the 19th century it caused the Golden Age of literature to burst into bloom. But, notwithstanding all the literature of the Golden Age, it is the Icelandic sagas which today stand unsurpassed in purity, virility and power. These sagas are the earliest truly democratic literature in the world.

The Danish language was, at one time, a world-language. All the Nordic peoples called their language 'Dansk Tunge', Danish tongue. Philpotts says, "From the eighth to the thirteenth century, the Norse language became current over a large part of Europe. It was spoken, with small differences, in the whole of Scandinavia, in a considerable area of England, Scotland and Ireland, in part of France (for a time at least), on the southern and eastern sides of the Baltic, as far south as the great Swedish kingdom centered in Kiev, the mother of Russian cities. It became a recognized language in Constantinople, for it was the speech of the Emperor's bodyguard. It was probably used by traders on the shores of the Caspian, although there is no actual record of its being spoken farther east than the river Jordan, a verse still extant, uttered by an Earl of Orkney on pilgrimage. Its limit westward was no nearer than the coast of Massachusetts, for it was the first European language to be spoken in the New World ... Old Norse literature, then, belongs to a time when Norse was one of the most widely spread languages of Europe."

This tremendous expansion is comparable to that which the English language has undergone in the last two centuries. In the beginning, the Teutonic tribes carried their primitive language across Europe from the ancient Danish lands. Later, 'Danish Tongue' spread far and wide, and through its influence on the language of the English-speaking peoples, words of Danish origin resound today all over the world. It is not surprising that it was a Dane, Rasmus Rask, who founded the science of comparative philology. Half in jest, Professor Rubow remarks that it was a Dane who wrote the only work that might well be called world literature. Shakespeare, Molière, Goethe, and Cervantes are not read in

175

all countries, despite the greatness of their genius. Even the Bible, the Koran and Buddhist writings are read only in large, but not limitless, areas. The fairy-tales of Hans Christian Andersen, however, are translated into all languages.

The Danish tongue became the tool of the Nordic spirit. The meeting between this Nordic spirit and the type of Christianity represented by Catholicism was rewarding for both parties. The northman absorbed what he needed of Catholicism, altered and merged it with his own spirit, and from it created something new which was in many ways closer to the teachings of Christ than the dogmatic theology of the Catholic fathers.

The doctrine of the one, eternal, all-embracing God which Christianity brought, the living, invisible, creative God, was something new to the northmen, something grand, before which their moss-grown idols tottered and fell. In Vøluspá we see the eruption in an early stage. The simple message to 'do unto others as you would have them do unto you', was an extension and perfection of their own longing for righteousness. But the northmen never learned to understand the teachings of Sts. Paul and Augustine regarding original sin and misery, nothing of which was mentioned in the Sermon on the Mount, and not until later did they defer to it.

The 'White Christ' whom the northmen accepted was quite a different figure from that of Catholicism. He was more vigorous, more manly and resolute, and more akin to the Jesus who uttered the words, "He that hath no sword, let him sell his garment and buy one." Now these words certainly cannot be said to form the corpus of the teachings of Jesus, but they are a part of them, bespeaking a bold frown upon the gentle brow, and a virile trait often omitted in sermons. But the Viking, who knew that figthing has its place in the events of the world and the course of history, set out and continued his expeditions as crusader and holy knight of the sword.

*

The forms of civilization are varied in spiritual history. That which generally passes for civilization is not always an essential part of it. We are surely too inclined to measure the value of civilization by what it can produce in art and science, and to forget the sound and steady pursuit of trade, which is its very foundation. Artists, aesthetes, and philologists ennoble and embellish a culture, but it is the creative strength of practical life and the natural order of justice which form its base. Where religion, law and science are channeled into systems, structures, and ideologies, thus hampering initiative and the development of a culture, they will be pushed aside by the practical aspects of everyday living, or else civilization will suffer and disappear.

The northmen were never successful at building up systems. They faced the world and realities with open eyes, and their minds therefore remained plastic. They looked God, Heaven, Earth, and everything else straight in the eye.

In their strong sense of life, their practical ability, their freedom and integrity, the Vikings had something which, despite all their short-comings, was nearer to the truth in many respects than that which a thousand years ago was called Catholic Christianity. However astonishing it may sound, it is by no means unlikely that Jesus would have appreciated them.

The Nordic spirit was the most precious gift among all those the Vikings gave to the world. Freedom developed in Scandinavia in a manner surpassed only by ancient Greece, and its ability to give scope to all the creative faculties of mankind is what makes it so important. Where everything depends on a single man or a single class, organization, or party government, a certain firmness and solidity in operation may be attained for a time, but existence becomes poor, limited and more one-sided than when individual initiative is allowed to flourish. That is the perfect law of freedom. Grundtvig, that mighty and inspired prophet of freedom, was a typical Dane.

The northman's sense of justice, which found its expression in legislation and rules of the courts of law, led to men's abilities and actions being directed outward, or in cooperative ventures, rather than in conflict. The task of justice is to direct freedom so that it does not violate the rights of others. The sense of justice which prevailed in their own little world at home was spread by the Viking conquests, their commercial undertakings, and in their creation of states and codes of law. A Dane, Anders Sandøe Ørsted, laid the foundation for the modern science of jurisprudence.   *

The religion which emerged from the meeting between Catholicism and the Nordic spirit was somewhat peculiar, and from its beginning bore strong traces of Nordic influence which, at a later date, Wycliffe,

Luther and Grundtvig developed further. According to Grønbech, it had nothing to do with the modern concept of the nature of Christianity. It was a practical religion of a highly complex nature.

The Nordic religion, says Trevelyan, "was not a religion of dread, or of magic formularies to propitiate hostile powers. Instead of covering its temples with frescoes of the tortures of the damned, it taught people not to be afraid of death. Its ideal was the fellowship of the hero with the gods, not merely in feasting and victory, but in danger and defeat. For the gods, too, are in the hands of fate, and the Scandinavian vision of the twilight of the gods that was to end the world showed the heroes dying valiantly in the last hopeless fight against the forces of chaos—loyal and fearless to the last. It is an incomplete but not an ignoble religion. It contains those elements of character which it was the special mission of the Nordic peoples to add to Christianity itself.

"But, when all is said, the old Saxon and Danish faith was a religion of barbarism with no elements in itself of further progress, and the spontaneous conversion of its adherents to Christianity seemed a confession of this fact. The old religion was merely a traditional expression of racial character, not an outside force at work upon that character. It did little for learning or art. It did not preach humility, charity, or anything else that was difficult. It did not foster religious ardor in any form."

Ljungberg, in his book on Nordic religion and Christianity, has shown that the reason for the victory of Christianity over the faith of the northmen, in addition to the organized and state-supported propaganda of the missions and the mystical, picturesque splendor of divine services, lay principally in the fact that Christianity was tolerant on all matters of ritual, but intolerant on all questions of faith. The northmen were just the reverse. In their polytheistic religion one new god more or less made no difference. But they saw something essential in the sacred ancient cult-rites which brought happiness, life and fertility. Much of the cult of heathendom still exists.

Often, says Grønbech, the Church has arisen on the foundations of the old temple, so that men and women could continue to tread the accustomed road when the spirit moved them to seek strength behind their everyday life.

In one of Pope Gregory the Great's letters, the priests were openly recommended not to destroy the heathen sanctuaries but to transform them into churches, and they were advised to convert the heathen feasts into church festivals.

The northmen were able to combine their ancient practical ethics with the main tenets of Christianity. Grønbech says, "An ethical attitude is not a quality which can be shifted at will. Like everything that is erect and supple, it arises from the perfect interplay of the details which constitute the whole, and if it is to be re-erected on new postulates, this can only be achieved by a new formation of the personality. In England there were many examples of new Christians who surrendered and blindly cast themselves into the arms of a foreign church, in return to receive all their ethics dictated from without. Their life consisted in abandonment of the duties of practical life, in taking monastic vows, in making pilgrimages, and in the discharge of such good deeds as had been recommended. They forfeited their identities, and reaped the rewards of becoming good Christians. Here in the north the heathens effected the great achievement of becoming new men and of re-creating themselves in the conversion."

The reality of existence in the Nordic mind was embodied in life and luck and honor. Grønbech says, "Without honor, life is impossible, not only worthless, but impossible to maintain. A man cannot live with shame, which in the old sense means far more than now—the 'cannot' is equal to 'is not able to'. As the life is in the blood, so actually the life is in honor; if the wound be left open, and honor suffered to be constantly oozing out, then follows a pining away, a discomfort rising to despair that is nothing but the beginning of the death struggle itself.

"And 'life' meant first and foremost a firm cohesion among those born to be of the same ilk in the world. Life included a good personal reputation and recognition by men of experience and among friends. Life was bound up in honor, in man's vigorous self-assertion against wrong, his energetic defence through revenge of those bound to him by blood-ties, and his ability to prevent himself from committing such acts as might inwardly damage himself—'Niddingsværk', as it was called. Life itself had a future beyond the threshold of death. It was not sufficient to live in posthumous fame nor in the burial-mound. This immortality would sooner or later fade away unless the continuance of the kin were assured from generation to generation by a constant recrudescence of man in the form of noble deeds performed by his descendants." (Grønbech).

For the northman, existence was synonymous with holiness. He believed in an eternal life, in the force of personality, and in the perpetuation of kin in fame and deed.

> One thing I know
> that never dies:
> The judgment of a dead man's deeds.
>
> (Hávamál)

So profoundly did he feel that the body was a part of the soul that he saw immortality of an essential and intelligible nature in the continuance of a man's kin and in its unity. From this conviction came the custom of naming children after their deceased kinsmen so as to eternalize the dead and give the living a share of his strength, life and prosperity—a custom which still persists.

Family life made existence warm and enriching, and in practical everyday life became the nucleus of the community. The family was the foundation for the organization of practical life, and from it people derived the moral satisfaction of living with and for others. The sexual function, important though it is, was not the foundation of the family, because it can find release in so many other ways.

'Man shall follow upon man', says an old proverb. One of the things about the northmen which most bewildered the Catholic missionaries was their attitude toward death and the departed. Adam of Bremen complains a great deal about them, "The Danes can neither cry over their sins nor over their dead." Grønbech says, "The next of kin understood how a poor corpse would feel when everything had grown cold in the world around him, once warm human thoughts no longer coursed through him, and no compensation could be found in the company of saints and holy men. They therefore gave the departed his funeral and his feasts of remembrance. The heathens had been accustomed to celebrating the funeral ale with vigor, not as the sad commemoration of a dear friend, but as a tremendous feast of strength which put death to flight by the force emanating from the source of holy power through the companions in the sacrifice." This custom still lives, though in a weakened form, among the country people in the north.

Grønbech sketches the difference existing between north and south as follows, "In the south an almost perverted religious emotion prevailed. Much greater feeling was aroused by fumbling with saints' bones than by reflecting upon the saints themselves. It would seem easy, then, for

180

the realism of the northmen to merge into the materialism of the Romans, and yet strangely enough, the northmen did not entirely give way."

"One thing is certain," he continues, "that the religion which came into existence owing to the change of outlook in the north had its own character, one which can never be mistaken for the popular piety of the south. And it is equally certain that peculiarities in the faith of our ancestors can be traced through the course of history and still influence those of us who write and read about the past from points of view which have no validity farther than the Alps, and scarcely as far as that."

*

The devastations of the Vikings are a principal feature in their history. There are still, alas, some who consider that those who are able to destroy a city are at least as great as those who are able to build it. The Vikings could destroy a city but they could also build one, and the culture which they overran was in many vital respects an obsolete civilization, an effete indoor culture in contrast to that of the Vikings, which was characterized by the rough weather of reality. Violence, such a prominent feature in their make-up, was not simply cruelty and wildness: it was bridled and organized from the depths of their souls.

The Viking demonstrated to the world that he possessed values and had something to give which was needed, forces and ideals which operate and exist to this day in those countries where he trod and mingled with the blood of others. Grønbech says, "Wherever he goes, he carries within himself a social structure which manifests itself in definite political forms as soon as he is thrown together with a crowd of others speaking the same tongue. He is not of that inarticulate type which forms kalaidoscopic tribal communities. However small his people may be, and however slight the degree of cohesion between its component molecules, the social consciousness is always present and active. He is a people in himself, and has no need of building up an artificial whole by the massing of numbers together. It is not sufficient to say of these Vikings that they have character—they *are* characters. Their claim to be called civilized, in the exalted meaning of the word, rests on harmony. They possess themselves and their world in lordly right of determination. Their harmony may be poor in the measure of its actual content, but it is nonetheless powerful and deep."

*

The forces and causes which led to the Viking expeditions varied in their complexity in different periods.

Many of the causes were presumably the same as those which lay behind the numerous migrations from the north in the Stone and Bronze Ages and in the Migration Period. The distinction between Viking expeditions and migrations is not sharply drawn. Were not the Eruli who set out from Denmark in the 3rd century the Vikings' predecessors? Hugleik's expedition to Franconia and the other Danish raids in the 6th century were in a sense Viking expeditions, as were the plunderings of the Saxons and the Jutish tribes in the 4th and 5th centuries.

The Jutes, Angles and Saxons who crossed the North Sea to England anticipated the expansion of the Viking period. After the mighty burst of energy which triggered the conquest and colonization of Britain, it is only natural that there should have been a pause before the north was again ready for a fresh emission.

"In reality"—says Penka—"emigration from Scandinavia never ceased."

*

The term 'Viking Period' is not a particularly good one, partly because it is seldom used in contemporary sources, partly because the term 'Viking expedition' is specifically applied to small, individual plundering raids, and partly because, as a matter of fact, we do not know the actual significance of the word 'Viking'. From ancient times it was thought that the word came either from an old Nordic word for a fight, or from the inlets and bays where the Vikings lurked while awaiting their prey, whom they chose to engage in smooth water. But none of these suggestions is satisfactory, especially since it was not typical of the Vikings to keep to the creeks. Their tactics almost always consisted of settling on islands and thence undertaking their expeditions and conquests. Others have thought that the word has a connection with the Province of Viken in Oslo Fjord. But in the sources the inhabitants of Viken or Vestfold are never called Vikinger, but Vikverjer or Vestfaldingi.

The word pre-dates the Viking Period and appears as early as in Widsith and old Anglo-Saxon glossaries. Sophus Bugge therefore thought that it was a loan-word from Anglo-Saxon, formed from the word: 'wic', which means a fortified camp or town, in Latin: 'vicus'. Vogel has referred to the fact that centuries before, the Viking transit trade was carried on in market towns for distant trade, and that the names of these

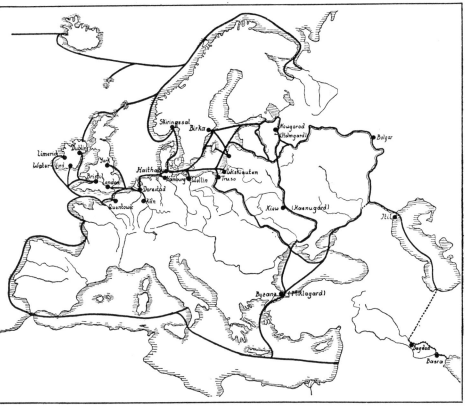

The trade routes of the Vikings. (Herbert Jankuhn).

settlements often end in: 'Wic'–as Slesvig, Quentowic and Bardowic. So the merchants who traded in these places might have been called Wicinger.

Now Fritz Askeberg, in a clear and profound philological treatise, has considered this question from its beginning and has arrived at the conclusion that none of the explanations advanced are possible, and that the word is of Nordic origin. It comes from: 'vige' (to yield), and therefore means a sea-warrior who swerves, diverges from a regular line of movement, makes a detour or travels far from home. The term was not used in ancient times for the large organized undertakings for conquest and colonization. The old sources also differentiate between the actual traders and the Vikings, who are often considered evildoers. Since the Viking period was a special Nordic phenomenon, it has been suggested that the term 'Norman Period' should be employed instead. But the term 'Viking Period' has a prescriptive right, and its meaning is clear.

Peaceful trade, raids, conquest and colonization overlapped each other. Stimulating trade and destructive plunder have in common that the purpose of both is to acquire the goods men can use; otherwise they have contrary interests and effects. Trade is to the benefit of both parts, while the benefit of plunder is one-sided. Import is the beginning of trade, and in times of normal exchange the imports required are paid for by exports. I do not defend piracy, but I do recommend common sense. The Vikings were realists because they were aware that their fundamental interest lay in imports. In the periods when traders turned pirate they only imported and refrained from paying with the equivalent export. If they had been educated in modern statesmanship they would have been content with exporting.

In the sagas we see how they sail away with their products and exchange them for other goods which they prefer to their own products, and then sail home with their merchandise. In between times greed or the sporting instinct asserts itself and the fighting spirit rises in men's minds. A brisk raid is sometimes the consequence. Egil Skallagrimsson sings as a boy, when his mother promised him a Viking ship,

> Stand up in the stem,
> steer the stately ship,
> penetrate into a port
> slaying one or the other.

Their appetite was keen for goods—whether it be trade and exchange, or plunder and exploits which brought them home. The need for the goods they lacked was the actual driving force behind their trade, as indeed it always is. But their appetite was also keen for fame. Fame and honor comprised a mighty thirst of the soul, the force which vitalized the kin and kept them together. Honor sprang partly from one's kin and partly from an individual man's actions and deeds, proving him a true descendant of his forefathers, one who did not dishonor his house or shame his kinfolk. In his individual life a mortal man was responsible for the immortality of his kith and kin.

184

The demand also embraced land, either on an individual scale for ploughing and dwelling-places, or on a larger scale for strategic points or realms to rule. Human beings usually go to war for two main reasons. These can be found in the peace treaties. The vanquished always have to give up land to the victor the source for food stuff and raw materials, or trading monopolies.

Various forces drove the northmen to seek for land. A profilic race requires space, and if the space were occupied at home, some of them emigrated. Vogel regards a surplus of population as having provided the main reason for emigration. When the older generation controlled all arable land the younger one was unable to obtain any to cultivate themselves: There have been periods in the north when there was great reluctance to split landed property. Frequently only one of the sons inherited the soil and so the others felt their roots to be less firmly planted in the homeland. This right of primogeniture was carried by William the Conqueror to England where it has been maintained until our day. The women, who otherwise occupied so free and honored a position in society, seldom inherited land, and among the landed aristocracy the marriage of a woman into a plain family was frowned upon right to the present time. Gradually, as royal power grew, the members of contesting dynasties and chieftains' families supplied the hordes of Vikings with high-born leaders who could not find room for their activities at home.

We must be aware that in Denmark, besides all these causes, a combination of high political problems plays an important part in the explanation of the explosive outburst of the Viking Period. The aggressive Carolingian Empire had subdued and destroyed the buffer states between the Danes and the Franks, threatening the Danish frontier. Arbman says, "The earliest connections between Scandinavia and the Continent seem to have been of a peaceful kind, based on trade." Charlemagne had hampered and restricted shipping and trade in the Frisian harbors with customs barriers and prohibitive restrictions on import, and traders were cut off from using the old natural roads up the rivers Rhine and Elbe. Denmark had a natural interest in using, consolidating and defending its important trade route across the neck of the Jutish peninsula, where impending dangers were growing darker and darker after the subjection of the Frisians and the Saxons. With this were mixed the religious-political factors, due to Charlemagne's forcible conversion of the heathens and its threat to old Nordic sacred creed and cult. Sir Charles Oman

185

emphasizes that the hostile advance of Christianity must have been a contributory cause to the inception of the Viking expeditions, the church often supporting high political and imperialistic undertakings. Sir Charles says, "Strange as the fact may seem, it would appear that the origin of the Viking raids must be sought in the hostile advance of Christendom, represented by Charles the Great, toward the north, rather than in any intention of the Scandinavians to attack the south."

Under Louis the Pious it became a conscious policy on the part of the Franks and Germans to paralyze the power of the north with the help of Catholicism. The idealistic pacification of human beings went hand in hand with an imperialistic advance and an attempt to distract people from the problems of this world by proclaiming the advantages of the next.

If one is to believe the contemporary accounts and loud complaints of the monks, the reasons for the Viking expeditions lay in the sinfulness of the Christian countries themselves, their resultant misfortunes being God's retribution. In that case there is not much for which to blame the Vikings. The monks are probably right, for Shetelig maintains that among the reasons for the Viking expeditions, the increasing population, desire for booty, and hunger for land were almost constant factors. These arguments are not sufficient, however, to explain the explosive force with which the expeditions developed. The actual provocation must have lain outside the permanent factors, outside the north, and must be sought in the vulnerability of the Western European powers resulting from internal disunity and disorganized systems of society. The powers of resistance and self–defence in these nations had been dissolved from within, and there appeared a weak spot, a *locus minoris resistentiae,* where the pressure from the primitive strength of the fresh Nordic nations suddenly broke through and split the old world order. As far as France was concerned, it seems that during internal disruptions King Lothar, son of Louis the Pious, had actually invited the Vikings to plunder those parts of the country which were ruled by his father and brothers.

Both in King Gudfred's war with Charlemagne and still more during the Jelling Dynasty, the foreign political factor moves into the foreground until it grows to the grand imperialistic plan of making the Baltic, the Kattegat, and the North Sea Danish lakes, where Denmark, through its central position, could unite and control the trade routes of North Europe. This was the idea realized by Svend Forkbeard and Canute the Great.

Stimulating activity, the sporting instinct, the youthful delight in superiority in speed and navigation, the pride of war and weapons, were also important factors in the development of the Viking expeditions. To these must be added the attraction of the culture and wealth of the Christian countries, that same force which magnetically drew the Celts to Italy and the Teutonic peoples to the Roman Empire and Byzantium.

As far as the sons of Regner Lodbrog were concerned, and later Svend and Canute, there was also present the desire for revenge which was so prominent a feature in the family feuds of the northmen. Regner Lodbrog's death in Ælla's snake-pit in Northumbria, and the mass murder of the Danes by order of King Ethelred on St. Brice's Day in 1002, when Svend Forkbeard's sister and brother-in-law perished, were deeds which impelled revenge.

When Charlemagne had finally subdued Friesland and destroyed the Frisians as a commercial power, and the mighty Frankish Empire began to disintegrate under Charlemagne's quarrelsome successors–then the opportunity suddenly presented itself. It was as though a golden America had appeared before their eyes. What a pity not to make use of it!

When the storm broke it was obvious that the western countries were more or less defenceless against the swift ships and insatiable energy of the northmen. Even as inner decay in the Roman Empires of the east and west was a strong contributory cause of the great migrations, so the internal decay and dissension in France, Germany, England and Ireland was a principal causative factor of the Viking expeditions.

The important progress made in the art and organization of ship-building, with the introduction of new and improved types, made long and rapid sea-voyages a technical possibility. The Viking Period is the age of the deep-sea ship, which created a revolution in the accustomed methods of warfare. Baker calls the sea-going ships, "the military answer of the north to the empire of Charlemagne."

All these reasons were combined in varying intensity and combinations throughout the Viking Period in the whole wide field of action. The transitions from trade to plundering raids, through conquest and colonization, to high political military expeditions and imperialism, are not clear-cut. The one merged into the other.

Voltage and tension accumulated. Lightning flashed.

THE SONS OF LODBROG

Gnyða mundu grisir, ef galtar hag vissi.
REGNER LODBROG.

The pigs would grunt grimly if the need of the boar were known.

Regner Lodbrog was the most celebrated sea-king of the Viking Period. He and his sons played leading roles in all the great events which took place in France, Germany and England in the 9th century and which brought large areas of those countries under Danish law. They were the prelude to the conquests of Svend and Canute the Great, but are in no way subordinate to the latter in the permanence and importance of their effects.

The figure of Regner is so thickly overgrown with legendary moss and mythical creepers that it is difficult to separate truth from fiction in what is recorded. However, certain dry facts emerge out of the mist and delineate themselves against the background of historical occurrences. The fact that England was almost entirely overrun by him and his sons, and that three-quarters of the country was actually conquered and colonized, presupposes that the mighty men who fashioned the course of events must have been outstanding personalities. We shall need good and sound reasons before rejecting these names. They are handed down to us by tradition, and found in contemporary English, Irish and Frankish sources as well as in the native Nordic sagas. Some historians tend to relegate Regner and his sons to the realm of fairyland, but when one considers the extent of such an exploit as the conquest of east, north and central England, and the impression it must have made at the time, it is highly improbable that the names of some of the actual participants should not have been preserved, as in the legends of Theodoric and Ermanaric. "Considering the prominence given to the story in Scandinavian tradition, it is difficult to believe that it is not founded on facts," says Mawer. We find much the same controversy surrounding the heroic figure of King Arthur. Here Collingwood thinks that the very fact that he has attracted fairy-tales and fables like a magnet need not necessarily imply that he is not an historical personage, but may be taken as proof of an original factual basis. Something similar applies to Regner Lodbrog.

It appears that Regner, in order to create a chain of military bases for later attacks on the Frankish Empire, consolidated himself in Ireland,

188

where Wicklow was established in 835 and Dublin in 836. Baker says, "The Irish question began with Regner." In 838 Regner consolidated himself in Cornwall, and in 842 he and his sons sailed up the Thames and conquered London.

The attacks on France possibly started from these bases. In 845 Regner and his sons sailed up the Seine and conquered Paris. Nobody can deny that they had a daring spirit, for to take London and Paris in three years is something.

Baker holds a high opinion of Regner. "He was a very famous man, whose memory fascinated the interest of succeeding generations just as that of Napoleon fascinates ours. His power was not the formal, official power, which accompanies the rulers and commanders of mature political states. It was a personal power, much more like that of an influential banker or company director. He had no more authority than he could at any given time get men to give him.

"He was the man who first realized the potentialities and the principles of naval war. He demonstrated the possibility of moving great fleets over immense stretches of sea. He conceived the first idea of those chains of naval bases which have since become the foundation of British naval power. He embodied that new world of the open sea which was the gift of his country and generation to mankind" (Baker).

All the sources, from the Frankish and Anglo-Saxon chronicles to the Icelandic sagas and the Danish history of Saxo, are filled with eulogies of Regner Lodbrog. Having regard to the uncertainty existing about the mutual relations and genealogy of Regner and the sons of Lodbrog, the names of Ivar and Halfdan are here generally employed as common denominators for those men who influenced the course of events, since it is the results of these events which are of lasting importance, and not the genealogical relationship.

Regner and his sons were of regal Danish blood. According to the fragmentary Irish annal, Regner's father was named Halfdan, and much suggests that he was a brother of Harald Klak and Hrorik, whom the sons of Gudfred had driven out of Denmark. Nordic sources state that Sigurd was his father and Halfdan his grandfather, brother to Gudfred.

Haarik I, son of Gudfred, was king from 813-854, and like his father, was a strong ruler. The attack on Paris and the Seineland—where Regner is found in 845 at the head of that fleet of 120 ships which on Easter

Sunday conquered and plundered Paris—was possibly a part of Haarik's policy toward the Frankish Empire, since Haarik at the same time sailed a fleet up the Elbe and laid waste to Hamburg. It is possible, though not certain, that Regner is identical with that Reginfred who was banished in 813, but it is more likely that this was the same Regner who destroyed Flanders in 858. Dysentery broke out in Regner's army in Paris, and he himself is said to have died of it after his return home. This information originates from a Frankish emissary under Count Kobbo, who was actually at the Court of Haarik when Regner returned. His references to the death of Regner do not inspire confidence, since according to other sources, Regner died later, in the snake-pit of King Ælla of Northumberland, uttering these famous last words: "The pigs would grunt grimly if the need of the boar was known."

In the preceding decade Friesland, especially Dorestad, was constantly besieged by Harald and Hrorik, banished members of the Danish royal family who established themselves in Rüstringen at the mouth of the Weser, and on Walcheren at the mouth of the Scheldt, holding these places in fief from the Emperor of the Franks. This was probably the Viking fleet which, under Asger's leadership, plundered Rouen in 841, and in the following year, London itself. Remarkable remnants of dragon-stemmed Viking ships, presumably Danish, have in recent years been found in the river Scheldt. One of them is now to be seen in The British Museum, a masterpiece in the art of woodcutting, with its long alert neck and the round head opening its cruel beak full of acquisitive energy. Another timber head is to be found in Nationaal Scheepwaarts-museum in Antwerpen. The loneliness of the endless sea, the sucking feeling of a sinking wave, and the nameless, indescribable horror of the deep-sea animal from the mud of the bottoms, is perfectly carved.

In the Frankish Empire the sons of Louis the Pious had divided the realm in three parts. Amid the confusing conditions prevailing, Hrorik succeeded in confirming his rule in Friesland. To this he added, after the fall of King Haarik in 854, "that part of the kingdom which lay between the sea and the Eider," which probably means Hedeby and the transit route across the base of Jutland.

Later, in 882, King Gudfred III succeeded in creating a kingdom in Friesland which included approximately the whole of Holland. Friesland had been ruled by Danes for several generations, though it was nominally a fief of France. It was for centuries a Danish sphere of influence, and

190

Dragon figure-head from a Danish
Viking ship found in 1934 in the River Scheldt
British Museum

Vogel says, "Gudfred's Norman Kingdom at the mouth of the Rhine is a quite peculiar historical formation that deserves our earnest attention. Here undoubtedly lay the germ of many forms of new kingdoms which, in the course of time, might have developed quite differently and achieved great importance had they not been destroyed by the downfall of Gudfred. Rollo's later foundation of Normandy was in a way anticipated here, and who knows whether a German Normandy might not have come into existence if the successful attempt on Gudfred's life had not prematurely checked its development. Meanwhile, this remarkable kingdom, one might say this kingdom afloat in the sea, could, under other circumstances have had a great future, and, in the course of time, become a colony of the same type as Normandy." In 885 the Emperor arranged the murder of Gudfred III.

Not all the Viking expeditions were successful. In 881 the Vikings suffered a severe defeat at San Court, and ten years later a still greater one at Louvain on the river Dyle. These defeats had considerable consequences, since they appear to have weakened Denmark to such an extent that the Swedes were able to establish themselves for a while in South Jutland, and Harald Fairhair was able to unite Norway from a nucleus in the provinces around Oslo Fjord, where Danish suzerainty appears to have been previously undermined. In the years around 900 Olof came to Hedeby from Sweden, and Harald Fairhair won the Battle of Hafrsfjord, vanquishing the west Norwegian petty kings.

The Viking attacks on England seem to have commenced with the Norwegians, who even before 800 had established themselves on the Shetlands, the Orkneys, and the Hebrides. They settled down in western Scotland, in Cumberland and Wales, and later made the Irish Sea a Norwegian sphere of interest. From their bases in Ireland—where they founded some of the earliest towns—their trade routes ran to west France, the raids on the Loire and Garonne being mainly Norwegian undertakings.

The Swedish Viking expeditions eastward to Russia and the Baltic States were mostly commercial-political undertakings on a grand scale, while any major colonization by an agricultural population does not seem to have taken place.

The Viking expeditions from Denmark which are historically known, commence in quite different guises, not as private voyages of discovery, but as regular military operations on a grand scale. Westward, the Viking forces evolved into well-organized armies. The fleets were admirably organized, with special supply corps and a regular commissary staff. Indeed, the great Viking armies in the latter half of the 9th century were veritable wandering states.

The long series of Viking operations which took place in France, Germany and England, will not be dealt with in detail here. Of special interest to us is not their progress, but rather the permanent effects they brought about. The first expeditions to England were somewhat of a reconnaissance nature, gaining footholds and bases in Ireland and Cornwall. After that followed the largescale attacks on Friesland and northern France where the Vikings began to settle in wintertime on islands along the coast, while the armies grew to tremendous proportions under their own sea-kings and special laws. There was scarcely a section of the country between the Rhine, Mosel, Saone and Loire that was not attacked. At length came the time when the Vikings felt themselves to be experienced, strong, and numerous enough for conquest and colonization. Behind England's green seawalls and white chalk cliffs, tempting soil awaited.

Regner Lodbrog appears to have been the first to attempt the conquest of Northumberland. In this he failed, while his sons were on a long and adventurous excursion along the European coastline to the Mediterranean lands where they plundered in Spain, North Africa, southern France and Italy.

Bjørn Ironside, son of Regner, is encountered from 855-858 commanding a fleet which ravaged the coasts of western France. Under the leadership of the chieftain Haastein, Bjørn Ironside, and the other sons of Lodbrog, the ships sailed out from 859-862 on their long and celebrated expedition which, as Hodgkin says, was an adventure standing out in this age like Drake's circumnavigation of the globe in the age of the Elizabethan sea-dogs. Haastein had sworn to conquer Rome and proclaim himself ruler of the world. This undertaking scintillates with youthful vigor and curiosity; up the rivers of Spain hand-fighting the Moors, down to the warm coasts of north Africa, to the rich districts of southern France around the River Rhone, up the rivers of northern Italy where Pisa and Fiesole were sacked, and to that white Tuscan city of Luna which was built entirely of Carrara marble. It was here that Haastein obtained entry by simulating illness, conversion and death, after which, during the solemn funeral ceremony, he rose from his coffin in the nave of the church, took the town from within, and plundered it in the joyous belief that it was Rome itself.

As early as 844 a Viking fleet of 100 ships attacked the coasts of Spain; first Asturia in the north, where the descendants of the Visigoths under Ramiro I repulsed them, and later Lisbon, Cadiz and Seville. It must have been a curious sight to see the tall, blond Vikings staring in wonderment from under their fair eyelashes in the brilliant sunlight at the flowering pomegranates and orange groves by the Guadalquivir.

Ibn Dihya, an Arabic source, states that after this expedition the Vikings sent an emissary to the Emir Abdurrhaman II (822-852). He then dispatched an ambassador with them to their homeland, a man of great charm and wisdom who, because of his graceful appearance, was called Al-Ghazal (the gazelle). There were presumably negotiations about trade. Al-Ghazal, who died in 860, states that he accompanied the heathens' fleet in his own ship, and that he came to their country after a passage from the Continent of three days' duration. The King's residence was on a large island in the ocean, and in it were running waters and gardens. Countless infidels lived there, and nearby were numerous other islands, both large and small, inhabited by heathens. The adjacent mainland also belonged to them. The manuscript, which dates from about 1200, states that the infidels were heathens at the time of Al-Ghazal, but had become Christians in the intervening years. Al-Ghazal made a deep impression on the Queen, whom he calls Noud, which could be one of the Nordic names Oddny, Idun or Aud. Thorgils, who at that time ruled over a Viking kingdom in Ireland, had a queen named Aud. Some therefore think that it was Ireland that Al-Ghazal visited. However, the Irish were by that time Christians, and furthermore, the description of the country does not fit Ireland at all, whereas it is a very good description of Denmark. Stefánsson therefore thinks that the goal of the journey must have been King Haarik's Court at Hlejre. Al-Ghazal unfortunately does not mention the name of the king or the name of the country, and it is not known what Haarik's queen was called. Probably the expedition to Spain was a continuation of the activity along the coasts of France. As early as the middle of the 5th century the Eruli had ravaged right down to the south coast of Spain. Later, the grand expedition to the Mediterranean took place from 859-861, and smaller Viking expeditions are mentioned in 910, 926, 951, 965 and about 970.

According to the saga, the conquest of England by the sons of Lod-

194

brog was carried through in revenge for Regner's death. Vengeance was of importance to the northmen, but more solid concurrent motives probably played a part. The large Viking army which operated in northern France sailed across to Kent and eastern England in 866. In the following year it entered the Wash and the mouth of the river Humber under the leadership of Ivar and Ubbe and Halfdan, and thence conquered York and the five 'Danish boroughs' which later became so famous– Lincoln, Derby, Nottingham, Stamford and Leicester. In York they took their revenge on King Ælla.

York was fortified and became the capital of the Danes. It was previously the largest city in England and had frequently been the seat of the government and residence of Roman Emperors. In the Danish Period it became, next to London, the largest and most important city in England. Its daughter New York, the largest and most important city in America, got its name in 1664 through the Duke of York, the later King James II.

After having consolidated their gains and procured horses for their army, the sons of Lodbrog advanced southward along the Roman roads and subdued both Mercia and East Anglia in the following years.

'Ferocious wolves take large bites' says an ancient proverb. In 872 they conquered London and now really only Wessex remained, the most remote, but strongest, of the English kingdoms. At that time the kings of Wessex were both warriors and statesmen. If Wessex had been like the other English states which Trevelyan calls "helpless East Anglia, decadent Northumbria and declining Mercia"–the course of history would have been different. It was owing to this accident of historical geography that the Vikings failed to complete their conquest of England, to the fact that King Alfred the Great and his brothers were the men they were, and that their kingdom lay in that part of England which was farthest from the invasion front.

But the Danes very nearly did succeed. Wessex was overrun at one time, and during the winter of 878 King Alfred controlled only the little fort on Athelney. With outstanding moral energy he succeeded once again in forming an army and defeating the Danish King Guthrum at Edington. Alfred succeeded in saving Wessex, but in saving Wessex he saved England, says Green. The Treaty of Wedmore–Alfred's and Guthrum's peace treaty–which is preserved in a venerable document, divided England between Alfred and Guthrum so that in the main

Alfred retained only the old Saxon districts. The frontier line ran more or less along the Thames and the old Roman road of Watling Street, and was much the same line that had formed the boundary between the Anglian districts and those in which the Saxons had settled. The Angles apparently found it easier to merge with the Danes than did the Saxons, and we see much the same thing happening again in the Danelaw after the conquests of Svend and Canute. The Danelaw, which made up about three-quarters of England, came under Danish law and became a territory for Danish colonization.

IVAR

We cannot but suspect, however, that on the side of the Vikings there was one who, if we knew more about him, would deserve mention with the Hannibals and Napoleons of history.

W. G. COLLINGWOOD.

These tremendous undertakings, which fundamentally altered the whole of England's national and social structure and eventually exercised a decisive influence on her future history, were more than mere piratical raids. Collingwood puts it thus: "When we consider the strategy of the invaders; the great war game which was going on; how fleet after fleet sought the weakest points; how on the failure of frontal attack, new attacks were made in flank; how the diplomacy of alliance with discontented dependencies was followed; how the maxim 'divide and conquer' was understood; how the net was drawn around England from point to point on either hand, until the time came for the final effort that should strangle the power of Wessex and make the British Islands wholly Scandinavian;—when we consider this, it is impossible to escape the idea that some great plan was in operation, some strong mind directing a warfare which, however originated, had become no casual scramble of independent adventurers, nor even an organization merely to exploit their sporting instincts, but a resolute scheme of conquest played with the skill of a chess-player on the field of Empire."

Collingwood continues, "The success of the Vikings was by no means a success of rude and savage force; it was a triumph of mental power as well as of moral endurance and physical bravery."

196

Green thinks that if the Vikings had succeeded in conquering Wessex, their scattered colonies in Ireland would have formed a Dominion and a large part of France would have then been theirs. In a word, Christendom would have seen the rise of a power upon its borders which might have changed the fortunes of the Western World.

Who was the draughtsman of the great plan whereby East Anglia, Deira and Mercia were gradually annexed? And why did the attempt to annex Alfred's kingdom fail? Collingwood thinks that it was Ivar, that half-mythical character who fought in Ireland in 857-862, who led the grand army through all its period of success. According to legends, he was the eldest of the sons of Regner Lodbrog and Kraka, daughter of Sigurd Fafnersbane, but the descriptions of him contain material which seems ascribable to the Norwegian-Irish Ivar of Dublin. He led the operations in England between 866-870, and is mentioned at the death of King Edmund of East Anglia in 870. This was the king who later adorned an English martyr-legend, where Edmund, like a second St. Sebastian bound to a tree, met his death under a rain of heathen arrows. The oldest source makes no mention of this incident. The village of Thetford, near Bury St. Edmund's, where Ivar established his headquarters, has recently been excavated.

It is probably the same Ivar who, according to Irish Annals, died in 873 and was then called King of the Norsemen of all Ireland and Britain. He was the first to bear such a title. Tradition has it that he was buried in a barrow at Cleveland in Yorkshire where, at a later date, William the Conqueror ordered the barrow opened and Ivar's bones burned.

Collingwood's research on the historical annals and chronicles reveals that for as long as the Vikings fought with success, Ivar is the only constant factor appearing throughout the shifting combinations of conquerors. Therefore, he concludes that Ivar was the brain behind it all, and this corresponds with the picture of controlled, coordinated, intellectual energy which characterizes him in the Nordic traditional legends. Collingwood says, "Wessex was saved by Alfred, but only after Ivar was gone."

HALFDAN

"The persistence of these Scandinavian innovations in law and agriculture, in monetary computation and personal nomenclature, is of more than antiquarian interest."

SIR FRANK STENTON.

The leading spirit after the death of Ivar seems to have been his brother, Halfdan. The first halfpennies in England were struck in London in 872–873, bearing Halfdan's name, and it was Halfdan who ordered the land in Northumberland surveyed and parcelled out in 875. The Anglo-Saxon Chronicle relates for the year 876, "In this year Halfdan shared out the lands of Northumbria, and they were engaged in ploughing and in making a living for themselves." Three years later the land in Mercia was similarly distributed and Guthrum followed suit in East Anglia in 880.

De Vries considers Halfdan to be the one who can most surely be regarded as a son of Regner, and thinks that he is the same person as that King Halfdan who is referred to in the Fulda-annals as being King in Denmark in 873.

After having carried out the land-reforms in Northumberland and Mercia and founding the five Danish cities–the Five Boroughs–Halfdan is said to have been deposed by his men because of his despotic rule. It was therefore presumably King Guthred or Hardeknud who continued and consolidated Halfdan's brilliant policy. De Vries believes that the distorted account of Halfdan's behavior was later invented by monks.

LANGUAGE AND PLACE-NAMES

"It is precisely the most indispensable elements of the language that have undergone the strongest Scandinavian influence."

OTTO JESPERSEN.

The parcelling out of land was an extremely important event which has influenced the fate of England right down to the present time. Stenton calls it a revolution. One can study the intensity of the colonization on the map of England, which has been aptly called the most wonderful of all palimpsests. Race after race has left its mark in the place-names of England but, with the exception of the actual Celtic districts, Celtic place-names have as a rule been preserved only in names

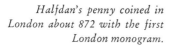

*Halfdan's penny coined in
London about 872 with the first
London monogram.*

of rivers and a few cities such as London. The Roman Empire, in the course of its three centuries, left but few traces in places-names. In southern England practically all place-names are Anglo-Saxon—a proof of the compact nature of the Anglian and Saxon colonization. But in the Danelaw, Nordic place-names are found by the thousand, and the English Place-Name Society is constantly unearthing fresh ones. The Nordic places-names are generally those which end in -by, -garth, -thorp, -thwaite, -force, -fell, -ey, -ness, -wick, -ford, -beck, -dal, and -holm. The most common are names ending in -by, and their first syllable is almost invariably an ancient Nordic personal name. Thus Grimsby and Derby bear the old Danish man's names of Grim and Dyre. In the north, Norwegian names are prominent.

The actual forms of the personal names in the first syllables suggest that they arose for the most part in the period just after the conquest, when the army divided up the land. Therefore they correspond in a way to the -lev towns in the Skjoldung Kingdom.

While England has thousands of Nordic place-names, there are only a few to be found in Ireland. In contrast to the large number of Danish names, it is noticeable how few Norman-French place-names exist in England, despite the fact that French was the language of the rulers after 1066. This is due to the fact that the Normans were not colonizers and settlers, as were the English and northmen. They formed an aristocracy of barons, magnates, officials, prelates and landlords.

In addition to place-names, the ancient records are filled with Nordic personal names appearing on deeds and other documents. In the northern part of the Danelaw, Nordic names of both men and women are more numerous than the original English. This proves that it was not merely an army which seized the land and intermarried with natives, but the veritable migration of a people, which took place in the 9th century. Nordic personal names were retained for at least three centuries after the Norman Conquest had caused direct communication with the Scandinavian countries to dwindle.

The English language, as spoken today, bears clear traces of strong Danish influence. Chadwick says that English occupies a position midway between Nordic and German. French words introduced by the Normans outnumber the Danish, but the latter are those largely used in everyday speech by the people, and have thus become more a part of the living language. The French words are preponderantly aristocratic, in contrast to the democratic Danish ones. "An Englishman cannot *thrive* or be *ill* or *die* without Scandinavian words; they are to the language what *bread* and *eggs* are to the daily fare. It is precisely the most indispensable elements of the language that have undergone the strongest Scandinavian influence."

The pronouns af daily speech—they, them, their, our,—are Danish, as are adjectives such as same and both, and the adverb fro, and certain auxiliary verbs and prepositions. This is further evidence of the massive scale of the colonization, since so many traces could not otherwise have been preserved in the language. Some Danish words came to England indirectly, brought by the Normans from Dano-French Normandy.

As late as the 18th century a Nordic language, mainly of Norwegian origin, was spoken in the Orkneys, Shetlands, and Caithness. Indeed, it is said that the fishermen still use Scandinavian words when setting forth, to ensure a good catch. At Maeshowe in the Orkneys there is a late Runic inscription which mentions the barrow of the Sons of Lodbrog and provides evidence of their contact with these islands.

The word most characteristic of the English conscience and moral qualities in games, politics and love—the little word *fair*—is one which has a common origin in English and Danish. Fair is the same as the ancient Danish word *fager*, in that it means light, blond, honorable, clean and just.

In the realm of art the northmen were by no means inactive. Their vivid and forceful styles and entwined animal ornamentations had been developed to great perfection and originality and these exercised considerable influence in England. They reached their highest attainments in the arts of wood-carving and wood-working, of which, alas, so little has been preserved. The Norwegian wooden churches, for example, and the rich finds in the Oseberg ship, compare favorably with the best of the world's art. Strasser says, "Nordic art is even more fragmentary than is the Greek. But its remnants are glorious and all the more deeply do we deplore its vanished beauty. That which has been preserved is equal to the masterpieces of the great civilized peoples. Would that the public paid half as much attention to the Nordic royal graves as they do to the Egyptian.—Nordic art was great, even though it did not achieve as many forms as that of the south, and its conception was different. But the few still recognizable twigs of its tree surpass every conception in the variety of their ramifications, and make Greek art appear meager and Egyptian cold. On the other hand India, with its pagodas and columns swarming with pictures, shows a certain relationship with it. Therefore this wood-workers' art became also the actual mother of the classic art of the European north—the Romanesque and the Gothic."

LAW AND JUSTICE

So far were they from enslaving their neighbours, that their Danelaw contained many freemen and no slaves, in sharp contrast to Wessex.

GEORGE MACAULAY TREVELYAN.

With them the northmen brought a new concept of personal honor which exercised influence on the English notion of what constitutes a gentleman, and expressed itself in English legislation. It is interesting that the English word 'law', of Scandinavian origin, replaced the earlier Anglish synonym 'doom'.

'The legal instinct'—says Mawer—'was strong in the Scandinavian mind, and English law bears deep marks of its influence. Unfortunately, it is only within the last few years that the question of Danish influence on our social, political and legal systems has been treated at all seriously and much work still remains to be done, but we can already see that the Danes affected English life more deeply than a superficial glance might suggest. Doubtless the Danish invasions struck a heavy blow at learning and literature, a blow from the effects of which not even the heroic activities of an Alfred could save them, but there can be no question that in the improvement of organization and administration, and in the modification of legal procedure the invaders conferred great benefits on the country as a whole."

This is something not discerned by earlier English historians. Conversely, early Danish historians such as Worsaae and Steenstrup realized this much more clearly than later Danish historians appear to have done.

201

The ancient God Tyr seems to have been the god of the law courts, 'Mars thingsus', as the Romans called him. The origins of the law court as an assembly place for the population of the district is lost far, far back in the mists of antiquity. It was the center from which justice and peace radiated, and the embryonic cell of a system of legislation which grew out of the people's own sense of justice and the actual demands of everyday life.

Law and justice developed naturally in Denmark. In forceful and vivid sentences—with alliterative verse to assist the memory—the rules of law were formulated long before they were written down. "With law shall the land be built," runs the Jutish Law, or as Njal puts it, "With law shall the land be built, lawlessness lays it waste."

From the depths of the personality this sense of justice made its way to the surrounding world. Grønbech writes, "Justice has to be felt in man or it does not exist.—As soon as he has settled in a place for a short while or for some length of time, a 'law-thing' shoots up out of the ground, and around it grows a community. Whether his sense of social order finds scope to form a kingdom, or is constrained within narrower bounds, it is a deeply rooted tendency, part and parcel of his character itself."

The northman's sense of justice was more a moral and practical compulsion than a logical construction, and therefore has a warmth lacking in Roman law. It is gravely concerned with the rights of the individual, his kindred or the nation, in contradistinction to Roman law, where the main interests lie in property and possessions.

The instinct for justice found a source of strength in the interacting solicitude of kinship and people. A sense of fellowship stood behind the statutes of the law, and during legal proceedings companions and relatives were present to help support a claim. The English word—'fellow' is the same as the Danish word—'fælle', and the English word 'friend' is the same word as the Danish word 'frænde'. So strong was the bond between kinsmen that Grønbech says, "When the Church brought legislation under its control it brought to light an essential defect in the old jurisprudence: it contained no provisions concerning homicide among kinsmen."

The place of assize (Thing-sted) was generally an exposed hill in the Herred. Herred (hundred) is an ancient word that actually means army-following; army, in this case, may have had a military significance or

202

Silver brooch with the Anglian Beast in the Urnes Style. From a Viking grave in Lindholm Høje. Jutland.

merely denoted a crowd. The Herred probably pre-dates the Migration Period and was in part a judicial area, in part determined by geographical conditions, and partly a center of religious cult, as the place–names suggest. The Herreds correspond to some extent to the English 'hundreds' and 'wapentakes'. The English 'Ridings' were superior Herred-courts, originally called' Thrithings', but came to bear their present name simply because the later Norman-French lords could not pronounce 'th'.

Ancient, undated laws, which must go back to the time of Halfdan, exist in northern England, according to Sir Paul Vinogradoff. They give the impression that a certain superiority complex existed among the conquerors, since the fine paid for homicide–'Wergeld'–was twice as large for a Dane as for an Englishman. It is, however, probable that it was more a practical measure designed to protect the new colonists, who can scarcely have been welcomed everywhere. In the peace treaty between Alfred and Guthrum the fines were equalized, but in such a way

203

that a Danish commoner was considered the equal of an English nobleman.

Even if the northmen came from very different social strata in their native land, equal rights were secured for them in their new homes. Their service in the army had cut across caste lines in mixing them together and had raised them all to the same social and democratic level, and colonization was arranged on military lines. In the Danelaw it was everywhere 'the army' which settled in and divided up the land.

Clear traces of the Danish system of law are encountered in the Danish towns of England. There are 'Things' and 'By-laws' and we find 'Hus-tings' in the large cities such as London, York, Lincoln and Winchester. The highest court in the City of London is still called 'Husting'. In political life the platform for nomination of candidates before 1872 bore the old Danish name of Hus-ting.

The ancient Nordic duel 'Holmgang', the challenge to battle fought on a holm, was regarded as a sort of judgment of the gods. It was introduced into England as a legal means of proof and was not abolished until 1818, when an enterprising person demanded the right to avail himself of the ancient statutory provision that a lawsuit could be decided by duel.

The northmen's love of freedom created a vital difference between the Danelaw and the ancient Anglo-Saxon districts. Two hundred years later, William the Conqueror's survey—the Domesday Book—brought to light this important distinction, the documents showing a free peasant population in Scandinavian England which had no parallel in the south and west. In the latter districts estates were large, serfs and bondsmen numerous, and there were few freemen. In the Danelaw the estates were evenly divided, the peasants free and independent, and the serfs few. Sir Paul Vinogradoff draws attention to the fact that even though the Danish invasions were marked by cruelty and ruthlessness, they nevertheless did not lead to the formation of an oppressed slave-caste in the Danish districts—the slavery which existed was to be found toward the south and west. Maitland's investigations have shown that at the time of the Domesday Book there was not a single serf in the whole of Lincolnshire and Yorkshire, but some tenants and freed-men who had obtained small plots of ground for cultivation. This sense of freedom has been of invaluable importance to the development of democracy in England. It is an expression of the northmen's realistic awareness of the

204

simple fact that the more free people there are who have scope to develop their abilities and initiative, the better people will work, with the result that greater production and exchange will be carried on, and the entire nation's standard of living and strength will be improved.

In Ireland, serfdom was so much a part of the system that the 'cumal', the female slave, appears as a standard article of trade and a unit of reckoning, as Vinogradoff remarks. The slave was outside the Law, and the owner had possession of him as of his live stock. Poul Johs. Jørgensen says, "He was actually and legally subordinated to the unrestricted authority of his lord as though he were a domestic animal."

The northmen had also kept slaves, 'with bent backs and long heels' as it is written in Rigsþula, but in the interests of the common good they mostly liberated them and gave them a certain economic independence. The Nordic peoples never took slaves from among themselves, even though they formerly had carried on a slave-trade.

*

As has already been stated, the foundations for the Jury Courts of later days were laid in the Danelaw, under the influence of the ancient 'næfn' and 12-man courts. Worsaae writes, "It is certain that the earliest definite traces of a jury occur in the Danelaw among the Danes who had settled there." Steenstrup writes, "A decision on legal cases by verdict of a jury, the English institution which has in recent times spread through many countries, did not attain full development until long after the cessation of Danish rule, although its inception was noticeable as early as those times within the era of the founding of the Danelaw. Here 12 men had a corresponding task, and Saxo also relates that Regner Lodbrog, the great Viking king and conqueror, promulgated the law that legal actions were not to be decided through proof brought by either of the parties, but by the judgment of 12 jurors." Trevelyan says that it was the Danes who introduced the custom of appointing a committee among the free men in the Court, and that this very closely resembled the mediaeval juries; even if it was not their actual prototype, it prepared the way for the Frankish jury system of the Normans.

Stenton says that the sworn jury was unknown in the original English law, and that it is first met with in the Scandinavian districts of England. The legal provision that judgment should be valid when 8 out of 12 jurymen concurred, he calls the first assertion in England of the principle that where opinions differ, that of the majority shall be decisive. Pollard attributes such great importance to this principle that he says that an English state could scarcely exist until people had built roads, and it had just as little chance of continuance until they had won that great victory of civilized government by which a minority agrees, for the sake of peace, to submit to the majority.

In innumerable ways the northmen influenced the legal system so thoroughly that, as Stenton remarks, the late Professor Lieberman could fill two columns of a quarto page with an index to the legal peculiarities of the Danelaw, printed in small type and with much abbreviation of words.

The northmen were practical law-makers and forceful jurists. They were not devoid of love of litigation but they had no professional jurists. Noach says, "The rules of court which the Nordic peasants built up are the most precious inheritance that the Nordic race has left behind it in western Europe."

The Nordic sense of justice and freedom could be over-emphasized, lose its flexibility and threaten social unity. In Iceland, says Mawer, one can best observe what the Viking culture was in a position to achieve when left to itself. But the northmen were much better at framing constitutions and enacting laws than in abiding by them, and the condition of Iceland has been vividly, if roughly, summarized as one of "all law and no government."

At the 7th Nordic Historical Congress in Copenhagen, the Icelandic State Archivist Bardi Gudmundsson, on August 10, 1939, gave a lecture on East Scandinavia's part in the settlement of Iceland (not available in print) in which he tried to show that East-Nordic, especially Danish, influence on Iceland's colonization must have been greater than has hitherto been believed. He referred especially to the fact that the legal 'Gode' institution appears to have come from Denmark, whereas the Norwegian 'odel' system of land-tenure does not exist in Iceland. There are also certain differences between Icelandic and Norwegian legislation and national customs, whereas there are many similarities in the folkways of Denmark and Iceland. Burial customs in Iceland resemble the Danish, while the Norwegian cremation burials were not used in Iceland. The Icelanders call their language 'Danish tongue' and Gudmundsson thinks that these examples are best explained by assuming that Danish and Swedish immigrants to South Norway and Trøndelag continued their wanderings to Iceland in the 'landnam' period; and he believes that in addition to the Norwegian share in the settlement of Iceland there was a considerable participation from east Nordic people, especially Danish. If this theory is correct it presupposes that these Danish-Norwegian immigrants in Iceland came mainly from the southern Norwegian districts which were under Danish rule before the Yngling-kings began the unification of Norway.

Ker says, "It is plain on the surface of European history, although often forgotten, that the spirit of the northern nations (commonly called Scandinavians) was needed to quicken all the rest." He continues, "Iceland was a political experiment of another sort, and the meaning of it was to show what the northern genius could do on bare, unbroken ground, picked out and colonized by a few adventurous families from Norway. Here in Iceland, they were to show what they could do when left to themselves. The Icelandic settlement was (and remains in history) a protest against all the ordinary successful commonplaces of the world. They made a commonwealth of their own, which was in contradiction to all the prejudices of the Middle Ages and of all ancient and modern political philosophy; a commonwealth which was not a state, which had no government, no sovereignty. And this republic, or association, without political coherence, likely, one might have thought, to fall into mere disintegration from its want of proper equipment in the struggle for existence, was held together and survived by force of intellect; and proved itself superior to Norway, took the lead of Norway in certain important matters belonging to Norway itself. Their own origin and way of life were a protest against kingdoms, even against all politics, as usually understood."

The Nordic sense of freedom and justice made one of its most praiseworthy and unique contributions in Iceland's outstanding intellectual culture. But, says Mawer, "It was anarchy without a police-constable. The result was that the rich men grew richer, the poor became poorer, the smaller gentry died out and the large estates fell into fewer hands. The great men quarrelled among themselves, intrigued against one another and played into the hands of the Norwegian Kings who were only awaiting their opportunity."

It is said of Njal, the wise Icelandic chieftain, that he had a lot of money tied up in farm mortgages. That is the same procedure reflected in 'Konongsskuggsjá' (The Mirror of Kings) wherein the father gives his son this advice, "If you see that your property begins to increase considerably through your trading journeys, then take two-thirds of it and utilize it to buy up good land, for that type of wealth is most generally looked upon as being secure, whether it be one's own self who enjoys it or one's relatives."

What attracted the newcomers to Iceland was simply the free availability of the soil and the personal independence it brought—exactly as was the case in a later age during the colonization of North America. When both free soil and independence disappeared after the developments which followed, then also the foundation for Iceland's civilization and independence vanished. The wise Njal had endeavored to democratize and transform the law courts of Iceland to an elective popular body, but had not succeeded because of the desire for power of the large landowners. As a consequence, in the Sturlung Period during the 13th century, virtually all land in Iceland was collected in the hands of six families who tried to evict, murder, and burn each other in their houses. The great historian and saga-writer Snorre Sturlason was a millionaire, Iceland's richest man, and the Norwegian King Haakon Haakonsen arranged his murder in 1241.

"The desire for power and covetousness of the individual chieftains," says Valtyr Gudmundsson, "was so limitless that they had no time to think about their country. They considered only their own power and wealth, and therefore fought one another with all their might, so that a general civil war arose in which even brothers and other near relatives fought and slayed one another. These fights were not conducted with honor and decency, as in the saga-period. All means were considered fair. Cunning ambushes, night attacks, and even arson and murder became the order of the day. The cruelty which characterized these quarrels was appalling. They were not content, as in olden days, to kill their enemy in an open and honorable manner, but took the greatest pleasure in mutilating and maltreating him in the most abominable ways. They kept neither their word nor their oath. One day a man would swear peace and loyalty to his opponent, and then on the following day would attack him. Since no single chieftain or family succeeded in obtaining complete superiority, and there was no central authority in the country which could intercede to assume control and establish peace, the way was opened for foreign influences and these came swiftly."

Sir Allan Mawer draws the following conclusions about the Nordic civilization, "Powerful and highly developed as that civilization was in many ways, it only reached its highest and best expression when brought into fruitful contact with other and older civilizations. There it found the corrective for certain inherent weaknesses, more especially for certain tendencies of too strongly individualistic characters leading to political and intellectual anarchy, while at the same time, by its own energy and vigor, it quickened the life of the older civilizations where they were tending to become effete or outworn. The Germanic peoples had done much for the development of European civilization in the time of the wanderings of the nations, but by the end of the 8th century they had lost much of their pristine vigor through contact with the richer and more luxurious civilization of the Roman world. It was reserved for the North Germanic peoples, or the northmen, as we can more fitly describe them, in the 9th and 10th centuries, to give a yet more powerful stimulus to European life, if not to European thought, a stimulus which perhaps found its highest expression in the great creations of the Norman race in the world of politics, the world of commerce, the world of architecture, and the world of letters."

Professor Green says, "No race has ever shown a greater power of absorbing all the nobler characteristics of the peoples with whom they came in contact, or of infusing their own energy into them."

COLONIZATION

It was upon the land and not the person that the service was imposed.

A. F. POLLARD.

After the sword came the plough.

The most remarkable performance of the Danes under the Sons of Lodbrog was the manner in which they planned and carried out the colonization of England. It had a lasting effect on England's life. Sir Winston Churchill says:

"Here I may mention—in speaking of the character of the British people—that that which the British people owes to the ancient Danes we did not regard as a debt at that time, and there was considerable controversy on what was going on.—The Danish sailors from the long ships who fought ashore in England as soldiers brought with them into England a new principle represented by a class, the peasant-yeoman proprietor. The sailors became soldiers, the soldiers became farmers. The whole of the East of England thus had seen a class of cultivators who, except for purposes of common defence, owed allegiance to none; independence and discipline were thus conjoined. Particularly in East Anglia did this sturdy, outstanding stock take root."

Sir Frank Stenton writes, in the introduction to his edition of the Documents of the Danelaw, "It was in the Danelaw that the traditions of the age before the Conquest influenced most deeply the social order of mediaeval England. The men of this region had developed among themselves a form of society which could resist even the shock of foreign invasion. They escaped as a whole the process which, before the end of the eleventh century, had reduced the mass of the southern peasantry under seignorial control. The spirit which preserved their liberties preserved also their terms of law, their land division, and their ancient inheritance of personal nomenclature. The contrast of north and south, fundamental as it is throughout English history, is nowhere revealed more clearly than in the private charters of the twelfth century."

The sources show that the Viking armies divided up the land among themselves, and for a long time the districts continued to be called armies. Villages were given Danish names but the large estates were not, which implies that the leaders themselves took these over while their men colonized the surrounding territory. Aakjær supposes that the thanes and their servants, who are mentioned both in English documents and on Danish runic stones, were a kind of officiating nobility corresponding to knights and squires later on—a sort of gentry who paid rent for their lands. They were probably the people who took over the former estates. In the northwest the place names are mainly Norwegian, indicating a colonization issuing from the Norwegian settlements in Ireland.

Stenton says that the free peasant population in the Scandinavian part of England, for which there is no parallel in the south, is more than just an interesting exception, "Individually, they were men of small estate, possessing only one or two plough oxen and farming on an average some twenty to thirty acres. But they were certainly independent of anything that can be called manorial discipline. The plan of the Domesday survey shows that they were responsible for the taxes due from their land, and they were scattered over the land in a way which shows that

210

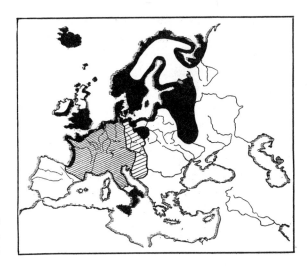

*Europe in the
Viking Period.
(Herbert Jankuhn).*

they cannot have been subject to any heavy agricultural services to their lords. It is easy to underestimate their numbers.–The sokeman, and not his lord, paid the geld charged upon his tenement.–They gave no opportunity for any general extension of seignorial control nor for the development of severer forms of customary labour."

The English Soke (parish), is the Danish 'Sogn', carried over to England. The word 'Sogn' was probably used in pagan times to denote districts sharing the same sanctuary and assembly, Ting (as the use of the word in the Danelaw seems to suggest). Stenton says, "To the very end– and the end of many sokes only came in the eighteenth century–the average tenant on an estate of this kind retained much of his original independence. There is much to suggest that estates like these had already arisen before any king of the English had won effective power in the north, that, in fact, they result from the settlement of the rank and file of the Danish armies around the men who had led them in the invasion."

Concerning these Sokemen, who constituted more than half the population in a widespread area, Stenton says, "He had his own recognized place in the courts of wapentake and shire. He could alienate his land or any portion of it by gift, sale or exchange. He paid his taxes, such as the Danegeld or the sheriff's aid, directly to the officers of the king or the sheriff. Above all, he was usually free from the villein's duty of working two or more days each week on his lord's land. He was therefore free from the compulsion of manorial discipline." He played an important part in local government during the seventeenth and eighteenth centuries. As Pollard says, "It was upon the land and not the person that the service was imposed."

A man could place himself and his land under any overlord he chose. "Such a liberty was the most obvious proof that a man was the master of his own land, and therefore might be expected to answer for the taxation levied upon it." (Stenton).

In the century following William the Conqueror's Domesday Book of 1085, there is only meager information available concerning land tenure conditions in the Danelaw. But, says Stenton, "When at last the darkness lifts, the free peasants of the Danelaw reappear, unbroken by royal exactions or seignorial oppression. They stood to gain more than most people by the great innovation of the age, the opening of the king's court to all free men of every condition."

From a purely materialistic viewpoint they had survived the time that followed the Norman Conquest and also that period in the 10th century during which Alfred's son and grandson had formally recovered suzerainty over the Danelaw. This reconquest showed that ashore, the Viking colonization had not been able to create the political unity which the conquering armies had possessed. But the Danelaw preserved its individuality and character even under the formal suzerainty of Wessex. It remained a Danish, not an English, land. The laws continued to recognize Danish statutes and the liberties of the people; the Danes' loyalty to English kings was reciprocated by the latters' recognition of their self-government and customs. According to Collingwood, East Yorkshire and Lincolnshire were Scandinavian districts 800 years after the Normans, even as they had been 300 years previously.

This land-system, the parcelling-out of land into small holdings with the preservation of only a few large estates, the freedom to dispose of their property, and the duty of paying land taxes, was something typically Danish, a custom which the settlers had brought with them. Stenton says, "That the Danes brought to England their own distinctive forms of agricultural tenement, the ploughland and oxgang, seems certain. Not infrequently, English texts of the eleventh or twelfth centuries supply a direct answer to questions which in Denmark, Norway or Sweden can only be approached by way of inference from materials of the later Middle Ages. In all the Scandinavian countries, the ancient forms of land division are commonly overlaid in medieval records by a new terminology of a highly artificial character based on taxation, rent, or the seed with which a given area is sown."

This interesting English material which may help to throw light on a period in Denmark for which Danish sources are lacking, has still not been fully utilized in respect to land legislation or legal history.

In the northern Danelaw the land was measured by a unit called 'ploughland', corresponding to the old Danish 'Bol' (hide-of-land) valuation. Each plough was divided up into eight 'ox-gangs' (ox-tracks) corresponding to the Danish 'ottinger' (eights). This is a system which reflects the fundamental factor in land economy of that period—the large plough-team of eight oxen. Henrik Larsen says of Danish Bol valuation, "Division into Bol must refer to a time when there was a need for it, and it is likely that it was introduced during the Viking Period, possibly in its later years under Svend Forkbeard and Canute the Great, about 1000 A.D."

It should be observed, however, that it must also have been needed in the early Viking Period when the colonization of England took place, at which time it left clear traces in England. Rigsarkivar Svend Aakjær, the Danish State-Archivist, writes in his treatise on Weights and Measures, "The Bol-division goes back before 1085, and inasmuch as the ancient irregular division of fields, called Forn-division, is still older, the measurement of width they employ must also be earlier than 1000 A.D." It is therefore reasonable to reckon that for centuries before 1000 A.D., Denmark had a system of land-valuation and taxation corresponding to the land division and land-value taxation in the Danelaw.

Stenton says of this system, "Nothing in the routine of common life offers a more massive resistance to change than agriculture. The introduction into a third of England of the system which has been described was a revolution."

The ancient Danish revolving division of village-land (the 'Solskifte') strikingly illustrates, according to Vinogradoff, that no compulsion on the part of people in authority was necessary to create a systematic division of land. It was effected in England, as in Denmark, by free village communities without intervention by a superior landlord.

With the exception of the tax on their land, the northmen did not like to pay taxes. The Norwegian chieftain Asbjørn of Telemark, on

213

being asked for payment of taxes by his king, replied, "We will have nothing to do with taxation, but we have no objection to sending friendly grants to the king."

The Anglo-Saxons, on the other hand, were quite accustomed to taxation. Trevelyan describes how the power and influence of the Church had advanced feudalism and aristocracy, and how the Church taxes and heavy fines had resulted in many peasants being reduced to poverty and serfdom.

Nordenstreng compares the circumstances in Lincolnshire and Yorkshire, where no serfs were to be found, with the conditions in Devonshire, where Domesday Book shows that in the countryside there was not one single free man. He points to the difference between the free Nordic peasants and the population in France and Anglo-Saxon England and says, "One of the reasons for the unfortunate conditions in these countries was that of the soil seldom being cultivated by its owner but by serfs or tenants who had to pay rent to the landlord and who were not allowed to leave without his permission."

Poul Johs. Jørgensen writes, "In the beginning, actual taxes to the king were unknown. The duty to furnish personal rents was certainly considered incompatible with full personal freedom, and land-taxation as irreconcilable with full rights of possession of the soil." But Professor Jørgensen's judgment in regard to land-taxation is unconvincing because he does not include in his premise the conditions in the Danelaw and at Viken in Norway, then part of the old Danish kingdom. He refers to Svend Aggesen's account of the construction of the ramparts of Danevirke, where the king's summons for men from the whole kingdom to work on the ramparts was excused on the score that the king owned all land in the kingdom with rights of possession, as was the case in England. Perhaps the words of Svend Aggesen more clearly reflect the view of his own time—the 12th century—than the 10th century of Gorm and Tyre, but there is good reason to suppose that a similar practical arrangement existed even in the days of King Gudfred, about 800. The actual construction of great engineering works such as the ramparts of Danevirke would have required a well organized contribution of man power. The army arrangements in ancient times appear to have been based on a land-valuation, and the difference between a tax in service and a tax as impost is more formal than real.

In the period following the death of Canute the Great, it is related

The first English halfpenny.
Coined by Halfdan in London.

of King Harold Godwinson's brother Toste Godwinson, that he, as earl of Northumberland, wished to set aside the laws of Canute and impose taxes on the Danes in Northumberland. The population unanimously opposed this and replied, "We are born free and brought up as free men. We will not tolerate a domineering and haughty chieftain, having learned from our fathers to live as free men or die."

*

The northmen were great founders of cities. They combined military and commercial-political considerations in their fortified towns, which were open insofar as commerce was concerned. Each of the Five Boroughs in the Danelaw: Lincoln, Nottingham, Derby, Leicester and Stamford, those early-founded Danish cities in England, was the center of colonization by an army group, and they all became flourishing commercial cities with the possible exception of Stamford. The Five Boroughs had a common general assembly which controlled the firmly constructed organization which had no doubt originally been a meeting between representatives of the armies that had settled down around the castles. This organization strengthened the Scandinavian influence far into the future.

There were no cities in Ireland before the Vikings arrived there and shipping had been of no consequence. Dublin, the capital, together with the ports of Cork, Limerick, Wicklow and Waterford, was founded by them. London was rebuilt by King Alfred on Danish lines. Trevelyan writes, "Learning had indeed received a terrible blow in the sack of the Northumbrian and Mercian monasteries, but at least Alfred had set recovery afoot, and the new growth of city life due to the Danes would in the end do more for the higher civilization than monasticism at its best."

York was the center of Danish power in England, and in Canute's time was a city of about 30,000 inhabitants. It was filled with merchants from all parts, especially Danes, who brought in goods and wealth.

Later, during the Danish rule, city life made great progress owing to the vast territories which Canute's policy had opened up for England, and this was especially noticeable in London.

*

Just as in many other spheres, Danish influence can be felt in the system of currency. Arbman writes that the quality of Viking coins was remarkably high and Nordic mint masters were evidently appreciated even by the English. Stenton says, "The modern inquirer is continually baffled by the perverse ingenuity of pre-Conquest methods of reckoning, which could maintain a shilling of four pence north of the Thames beside a shilling of five pence to the south. With increasing clearness, as time goes on, a new Scandinavian system can be discerned cutting across the complexities of Anglo-Saxon reckoning and leaving traces which can still be recognized today. The persistence of these Scandinavian innovations in law and agriculture, in monetary computation and personal nomenclature, is of more than antiquarian interest. It affects the whole interpretation of the last, critical phase of Early English history."

Sir Winston Churchill concludes, "The Danish settlement differed entirely from the Saxon settlement four hundred years earlier. There was no idea of exterminating the older population. The gulf between the Danes and Saxons in no way resembled that which had divided—and still divided, in those days—the Saxons from the British. Human and national relations were established. The blood-stream of these vigourous individualist invaders, proud and successful men of the sword, mingled henceforward in our island race; a vivifying, noble, lasting and resurgent quality was added to the breed, and as modern steel is hardened by the alloy of special metals in comparatively small quantities, this strong strain of individualism, based upon landownership, was afterwards to play a persistent part not only in the blood, but in the politics of England. Centuries did not destroy their original firmness of character in this part of the Danish settlement, nor their deep attachment to the soil. All through English history this strain continued to play its part, and to this day the peculiar esteem in which law and freedom are held by the English-speaking peoples in every quarter of the globe, may be shrewdly and justly referred to a Viking birth."

Hodgkin sums up the importance of the colonization thus, "In particular, the migration of the Danes went on silently and without record, transplanting to the east of England some of those characteristics which we saw existing among the Scandinavians at the opening of the Viking period—their independence, their energy, their fierceness, their worldly wisdom."

THE NORMANS

"Trade and commerce were fostered here as everywhere by the Vikings. It was the Normans who first taught the French to become a power at sea, many French naval terms are of Norman origin and from the Norman province have come some of France's greatest sea-captains."

SIR ALLEN MAWER.

Normandy, the second Danelaw, was founded by Rollo and his Vikings in 911. A century and a half later the Normans made themselves masters not only of the first Danelaw but the whole of England. It was the Danes from Rouen, Caen and Bayeux, with their traces of Franco-Roman blood and culture, who harvested the fruits of what had been planted and pruned by the Danes in England.

As a continuation of the Viking raids—which since the days of Hugleik and Gudfred had brought the Danes to Friesland and northern France and had finally created the great Viking armies in the west—Rollo and his men one fine day came sailing up the Seine, after a series of hostilities which had lasted for many years.

The chieftain Haastein, who had entered the service of the Franks, shouted across the water to the ships, "Who are you, where do you come from, and what do you want?"

They replied, "We are Danes. We come from Denmark, and we are going to conquer France!"

A clear answer. No false, ingratiating phrases or slippery non-aggression pacts. One at least knew where one stood with them.

Haastein then asked, "What is the name of your lord?" They replied, "We have none. We are all equal!"

A classic answer. It reflects the northmen's whole attitude to king and chief—the first among equals.

However, it was admittedly not the whole of France that was conquered—a part sufficed. Neustria, later Normandy, which Charles III had to cede to Rollo, was one of France's loveliest provinces. Formally, Rollo

217

received it only in fief, but he was, in point of fact, independent. The peace which Rollo and Charles the Simple concluded at St. Clair-sur-Epte in 911 was reminiscent of Alfred's and Guthrum's peace treaty a score of years before. The settlement also resembled that system of semi-independent fiefs which Danish Viking-kings had had on Walcheren, in Rüstringen and in Friesland. Rollo was baptized just as Guthrum had been, and also like him obtained the princess and half the kingdom.

In addition to its nature, Normandy was of great commercial-political and strategic importance. Its location was excellent, and the short distance across the channel to England partly explains why it was easier for the Normans to conquer and maintain mastery over England than it was for the Danes, on the other side of the North Sea.

•

The islands of Normandy, which lie off the Cotentin Peninsula but belong to England, were probably starting-points and auxiliary posts for the Danes, inasmuch as they are the only islands along the French coast which in their names contain the Nordic suffix -ey: Jersey, Guernsey, Chaussey and Alderney. But within Normandy itself one comes across Danish place-names by the hundred, and the type of people north of Paris differs from that of the south. They are tall, strong and independent, and in many districts on the Cotentin Peninsula one meets the blond, blue-eyed type. The styles of buildings in Normandy with their brick-nogging, thatched roofs, and mud walls, are like the Danish, as are also the beer and porridge which the people still appreciate to the undisguised amazement of other Frenchmen. Love of freedom and justice is pronounced—so pronounced that the Normans are accused of being opinionated. The old Nordic sense of freedom was a living thing throughout the Middle Ages in the towns of Normandy, which were also prominent centers of republican spirit and movements.

A very large proportion of the Protestants driven out of France in the time of Louis XIV, during his cruel religious persecutions, were of the blond type. The 200,000 Protestants who migrated to Brandenburg came mainly from Normandy, and were a considerable factor in Prussia's rise to a powerful state. Mac Dougall says that their exodus is one of the greatest losses that France has ever suffered. The numerous protestants who nonetheless fled to England were received there with hospitality. They took with them to England their skill, craftsmanship and manufacturing secrets. In England they laid the foundation for a great part of that country's future industry.

*

When Rollo acquired control of Normandy the country was almost devastated–plundered as it had been by the Vikings. His task was to rebuild it, and his first undertaking was to rope-measure the land and partition it out among his companions. Surveying by rope was a peculiarly Danish custom. The land distribution which Rollo carried out in Normandy was, however, somewhat different from the land policy of the Sons of Lodbrog in the Danelaw some decades previously, as the land seems to have been apportioned into larger estates; Normandy therefore quickly became feudalized, and a feudal nobility was established. Yet the estates were not as large as in the rest of France. The great baronies which had weakened the power of the French kings and helped disorganize the country from within were not permitted by the Norman dukes, nor did the large earldoms exist here. This made possible the effective power of the Norman dukes and was a feature peculiar to Normandy. The Norman State rapidly became the best organized one on the Continent. It differed from the French, whose large baronies were to some extent set up as a defence against the Vikings, but were founded on ancient customs in western France, which was preponderantly Celtic and aristocratic. The baronies proved, however, to be of more advantage to the barons than to France, and were used for internal and private petty quarrels.

Rollo rapidly established public security in the country. What we know of his laws shows considerable resemblance to those which King Frode, according to Saxo, laid down in Norway and Denmark; indeed, the actual account of the peace of Frode and the golden ring is repeated in the account of Rollo. Rights of property and public security in the fields were maintained so thoroughly that the law prohibited people from taking their ploughs home at night or locking up their treasures. In return, Rollo pledged himself to replace anything stolen. This respect for public security and confidence in mutual integrity are characteristic of Denmark to this day, where full milk-churns stand on the highway and doors are often left unlocked.

'A word is a word and a man is a man'–this old Danish proverb reflects something that is socially very precious, namely the belief that people improve by being shown confidence. Certainly commercial life functions more easily in a climate of mutual trust than when constant suspicion and uncertainty poison relations. It has always been customary in Normandy to conclude a business transaction with a handshake—just as is done at Hjallerup market in Denmark today.

Steenstrup says, "It was soon said of the Norman Kingdom, as of so many other Viking colonies, that here ruled security and respect for law and justice. Far down the ages the Normans in France retained the sole right of having their cases decided in Normandy."

"These Normans," he continues, "had manifestly a special ability to organize society and construct solid and comprehensive codes of law. This faculty, which appeared wherever they went, could have easily degenerated into love of litigation and cavilling, but far more often it was the saving and progressive element when decadence threatened. Thus it succeeded in manifesting itself when, at the commencement of the 11th century, the Normans occupied the provinces of southern Italy and half a century later, when they made themselves masters of England. Without this respect for the laws that existed in Normandy and diligence in carrying them out, the country would never have been able to thrive economically, and it was in economic matters that the Danes had put forth their greatest exertions. As a result, trade and shipping soon flourished, the country was cultivated and its splendid natural resources utilized. Here the value of the work of free men was understood and slavery died out in Normandy several generations earlier than in the rest of France. This country soon became one of France's most flourishing provinces, and to its progress in material matters was linked a living spiritual movement, a sense of poetry and art, and a deeply religious life, but above all a strong inclination for work and a continual urge for fresh undertakings." In Normandy slavery had already disappeared by the year 1100, while it remained, for example, in Champagne and Burgundy until about 1300.

Arbman writes that conditions in the Frankish Kingdom proper were far from satisfactory. The wars and quarrels of the aristocracy were fully as destructive to the country as were the devastations of the Vikings. The chief concern of the magnates was the continuation of the feudal system which gave them the opportunity to carry out a policy profitable to them—the fleecing of the population. This policy was carried so far that even when the peasants within restricted areas joined together to repel the Vikings, they were forcibly dispersed by the lords. Under such conditions it was inevitable that a certain amount of contact would take place between the population and the Vikings.

The Norman control of finance was the best in all Europe. Workers and craftsmen flocked there in great numbers, since public security, and therefore price conditions, were better than elsewhere. This, together with the Norman's increasingly large families, in 100 years' time produced a population which found an outlet in fresh conquests—the expeditions to Sicily, southern Italy and later England.

Sir Allan Mawer says, "Trade and commerce were fostered here as everywhere by the Vikings. It was the Norman who first taught the French to become a power at sea, many naval terms are of Norman origin and from the Norman province have come some of France's greatest sea captains."

"One of the northmen's greatest merits is that they gave France a fleet," says Depping.

Architecture flourished in Normandy and created a special Norman style. Their hexagonal cross-vaulting is one of the germ-cells of Gothic. The writing of history thrived at a period when elsewhere in France there was no interest in it, while the Norman Trouvéres vied with the lyric Troubadours from Provence. "Norman literature, chivalry, and architecture became the envy of Europe."

The Norman Abbey at Bec was one of the most celebrated Christian schools of learning during the Middle Ages. Here the philosophy and scholastic theology of those days flourished, especially under the Langobards—Lanfranc and Anselm—both of whom became Archbishops of Canterbury under William the Conqueror. Here the most trenchant religious theories were evolved and elaborated with logic and elegance.

"The Roman civilization in France did not succeed in curbing the vigor and enterprise of the Normans. The province which their Viking ancestors had carved out of France as another 'Danelaw' became the citadel whence the language, arms and manners of French feudalism sallied forth to the conquest of the world, more particularly of Naples, Sicily and the British Isles." (Trevelyan).

In Italy and Sicily—which had been battlefields for Greeks, Romans, Carthaginians, Byzantines, Vandals and Arabs—the Normans created a state under Robert Guiscard, Godfred, and Roger, the sons of Tancred. By the middle of the 11th century, Roger's son had united the Kingdom of the Two Sicilies which endured until as late as 1860. The Norman state in Italy became an example of tolerance and equality without parallel in those days. Art and literature thrived at the Courts of Palermo and Monreale, and here Italian poetry found its first expression.

*

Norwegian sagas relate that Ragnvald Møre-Jarl had a son called Ganger-Rolf who was so large and powerful that no horse could carry him. On one occasion, despite Harald Fairhair's injunction, he raided Viken and was consequently outlawed in Norway. He emigrated, and later went via England to Valland, where he founded the Duchy which is called Normandy.

Around 1130, a private person in England added a note to a collection of Edward the Confessor's laws. There it is stated that William the Conqueror preferred the laws in the Danelaw, not because they were better than those of the Britons, Angles and Picts but, as he said, because his family and almost all the barons in Normandy were descended from Norway. William the Conqueror was Rollo's great-great-great-grandson, and the word 'Norwenses' in this source is a designation common to both Danish and Norwegian, with the meaning northmen or Vikings. A similar interpretation may be given to the theory that the Normans came originally from an island called Nora—the source of this information being the Norman Abbey at Monte Cassino, Italy.

To this can be added the fact that there is no tradition in Denmark that the conquerors of Normandy were Danish, except for an utterance by the Danish chieftain Esbern Snare, some remarks in historical annals from the 12th century, and also in the Chronicon Erici from the 14th century, wherein Rollo is called a Danish Duke. Saxo does not mention Rollo. This is a strange state of affairs, but not more remarkable than that there is no tradition in Sweden concerning the conquest and foundation of the Russian Kingdom by the Swedes, though that is a matter about which no one today has any doubts. It seems that the dead leaves of tradition settle themselves more easily to leeward than to windward of events.

On the basis of these facts it is natural that many Norwegian historians—with Alexander Bugge at their head—consider Rollo to be of Norwegian descent. This would be justified if other sources did not exist. It should be noted that the Icelandic Sagas were committed to writing very late—two or three centuries after the foundation of Normandy. Theirs is not merely a late tradition but also a poor one because it makes no mention of the conquest of Normandy in 911 other than that it occurred, and that the man was called Ganger-Rolf. The names of Ganger-Rolf's Norwegian relatives are not known in Normandy, nor was the so-called daughter of Ganger-Rolf, Kathleen, born in Scotland. The relatives who are known of in Normandy are not mentioned in the Sagas, which make no reference whatsoever to Norwegian emigrants to Normandy, though a number of expeditions to many other countries are recorded. In France itself, the ducal family's descent from a Norwegian family is not mentioned until a thousand years later—in the 19th century.

Everything considered, the most important sources for Rollo's descent must then be those which are most nearly contemporary, those that originate from Normandy itself, and those which come from the nearest relatives. Dudo, the Canon of St. Quentin, who was born about 960, wrote the history of the Norman dukes at the direct invitation of Rollo's own grandson, Duke Richard I, while the latter's brother, Count Raoul d'Ivri, and Richard's son, Richard II, were also his authorities. Gunnor, Richard I's widow, who was of Danish birth, gave him details, and the Duke's men were also bearers of a living tradition. Although Dudo was a poetical, prolix writer who, like Saxo, never gave tiresome dates, and

English men and Norman horses crashing down in wild confusion in the battle at Hastings on October 14, 1066. The Bayeux Tapestry.

while his writings are a romantic and apologetic glorification of the dukes, they remain, nonetheless, a source which, compared with the poetical, legendary material of the Icelandic Sagas, must be assigned primary importance. It is difficult to imagine that in Normandy such a large and well-informed circle would have accepted entirely erroneous information.

To completely eliminate the oldest and closest source, as Prentout and Douglas do simply because Dudo is often unreliable, and to rely solely on the unreliable late Icelandic Sagas, is methodologically incorrect.

"Rollo, as well as his followers, came originally from Denmark," says Steenstrup. "This is a well-established tradition which, for 150 to 200 years after the conquest, was never disputed. It was recounted by Rollo's grandson and by other members of the family. All the dukes looked on Denmark as their native land, and on several occasions sought the support of Danish kings and warriors."

Dudo has reported the exchange of words between Haastein and Rollo's men on the Seine. By their abruptness they give the impression of a Nordic origin, and do not in the least resemble Dudo's own Gallic verbosity. The words 'We are all equal' make a genuine impression because they are not flattering to Rollo.

The words, 'We are Danes, and we come from Denmark' are clear and precise.

*

In 942 William Longsword, the son of Rollo, held a meeting at Visé with King Louis and King Otto. Dudo relates that during the meeting Otto's Saxon followers stood around muttering sinister remarks about Duke William, and because of his knowledge of the Danish language he understood them and took offence. Saxon and Danish were in those days still closely related languages.

During the meeting, the Saxon Duke Herman Billung addressed himself to William in Danish, whereupon the latter exclaimed, "Who taught you Danish?" And Herman replied, "Your pugnacious kinsmen instructed me in Danish against my will. They conquered the castles of my duchy and, when I was taken prisoner and carried off to their country I learned the language against my will."

This account must also reflect what was then a living tradition, probably reported by the Duke's bodyguard who were present at the meeting. That Herman refers to the Danes as the Duke's 'pugnacious kinsmen' is of great significance. We know that at about that date the Danish king, Harald Bluetooth, was fighting in Holstein, and other data also suggest a relationship between Rollo and the Danish Royal House, one example being that King Harald's father was called Gorm, as was Rollo's brother. By a strange coincidence, the Norman Kings in England bore the same three lions on their coat-of-arms as do the Danish Kings. This crest is known in England from the time of Richard the Lionhearted, and in Denmark from the time of Knud VI.

Later in the year 942, at the instigation of the Emperor, William Longsword was murdered by the Franks at a meeting on an island in the Somme. Dudo relates that the chieftains in Rouen forthwith sent appeals for help to the Nordic lands and dispatched trusted men to Denmark to beg King Harald to come to the aid of his kinsman, young Duke Richard. King Harald assembled a military force and sailed to Normandy with his fleet, putting in at the mouth of the Dive near Caen, and setting up headquarters in Cherbourg. This took place in 945, exactly a thousand years before another invasion of Normandy.

Saxo does not refer to any expedition to Normandy led by Harald Bluetooth, but he mentions him in connection with King Athelstan in England, while Harald Bluetooth's brother, Knud Dana Ast, is noted in another source as being at the Court of Flanders where he is referred to as Knud, "the Danish King's brother."

This Harald is not referred to by Floduard as King, but as Chief, in Bayeux. Doubts have therefore arisen as to the probability of this Harald's being the Danish Harald Bluetooth. At that time the name Harald was used exclusively in the Nordic royal families and never in commoner families or those of petty chieftains. Harald Bluetooth is the only one of the Nordic princes of that name and date who can be considered, inasmuch as King Harald Graafeld was then still a child, and Harald Grenske had not yet been born. Guld-Harald and Strut-Harald were only petty kings or large landowners with the title of king and could hardly have given effective support to the Norman Duke against the Emperor of the Franks. Wace and William of Jumiéges expressly mention Harald as being the father of Svend, which strongly indicates that the reference is to Harald Bluetooth, Svend Forkbeard's father. The Danish King Svend Estridsen, in telling Adam of Bremen about his great-grandfather King Harald, said, "It is certain that Harald Bluetooth gave the Holsteiners and Frisians laws and courts which, because of his reputation, they still zealously preserve."

A score of years after King Harald's presumed intervention in Normandy, when Richard I (942-996) was fighting Thibaut of Chartres, the former sent requests for help to King Harald of Denmark who replied by dispatching troops to him in Normandy. This might suggest that there had been precedents for such action. When to this is added that Harald Bluetooth was at war with the Kingdom of the East Franks in 974, it may be said that Harald's activity and interests in the west are well certified, and that there is a strong probability that it was indeed Harald Bluetooth of Denmark who came to Normandy and arranged matters for the young Duke Richard. This fits in logically with Denmark's westward policy. As late as 1003 Harald's son, Svend Forkbeard, travelled to Normandy and concluded an alliance with Richard II. Mawer remarks that the Normans still looked to Denmark as their homeland up to the 10th century.

William Jumiéges, who wrote in the time of William the Conqueror, was himself of Norwegian descent, and yet he, like Dudo and other Norman sources states that Rollo came from 'Danamarcha'. Jumiéges further adds, as do Wace and Benoit, various details to the account not to be found in Dudo, and these show that in addition to Dudo they must have used an independent source. It also proves that the theory expounded by adherents of the Ganger-Rolf hypothesis cannot be correct. This theory is that the story of Rollo's Danish birth was invented in Normandy for political reasons because in those times it was more desirable to be descended from Denmark than Norway, due to the glory which the Empire of Canute the Great had reflected on the name of Denmark. Such a widespread, unanimous participation in the falsification would not have been possible. In fact no motive can be cited as to why the dukes and Dudo together should concoct an entire book as a circumstantial fraud in order to explain away a Norwegian descent. The doubtful political advantage this would entail was disproportionate to the risks they ran if it were discovered, and this it undoubtedly would have been in a circle and country aware of the facts. And finally, Norwegians are usually and justifiably very proud of their country. The tradition existing in the Ducal family and the Norman circles concerning their heritage is of great importance and therefore this evidence is of great weight.

226

Dudo states that Rollo was born of the proud blood of dukes and kings, and that his father was a mighty man in Denmark whose sons Rollo (Hrolf) and Gurim (Gorm) inherited his lands after him. As the King of Denmark at that time wanted to evict a portion of the youth of the country owing to overpopulation, many sought refuge with Rollo and Gurim. The King marched against them with an army and killed Gurim, while Rollo fled to Skaane. From there he sailed to England to King Athelstan, by whom is meant the Danish King Guthrum (Gorm) in East Anglia who, at his baptism, had been christened Athelstan. He supported Rollo and it is not unlikely that kinship existed between them. Later, Rollo sailed to Walcheren and fought for many years in the great army in Friesland and northern France until he subdued Normandy in 911. That Rollo was at the head of this undertaking also supports the theory that he was a man of noble birth.

Benoit de St. More states that Rollo was born in a town in his native country called 'Fasge'. This is presumably Fakse in Stevns in eastern Zealand, which agrees very well with Dudo's account that Rollo fled to Skaane, just on the other side of the Sound.

Dudo's statements about Rollo's Danish past have a certain interest, albeit he does not specifically mention the names of Rollo's father or of the King of Denmark (Richer of Rheims calls Rollo "Filius Catilli", Ketils son), for Dudo's writings are otherwise one continuous eulogy of the ducal family. According to the code of that period, it was dishonorable to loose in battle or be hunted out of one's country—to have fled from it all without even making an attempt to wreak revenge or obtain compensation on behalf of a murdered brother or forfeited lands. Professor A. Stille of Lund has asserted therefore, that when in a panegyric one comes across an account which is unfavorable to the hero, it must be regarded as authentic and not fabricated. That Rollo's grandsons should not know where their grandfather came from would, according to Walberg, be just as extraordinary as if King Oscar II of Sweden were uninformed as to whether his grandfather Bernadotte came from Switzerland or southern France.

The very names Rollo and Gurim—Hrolf and Gorm— sound Danish and confirm Duke Herman's reference to the Danish royal family as Duke William's kinfolk. The concatenation of evidence supporting the theory of Rollo's Danish birth is so strong that the late Icelandic saga's data implying that he was of Norwegian origin must be considered a misunderstanding. This arose partly because of the two Rolfs' identical names, and partly because in French usage the word 'Norman' was a common designation for all Nordic peoples, whether Norwegians or Danes.

*

The majority of historians agree that the bulk of the colonists in Normandy was Danish. But inasmuch as Normandy was located in the middle zone between the Danish sphere of interest in Friesland and that of the Norwegians in western France, it is probable that the Danish Viking army which operated in northern Germany, Friesland and northern France, received reinforcements from the Norwegian Vikings. Members of the fleet which attacked Nantes in 843 called themselves West-faldingi–people from Vestfold, in Norway. But as Vestfold belonged to the Danish kingdom in the time of Gudfred and Harald Klak it is probable that it was also under Danish rule during King Haarik's reign in 843.

The place–names in Normandy speak a very clear language. Those bearing the suffix 'ville' are a peculiarity of this province and there are hundreds of them. The termination itself is French, but it corresponds to the Danish place-names which end in 'by' (town). The personal names which generally constitute the first syllables are emphatically Nordic ones such as Bram, Grim, Hugleik, Haarik, Harald, Helge, Kraki, Hrolf, Hroar, Skjold, Saxe, Regner, Ivar, Krok, Toke and Ulf. Many of the Norman place–names have obvious parallels in Denmark or in the Danelaw.

The towns with the termination 'tot', the Danish 'tofte' (field), are found in France only in the province of Normandy, and almost all these village names have parallels in Denmark, for example, Apletot-Æbeltoft, Beltot-Beltofte, Epretot-Espertoft, while they have no parallels in Norway and Sweden. The same is the case with the towns ending in 'bec', the Danish 'bæk' (brook). There are hundred of these: Carbec-Karrebæk, Houlbec-Holbæk, etc. The large Norman port of le Havre, which means: haven (havn) and Dieppe, which denotes: 'dyp' (deep) are also Danish place names.

Many cognomens which form the initial syllables of place names are also found on Danish runic stones, whereas characteristically Norwegian masculine names are rare, a specific example being the widespread and popular Norwegian name Olav, which occurs nowhere in Normandy.

228

The place-name suffixes which are pronouncedly Norwegian and occur in the Norwegian colonization areas to the west, for example, -seter, -sta, -bolst, -gja, -vagr, do not exist in Normandy. Investigations by the Faeroese place-name expert. Dr. Jakob Jakobsen, show that Norman place-names have an unmistakably Danish slant, and the Swedish romanist Walberg says, "As far as I know there is scarcely a single place-name in Normandy which in form or meaning betrays a Norwegian origin."

Worsaae drew up a list of place-names in Normandy in France, the Danelaw in England, and ancient Denmark. Here is an extract from it which speaks for itself:

Normandy	The Danelaw	Denmark
Carquebu	Kirkeby	Kirkeby
Tournebu	Thornby	Tornby
Tourp	Thorpe	Torp
Thuit	Thwaite	Tvede
Longetuit	Longthwaite	Langtved
Braquetuit	Brackenthwaite	Bregentved
Languetot	Langtoft	Langtoft
Bec	Beck	Bæk
Houlbeck	Holebek	Holbæk
Le Houlme	Holme	Holm
Auppegart	Applegart	Abildgaard
Londe. Lon	Lont. Lund	Lund
Nez	Ness	Næs

Half a century before Dudo, Widukind the Westphalian called the city of Rouen: 'Urbs Danorum' and in Normandy itself, where the word Normans means northmen, and not Norwegians, there are no less than fifty place names which contain the name Dane in the form of Danne or Denne, as for example, Danneval, Danneville, le Danois, etc.

The same is true of patronymics, for in Caen and Rouen such names as Dan, Ledan, Danne, Ledanois, etc., frequently occur. The language of the place name is important evidence of the Normans' Nordic homeland: Denmark.

As late as the 13th century Denmark enjoyed commercial privileges and lower customs duties in the harbors of Normandy—an interesting piece of evidence. It may also be mentioned that in 1270 the Danish

Archbishop Jacob Erlandsøn presented an altar to Rouen Cathedral, where Rollo is interred.

When all these indications are assembled, plus the fact that Friesland and northern France had long been Danish spheres of interest in political, commercial-political and geo-political matters, the probability is so strong that Rollo and his men were Danish that only a very slight possibility remains that Norwegian Saga-tradition may be correct. Otto Scheel says, "The deeds and renown of the Norwegians are so great and resplendent that they can well afford to waive any claim that Rollo was one of them, if proof that he is the same person as Ganger-Rolf is uncertain."

*

The Normans came to exercise a very strong influence in France, Italy and England, and at the same time themselves absorbed the best of the culture of those countries. Trevelyan says, "The Norman aristocracy, Scandinavian by origin, retained all the Viking energy in colonization and in war, but had become converts to Latin culture. For that or other reasons the Normans were distinguished by a quality which the Scandinavians at home and in England lacked, the instinct for political unity and administrative consolidation. That instinct was the most valuable of the Conqueror's many gifts to England."

John Richard Green maintains, "The conquests of Ivar and Guthrum and Halfdene in the days of Ælfred were in their turn but the prelude to the bowing of all England to a foreign rule under Swein and Cnut. But in the end the fruit of the long attack slipped from Danish hands. The harvest was reaped, but it was reaped by northmen who had ceased even in tongue to be northmen at all. Not the Danes of Denmark, but the Danes of Rouen, of Caen, of Bayeux, became lords of the realm of Ælfred and Eadgar." The greater part of the English aristocracy is descended from these Norman Danes.

The decisive influence wielded by William the Conqueror and his barons on the history of England and ultimately on that of the world, will not be examined here. Succinctly stated, if one adds up all that England received from the ancient Danish lands through the Angles, Jutes, Vikings, and lastly and indirectly through the Normans, it is by no means insignificant. Grundtvig said a hundred years ago, "Were I not a Dane I would wish to be an Englishman."

Normandy was the second Danelaw. In 1066 William the Conqueror's Norman army conquered all England, even as the Danes had conquered it before them. They can be seen as in a film-strip on the 75-yard-long Bayeux Tapestry, preparing for invasion, crossing the Channel, and carrying out the Conquest. The way was prepared and everything arranged beforehand. "William accepted the crown in the spirit of Cnut," says Green.

"William's was the third and decisive Danish conquest of a house divided against itself," says Pollard "for his Normans were northmen with a French polish, and they conquered a country in which the soundest elements were already Danish. The stoutest resistance, not only military but in the constitutional and social sense, to the Norman conquest was offered not by Wessex, but by the Danelaw, where personal freedom had outlived its hey-day elsewhere; and the reflection that, had the English re-conquest of the Danelaw been more complete, so too would have been the Norman conquest of England, may modify the view that everything great and good in England is Anglo-Saxon in origin."

In the 900 years which have since passed, England has not been subjected to conquest. She has become the hammer instead of the anvil.

KING GORM

The story of Denmark's development into the formidable king-dom ruled by Svein begins in the days of his grandfather, Gorm.
                                          SIR THOMAS KENDRICK.

When standing between the venerable royal barrows at Jelling in Jutland, the musty smell of grey remoteness which strikes one is a compound of feelings aroused by the solemnity and age of the barrows and the runic inscriptions on the two scarred stones which bear the names Gorm, Tyre and Harald. They mention the name of Denmark for the first time in Denmark itself. Together they form one of the mightiest monuments of antiquity in northern Europe. Powerful rulers of great achievements had erected these tombs.

After all the continuous migrations westward in the 9th century, and following upon the great defeat which King Arnulf inflicted on the Danes by the River Dyle one wet November day in 891 when King Sigfred and King Gudfred, together with thousands of their men, fell

231

at Louvain, Denmark must have been weakened internally and lost much of its power abroad. It was probably in this period, around 900, that southern Denmark–between Hedeby in Slesvig, and across the southern islands Langeland, Laaland, and Falster, to Blekinge in the east–perhaps came under Swedish chieftains' rule. Ramskou questions this. In the north, Danish suzerainty in the Norwegian Vestfold ebbed, while at the turn of the century, Harald Fairhair united the West and East Norwegian Kingdoms after the Battle in Hafrsfjord.

It is possible that a Swedish dynasty for one generation ruled in Hedeby and controlled the transit-route between the Baltic and the North Sea, as well as the route through the Baltic to Sweden and Russia. Behind this there was further Swedish expansion in Russia, where a network of trading stations along the mighty rivers had put Swedish commerce in active contact with Arabs, Persians and Greeks. When the Arabs had closed the Mediterranean, the trade routes connecting the Caspian and the Black Sea with the Baltic became more important. In Uppland and on the islands in the Baltic–Gotland, Øland and Bornholm –considerable finds of Arabic silver coins testify to these distant connections. The Byzantine golden coins are not so numerous due to the strict Byzantine currency restrictions. Necklaces made of snail-shells from India and a purse made of lizard skin from Baluchistan have been found, as well as remnants of Chinese silk. In the estuary of the river Dnieper is preserved a runic stone in memory of a man from Gotland. On Gotland is preserved a runic stone in memory of a man who perished in the river Dnieper. During an investigation of a Viking-grave on Helgö near Stockholm in 1955 there appeared a bronze figurine of a Buddha seated on a lotus flower in the mudra called Mara vijaya. It is presumably from Northern India from the sixth century A.D. The writings of Arabic merchants and geographers, especially Ibn Rustah and Ib Fadlan, provide scraps of information about these Swedes. In Russian as well as in Byzantine and Persian manuscripts they are called Rus, a Finnish borrowed word originally deriving from the name of the coastal province of Roslagen in Uppland, Sweden.

Most scholars agree that it was the Swedes who gave their name to Russia. They also agree that the mighty Russian Empire was first founded by the Swedes. Not all of them agree that the Swedes ought to have done so.

Important Russian towns such as Novgorod, Rostov, and Kiev were

King Gorm's runic stone. Jelling. Jutland. About 935.
"Gorm the King made this monument to Tyre, his wife,
the adornment of Denmark."

233

founded by Swedish Vikings as trading colonies, their export of furs and slaves being counterbalanced by the import of cloth and spices as well as silver, when export exceeded import. From the days of the Bronze Age, northmen have taken a special delight in costly glittering metals which—as far as Denmark is concerned—they did not possess in their own countries.

Westward the Danes appear to have imported more from Friesland and Franconia than they exported, and through transit eastward, a part of the silver and gold of the north travelled westward. This explains the wealth of metal in the Baltic islands at that time and the Swedish interest in the trade of Hedeby. When later on Swedish trade southward through Russia ceased, partly due to the lack of the Arabs' purchasing power and partly because of the reawakening in Mediterranean trade, commerce in the Baltic by preference frequented the Novgorod-Øland-Hedeby route south of Uppland, and the wealthy provinces of Upper Sweden again sank into relative obscurity, while Denmark once more became the leading country in the north.

*

About 1075, Master Adam of Bremen relates that the Danish King Svend Estridsen told him that Olof, who came from Sweden, usurped the Kingdom of Denmark by force of arms after he had killed King Helge, and that Olof was succeeded by his sons Chnob (Gnupa) and Gurd. We know that in 934 King Gnupa was vanquished at Hedeby by the German King Henry the Fowler, and Gnupa's name can be found on the two runic stones which his Danish Queen Asfrid, daughter of Odinkar, erected at Hedeby in memory of King Sigtryg, her son by Gnupa. It was believed in Italy that this defeat had been inflicted on the Danes, and therefore Liudprand lauded it as the most celebrated deed performed by King Henry. A ship burial has been discovered in Hedeby which Knorr thinks may be that of one of the Swedish inhabitants, while Kossinna surmises that it might be the grave of King Gnupa himself.

Everything suggests that it was this important frontier-land of Slesvig, with its great commercial possibilities, which tempted the Swedes and King Henry. As Wessén says, "South Jutland was the key to the economic control of the whole of the Baltic area." But the Swedes can hardly have ruled over more than the important frontier-land, with adjacent

234

districts in Slesvig and Holstein. And so the rest of the Danish kingdom, in a tattered condition, and perhaps weakened by inner strife and independent petty kings, was restricted to the northern, main portion of Denmark. It became united and strong again under the Jelling kings. When Bishop Unni visited Denmark in 936, Gorm was King and no reference is made to the Swedish rulers. Dr. Lis Jacobsen therefore thinks that Gorm's conquest of Hedeby and his victory over Gnupa took place between 934, when Gnupa was made tributary to King Henry, and 936, when Gorm is mentioned as being king.

These Jelling kings were certainly of the ancient Skjoldung stock, but where they came from is not definitely known, as the sources are confused. In Adam's account it is stated that Hardegon, son of Svend, who came from 'Northmannia', drove out Sigerich–surely the same as the Sigtryg, son of Gnupa, of the runic stones. But who was Hardegon, the son of Svend? Some authorities think that the name means Harde-Gorm, and that it was thus Gorm the Old who reunited Denmark; others are of the opinion that it must be Gorm's father, Harde-Knud; and still others feel that he is an independent personage, Harde-Gunni, a descendant of the Royal House. In another chapter, Adam refers to King Gorm as Hardecnudth Vurm. It is thought that a word may have been left out here and that 'filius' should have been put in front, thus: Gorm, son of Hardeknud.

What Adam means by the word 'Nortmannia' is also disputed. In Adam it generally means Norway but may also indicate Normandy, and again it may possibly be a slip of his pen or memory in referring to Northumbria, assuming that Adam took careless, indistinct notes in abbreviated form, of his conversations with the Danish King Svend Estridsen, who was his authority. The Danes had been masters in Norwegian Østfold and Vestfold, and westward in Normandy they displayed great activity in these years, where Rollo–whose deceased brother was called Gorm–set himself up as lord and master. Storm, Curt Weibull, Arup and Bolin consider it most likely that the Jelling Dynasty came from Norway, partly because 'Nortmannia' in Adam generally means Norway, and partly because three of the Jelling kings–Harald, Svend and Knud –later ruled as kings in Norway. On the other hand, Lis Jacobsen maintains, "That Hardeknud's native place was *Denmark* is proved by the close connection that he and his family had with the country; about *fifty* of its members having since then ruled in Denmark in uninterrupted succession. Facts in the study of the history of names exclude the possibility that *Hardeknud*–the son of *Svend* and father of *Gorm*–could have come from Norway. Both *Svend, Knud* and *Gorm* are, to a marked degree, peculiarly Danish names.–It can be stated with complete philological certainty that the succession *Svend-Knud-Gorm* of persons born at the latest from 850-900 *cannot be Norwegian*."

In addition, Viken in Norway was probably under Danish rule from the Migration Period, so it must be assumed that it could only have been from there, and especially from Østfold, that they came; that is if they came from Norway at all. That it was the districts east of Oslofjord which were particularly subject to Danish rule in these periods is suggested by the clear indications of land division into 'skipæn'. This classification of 'skipæn' or 'skibsrede' (ship-money) was a political division established for military and taxation purposes which can be traced back to the time of King Gudfred. Harald Fairhair, who in about 900 united Norway from his kingdom in Vestfold appears, according to the Sagas, to have been connected with the Danish Royal House. His mother Ragnhild, a granddaughter of Harald Klak, was Danish, his wife Ragnhild, daughter of Erik, was a Jutish Princess, and his son, Erik Bloodaxe, was married to Gunhild, daughter of Gorm the Old.

Actually, only the word 'Nortmannia', as used by Adam, seems to indicate Norway, for other signs point toward the west. The Danes displayed great activity in Normandy during the years when Rollo's kingdom was established. We know that in about 943 a king named Sigtryg fell in Normandy, and some authorities identify him as that son of Gnupa and Asfrid who was driven out by Hardegon, and who is mentioned on the Hedeby stones. Dr. Lis Jacobsen thinks that by error, Adam has linked the remark about 'Nortmannia' with Hardegon, instead of with Sigtryg, but there are no definite indications that Gorm came from Normandy.

In the old English chronicles and Icelandic Sagas there is a series of genealogical data which have a certain interest concerning Gorm's origin. The same names reappear in the sources, but in varying combinations. The pieces are there as in a jigsaw puzzle, but the original order has been disrupted. The authors, probably unable to distinguish between ancient lists of kings from Denmark proper and those from the Danish colonies in Friesland, Normandy, East Anglia and Northumberland, mixed them up at random. The greater Olav Trygvason Saga and Joms-

236

vikings Saga tell of a childless Danish king named Gorm who adopted a boy whom Arnfinn, his Earl in Saxony, a vassal of Charlemagne's, had begotten by his own sister. This adopted son was given the name Knud, and was called Knud the Foundling. He had a son named Gorm who ruled a kingdom under the sons of Lodbrog. This Gorm became foster father to a son whom Regner Lodbrog's son Sigurd Snake-eye had had by Blæja, daughter of King Ælla of Northumberland. Sigurd's son was given the name of Knud, and was called 'Hørda-Knud' or 'Harde-Knud' because he was born in Hardsyssel in Jutland. Harde-Knud's son was Gorm the Old, named after his foster father. The Jomsviking Saga, however, maintains that it was the first Gorm, the son of Knud the Foundling, who was Gorm the Old.

We do not know on what old tradition the sagas rely, but perhaps it was Northumbrian lore and ancient lays. Dr. Lis Jacobsen thinks that such ancient songs about Gorm and his victorious battles did exist and that they are source for the data in the sagas about Gorm's conquest of Denmark. According to general opinion, the 10th century was the flourishing period of old-Danish poetry.

The Roskilde Chronicle, which dates from about 1140, relates that Svend, "Normannorum transfuga", conquered England, and that Svend's sons, Gorm and Harde-Knud, invaded Denmark and killed King Half-dan, after which they divided the kingdom so that Gorm was conceded Denmark and Harde-Knud, England. This presumably reflects a tradition concerning the expulsion of Halfdan, the son of Lodbrog, from Northumberland.

In the opinion of Sir Charles Oman, Simeon of Durham, who wrote in the 12th century, relies on an earlier Northumbrian chronicle. He relates that after Halfdan's expulsion of Northumberland, St. Cuthbert appeared in a vision to Bishop Eardulf of the Abbey of Lindisfarne and directed him to seek out a boy named Gudrød, serf to a widow in Hwittingham, but in reality a son of Harde-Knud. He located the boy and had him proclaimed King over the Danes in Northumberland.

Cnut's coin from York about 880-890.

237

Gudrød, or Guthred proved a good king who zealously supported the Church and apparently ruled in a prosperous period. Athelwerd says that King Gudrød died August 24, 894, and was buried in York Cathedral, which he had rebuilt.

The different traditions, when compared with what Adam of Bremen and Svend Aggesen relate, do not give a clear picture. But even though the data are hazy and confused they have perhaps a certain interest as remnants of a partly destroyed tradition, inasmuch as they are reinforced by something as tangible as a find of coins. In 1840, at Cuerdale near Preston, about 7,000 coins were discovered, all dating from the 9th century, in particular its latter half. They must have been buried in the opening years of the 10th century, before 905. A large part of the coins was Northumbrian, and among those, about fifty per cent bore the inscription: 'Cnut Rex'. Some of these inscribed with Cnut's name bear on the reverse side the name of Alfred the Great, 'Elfred Rex', while others, on the reverse, have the name 'Siefridus'. There are, however, no coins bearing the name Gudrød. English numismatists agree that these coins are Northumbrian and date from the time immediately following Halfdan, or when King Gudrød reigned. They conclude that Cnut must be identical with Gudrød, since it was common practice for christened Vikings to receive a fresh name at their baptism. Others lean more to the view that Cnut is a son of Gudrød. If Gudrød actually died in 894 and Harde-Knud appears as conqueror of Denmark in the beginning of the 10th century, this suggests that Gorm's father, Harde-Knud, must be either a son of Gudrød or a descendant of the same family.

The fact that the name of Alfred the Great is found on the reverse of some of Cnut's coins indicates that at a certain date Alfred had obtained suzerainty over Northumberland, a circumstance confirmed by the Anglo-Saxon Chronicle for 894. That the name Sigfred is found on some of Cnut's coins must indicate that at one time they ruled jointly. Sigfred is thought to be the son of Ivar and it is believed that he reigned after Gudrød, from 894 to about 898. Whether Cnut is identical with Gudrød or one of his sons, he could be the Harde-Knud of the tradition said to be the father of Gorm, as the Olav Trygvason Saga and Adam appear to believe. The fact that the Jelling kings are called 'Knytlinger' may also suggest that their descent derives from this Knud or Harde-Knud. The traditions are uncertain, but the coin discoveries give them a certain foundation.

*

238

The same uncertainty which veils the origin of Gorm also hangs over his consort, Queen Tyre. According to the Sagas, she was a daughter of Harald Klak, who died about 843. For chronological reasons Erslev considers this to be an impossibility, but the fact that one of the sons was called Harald might support the supposition that some ancestor bore the name of Harald, even as the fact that the other son was called Knud Dana-Ast could support the assumption that Gorm's father had borne that name. The names Knud (Canute) and Harde-Knud (Hartha Canute) both appear in the family at later dates.

Saxo affirms that Tyre was a daughter of the English King Edelrad or Ethelred, but Erslev thinks that this is also an error, for at that time there was no English king of that name. Erslev makes a mistake, because Aethelwulf, who reigned as king of England from 839 to 857, had four sons, all of whom succeeded him: Aethelbald, Aethelberth, Aethelred, Aelfred. Ethelred I, the third of the sons, ruled from 866 to 871 and established peace with the Danes at Nottingham in 868. He died at the Battle of Ashdown, being succeeded by his younger brother, Alfred the Great (871-901). In King Alfred's will, Ethelred's son Ethelwald is mentioned, and he maintained that his rights to the throne anteceded those of Alfred. But as regards Tyre, no daughter of King Ethelred is mentioned in the English sources.

If Cnut were Gorm's father and Ethelred Tyre's father, then a marriage between Gorm and a niece of Alfred would have been an obvious political possibility at a date when Alfred had won suzerainty over Northumberland. As a matter of fact, a similar political expediency occurred some years later, when King Sigtryg of Northumberland (923-926) married the sister of the English King Athelstan. The fact that King Ethelred's mother is said to have been of Jutish descent would explain Tyre's Nordic name.

Rason maintains that if Tyre were indeed a daughter of King Ethelred I, then according to the English laws of succession, her grandson Svend Forkbeard would be closer to the throne of England than King Ethelred II, King Alfred's great-great grandson. Rason therefore, somewhat naively, interprets King Svend's effort to gain England's crown less as a conquest than as a dynastic struggle, similar to the Wars of the Roses between the Houses of Lancaster and York. He refers also to the fact that Saxo has preserved a report that Gorm's sons, Knud Dana-Ast and Harald Bluetooth, tried to take over England after the death of their maternal grandfather, and that Harald Bluetooth advanced a claim to his hereditary right to England. Perhaps he did not aspire to rule the entire country, and was concerned only with Northumberland —as stated in an Icelandic Saga.

Saxo and Svend Aggesen give Tyre credit for building Danevirke, the great earthwork in Southern Slesvig—an achievement which modern historians have doubted. But the fact remains that Danevirke was built on the same lines as the earthworks built in England by Ethelfled of Mercia, and if she were cousin to Tyre it is conceivable that there is a connection.

Rason's view is not well-founded, but is nonetheless a theory worth considering. It may perhaps explain a number of difficulties in the English history of that period; for example, the numerous instances of treachery among the Anglo-Saxons, and especially the Quisling attitude of Eadric Streona. Varying sympathies with contending pretenders to the throne is not the same as treason.

Several things intimate a close connection between the Danish royal family and Northumberland. It is quite a remarkable coincidence that the names Svend, Knud, Harde-Knud and Gorm appear in the sources, and that in particular the unusual name Harde-Knud is mentioned in English, Icelandic and Danish sources, and later emerges as the name of Canute the Great's son.

The sons of Lodbrog in Northumberland are generally regarded as being of royal Danish stock, and the Sagas relate that Sigurd Snake-Eye ruled over a part of Denmark and in the Norwegian Viken. King Gudrød of Northumberland is said to have been brother to King Gorm (Guthrum) of East Anglia who died in 916 and whose predecessor of the same name was the Guthrum christened Athelstan, one of Alfred the Great's chief opponents, who died in 891. It is certainly one of these two, and probably the former, who appears in Saxo as King Gorm the Englishman. A number of the Northumbrian coins bear a picture of a bird, believed to be a raven, or a triangular banner which also seems to portray the same device. This is again found in the Bayeux Tapestry. Worsaae has advanced the suggestion that this is a representation of the celebrated raven banner of the Sons of Lodbrog, and he also thinks that the characteristically Danish swallowtail flag is patterned after this ancient fringed banner.

When Alfred the Great died about 901, a strange thing occurred.

Ethelwald, the youngest son of King Ethelred I, immediately marched to Northumberland, where he was proclaimed King of the Danes. Here he laid claim to the English throne and endeavored to acquire it. According to English laws of succession, he had a clearer title to it than Edward the Elder, the son of Alfred. Ethelwald ruled in Northumberland from 901 to 903, and coins struck by him exist. Attempting to conquer England, he fell in the Battle of Holme in 903, together with King Erik of East Anglia. It seems extraordinary that Ethelwald should thus have fled straight to the Danes in Northumberland and been hailed at once as king there, despite the hostile relations usually prevailing between the Danes and English at that time. In his attempt to get the better of Edward he had the support of the Danes in Northumberland and East Anglia. But if he were indeed Tyre's brother, their support becomes more understandable.

Edward the Elder's son, King Athelstan, who reigned from 925 to 940, and who as king acquired suzerainty over Northumberland, had at some time in his youth visited Gorm the Old in Denmark, according to John of Wallingford. In 948 the Norwegian King Erik Bloodaxe, the husband of Gorm's daughter Gunhild, turned up in Northumberland and made himself king there. Shetelig thinks Erik's immediately turning to Northumberland after his expulsion from Norway must be based on a claim of inheritance from the sons of Lodbrog, Gudrød and Cnut. One of the sons of Erik and Gunhild was in fact called Gorm, another Gamle and a third Gudrød.

It appears that at the beginning of the 10th century the Norwegians from Dublin, Ireland, made themselves masters for a time in Northumberland. This would then explain why Harde-Knud and Gorm returned to Denmark. Whether Harde-Knud is the same as Gudrød or another descendant of the family remains indefinite. But the very fact that they returned to Denmark suggests that they had hereditary claims to advance.

The so-called ornamental Jelling style as we know it from finds in Gorm's and Tyre's barrow, and which is a form seen in Denmark at the commencement of the 10th century, clearly denotes a connection with Irish and northern English ornamentation. Brøndsted thinks that the Jelling style is earlier than 900, while Paulsen and Shetelig aver that it first appears at that date. The style to be seen on the large Jelling stone which King Harald caused to be raised over Gorm and Tyre, the great animal style, together with the arrangement of the inscription, shows that it was cut by a Northumbrian runemaster.

There are thus many signs pointing to a close relationship between the Jelling Dynasty and Northumberland, and even though it cannot be proved, there is nonetheless a possibility which merits further investigation, that the Jelling Kings are descended from the Danish royal house in Northumberland.

*

There is doubt as to whether Gorm the Old was a great ruler and an energetic conqueror—or a stupid and incapable person. Both the sources and scholars are at variance on this point, though both may be correct, if it be the young Gorm who performed the deeds and the old Gorm who experienced premature arteriosclerosis and senility. In any case it looks as though it were Gorm or his father who defeated Gnupa at Hedeby the year after Gnupa became enfeebled through his defeat by Henry I. According to Norwegian-Icelandic tradition, Gorm was a mighty tribal-king, and Dr. Lis Jacobsen considers this report to be well founded. Olav Trygvason's Saga and Hauksbok state that Gorm marched into Jutland, defeated Gnupa and advanced against a king named Silfraskalli. Next, Gorm went into northern Jutland, destroyed all kings as far south as the Sli, and similarly conquered a great kingdom in Vindland–Vendic lands. King Gorm fought many battles with the Saxons and became the mightiest of kings. Laurence M. Larson says, "It was Gorm's work and great achievement again to unite the Kingdom and secure its ancient frontiers."

There is still no general agreement as to the meaning of Queen Tyre's nickname: 'Tanmarkar but' (Danmarks Bod) on the small Jelling stone which Gorm had placed over his queen. The tradition from Svend Aggesen's time interprets the words as 'Denmark's Amends', but Brix has shown that from the way in which they are written the words seem to point not to Tyre, but to Gorm himself. If the meaning is: 'The one who has repaired Denmark', it is almost inconceivable that a huge, bear-like Viking king would record on a stone that it was really his deceased wife who had restored the Kingdom and secured it against dangers from without. But if the words mean: 'Danmarks Pryd' (the adornment of Denmark) they point most naturally to Tyre, but in that case it is merely a courtly compliment without political significance.

242

There are indications that Gorm readopted Gudfred's policy in the Vendic lands, and that it was he who laid the foundation for the mastery which his son Harald secured at Jomsborg on the Oder. The marriage policy of the Jelling kings implies great interest in the Vendic lands south of the Baltic, Gorm's son King Harald, for instance, marrying a Vendic princess. But the age in which Gorm lived looms through an historical twilight in which it is difficult to distinguish things clearly.

HARALD BLUETOOTH

The great barrows still speak in loud tones of Harald, son of Gorm. The massive stone midway between them gives in words and pictures the basic elements of the royal achievements performed by this Nordic Pharaoh.

LAURITZ WEIBULL.

King Harald had a runic inscription cut on the sides of the large Jelling stone erected in honor of his parents, Gorm and Tyre–but chiefly of himself. On the stone King Harald refers to his three great achievements: he won the whole of Denmark, he won Norway, and he converted the Danes.

The stone is three-sided, and on the east face is found the main portion of the inscription, set in horizontal bands. On the south side is a picture of the all-embracing Christ–the earliest depiction of Him in the north–with the statement that Harald converted the Danes. On the north side is a picture of 'the great animal'–a lion entwined with a snake–with the reference to Norway. The significance of this picture is unknown, but it is reasonable to suppose that, like the Christ picture, it has some connection with the accompanying inscription. It might then symbolize Harald's victory over the King of Norway–Haakon Adelstensfostre or Harald Graafeld–and the lion may then portray the symbol of regal sovereign power.

Harald was a great king, and the stone is a monument which, in its dull-reddish granite crystals, testifies to the blazing flames of a departed age. Harald strengthened the position of royalty in Denmark and based the authority of the State upon cooperation between royal power and that of the Catholic Church. He was the second of Gorm's sons, the eldest of whom, Knud Dana-Ast, had been killed on a Viking raid in

Ireland. There are indeed those who think that Toke, son of Gorm, was a third son. He is named on some runic stones in Skaane in connection with the expedition to Uppsala, and appears to have been Earl in Jomsborg and father of the younger Bishop Odinkar.

It is not known when Harald became king after Gorm's death. As we have seen, Gorm gained a victory over Gnupa about 935, and Harald appeared in Normandy in 945 to help Rollo's grandson Richard I. It was probably between those dates that Gorm's death took place, even though some scholars hold the opinion that he died about 950.

*

Northward in Norway, Harald Fairhair's family had created a united country by virtue of their royal power. Erik Bloodaxe, son of Harald Fairhair, was married to Gorm's daughter–'Gunhild, mother of kings.' Gunhild seems to have represented a pledge of peace between Denmark and Norway, inasmuch as it appears that Harald Fairhair and Erik had relinquished their claims to Østfold, east of the Oslofjord. Erik and Gunhild together had systematically endeavored to dispose of the rest of Harald Fairhair's sons, gaining little popularity by this course of action. When Egil Skallagrimson had killed one of Erik's sons in a quarrel, he composed the caustic lines: "We greatly assist the Blood-axe in the murder of his family."

Haakon Adelstensfostre–Erik's youngest brother–had been brought up in England by King Athelstan, no doubt as part of a political scheme on the part of Athelstan and Harald Fairhair, so that by mutual help they might come to grips with the Vikings. Athelstan might thus also be in a position to drive a wedge between Denmark and Norway. Around 945 Haakon sailed home to Norway, usurped the crown with the support of the great chieftains, and expelled Erik Bloodaxe, who then sailed westward and in 948 made himself master in Northumberland–where he held forth, with interruptions, until 954. When Erik was driven out of Northumberland, and was shortly afterward killed, Gunhild and her sons sought the help of her brother, King Harald of Denmark, in conquering Norway for Gunhild's son Harald Graafeld. Around 955 the Dano-Norwegian war broke out. At the outset, King

244

King Harald Bluetooth's runic stone. Jelling. Jutland. About 98
"Harald the King caused these monuments to be ma
to Gorm his father and Tyre his mother, the Harald who w
all Denmark and Norway and made the Danes Christian

Haakon Adelstensfostre won several victories and enthroned Trygve Olavson, the father of Olav Trygvason, as viceroy of Ranrike in Østfold. Guttorm Sindre's Lay relates that King Haakon subdued Zealand and that the sons of Gunhild made fruitless attacks on Norway in 957. But in a following year, about 960, Harald Bluetooth won a victory at Fitjar, where Haakon Adelstensfostre was killed. Norway came under Danish suzerainty with Harald Graafeld as tributary king. He doubtless received the name Graafeld (Grey-pelt) in recognition of his establishing Norway's important fur trade with the north.

The sons of Gunhild endeavored to insure their power in Norway by killing the powerful Sigurd Jarl of Hlade, and his son Haakon Jarl forthwith sailed to Denmark. Here he succeeded in gaining the confidence of Harald Bluetooth, who was predisposed in his favor because Gunhild and Harald Graafeld were unwilling to continue payment of tribute.

At this time Knud Dana-Ast's son Guld-Harald (Gold-Harald) returned to Denmark and demanded a share of the kingdom. To this proposal Harald Bluetooth replied that nobody had ever dared to advance such a claim against Gorm, Harde-Knud, Sigurd Snake-Eye, or Regner Lodbrog. Haakon Jarl then formulated a plan for securing Norway by means of enthroning Guld-Harald there instead of the unconciliatory Harald Graafeld, thus at the same time solving the difficulty with Guld-Harald. Harald Graafeld was therefore lured down to the Limfjord where Guld-Harald, probably in about 970, succeeded in killing him in an engagement at Hals–the eastern entrance to the Limfjord.

After this event Haakon Jarl persuaded Harald Bluetooth that he would be better served if he were Jarl in Norway instead of a powerful and dangerous rival such as Guld-Harald. Guld-Harald was killed by Haakon Jarl after a hard battle, and through these harsh expedients Harald Bluetooth secured his power over Norway. There can hardly be historical fact substantiating the Sagas' tale that King Harald sailed to Norway with a large fleet, inasmuch as Harald had won Norway for himself before Harald Graafeld was enthroned as king. Nor can it be correct that Norway is said to have slipped out of Harald's hands again, as nothing suggests severe friction between Haakon Jarl and Harald Bluetooth. North Norway appears to have been governed by Haakon Jarl, while South Norway was brought directly under Danish control with young Svend Forkbeard as viceroy.

As Harald Bluetooth's royal power had now reached its zenith, it is probable that he erected the runic stone at this time. Lauritz Weibull says, "On the great picture-stone between his parents' barrows at Jelling, he set up in proud self-esteem the inscription which was to serve as a testimonial to his deeds for his own age and for posterity."

*

Styrbjørn Starke, who was the nephew of King Erik Sejrsæl (Happy in victory) of Sweden, married Harald Bluetooth's daughter Tyre. According to late and doubtful accounts, it appears that he had tried to gain the Swedish throne by means of an expedition to Uppsala which ended, however, in a serious defeat. Styrbjørn's connection with this battle has been much disputed. The runic stones in Skaane which refer to such a battle do not mention him, but rather Toke, the son of Gorm.

On one of the Hällestad stones is written, "Askel erected this stone to Toke, Gorm's son, his loyal lord. He did not flee at Uppsala." The Sjørup stone reads, "Saxe erected this stone to Asbjørn, his friend and follower, the son of Toke. He did not flee at Uppsala but fought as long as he held a weapon." In Bjørn Bredvikingskappa Aasbrandsson's Lausavers, Styrbjørn is referred to, but not in any definite connection with the battle of Uppsala, "My deeds under Styrbjørn's gold-embroidered

The Viking ship from Ladby on Fyn. Reconstruction in Ladby.

banners were well known; Erik with the iron helmet slew the men in battle." Styrbjørn is also mentioned by Odd, by Saxo, and in the Knytlingesaga.

P. A. Munch and Wimmer have combined the accounts about Styrbjørn, the Uppsala battle and the runic stones. These unified versions are theories which are criticized by Lauritz Weibull. Wimmer maintains that since Toke, the son of Gorm, is clearly defined on the runic stones as being a princely lord with a bodyguard, and inasmuch as he, like Harald Bluetooth, bears the name 'Gorm's son', it is reasonable to suppose that they were brothers. Adam of Bremen informs us that the younger Bishop Odinkar—who exercised such a powerful influence on Church policy under Svend Forkbeard and Canute the Great—was son of an Earl or Duke in Vinland, which means Jomsborg in Vendland. Since Odinkar's father was called Toke and was an influential member of the royal family, while Odinkar's mother was probably the elder Odinkar's sister Aase, there seems to be support for Wimmer's supposition. In addition, the nickname of Erik Sejrsæl (happy in victory) seems to show that the assaults on the Kingdom of Sweden were actually serious, large scale attacks, and not merely small piratical raids.

Presumably, the Styrbjørn battle occured after the killing of Harald Graafeld and Guld-Harald, about 970-980, and one glimpses in vague outline an attempt on the part of Harald Bluetooth to repeat his policy toward Norway in order to unite the three Nordic kingdoms under his sway, with the help of Toke and Styrbjørn.

*

Both Toke, Gorm's son, and Styrbjørn Starke appear to have been closely connected with Jomsborg, and the brothers Sigvalde and Thorkild the Tall were both Earls from Skaane and chiefs in Jomsborg. The mouth of the Oder lies just opposite Skaane.

Jomsborg, that outpost to the south so wrapped in legend, is said to have been founded by Harald Bluetooth. Its purpose was to create a strong-point for the Baltic trade and to open routes along the Oder which had been sealed off by the Vends, who were not merchants but principally hunters, shepherds and farmers. One never hears of their being merchants in the north and they had no market-towns of importance. Steenstrup says, "The Vendic people lived a very secluded and isolated life, preferring to reject that civilization which they saw develop-

248

ing among their neighbors. They despised the religion of these Germans and found them unattractive and perfidious in character. The Germans looked down on the customs and religion of the Vends with no less contempt, and a national hatred developed between the two peoples which gradually mounted to a passion."

Steenstrup writes the following, "King Henry I gave to those divisions of his army to which he had assigned robbers and thieves, permission to exercise every sort of rapine among the Slavs, and once when he had conquered a Slavonic town in the region of the Elbe, he permitted the massacre of the entire adult population, and boys and girls to be sold as slaves, while everything in the city was allotted as booty to the soldiers."

Laurence M. Larson says that the Danes' interest in Vendland seems to have been purely commercial; horses, cattle, game, fish, meat, timber, spices and hemp are mentioned as being important articles of trade with the south, where a market for Danish products had opened up. Relations between the Danes and Vends seem to have been peaceable at that time and they lived side by side in perfect amity. But the Germans were not regarded with much friendliness by their Slavonic neighbors, while in the opinion of the Germans, the Slavs did not even fall within the category of human beings, and consequently enmity and hatred were the order of the day between the two peoples. On the other hand, says Larson, the Vends appear to have become quickly accustomed to Harald's rule, protecting their coasts from piracy as it did.

Harald also provided himself with fortifications at other points along the Baltic coast. In East Prussia his son Haakon conquered Samland–between Frisches Haff and Kurische Haff–a coastline rich in amber. Ivar Vidfadme is said to have held dominion there. The Jelling Dynasty's policy of marital alliances with Abodritish and Polish princely houses reflects their interest in the Slavonic trade.

Tradition has it that Danish kings often held suzerainty in Holstein, and according to Svend Estridsen's statements, King Harald had promulgated laws which were in force for many years in Holstein and Friesland. Green thinks that Harald's intervention in Normandy must be regarded as an attempt to create a strong-point there for further operations which were fulfilled to some extent by his son Svend. Harald's administration in Vendland, Samland, Holstein, Friesland and Normandy can be considered an extension of Gudfred's policy, but this could not be carried out until after the reconquest of Hedeby in 935. The Saxon Duke Herman's words to Rollo's men in 942 may be interpreted as having reference to these battles. Harald's overall plan, when further developed by Svend and Canute, had England as the final goal.

When the German Kaiser Otto I died in 973, Harald must have deemed the moment favorable for aggressive action in Holstein. However, he miscalculated, and his plans were foiled by the young Emperor Otto II who, in the following year, led an army against Danevirke, forced his way through Wieglesdor and built a castle on the frontier. Adam thinks that Otto advanced right up through the peninsula to the Limfjord, because to his German ear it seemed obvious that 'Oddesund' must have been called after Otto—an early example of a lively imagination in research on place-names.

Adam again indulged in fantasy in stating that both Otto I and Otto II undertook warlike expeditions into Denmark, inasmuch as Otto I's campaign is not an historic fact. The primary motives of Otto II's military campaign were to seal off Harald's advance, to insure the Hedeby trade, and to neutralize the center of power which the sallyport constituted. But German rule held sway there no more than nine years. While in 982 the Emperor was fully occupied with fighting in Italy and the entire German Empire threatened to collapse, Harald reconquerred the lost frontier land, possibly with his son Svend as army commander. Some think that it is this transference of the frontier which is alluded to on the Jelling stone, while others are of the opinion that as early as 935 Harald may have held leadership of the army, or that it is the reconquest of Zealand from Haakon Adelstensfostre to which reference is made. Curt Weibull ascribes to Harald Bluetooth the foundation of the Danish Kingdom, but everything suggests that Denmark was a united kingdom even before King Gudfred's time. Elsewhere, Weibul writes, "Unfavorable internal boundary conditions impeded and delayed Sweden's development into a firmly unified state and facilitated the provinces' furthering their own special interests contrary to those of a united kingdom, right down to recent times. Conditions in Denmark, however, were so favorable that she overcame provincialism and grew together in unity perhaps earlier than any Germanic state. The lead which Denmark held over Sweden in culture and political strength throughout the whole of the Middle Ages is to a large extent due to this."

Perhaps Haakon Jarl had a free hand in Norway after Harald's defeat

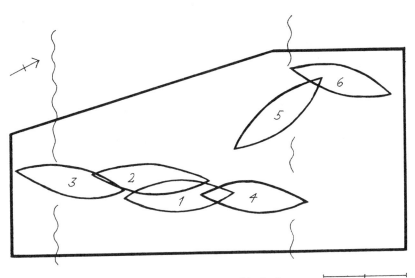

Diagram of the submerged Viking ships blockading the original navigable channel of Roskilde Fjord, Zealand. The stone-filled ships are now being excavated (1962). The frame indicates sheet piling.

5y.   10y.

by Otto II in 974, but it does not appear that he made himself independent. The celebrated expedition of the Jomsvikings to Norway, and their glorious defeat at Hjørungavaag, most likely occurred at the close of Harald's reign and it is probable that Harald himself was instrumental in the undertaking and that its aim was to clip the wings of Haakon Jarl. At all events, the consequences of the defeat seem to have affected Harald. Dates are uncertain, and there are those who think that the expedition did not take place until the beginning of Svend Forkbeard's reign.

There are few warriors in the history of the world who shine with such metallic luster as did Vagn Aagesen and his men when they stood captive before the victorious Norwegian Earl Haakon and his magnanimous son, Erik. Their experience is related in 'Jomsvikinga Saga'. It is a good story, but too long to be related here. One must go back to Thermopylae to find its counterpart. Fearlessness in death has given these warriors eternal fame, and their sharp, biting words still ring fresh as on a frosty day, giving them in death a spiritual revenge over their slayer.

251

Earl Haakon had ordered his executioner, Thorkel Leira, to cut down some of the captive from the battle, found wounded and exhausted on a skerry in the sea. Before he gave the sword cut, Thorkel Leira asked each one how he felt about dying. One of them answered, "My death seems good to me. It will happen to me as to my father that I shall die." Another replied, "I should be unmindful of the law of the Jomsvikings if I dreaded death or spoke words of fear. Everyone must die sometime." A third retorted, "It pleases me to die with honor, but you, Thorkel, will live on in shame." There was also one who replied, "I think it fine to die like my comrades, but I do not want to be slaughtered like a sheep. Cut straight into my face and watch well if I flinch!"—He did not flinch.

Vagn Aagesen, by his quickness and adroitness, succeeded in killing the executioner himself. Of course the Earl was furious, but his noble son Erik saved Vagn's life by offering him peace. Vagn Aagesen answered, "Only on this condition, that all my comrades who are still alive are liberated too. If not, we will all go the same way together."

After some years in Norway, Vagn Aagesen returned to Fyn, and many prominent men are descended from him. Johannes V. Jensen suggets that it is he who lies buried in the Viking ship in Ladby on Fyn.

*

The might of the regal power which Harald established in Denmark was perhaps in part the result of his third great achievement—the conversion of the Danes. This transition from Nordic paganism to the Catholicism of Rome seems to have taken place without great disturbance. Whereas Charlemagne baptized the Saxons with fire and sword, and religious fanatics such as Olav Trygvason and St. Olav swept through the Norwegian valleys tearing out the tongues of those who refused baptism, the change of faith in Denmark was effected without major excesses, without martyrs and persecutions, and without loss of spiritual balance. For example, Snorre Sturlason, in referring to Olav Trygvason's treatment of the Norwegian chieftain Ejvind, who refused to be converted, relates that Olaf caused burning coals to be laid on the skin of his belly until it began to smolder, and then asked him, "Now will you believe in Christ?"

The Gospel of justice and love brought by Christianity was a new inspiring power, and the streams of learning and culture which followed in its wake were later to produce rich results in the medieval Valdemar Period. But these spiritual forces were linked up with a set of political ones which appear to have been of great importance.

King Harald's baptism, which took place about 960, was referred to by Ruotger, who wrote as early as the years between 966 and 969, and it could therefore have no connection with the Emperor's campaign against Denmark in 974. Nonetheless, relations with Germany were certainly a contributing cause, so that foreign policy motives did play a part. The conversion of the Danes deprived the Germans of the excuse for making religious crusades into Denmark.

In the archives of the Church of Bremen there are two much disputed missives from 965 and 988 in which the German Emperor exempts the Danish churches in Ribe, Slesvig and Aarhus from taxation on their lands. Most scholars consider these two letters to be ecclesiastical political forgeries, and at all events they do not appear to have been drawn up in the German Chancery. Sofus Larsen writes that the Church of Bremen made systematic use of that kind of forgery and Steenstrup says, "While it can scarcely be proved that throughout the Middle Ages more than a few Danish documents were forgeries, yet false or forged documents appear literally by the score from the first centuries of the history of the Church of Bremen." It must have been a curious spiritual influence which came to the Danes from the German Church of Bremen. It is easy to understand why Svend Forkbeard and Canute the Great tried to forestall its influence in Denmark.

But other scholars regard the letters as genuine and consider them to be proof of German influence in Denmark at that time. Brøndal has pointed out that if the letters are authentic they do not signify that the Emperor wielded any actual power in Denmark, there being no indications that Denmark had been bound in any way to render taxes or military services. But in that case the letters merely denote that the Emperor exempted the Archbishop of Hamburg-Bremen from levying taxes and services on the churches in Denmark, due to the difficulty or impossibility of collecting them on the soil of a foreign power.

Added to the purely foreign-political causes was a certain commercial-political factor. Many Vikings, on their long commercial voyages or plundering raids, had come in close contact with a number of Christian cities and countries. There they quickly learned that it was easier to make binding commercial agreements when they had at least been given the 'prima signatio'.

If one recalls the powerful and decisive role played by land-political interests during the Reformation Period in Denmark, Germany and England, it is natural to suppose that similar factors came to the forefront in the changeover of religion in the north. A series of remarks, culled at random from the writings of historical authors, forms a picture when assembled. Their purport is as follows:

Valtyr Gudmundsson, writing about conditions in Iceland, "It was only the richer, and as a rule, the leading colonists who had the wherewithal to erect a temple for use of public worship. The less well-to-do, among whom the urge to participate in devotions might be just as great and was often greater, were obliged to resort to these temples and pay a tax in return for their use, a temple tax, to the owner of the particular temple."

Svend Aakjær has shown that the words 'Hovgaard' and 'Hoveri' (Hov-Aervid) are associated from heathen times with the fact that it was the class of chieftains in antiquity who officiated as temple-priests (Hov-goder) at the sacrifices in the heathen temples. The lands belonging to churches and vicarages often bear names originally connected with heathen sacraments.

Gudmund Hatt says, "The earliest development of the State is thus closely linked up with the religion of the farmer. The esteemed ritual centers were at the same time foci of political power. Spiritual rites gradually produced a religious and political upper class, the status and temporal power of which depended to a great extent on its upholding the cult considered essential to the fertility of the fields and herds."

Trading markets were generally associated with the great sacrificial feasts to which people came from long distances, and these festivals must have constituted a permanent source of income for the landowning chiefs. Paulsen says, "At the ancient heathen centers of holy ritual a 'Kaup-fridr', or trading peace synonymous with sacred peace, prevailed during the great feast-days. Churches and abbeys were usually built at traffic and trade intersections and frequently at ancient heathen ritual-places where, by ancient custom, people gathered on certain occasions."

Concerning conditions in the time of Harald Bluetooth, Steenstrup writes, "Buildings, property and anything else formerly used in the

254

King Harald Bluetooth baptized by Poppo.
Detail from the golden altar in Tamdrup Church. Jutland.

worship of heathen gods should from that time on rightly pass into the realm of the Christian cult, its community and priests. We know that such a command was issued once at the beginning of Harald Bluetooth's reign."

Arup says, "The internal political importance of Harald's conversion therefore shows up with great clarity. The chieftains throughout the country had acquired for themselves, in their role as priests, averters of

255

the anger of the old gods, and through their sacrifices, procurers of peace and good harvests, an influence over the people which the King would now assume with the help of his new God. If the God of the King proved to be mightier than the gods of the chieftains, the King would then be more powerful than they–and Poppo had produced incontestable proof of the new God's omnipotence."

On Fyn the crown property of later days is found clustered around the ancient ritual-places–the 'Vi' (places of sacrifice). Lundbye points out that they appear to have been confiscated estates. This seems associated with Harald's taking over the ancient ritual-places and causing the Churches at Odense and Roskilde to be erected.

Sofus Larsen thinks that the great chieftains' initial opposition to Christianity was because it deprived them of the authority and income they had undoubtedly possessed as heathen priests in the temples of their homesteads."

Hans Olrik is of the opinion that the king must have had control over the temple property, thus enjoying considerable power.

In writing of conditions in Norway, of the land-political strife between chieftains' families over their free property rights to the soil (the Odel right) and the monarchy's insistence on the overlordship of all land in the country, Halfdan Koht says, "The main point in the introduction of Christianity was that it took away a large measure of power from the old aristocracy, and the monarchy became Christian-democratic. Monarchy gained a firm legal foundation."

The land-political factor deserves a more central position and a closer examination. It appears to have played just as great a part in the religious change-over as it did later in the Reformation, and is probably one of the main reasons why Harald was opposed by the chieftains before they began to ally themselves with the two great, expanding forces in society–the Monarchy and the Church.

The German-orientated Church policy and the various military and political repercussions against Germany, Sweden and Norway, must have increased the disagreements in religious and economic matters which existed between Harald and the leading representatives of the old faith. Tension grew until it brought open revolt. At first, Svend does not appear to have led the opposition, nor does he seem to have been its initiator, but when the events caused a landslide, the momentum carried him to the forefront. The many evil plots which Adam of Bremen ascribes to

Svend must be considered in the light of Adam's serving the interest of the Church of Bremen, which Svend certainly did not.

During the altercation which broke out between the King and the opposition, it was, according to tradition, the mighty chieftain Palna-Toke who mortally wounded the King in revenge for his having compelled him to shoot an apple from his son's head. It is probably no more than a legend—equating with the myth about William Tell in Switzerland—though Saxo told the tale a hundred years before the Swiss episode supposedly occurred.

The wounded King was carried by the Jomsvikings to Jomsborg, where he died on November 1, probably in the year 986. He was later buried in his own newly-built Trinity Church at Roskilde. He was succeeded by Svend of the forked beard who, on the foundation his father had laid, was to carry Denmark forward into the first rank of European statecraft.

SVEND FORKBEARD

The rapidity and precision of his movements place him as a general above every other Viking leader of his time.
Sir Frank Stenton.

"The accession of Svend Forkbeard to the Danish throne marks an era in the history of Denmark. Harald Bluetooth had not been a weak king; he had enlarged his territories; he had promoted the cause of the Christian faith; he had striven for order and organized life. But his efforts in this direction had brought him into collision with a set of forces that believed in the old order of things." Thus writes Laurence M. Larson.

"But Svend was no ordinary man. If greatness consists in mere skill and steadfastness in carrying out an object, irrespective of the moral character of that object, he may even be called a great man. His purpose was doubtless fixed from the beginning; but he knew how to bide his time, how to mark and to seize his opportunities. Of that species of glory which is won by steady and skilful destruction of one's fellow-creatures, the glory of an Attila or a Buonaparte, the first Danish conqueror of England is entitled to a large share." Thus writes Freeman.

The English regarded Svend only as a conqueror and tyrant, never having the opportunity to know his great qualities in days of peace, as they did those of Canute the Great, at a later date. Svend was a man of great parts, and it would have been impossible for him to achieve all that he did if he had been merely a furious Viking with a blood-stained mist before his eyes.

In his youth Svend had been in England as a Viking. There he had noted England's weak points and internal disintegration, and he seems to have formulated plans for conquering England at a very early date. As a young man he had been viceroy in South Norway, and it is possible it was he who, in 983, led the army in the reconquest of Hedeby from the Germans.

It is interesting to observe the statecraft with which he slowly built up his plan, carried it through and brought about its success. Even though the accounts in the Sagas are late and full of errors, his plan has been outlined.

Denmark was surrounded by enemies. To the north, Haakon Jarl in Norway had actually freed himself after the victory over the Jomsvikings and the death of King Harald, while the Jomsvikings themselves represented a danger toward the south, their loyalty to Harald Bluetooth not having been transferred to Svend. They transported the dying King from Helgenes to Jomsborg, where he expired. Early in the reign of Svend they had had the good fortune to take him prisoner. The story that the women of Denmark ransomed him by sacrificing their jewels is supported by legal historical evidence. In return they were accorded a half-inheritance in landed property with men, which was almost a unique law, there being only a few parallels within the Teutonic nations.

Toward the east, Sweden was inclined to be hostile, and King Erik Sejersæl attacked Denmark while Svend was in the west on Viking raids. Adam of Bremen's statement that Erik twice exiled Svend, each time for a period of seven years, is improbable but has the foundation that Svend was in England in 994, where he besieged London, together with Olav Trygvason. Adam is also contradicted by numerous facts. It was probably in Hedeby that Erik Sejrsæl settled, as had the earlier Swedish conquerors at the beginning of the century. At Hedeby, the runic stones which bear Svend's name probably date from Svend Forkbeard's reconquest of that disputed trading city. There is a possibility that they may originate as early as Hedeby's reconquest in 983 or, as Lis Jacobsen thinks, from Svend Estridsen's battles with Harald Haardraade. But la Cour deduces that the inscriptions on the stones show that they were raised by a Svend

Viking sword.
Bjørnsholm. Jutland.

who was besieging the city, and in Harald Haardraade's time it was
Svend Estridsen who was the besieged. Wimmer has guessed that the
man Skarde who is named on the stone is perhaps identical with Skarde
the Jomsviking who, along with Vagn Aagesen, survived the battle of
Hjørungavaag. Svend Forkbeard's battles with Erik Sejrsæl probably took
place around 995 and thus help to explain why Svend was so ready to

accept the peace offer of King Ethelred in England during the winter of 994-995.

Svend Forkbeard inaugurated his policy by marrying Gunhild, the Sigrid Storraade (Sigrid the Haughty) of the Sagas whose name is so wrapped in legend. She was a daughter of the Polish Duke Miesco, who is mentioned in some documents by the Nordic name of Dagr and is believed to be of Nordic descent. Gunhild had been married to Erik Sejrsæl and was the mother of King Olof Skotkonung of Sweden. She had been cast off by Erik, no doubt after the death of her father in 992. Through her marriage to Svend she became the mother of Harald, Canute the Great and Estrid, from whom the later Danish Kings are descended. According to the Sagas, Sigrid Storraade was a daughter of the wealthy Swedish chieftain, Skoguls-Toste, undoubtedly the Toste mentioned on the Yttergård runic stone, where it is said of Ulf that he collected Danegeld three times, first under Toste, then under Thorkild and a third time under Knud. Thorkild must be Thorkild the Tall, and Knud, Canute the Great.

L. Weibull does not think that the Sigrid Storraade of the Sagas was an historical personage, but various indications suggest that she actually existed. In the family of Ulf Jarl, the names Sigrid and Toste occur as hereditary names, and the large Swedish estates owned by the Danish royal family–which are called 'Sigridlev' (Syghridleff) in the Domesday Book of the Danish King Valdemar the Victorious–are also mentioned in a Swedish register of 1333, where 'Sigridlev' are said to originate with the mother of Olof Skotkonung. The problem, therefore, is not so simple. Beckman emphasizes that questions of heredity and names of inheritors are among the things most stubbornly maintained in family tradition, especially with something as intricate in its ramifications as the estates of Danish Kings on Swedish territory; he therefore attributes a certain importance to the tradition in the Saga. Hans Toll's investigations make it probable that Sigrid Storraade is an historical personage. He thinks she was married to Thorgils Sprakaleg, a son of Styrbjørn Starke and father of Ulf Jarl, and he believes that 'Sigridlev' came into the ownership of the Danish kings through Svend Estridsen, the son of Ulf and Estrid. Sigrid Storraade is real enough then, but she was neither a Swedish nor a Danish queen.

At all events, the Queen of Erik and Svend was a lady who herself knew who she was. It was she who, according to the Sagas, caused

260

Harald Grenske to be burned to death in his house when he came to court her with all propriety. She gave the excuse that she wanted, as she said, "to discourage petty kings from proposing to me!" Harald Grenske was the father of St. Olav and himself Viceroy in Viken.

She was more interested in King Olav Trygvason's proposal of marriage. He was a blond, blue-eyed hero, the first in sport and use of arms. He had recently been baptized and his frenetic zeal for missionary activity was stimulated by the general eschatologic anticipation of the Second Advent in 1,000 A.D., the Day of Judgment and the arrival of the Millennium. Therefore there was an all-out effort made to hurry up and baptize everyone before it was too late.

King Olav asked Sigrid if she was christened. She answered, "I will not depart from the faith which is mine and which my kin have held before me. But I shall not object to your believing in any God you may wish to." King Olav became exasperated and struck her in the face with his glove, saying, "Do you think I will have you when you are heathen as a hound?" She then stood up and replied, "This may well be your death." She then married the Danish King Svend Forkbeard. Perhaps Canute inherited some of his strong character from her.

During the Viking expeditions westward, Svend had been in league with Olav Trygvason at the siege of London. In the seething discontent at the close of Haakon Jarl's violent rule in Norway, Svend had a possibility of conquering the country, but this opportunity was, in 995, seized by Olav, who was a great-grandson of King Harald Fairhair. Perhaps Svend was occupied at that time with Erik Sejrsæl's attack on Denmark.

When Erik Sejrsæl died, his unwarlike son, Olof Skotkonung, became King of Sweden. Through his politic marriage with Olof's mother, Svend had ensured his position in the rear. Olav Trygvason's shining heroic figure stood threateningly in the north, especially after Olav had initiated a marriage policy which Sweden and Denmark could not regard as friendly. Olav had married Svend's sister Tyre against her brother's wishes. She is said to have first been married to Styrbjørn, grandfather of Ulf Jarl, and later to Miesco's son, the Polish Duke Burislav. When quite young, Olav had served under the Slavs and taken part in their battles against the Danes and Saxons. In those early days he already appears to have had some connection with Jomsborg. This marriage gave Norway the opportunity of forming an alliance with Poland and Vendland in the south, and an entente with the Jomsvikings on the Oder, so that Denmark could be threatened from both south and north. At the same time, Olav had given his sister Ingeborg in marriage to Ragnvald Jarl in Väster Götland, which appears to have still been independent of Sweden and hostile to Olof Skotkonung. This might have resulted in a closer collaboration between Svend and his stepson, Olof Skotkonung.

Most likely as a countermove to the Norwegian policy, Svend had received Haakon Jarl's magnanimous son Erik Jarl and given him his daughter Gyda in marriage, while the brother of Erik, Svend Jarl, married the sister of the Swedish Olof. By these alliances the support of the Earl party in Norway was ensured and the position of Olav Trygvason weakened.

Later, in the summer of 1,000 A.D., Olav Trygvason sailed a large fleet into the Baltic and opened negotiations with Poland and Jomsborg. In Poland he arranged Tyre's inheritance claims, and Vendish ships were placed at his disposal. At Jomsborg, Sigvalde kept the negotiations alive while at the same time holding open the door to discussions with Svend, whose powerful Danish-Swedish-Norwegian alliance he seems to have feared.

Svend did not let the opportunity pass. Here was a chance to prevent the return of Olav to Norway. He collected his naval forces, together with those of Erik Jarl and Olof Skotkonung, induced Sigvalde to protract the negotiations, and then fought the Battle of Svolder, probably in the Sound between Helsingborg and the island of Hven. Later Icelandic accounts locate the battle, probably incorrectly, at Rügen, near the island of Hiddensee, or in Gristower Wick.

The year 1,000 came, but Christ did not appear among the clouds, nor did the Day of Judgment come. The non-culmination of the expected events may have shattered King Olav's self-confidence. His luck of leadership was lost, the blessing of kingship withdrawn and in the battle of Svolder the Kingdom of Norway broke in his hands.

After the fall of Olav Trygvason, his Kingdom was divided among the victors. Svend obtained southern Norway, Erik received northern Norway as an earldon, and the Swedish Olof Skotkonung received land in the Province of Trøndelag as well as Ranrike and Bohuslen in Østfold, which formerly had been under Denmark, and where Olav Trygvason's father had been Viceroy under Haakon Adelstensfostre.

This was probably the price of Olof's cooperation in the alliance. Swedish suzerainty in Väster Götland is not known historically until after the Battle of Svolder. Olav Trygvason's alliance with Ragnvald Jarl in Väster Götland perhaps entailed these political consequences.

"The actual victor at Svolder was the King of Denmark," says Noach, and Larson says, "The diplomacy of Svend, culminating in the partition of Norway, had made Denmark a state of great importance. The Battle of Svolder was of great importance to the policies of the Knytlings. The rival Norse kingdom was destroyed. Once more the Danish King had almost complete control of both shores of the waterways leading into the Baltic. Danish hegemony in the north was a recognized fact."

After having thus made himself secure on all sides, Svend could resume his activities westward. During the years from 995 to 1,000, when the tension between Olav Trygvason and Svend kept the Danish forces in home waters, England had, to some extent, been left in peace. "During most of the tenth Century the Viking movement was in abeyance. Emigration from the Baltic lands fell off, and the Scandinavian colonists spent their time in building up towns, farms and institutions in the land which their fathers had won with the battleaxe. It was due to this ebb in the tide of invasion that Alfred's children had been able to effect a nominal reconquest of the Danelaw, on condition of leaving its Scandinavian character untouched. The era of Edgar and Dunstan followed as a brief period of peace and prosperity. And then, during the reign of the incompetent Ethelred the Redeless, the storm broke once more.

"The Vikings were again on the warpath, and this time, under Sweyn Forkbeard, King of Denmark, they made South England the special object of their attack. Normandy and the English Danelaw, being under Scandinavian rule, they naturally spared, while their cousins in Yorkshire and East-Anglia equally naturally did nothing to thwart them or to help the decadent Saxon King to save his Wessex. The unity of Saxon and Dane in the island was still incomplete, and the weakness of the new Kingdom of England stood revealed. The Danelaw has been called 'the rock on which the old English Nationality foundered'." (Trevelyan).

According to Green, the Danelaw preserved its character and individuality, even during the suzerainty of the Kings of Wessex. It continued to be a Danish, and not an English country, and at a later date it rose to assist Svend so that half of his work was completed in advance. In the suppression of the free man and the growth of the large estate-owner's power, Green sees the chief reason for the destruction of the

263

sense of freedom and decline of the old English nation. He says, "From Ælfred's day it was assumed that no man could exist without a lord. The ravages and the long insecurity of the Danish wars aided to drive the free farmer to seek protection from the thegn. His freehold was surrendered, to be received back as a fief, laden with service to its lord." Gradually the 'lordless man' became a sort of outlaw in the realm. The free churl sank into the unfree villein, and changed from the freeholder who knew no superior but God and the law, to the tenant bound to do service to his lord, to follow him to the field, to look to his court for justice, and render days of service in his demesne. While he lost his older freedom he gradually lost, too, his share in the government of the state.

Dorothy Whitelock says, "The slave had no wergild. He was a chattel, and if anyone killed ham, he had merely to pay his value to the owner.– It proved particularly difficult to prevent slaves from running away to join the Danish forces during periods of Viking ravages.–The English slave who joined the Viking forces ravaging his district might seize the opportunity to turn the tables and pay off old grudges on his former master; Wulfstan laments that 'often a thrall binds very tight the thane who was formerly his master, and makes him a slave'; or it might happen that the slave killed his former lord in a fight, and no wergild was paid to the kindred."

"It is in the degradation of the class in which its true strength lay that we must look for the causes of the ruin which already hung over the West-Saxon realm." In this sentence Green hits an important problem, because it shows that the civilization which the Danes overran was in many respects undermined and outworn. A society which ended by being ruled by great landlords and sanctimonious abbots met a civilization of which the foundations were the freedom of the peasantry and independence of the individual. The England of those days was a rickety realm, and Ethelred an unready and irresolute monarch. But the blame for England's ruin was not Ethelred's alone. Larson writes, "In the early years of the eleventh century, only statesmanship of the highest order could have saved the dynasty; but England had neither statesmen nor statesmanship in Ethelred's day."

King Svend was aware of this from his expeditions to England in the 990's, when the attacks and levying of Danegeld had begun to undermine the country. Arup writes, "Svend organized the Viking wars. In the 90's the Isle of Wight was the winter-quarters for himself and his army,

264

and there the peasants of Wessex supplied them with provisions. He drew up definite regulations for the levying of contributions and arranged for the commandeering of horses, thus giving the army the wherewithal to undertake major raids on the wealthy towns of the interior which had hitherto escaped plunder. He understood how to gauge when fatigue spread through his army, this being the moment to force through the payment of Danegeld by the weak English Government, thus enabling him to discharge to their satisfaction those who were weary." Except for these admissions, Arup seems to regard King Svend almost as a person of limited ability, on a par, for example, with that portrait which Bengtson draws in his book 'The Long Ships' ("Røde Orm"). But if anybody endeavors to plan and carry through a conquest of England or to build up an Empire, he will discover that a certain combination of virtues is required—namely, energy, perseverance and the faculty of reflection.

Normandy had given the Danes considerable support by providing them with a stronghold. Ethelred tried to prevent this by an attack on

The Viking fortress Trelleborg. West Zealand.

265

Normandy, but without much success. He did, however, secure an agreement which was in the nature of an alliance, and early in 1002 he strengthened the bond by marrying Emma, sister of the Norman Duke Richard II, and daughter of Richard I and the Danish-born Gunnor. Emma was a great-granddaughter of Rollo, and it was this marriage which later directly prepared the way for the Norman Conquest of England. Emma was later wed to Canute the Great, but it was the son of her first marriage, Edward the Confessor, who as king paved the way for William the Conqueror's claim to the throne of England.

In 1002 the confused and worried Ethelred adopted a fatal expedient. He instigated a St. Bartholomew's Eve massacre of the Danes who had settled in the English districts. "On Saint Brice's Day, November 13, the English rose, not to battle, but to murder," says Larson. Countless Danes were the victims of this slaughter and among those murdered was Svend's own sister Gunhild, who had to look on while her husband, the Ealdorman Pallig, and their child, were murdered before her eyes. She herself was struck down uttering the prediction that vengeance would follow. Green calls St. Brice's Day 'an act of basest treachery' and Freeman describes the deed as 'both cowardly and foolish'. With an expression which savors of Talleyrand, he says, "The Vespers of Saint Brice were not only a crime but a blunder."

"But brief is the hour that striking hands are happy," runs an ancient Danish saying. St. Brice fanned the flames, and revenge for his kin became an additional driving force in Svend's mind. He did not lose his head but bided his time. In the Nordic countries the St. Brice's Day massacre must have been looked upon as a 'Niddingdaad' (a dastardly outrage) contrary to all unwritten laws of fighting and conceptions of honor. A cooling-off in Normandy's relations with England resulted. So, in 1003, Svend sailed to Normandy and secured a dissolution of the alliance with England and an agreement with Richard II to open Normandy, partly as a market for the booty from England, and partly as a haven of refuge for sick and wounded Danes. The most important result that Svend thus gained was security for his Norman flank during the attacks on England.

London had already been taken and burned in 842, 871 and 982, but at a later date the city bravely withstood several attacks and sieges by Svend Forkbeard and Olav Trygvason. Paris had been plundered by Regner Lodbrog in 845, by Bjørn Ironside in 857, and besieged by

Sigfred in 885. As late as 1349, Berlin was attacked by Valdemar Atterdag.

Westward, Svend carried through his systematic attacks on England with constantly recurring levy of Danegeld. Thousands of pounds of silver were collected and much of it has been discovered in large concentrations of coins in the soil of Denmark. In the years between 991 and 1014, 158,000 pounds sterling were paid over, an enormous sum for those times, and in addition, there was what was seized by direct plunder. The year 1000 was the only one in which no raiding took place in England, hostilities with Olav Trygvason having kept the forces at home. Nor was there any pillaging in 1002 and 1005, the first year because the Danegeld was paid immediately, the second because there was a failure of crops with resulting famine in England.

In 1009 the Jomsvikings left the Oder and settled down by the Thames under the leadership of Thorkild the Tall. His brother Sigvalde had previously fallen in England, perhaps as a victim of the St. Brice massacre. In the following years Thorkild appeared as leader of the army, repeatedly collecting Danegeld. In 1012 he received a total payment of 48,000 pounds, disbanded a part of the army, then took service under King Ethelred, bringing with him forty-five of his ships. Accompanying Thorkild was the Norwegian Olav the Stout—the Olav of the Battle of Stiklestad, who was later canonized. There were probably cogent reasons for Thorkild's entering English service and not wishing to return to Jomsborg within Svend's reach. He certainly had great ambitions, but what his ultimate plans may have been is unknown. He seems to have been loyal in his allegiance to Ethelred. Meanwhile, the decisive operations against England were planned in Roskilde. Thorkild's defection was probably a determinant in Svend's decision to strike just then. He had made his position secure from behind and on the flanks, and the fruit was ripe for plucking.

Larson describes the situation thus, "In many respects the time was exceedingly favorable for the contemplated venture. A large part of England was disposed to be friendly; the remainder was weak from continued pillage. Denmark was strong and aggressive, eager to follow the leadership of her warlike king. Svend's older son, Harald, had now reached manhood, and could with comparative safety be left in control of the kingdom. Denmark's neighbors in the north were friendly: Svend's vassal and son-in-law controlled the larger part of Norway; his stepson

Olof ruled in Sweden. Nor was anything to be feared from the old enemies to the south. The restless Vikings of Jom were in England. The lord of Poland was engaged in a life-and-death struggle with the Empire. The Saxon dynasty, which had naturally had northern interests, no longer dominated Germany; a Bavarian, Henry II, now sat on the throne of the Ottos. In the very year of Svend's invasion of England, the German King journeyed to Italy to settle one of the numberless disputes that the Roman See was involved in during the tenth and eleventh centuries. He remained in Italy till the next year (1014), when the victorious Pope rewarded him with the imperial crown."

A regency was set up at home under Harald, and in July of 1013, Svend sailed with a powerful fleet to England. The Monk of St. Omer describes its magnificent equipment—the prows of the Vikings' ships decorated with gold, silver and bronze, the ships' sides resplendent in color. "Then one could see the blue sea foam far and wide as it was whipped by countless oar-strokes, and the sun sent double rays into the air as its light was reflected from the shining metal."

After a feint on Sandwich in Kent, the fleet turned north, ran into the Humber and sailed up the Trent to Gainsborough. Svend counted on a peaceable attitude in the Danelaw and he was not disappointed. The whole country north of Watling Street submitted to him and escaped plunder. Recruits flocked in, horses and food were assembled, and late in the autumn Svend crossed the Thames at Oxford and marched down into Wessex. Oxford and the capital city of Winchester surrendered and Svend then moved toward London. Under Thorkild and Olav London defended itself successfully. Svend was too good a strategist to waste his strength beating his head against London, so he turned resolutely westward and marched on Bath, without meeting serious opposition anywhere. In Bath the English magnates assembled and submitted, and Svend again marched north to Gainsborough, where he set up winter quarters. The Anglo-Saxon Chronicle says, "All the nation accepted him as king; and later the borough-men of London submitted to him and gave hostages; for they feared that he would destroy them."

Meanwhile, King Ethelred fled from London on board the ships of Thorkild the Tall. He had previously sent Queen Emma to Normandy, probably to enlist help, and somewhat later had sent away his sons Edward and Alfred. Ethelred celebrated Christmas on the Isle of Wight,

268

then in January followed the others to Normandy where his Norman brother-in-law received him but did not proffer any assistance against Svend.

Thorkild is a character of much interest, says Freeman, "in many points resembling, on a smaller scale, his wonderful countryman Cnut." He remained faithful to King Ethelred and kept his pledge toward him. "He fought valiantly for England, and his ships for a while were the only refuge where the native king of the English could find shelter."

Thorkild and his Jomsvikings were in a difficult position after Ethelred's flight. They spent the winter at Grimsby, and then something unexpected occurred early in 1014. King Svend died on February 3, on his way from Gainsborough to Bury. He had been King of Denmark for about 30 years, and perhaps the exertion of the campaigns had been more than his heart could stand. He is supposed to have been 54 years of age, and he had never spared himself. Shortly before his death he summoned his young son Canute, who had guarded the camp and hostages at Gainsborough while Svend was on his victorious campaign, and instructed him about his plans and the secrets of the art of government, impressing upon him the necessity of linking his policy with the English Church.

By his statesmanship and abilities as military commander, Svend had carried the dynastic plans of the Jelling Kings a good stage further. "The story of Denmark's development into the formidable kingdom ruled by Svend begins in the days of his grandfather Gorm, a monarch whose achievements history has unhappily failed to chronicle, although his reputation as a mighty man has survived into saga-tradition," says Kendrick. And Steenstrup says, "King Svend was the epitome of the new age which had dawned in Denmark. He was as brave as he was enterprising. Adversity did not diminish his delight in action or hope of ultimate victory, and if he was fierce and cruel as a warrior his enemies nevertheless realized that they faced an able army commander and a strong ruler, and could understand why his own people loved him."

In England, therefore, Svend was able to obtain a large measure of voluntary submission among many sections of the people against whom he fought. At his side were able men whom he knew how to use wisely. It was also easy for him to reconcile himself with his enemies, and he was always generous and friendly toward the crowds of warriors who flocked to him.

He was a great king. Larson characterizes him thus, "Svend's virtues were of the Viking type: he was a lover of action, of conquest and of the sea. At times he was fierce, cruel and vindictive, but these passions were tempered by cunning, shrewdness, and a love for diplomatic methods that was not common among the sea-kings. He seems to have formed alliances readily, and appears even to have attracted his opponents.—His third expedition to Britain was eminently successful and when Svend died he was king not only of Denmark but also of England, and overlord of the larger part of Norway, besides."

The English did not cherish his memory. L. Weibull says, "In the Anglo-Saxon Chronicle's account, a picture is drawn in clear lines of this Nordic conqueror who, on his marches, crushed all opposition and subdued the country. The account is dispassionate and impartial, no personal judgment of Svend being expressed."

It is only later sources which enlarge upon and exaggerate the descriptions of his cruelty, which was doubtless no greater than was made necessary. His body was saved from the English, who appeared determined to seek out and dishonor his mortal remains. Some women, apparently English, rescued his corpse and brought it to Roskilde late in the summer of 1014, where it was buried in the Church of the Trinity. Harald Bluetooth also lay buried there. That the Jelling Kings, with the exception of Gorm, sought their last resting-place at Roskilde, suggests that the old seat at Hlejre was still regarded as the center of the kingdom.

Svend had raised Denmark's status abroad. Green says, "It was the aim of Swein to unite them in a great Scandinavian Empire, of which England should be the head; and this project, interrupted for a time by his death, was resumed with yet greater vigor by his son, Cnut."

The great constructive idea was to make a Danish lake of the North Sea in order to control the trade-routes in northern and western Europe, a large-area-policy which Denmark's absolute mastery at sea made possible. So absolute was this mastery that in the centuries of the Viking Period not one single naval attack was made on Denmark by the English, Germans or French.

Internally, Svend tried to put an end to the Church's dependence on the German Church and to orient ecclesiastical policy toward England. He was scarely a pious soul, but the words of hatred which Adam of Bremen ascribes to his grandson, Svend Estridsen, are only to be understood as an expression of the petty enmity which the Church

The Viking fortress Fyrkat. East Jutland.

of Bremen felt toward the man who endeavored to free Denmark of its grip.

Svend's organizing ability, as demonstrated in his great undertakings abroad, presupposes his concern in the domestic side of those undertakings—the arrangements for contributions of men and taxes, and the land policies on which they were based. It has also been supposed that the land-valuation in bol (hides) dates from Svend Forkbeard's time, though some think it may be earlier. At all events, a technically sound solution to that aspect of the business was a prerequisite for military success abroad.

As far as actual military organization is concerned, the building of ships, the equipping of large fleets, the commissariat, and the actual leadership of these Viking armies, composed as they were of bluff, sturdy desperadoes with a strong sense of freedom and pride—must have been a most remarkable achievement which, against the background of conditions at that time, can hold its own with Eisenhower's coordination of the great invasion convoys of the Allies in Africa and Normandy in 1944. The ancient Viking camps and fortresses at Trelleborg on Zealand, Aggersborg and Fyrkat in Jutland and Nonneborg on Fyn dating from

271

that time, prove that the organization of the army was not inferior to that of the navy. These fortresses have astonished a world with their amazing size, organization and precision. The ellipsoid halls, looking like ships, laying in quadrangels or radiating from the center of the circular wall, are imposing. In Trelleborg there are 16 of these great halls inside the wall, in Aggersborg 48. In Trelleborg alone 8000 great trunks of trees have been used. According to Brøndsted, "It is right and proper to describe the men who built Trelleborg as engineers, so mathematically precise were their methods of construction.–Only the king would have had the means and power to construct such large establishments." Nørlund, who found and excavated the fortress says, "It is most likely to suppose, that the king himself, Svend Forkbeard, the mighty Viking Prince, the conqueror of England, has ordered the construction of Trelleborg."

A dense and vigorous population was another prerequisite for the success of those great undertakings which of course sapped the home country of much of its best blood and enterprising youth. Many remained abroad. On the Valleberg runic stone one gets an impression of the international atmosphere of that period. The inscription in honor of the dead men ends, 'God help their souls, but they lie in London'.

CANUTE THE GREAT
"He had built an empire."
LAURENCE M. LARSON.

The Viking Period was at its zenith when Canute was a young man. Before his death he himself brought it to a close.

He began as a Viking at Jomsborg and ended as a statesman of world fame.

He had inherited the dynastic plans and imperialistic ambitions of his ancestors, and realized them. When his father died, he was a prince without a country. When he himself died he was King of Denmark, England and Norway, part of Sweden, the Slavonic coast of the Baltic from Jutland to Estonia, and in addition was suzerain over Scotland, Wales and perhaps Ireland. As King of Norway he held suzerainty over the Orkneys and Shetlands, the Hebrides, and most probably was recognized by the distant colonies in Greenland.

One of the few men to whom the world has given the title 'The Great', he was an emperor of Charlemagne's type, and in England followed in the tracks of Alfred the Great.

*

Danish horse-collar. Mammen. Jutland.

'No King came younger of years from his homeland'.

Thus sings Ottar Svarte. Canute was between sixteen and nineteen years of age when in Gainsborough the dying Svend tutored him in the secrets and arts of governing. The army immediately chose him as king, but England itself was an elective monarchy and the English nobles decided to send for King Ethelred again because, as they said, "No king was dearer to them than their natural lord—if he would but rule them better than he had done before." Thorkild the Tall seems to have played an important role among the English nobles because of his sagacity and the fighting forces he controlled, and when Ethelred returned on board the ship of Olav the Saint, he advanced northward with an army under the leadership of Thorkild.

Canute found himself in a precarious position. His elder brother Harald had inherited the throne of Denmark, and the northmen in Ireland had just suffered a heavy defeat at Clontarf, which made it difficult for Canute to obtain reinforcements for his army. He embarked all his forces and sailed southward to Sandwich with his English hostages, and there mutilated them by cutting off their noses, ears, or hands, putting them ashore afterwards. This barbarous behavior cannot be justified, albeit Canute may have considered the hostages a pledge for the security of the dynasty which, due to the deceit of the English, had incurred his wrath. It is amazing that although his relations with the English began so inauspiciously, he later became one of their most beloved kings.

Canute sailed back to Denmark, where King Harald refused to share the kingdom with him, but in other respects appears to have received him well and offered him assistance in conquering Norway. Erik Jarl's readiness at a later date to accompany Canute to England perhaps hinges on this.

Canute and Harald sailed together to Poland and brought home their mother, Queen Gunhild, whom Svend had exiled.

Preparations were actually being made to equip a fleet against England when Thorkild the Tall, with nine ships, unexpectedly landed in Denmark, seeking reconciliation with Canute. It had so happened that in England King Ethelred, who now felt himself to be safely in the saddle, considered the Jomsvikings to be both dangerous and expensive friends. Therefore, during Christmas 1014-15, he ordered his men to fall upon their garrisons in London and Slesswick, a town presumably situated in East Anglia. The men in London escaped, but the garrison at Slesswick, with Thorkild's brother Hemming at its head, was cut down to the last man.

By this fresh act of perfidy, Ethelred had tried to kill the very men who had stood by him in his days of misfortune and had helped him regain the throne. Thorkild had now another brother to revenge in England, and considered himself released from his oath of loyalty to Ethelred. He offered his services to Canute.

Canute obtained help from King Olof in Sweden and from Erik Jarl in Norway and the fleet he thus collected was immense. The sources do not agree as to its size. Encomium Emmae—which is the earliest—says 200 ships, the Jomsviking Saga 960, and Adam of Bremen, whose data come from Canute's nephew Svend Estridsen, says 1,000. The troops were selected and well-trained; only the well-born were on board and not a single serf or freed slave. Late in the summer of 1015 this magnificently equipped fleet, with its gilded dragon-heads, sailed westward to England.

At the same time another Prince sailed in the opposite direction. Olav the Stout—later the Saint—took advantage of the favorable opportunity to cross the North Sea in order to conquer Norway, the kingdom of his ancestors, where he later won the halo of glory. In the same year in which Canute conquered England, Norway slipped from his hands, and he did not regain it until 1028.

Canute landed at Sandwich. Thus sings Thord Kolbeinsson:

> Knut on the keel's way
> Rushed against kings in the country.
> He let his long ships land
> On the low banks of the sea shore.

Shortly afterward he received a reinforcement of forty ships commanded by Eadric Streona, who deserted his English king after having been in conflict with Edmund Ironside, the king's son. Eadric's story is one of a continuous series of perfidious and questionable deeds unless, in company with Rason, one hesitatingly seeks to justify his actions by supposing that he recognized the claim of the Jelling dynasty to inherit the throne of England through Tyre, Gorm's Queen. Rather a lame excuse.

Canute began by attacking southern England. It was late in the year and the English seem to have expected that he would soon go into winter-quarters. However, to everyone's surprise, and contrary to all calculations, he launched a winter campaign, quickly subduing Wessex and then, shortly after Christmas, advancing northward to the old Danish cities of Lincoln, Nottingham and York. After this Northumberland sided with him, and Erik Jarl, who meanwhile had lost his Earldom in Norway, was appointed Earl of Northumberland. Canute marched south again, journeying west of the Danish Mercia, and by Easter there actually remained only London, which Ethelred and Edmund held with their army. Ethelred, who was a sick man, died there April 23rd, 1016.

The citizens of London proclaimed Edmund Ironside as king while the remainder of the country swore allegiance to Canute at Southampton. As early as May, Canute surrounded London and had a canal dug outside the city so that his ships could sail up the river and around the walls. He then built a rampart north of the city so that is was completely encircled.

In a lay composed by one of Canute's house-carls during the siege of London, this picture of the attack is given:

> Bold and ambitious, oh young King!
> You came in a rush to the ramparts.
> Flashing brightly, your keen sword
> Clashed against British byrnies.

But Edmund slipped out before the fortifications were completed and began a stubborn resistence against Canute. He won a couple of engagements in the west against Thorkild; then Eadric Streona rejoined him and his forces increased. Canute had resolutely raised the siege of London and embarked in his ships, while Edmund defeated his rearguard at Brentford. He later defeated a section of Canute's forces which was out foraging, and the latter's position was at one time critical.

In the middle of October the armies met for the decisive battle at Ashington in Essex and here Canute gained the victory, supported as he was by a further act of treachery on the part of Eadric Streona. The Anglo-Saxon Chronicle says, 'All the flower of the English race was there destroyed'. After the battle the magnates arranged a compromise and the Kings met on the island of Olney in the Severn, near Dearhurst. They agreed to divide the country and, in the event of the death of one of them, the survivor should inherit the other's kingdom in the same way as Hardeknud in Denmark later arranged matters with the Norwegian King Magnus the Good, the son of St. Olav. Edmund got East Anglia, London and the southern provinces, while Canute received Mercia and the north country.

But as early as November the 3, King Edmund died and Canute was elected King of all England. Late sources insinuate that Canute arranged that Edmund be murdered by Eadric Streona, but no contemporary English source suggests anything of the kind, and the authorities therefore agree that Edmund died a natural death.

Canute was now England's legitimate king. "It was the hour of the greatest triumph in the whole history of the Vikings," says Kendrick. "A Danish king ruled the country and the Danish army and the Danish fleet were masters of the English lands and the English seas. There could be no rallying, no hero of this last and desperate danger to rescue England, no Athelney to shelter him. For the end had come and the victory was to the Danes."

Edmund Ironside was a brave man and had fought dauntlessly. "Edmund was victor in numerous important engagements but not in any major battle. He was an English Viking—passionate, brave, impulsive, but unruly and uncontrollable." (Larson).

Canute, on the other hand, was an army commander of a quite different type. Green says, "He was indeed a born general, as great on the battle-field as in the planning of his campaign." He sacrificed nothing

276

Edmund Ironside and Canute the Great.
(Matthew of Paris.)

in order to pose as a hero, but took care to win the final battle. Larson calls him, "one of these commanders who are not attracted by great battles. Fate had been kind to Canute; still the outcome must be chiefly ascribed to the persistent activity of the invader, and we should not forget that he was surrounded and assisted by a group of captains who probably had no superiors in Europe at that time." Thorkild the Tall seems to have been an outstanding personality. Freeman says of him, 'Thorkild is a character of much interest, in many points resembling on a smaller scale his wonderful countryman, Canute'.

*

The manner in which Canute began his reign was surprising and quite unexpected. It was common custom and practice in those days to oppress the inhabitants of a conquered country, seize their land, sell or enslave them and create a new upper class from the ranks of the conquerors. Nothing of this sort occurred. With prudent wisdom, Canute tried to frame his policy so that he not only made his position secure but at the same time won the favor of his new subjects. Kendrick says that "Canute was a prince who in respect of his achievement, in respect of wisdom, statesmanship and military genius, must take the rank as the greatest of

277

all the Vikings. He ruled until the day of his death supreme and unassailable, a dignified and beloved monarch whose reign is an honorable page in the history of the two realms he governed".

The problem he faced was really an extremely difficult one. His sole right was that which his sword had won him. He had crossed the sea as a prince without a country. His elder brother Harald had Denmark, and the opportunities which might have been his in Norway were seized by Olav. From none of these countries could he claim assistance if a rebellion should threaten his position. Yet he went to work soberly, quietly awaiting his lawful election by the Witan, duly observing all legal formalities so that he should not challenge or offend.

When the election was over, he divided the country into four large earldoms held by Erik Jarl in Northumberland, Thorkild in East Anglia, Eadric Streona in Mercia and himself in Wessex. He next formed around the throne a group of magnates linked to him by family ties. Erik Jarl was married to his sister Gyda, Ulf Jarl became the husband of his sister Estrid, and Godwin–the Anglo-Saxon–was married to Gyda, the sister of Ulf Jarl. Ulf is said to be a grandson of Styrbjørn Starke who was married to the sister of Svend Forkbeard.

Eadric Streona, who now ruled in his old Earldom of Mercia, was capable and resourceful, but neither Canute nor anyone else trusted him. It would have been politically maladroit to remove him immediately, since he was married to Ethelred's daughter. However, he was killed by Erik Jarl in the following year, together with a couple of other Anglo-Saxon notables, presumably after conspiring against the young king. The murder of Eadric, which undoubtedly occurred with Canute's consent, was very popular in England, no doubt partly because a dangerous man who was a link with the former dynasty, was thus removed.

The relationship with the former dynasty was a difficult and delicate matter. Canute's solution was to send the young sons of Edmund to Poland. One source accuses Canute of having instructed the Polish Duke to dispose of them, but presumably if this had been Canute's intention, he would have found a surer method. At all events they were not murdered. The sons of Ethelred by Emma were in Normandy and that did constitute a dynastic threat which Canute solved by marrying Queen Emma, even though she was at least ten years his senior. By forming this matrimonial tie with the former dynasty he legitimized himself to some extent in the eyes of the Anglo-Saxons, and as Emma was by birth half-

Danish she also proved acceptable in Danish eyes. He secured the friendship of Normandy and at the same time neutralized the menace constituted by the king's exiled sons. Emma was a handsome, gifted and ambitious woman and the marriage seems to have been a happy one. Emma insured in advance that her children by Canute should receive inheritance rights to the throne, to the exclusion of her issue by Ethelred, and Canute's illegitimate offspring by the Anglo-Danish Elgifa. She and her sons Harald and Svend were sent to Denmark, but despite their removal from the scene they later came to play an important role—Elgifa and Svend as co-regents in Norway and Harald Harefoot as King of England. Of the children of Emma and Canute, Hardeknud became King of Denmark and England, and Gunhild was married to the later German Emperor, Henry III.

After these dynastic chess-moves with the large pieces, Canute made a couple of bold moves with the smaller chessmen. He had the temerity to send home his army after having paid it off with a tremendous Danegeld. He retained only forty ships with their selected crews of about 3,000 to 4,000 men. With them as a nucleus, he formed a standing army—the celebrated 'Tinglid'—his impressive and magnificently equipped bodyguard of house-carls, all of a build difficult to overlook. This Tinglid had its own law, the Veder-law, which has to some extent been preserved in the records of Svend Aggesen and Saxo. The army had a fixed rate of pay and was not rewarded with landed property as were William the Conqueror's barons later on.

Canute's bodyguard of house-carls was the first standing army in England and thus, in a sense, the precursor of England's present army. Similarly, Canute's fleet was one of the most important predecessors of the Royal Navy. King Alfred had formerly endeavored to create a fleet with the aid of Frisian mercenaries, but without lasting effect, and King Ethelred's flotilla consisted principally of Thorkild's hired Danish ships. Freeman says of Canute's army, "They were in fact the germ of a standing army, an institution of which we find no sign under earlier kings, but which later kings and great earls, English as well as Danish, found it to their interest to continue." And Green says, "Now for the first time the King had an armed force ready at his call." This gave the crown stability and executive power and was the instrument with which Canute established peace and public security internally and abroad.

The security of both Canute and England was increased when his brother, King Harald of Denmark, died in 1018 and Canute became King of Denmark as well. It strengthened his position in that he could now buttress his English throne with the whole of Denmark's military power and England was no longer attacked by Viking raiders, their base now being within the kingdom and under his control.

This can be seen in the Proclamation to the English People which he issued in 1020 after having spent the winter in Denmark settling affairs there and winning over such opposition as may have existed. The Proclamation runs: "Then I was informed that a great danger threatened us, greater than was well pleasing to us; and then I myself, with the men who went with me, departed for Denmark, whence came to you the greatest danger; and that I have with God's help forestalled so that henceforward no strife shall come to you from that country, as long as you stand by me, as the law commands, and my life lasts."

The following year Thorkild was sent to Denmark as Viceroy. The English Chronicle says that he was expelled and outlawed. This must, however, be a misunderstanding. Perhaps the fact that Thorkild had married Ethelred's daughter—Eadric's widow—led Canute to deem it safest to keep him at a distance, but he did require an able ruler in Denmark, being unable to absent himself for long periods of time from his new country.

Thorkild had been Canute's right-hand man in England, for he was sagacious and able and had over many years' time acquired an intimate knowledge of English conditions. Later, the Englishman Godwin became Canute's closest collaborator. We see that Canute gradually gave the English more and more access to high positions within the army and administration and the former Nordic assistants ultimately disappeared. Thorkild was sent to Denmark, Ulf Jarl to command at Jomsborg, Ulf's brother Eglaf had to leave the country after a disagreement and took service as a Varangian with the Greek Emperor at Byzantium, and Erik Jarl died after primitive surgery for a throat complaint. After Thorkild's death, Ulf Jarl rose to the position of Viceroy in Denmark and was succeeded at Jomsborg by Svend, son of Canute and Elgifa. Eventually it was mainly native-born Englishmen who occupied important posts in the Government and Church. There are indications of the beginnings of a division into political parties; indeed, Freeman says that one can glimpse from Canute's period the political division between Whig and Tory which has been so significant throughout English history.

It is proof of Canute's genius for ruling that he was able to win over the people whom he had conquered by force of arms. Steenstrup says, "He is also the first ruler to adopt the entirely new principle of permitting countries to continue their own national development and not to rule them through foreign chieftains and officials."

Sir James Ramsay says of him, "A foreigner living among a conquered people, he threw himself on their loyalty as if he had been born one of them, a signal instance of the northman's gift of adaption. Probably no conqueror ever ruled a vanquished nation as he ruled the English."

Freeman draws attention to his character, "This gradual change in the disposition of Cnut makes him one of the most remarkable and, to an Englishman, one of the most interesting characters in history. There is no other instance—unless Rolf in Normandy be admitted as a forerunner on a smaller scale—of a barbarian conqueror entering a country simply as a ruthless pirate, plundering, burning, mutilating, slaughtering, without remorse, and then, as soon as he is firmly seated on the throne of the invaded land, changing into a beneficent ruler and lawgiver, and winning for himself a place side by side with the best and greatest of its native sovereigns."

And Thomas Hodgkin writes of him, "The transformation of character which he underwent, from the hard, unscrupulous robber chieftain to the wise, just and statesmanlike king, is one of the most marvellous things in history. Perhaps the nearest approach to it is to be found in the change wrought in the character of Octavian. Both Canute and Augustus were among the rare examples of men improved by success."

Larson says, "He understood human nature better than did most rulers of his time."

Canute's methods of ruling in England later became characteristic of English statecraft. The English sail and trade and colonize, and, if a conflict arises, get their way by force, if necessary. After the discord is settled, the English have Canute's remarkable ability for obtaining cooperation and getting things to run smoothly.

*

In 1022, accompanied by Godwin and Ulf Jarl, Canute sailed a fleet down into the Baltic in order to secure and perhaps extend his strategic positions there. First of all he organized affairs at Jomsborg—that fortress which had been founded by Harald Bluetooth—and then sailed east where he confirmed his control of Witland, the part of East Prussia east of the Vistula, and Samland, in which Königsberg lies. His dominion probably extended farther along the east coast to the Esthonian districts on the Dvina, Riga and Grobin. A series of Nordic trading colonies and naval stations lay along the coasts of the Baltic, generally situated at the mouths of rivers—Jomsborg on the Oder, Truso on the Vistula, Grobin near Libau, and Riga on the Dvina—centers whence Danish and Swedish commercial enterprise pushed into the interior along the navigable waterways.

From ancient times the Baltic had been a Nordic sphere of interest, the Swedes concentrating in the eastern Baltic, as shown by archaeological finds. The Danes, however, also operated there at an early date and Ivar Vidfadme is said to have carved out territory over which he ruled. King Gudfred's influence had reached down along the Vendic coast to Reric, in the district around Wismar, and Gorm and Harald later extended and secured that influence. Haakon, Canute's uncle, had colonized Samland.

The extension of Danish influence in the Baltic countries had brought Denmark into closer contact with the German Empire even though German influence in the Vendic lands was still insignificant and had not as yet, to any considerable extent, reached as far as the Baltic. Germany at that time was having trouble with Poland, and Larson thinks that the agreement between Canute and the Emperor Conrad, therefore, dates from these years. The Emperor made certain of Canute's friendship by the betrothal of his son to Canute's daughter and at the same time renounced his supposed rights to South Slesvig between Hedeby and the Eider.

The Baltic policy of Canute and the Jelling Dynasty was the one which the Valdemar kings later adopted in their renewed attempts to turn the Baltic into a Danish lake. At a still later date this same policy was pursued by the Swedish kings from Gustav Vasa to Charles XII, and now it is the ambition of Russia. The east-Baltic countries had been a natural trading district for Swedish commerce ever since the trading period of the Varangs and Rus. By consolidating his Baltic and North Sea empires, Canute was able to insure the safety and prosperity of the trade-routes in the great Kingdoms which he had united.

*

Stone-head of a King from a house opposite the Cathedral of Slesvig, supposed to be Canute the Great. (Poul Kürstein.)

While engaged in these matters, however, he had not forgotten his ancient claims to Norway. Strangely enough, his Norwegian policy had considerable influence upon his Church policy. Canute was first and foremost a statesman, and though he became a serious and devout Christian, he never allowed his religious feelings to cloud his clear common sense. He was no unworldly Christian, as was, for example, the Danish King Harald Hejn (1076-1080), of whom Saxo writes, "He concerned himself solely with church practices, neglected the maintenance of the Law, was ignorant of the fact that direction of a conscientious government is more gratifying to God than the empty ceremonies of superstition, and that a firm maintenance of justice pleases Him more than does excessive prayer. God is worshipped better with laws than with incense."

The Danelaw and the Nordic countries were predominantly heathen, while the Anglo-Saxon districts were Christian. Canute therefore had to conduct his Church policy with care, in order to insure the strong support of the Church without driving the Nordic territories into a policy of opposition, the danger of which was to be seen in the fate of his grandfather, Harald.

In Norway, which King Olav the Stout converted by force, both the

283

adherents of the old faith and those notables who had been disturbed by Olav's power-policy were people on whom Canute would rely politically. In the first years of his reign, therefore, he tried to secure the support of the Church by magnificent gifts, by building churches, and by showing the clergy all due respect and consideration, but postponed his great ecclesiastical legislation until he had solidified his rule in Norway.

Olav's influence was not limited to Norway alone. All the Norse colonies in Orkney, the Shetlands, the Hebrides and Ireland and also the Norwegian elements in Scotland, could ultimately jeopardize the flank of Canute's English possessions–a weapon which Olav sought to utilize by ostensibly supporting the Scottish Kings in their opposition to Canute.

At first Canute's relations with the Church were in the nature of an entente, only gradually developing into an alliance. That he occasionally sought to use the Church for political purposes was perhaps not a strictly Christian approach, but when one recalls that the Catholic Church itself was well-versed in the art of using the power of the State in its worldly affairs and was often to be found on the side of the strongest, one can hardly object to Canute's conduct.

In Norway Canute tried to bind to him all the powerful but dissatisfied chieftains and did not hesitate to make use of money for this purpose. At all events, no less than 1,500 coins dating from the time of Canute and Ethelred were found close to the house that belonged to Erling Skjalgson of Sole, his strongest supporter. The scaldic verses also hint at this practice.

In 1024 Canute drove a sharp wedge into the Norwegian policy by despatching emissaries to King Olav asserting his claim to Norway, but in such a manner that he offered Olav the country in fief from him. Olav's violent and undiplomatic answer caused him to appear as the author of the troubles that ensued, for he replied, 'Things have now gone so far that Canute rules Denmark and England, and also parts of Scotland. Now he lays claim to my hereditary Kingdom. He should, at length, learn to put a limit to his greed. Which, I wonder, does he think is the easier–to be Emperor over all the north or to eat all the cabbage that grows in England?' At that time it was believed that eating cabbage made one stupid, so the answer was not without its sting.

As a consequence, in 1025 Canute visited Denmark, where he left his

284

Canute the Great's coin with the inscription:
"CNUT REX SV." Coined in Sigtuna, Sweden,
by the mintmaster of the Swedish
King Anund Jacob: "THORMOD ON SIHT."

son Hardeknud under Ulf Jarl's guardianship. He did not launch an attack however, but sailed back to England in 1026, for Olav had in the meantime persuaded Anund Jacob, the King of Sweden, that a Norway in Canute's hands would threaten Sweden's independence, and Olav and Anund therefore had formed a defensive alliance against Canute. Probably Canute hoped to dissolve the alliance and to win over Anund Jacob and Sweden, while perceiving that the time was not ripe in Norway.

Olav's and Anund Jacob's coalition gained confidence from this, and after Canute's departure they changed their agreement into an offensive alliance. It looks as though they tried to draw Ulf Jarl into their schemes, perhaps with some measure of success, for he, without Canute's consent, had the young Hardeknud proclaimed eventual king at a meeting in Viborg in Jutland. This is said to have occurred with the knowledge of Queen Emma, who was interested in promoting her son's cause at the expense of Canute's illegitimate children. Ulf Jarl gave as the motive for this step that the kingdom required a rallying-point in the tense situation then existing. It is also said that Ulf encouraged Olav and Anund Jacob to make the attack on eastern Denmark which followed. The two kings advanced into the country and occupied Zealand, while Ulf retreated to Jutland.

There seems to have been something fishy about the whole affair and in 1026, when Canute came sailing from England with his fleet into the Limfjord, the young Hardeknud had to beg forgiveness on bended knee. Ulf Jarl received curt directions to collect his forces and mind his own business.

The Norwegian-Swedish fleet lay at Helgeaa (Holy River) and there, after blockading the Sound, Canute sought it out. King Olav, a good engineer, had constructed dams on the lakes higher up the river which he caused to be breached at the crucial moment so that the flood waters, filled with drifting timber, suddenly swirled down, bringing confusion to Canute's fleet. This piece of strategy partly succeeded and Canute's mighty long-boat was for a moment in a critical situation from which Ulf Jarl is said to have rescued him.

In his Saga of Olav the Saint, Snorre describes the battle as a defeat for Canute, but several things suggest that this was not so. First, Ottar Svarte's Lay to Canute says:

> War-king bold in battle,
> Hard by Holy River
> You routed the Swedes and shook them.
> The she-wolf shall not starve.

Secondly, as a result of the outcome of the battle, Olav had to let his ships remain lying at Kalmar and himself march home overland to Norway—surely an unusual home-coming for a victor of a naval engagement. Thirdly, Canute shortly afterwards made a journey to Rome. It is hardly likely that he could have immediately left the north in the critical situation inevitably following upon a defeat. And finally, in his proclamation to the English People, despatched directly after his journey to Rome, Canute calls himself, 'King of all England, Denmark, Norway and parts of Sweden', and mentions a battle that had just taken place in which he destroyed the forces of his enemies.

There is a certain amount of mystery about a coin which was struck by Thormod of Sigtuna, the mint-master of the Swedish King Anund Jacob. It bears the inscription: 'Cnut Rex Sv', and the name of the mint-master: 'Thormod on Sith' i.e., Sigtuna in Sweden. The theory has been propounded that the words Rex Sv. might denote 'King of the Slavs' and not of the Swedes, but this is disproved by the fact that it was struck by the Swedish King's mint-master, and that in his letter from Rome, Canute calls himself 'King over parts of Sweden'. One is therefore justified in supposing that a part of Sweden had been ceded to Canute.

Around 900 A.D. Wulfstan told King Alfred the Great that Blekinge belonged to Sweden. This is written in his translation of Orosius. In 1050 the Västgöta Law states that Blekinge belonged to Denmark. Inasmuch as Helgeaa (Holy River) lies near the boundary between Blekinge and Skaane, and no other occasion is known on which Blekinge could have been Danish, it is permissible to suppose that perhaps Blekinge passed from Sweden to Canute after the Battle of Helgeaa. To this can be added the fact that the ancient Danish lev-towns do not exist in Blekinge.

Gudmundson holds the opinion that it was the newly won Väst-Göta-land that had to be ceded to Denmark.

The Swedish Professor Sture Bolin declares unreservedly, "Anund Jacob and Olav were driven off and Canute was left as victor. The Battle of Helgeaa had far reaching consequences. After the battle, Canute regarded himself as lord of Norway and called himself its King, though St. Olav was not driven out of Norway until 1028. Furthermore, Canute adopted the title 'King over parts of Sweden'. It was probably not without reason that a mint-master who worked for Anund Jacob in Sigtuna, struck coins on which–at the same place, as far as one can judge–Canute was called King of the Swedes. But Canute's rule in Sweden probably did not last long."

In a lecture in 1949, Dr. Adolf Schück suggested that the battle did not take place in Helgeaa in Skaane but in Heligaa, east of Sigtuna and Uppsala. Saxo relates that King Anund Jacob was beaten in a battle at Stangberg, and a town by the name of Staangberga is situated just east of Heligaa. This Heligaa must have been of great strategical importance, so near the Swedish capital. Canute's coin, struck in nearby Sigtuna, fits in well with this location. The Sjørup and Hällestad runic inscriptions which mention a battle near Uppsala, are connected with Canute, and not Styrbjørn Starke of fifty years earlier, according to Dr. Schück. This is supported by Dr. Lis Jacobsen's runological investigations. Twenty years later the Danish King Svend Estridsen–Canute's nephew–in his war against Norway, received help from the Swedish King Edmund Slema–the brother of Anund Jacob. Svend Estridsen was obliged then to repay with land, those districts won by Canute after the battle of Holy River.

After the battle, Canute played a famous game of chess with Ulf Jarl at Roskilde. Canute enjoyed playing chess, as statesmen of his stature often do. Through a bad move he was about to lose a knight and asked permission to retract his move, but Ulf Jarl, enraged, upset the whole board and rose to leave in anger. 'Are you running away now Ulf, you craven?' asked the King. The Jarl turned at the door and answered, 'You would have run farther at Helgeaa had you been able to, and you did not then call me Ulf Craven when the Swedes were beating you like dogs until I came to your help'.

The following morning Canute had the angry Earl cut down in church. That he suspected him of being a traitor seems certain, and Saxo says outright that he was. Ulf was an ambitious man to whom obedience did not come easily. It is possible that he was a traitor, indeed, it is probable, though not certain. The fact that afterwards, Ulf's son Svend Estridsen sought refuge in Sweden for twelve years, might suggest that more than a momentary passion had driven Canute to the murder of his brother-in-law.

Ulf's being murdered in church might easily have compromised Canute's relations with ecclesiastical authorities. He therefore placated Roskilde Church with considerable gifts, after which he went on a pilgrimage to Rome in 1027. This journey was no doubt more than an expression of piety and penitence, King Olav's zeal for the cause of Christianity being so highly appreciated in Rome that Canute's conquest of Norway might result in complications with the Papal See. He consequently felt it wise to discuss matters beforehand. It would also be reasonable to assure himself of the German Emperor's neutrality before his final attack on Norway.

The Emperor's enthronement happened to take place while Canute was in Rome, many great rulers being present at the coronation in the Cathedral of St. Peter on Easter Sunday. Next to the Emperor walked Canute and King Rudolf of Burgundy. The Roman Church had begun to reckon with the great power of the young blond King who was now, next to the Emperor, the most formidable potentate in Europe.

After returning to Denmark he sent his celebrated message to the English people. Such public proclamations were something hitherto unknown in England, and Green calls them, "memorable as the first personal address of an English King to Englishmen." Elsewhere he says, "Cnut's letter from Rome to his English subjects marks the grandeur of his character and the noble conception he had formed of kingship."

Canute writes, *inter alia,* "I have vowed to God to lead a righteous life in all things, to rule my realms and subjects justly and piously, and to administer just judgment to all. If heretofore I have done aught beyond what was just, through headiness or negligence of youth, I am ready, with God's help, to amend it utterly. No royal officer, either for fear of the King or for favor of any, is to consent to injustice in my realms; and if they would value my friendship and their own well-being, they are not to do wrong to rich or poor, but all men, noble or common, shall enjoy a just law, from which they must in no way depart, neither for favor nor pressure from any lord, nor for the sake of gathering money for me, for I have no need that money be heaped together for me by unjust demands."

This is a 'Speech from the Throne', a 'Government Program', the grandeur of which no ruler has yet surpassed. Liebermann calls it 'a forerunner of Magna Carta', and in spirit it is a worthy predecessor of the famous introduction to the Danish King Valdemar's "Jutish Law."

*

When Canute returned to Denmark he did not commence hostilities against Olav in Norway, but first sailed back to England, news of trouble in the north with Scotland apparently necessitating this journey, for as of 1027, King Malcolm of Scotland had to pay him homage as suzerain, and the Macbeth of Shakespeare–who was Earl of Moray, also had to submit to him. Perhaps Olav had a hand in the Scottish disturbances. It looks as though the Irish king in Dublin also had to pledge allegiance to Canute, so one may surmise that we have here the very first attempt to unite the whole of Great Britain and Ireland.

But Norway was not forgotten, and in the following year Canute was ready to strike. With fifty ships he sailed to the Limfjord, where an immense Danish fleet had been assembled, and proceeded northward with his united forces. The Sagas say that the fleet consisted of 1,440 ships. So powerful was this armada, and so well-prepared was everything both diplomatically and militarily, that not a single hand was raised to support Olav, who fled across the mountains to Sweden.

Canute received allegiance all the way up along the Norwegian coast. Steenstrup says, "If a military expedition be justified when nobody in the country under attack dares to take up arms in its defence, and when the notables and the common people immediately desert their king and voluntarily give allegiance to the new Prince, then King Canute's military adventure in Norway was of that nature. As when the Danish Kings took possession of England, everything was ripe and ready for a change of monarch; the people longed for a balanced and just rule."

Godwin was present in Norway and lost one of his men there, for on a runic stone is a memorial to Bjor 'who met his death in Godwin's army in the days when Canute sailed to England'. Ultimately Canute received homage as King of Norway in Nidaros, and here in 1028 was held what Larson calls 'the first imperial assembly'.

Two years later, in 1030, when Olav tried to recover his kingdom, he fell in the Battle of Stiklestad against the peasants' army. In popular fancy, and with the assistance of the Church, he rapidly became a saint, and a figure in Nordic popular belief standing somewhere between Thor and St. Michael—in spite of all Elgifa's sound arguments. She and her son Svend had been appointed by Canute as co-regents in Norway and she bravely countered the pleadings of the bishops for Olav's holiness, no doubt envisaging the political consequences that would follow his canonization.

*

Canute now stood at the zenith of his power. Freeman says, "The good fortune of Cnut had raised him up an Empire in Northern Europe to which there was no parallel before or after him.

"Cnut, King of five, or as some reckon, six Kingdoms, seems to have looked upon himself as Emperor of the North, and to have held himself as in all respects the peer of his Roman brother."

Larson says, "When the eleventh century began its fourth decade, Canute, was with the single exception of the Emperor, the most imposing ruler in Latin Christendom. Less than twenty years earlier he had been a landless pirate striving to dislodge an ancient and honoured dynasty; now he was lord of four important realms and the overlord of other kingdoms. Though technically Canute was counted among the kings, his position among his fellowmonarchs was truly imperial. Apparently he held in his hands the destinies of two great regions: the British Isles and the Scandinavian peninsulas. His fleet all but controlled two important seas, the North and the Baltic. He had built an Empire."

In spite of all this, not one single respectable monograph on Canute the Great has been published in England or Denmark. One has to cross the Atlantic to find such a book, "Canute the Great and the Rise of Danish Imperialism," by Professor Laurence M. Larson. Yet English and American historians unanimously regard "The Great Dane" with admiration. In Denmark Arup has made the following estimation, "Of more importance for Denmark than the conquest of the whole of England, was the fact that about the year 1,000 the population on the shores of the Sound began catching herrings in considerable quantities."

Even though it must be admitted that the tokens left by Canute were more lasting in England than in Denmark, his conquest of England was nevertheless of great importance to Denmark also, in the spheres of

Gilded bronze horse from a weather-vane on a Viking ship. Probably the only fragment that remains of the fleets from the time of Canute.

commerce, Church and finance. He threw open the north to the Christian culture of the west, pacified conditions in Denmark, put a brake on the influence of the German Church of Bremen, and instituted a controlled Danish monetary system. Surely the traces left in other countries by Denmark during Canute's reign also form a part of the history of Denmark.

The maritime, commercial, and national-political ideas in Canute's policy were sound and constructive. If he had been granted time to consolidate what he had created, the history of the world would have been different, and probably happier. He was a young man and, according to the laws of Nature, should have ruled for another thirty years. With his skillful mastery of diplomatic methods he would have accomplished great things in consolidating his possessions. But instead of thirty years he had just six allotted him, and in that short time could not succeed in binding the countries together and effecting a fusion. That the Empire disintegrated after his death is not surprising; indeed, the wonder is that it was ever built up. And yet the ethnic qualifications were present, created by former emigrations and geo-political factors. Moreover they are still present, and in other forms Canute the Great's idea may yet again be adopted as a considered policy; in some ways The North Atlantic Pact and Partnership reflects a further evolution of Canute's ideas.

*

Canute maintained diplomatic relations with most European countries. There was peace with Normandy for a long period, until Robert le Diable began to interest himself in the hereditary claims of the exiled sons of Ethelred. It is said that Canute then arranged a marriage between Robert and his sister Estrid, the widow of Ulf Jarl. But Estrid, though intelligent, was no beauty. Robert cast her off and the situation was very tense for a while until Robert became occupied with affairs on the Continent.

Canute kept peace with the German Emperor and it is probable that the Emperor's difficulties with Poland caused him to place such value on Canute's friendship that he signed away his supposed rights to the strip of Slesvig territory north of the Eider. Canute's domain along the Baltic coast can hardly have been a source of pleasure to the Emperor, but he was in no position to alter the *status quo*.

Even though Canute appointed English, Norman and Frisian bishops to Denmark, he did not consider it safe to break with the Church of Bremen, for his vast Slavonic sphere of interest lay within its diocese. The Church of Bremen therefore succeeded in retaining its ecclesiastical supremacy. Canute did not draft his great canonical laws in England until Norway had finally been conquered.

> Merry sungen the monkës in Ely
> When Cnut King rowed thereby.
> Row, cnichts, near the land
> And hear we these monkës sing.

Thus runs a little song which King Canute improvised while rowing near the monastery of Ely. His *entente cordiale* with the Church was transformed into an active alliance.

Canute says, in an edict which throws a clear light upon the practices of heathendom, "We absolutely forbid all heathenism. Heathenism is the worship of heathen gods, of sun and moon, fire and flood, spring or stone, or of any kind of forest trees whatsoever, or the conjuring up of magic, or any commission of murderous deed, or having anything to do with sacrifices or casting of lots or similar delusions."

In secular affairs Canute's legislative accomplishments were impressive. He caused the old laws from King Edward's time to be collected, edited and redrafted. But, as Larson says, "The Laws of Edward that the Norman kings swore to maintain were in reality the laws of Canute; for when the Anglo-Norman lawyers of the early twelfth century began to investigate the subject of Old English law, they found its most satisfactory statement in the legislation of the mighty Dane. So great was the Danish King's reputation as a lawmaker in the twelfth century that he was even credited with enactments and institutional experiments with which he never had any connection."

Thomas Hodgkin says, "Danish Canute, on the other hand, holds an honourable place in our legal history; for his Dooms, which fill one hundred pages in Liebermann's volume, show somewhat of the instinct of a codifier as well as a genuine desire to dispense equal justice to the Danish and the English inhabitants of the land."

Trading in slaves was forbidden and piracy was stopped. The Nordic conception of justice which had flourished in Scandinavian England for a long time was now formally recognized as being a part of the Kingdom's legal system, and with Nordic legislation a fresh interpretation of personal honor and a new expression for dishonorable actions–the word 'nidding' (scoundrel)–made their way into English life. Freeman says, "In one point the legislation of The Great Dane is distinctly more rational than the legislation of our own day." Every man had the right to hunt on his own land: "And I will that every man be entitled to his hunting in wood and in field on his own possessions and let every one forego my hunting." "As an English King he fairly ranks beside the noblest of his predecessors. His best epitaph is his famous letter to his people on his Roman pilgrimage.–The tone of the letter is that of an absent father writing to his children.–The same spirit reigns in the opening of his laws," says Freeman.

In Canute's laws we find the following: "Many a powerful man will, if he can and may, defend his man in whatever way it seems to him the more easy to defend him, whether as freeman or as serf. But we will not suffer that injustice." Larson says, "The principle of equality before the law is distinctly stated; the magnates were to have no unusual privileges in the courts of justice."

"Having won Kingship over the English by force of arms, he put them on a real equality with the Danes, and was loved by all his subjects alike," says Trevelyan.

Canute believed in a strong and well-ordered administration and built its foundation by improving the old form of land-value taxation in the Danelaw which had been in existence since the time of the sons of Lodbrog. Strangely enough, the Danegeld which the Viking kings had levied was charged as a land-tax. This Danegeld was remodelled by Svend and Canute into a permanent and national system of land-value taxation.

Concerning the Danegeld and William the Conqueror's great land valuation of 1086, the Domesday Book, Trevelyan says, "The sums extorted from the peasantry were ruinous, and hastened the decline of the freeholder into the serf. The Danegeld holds indeed a great place in our social, financial and administrative history. Direct taxation began in this ignominious form. Under the weak Ethelred it was the normal way of buying off the Danes. Under the strong Canute it became a war tax for the defence of the realm. Under William the Conqueror its levy was regarded as so important a source of revenue that the first great inquisition into landed property was with this end in view. Domesday Book was originally drawn up for the purpose of teaching the State how to levy Danegeld."

Green says, "They were in fact the first forms of that land-tax which constituted the most important element in the national revenue, from the days of Ethelred to the days of the Georges. As a national tax levied by the Witan of all England, this tax practically brought home the national idea as it had never been brought home before.

"The establishment of a land-tax had been attributed in popular fancy to the need of paying Danish tribute, as its name of Danegeld shows. But its continuance from this moment, whether Danes were in the land or not, shows that the need of meeting their demands had only forced to the front a financial measure which had become inevitable, and which was necessarily carried on under Ethelred's successors. The land-tax thus imposed formed the chief resource of the crown till the time of the Angevins; and though the taxation of personality was introduced by Henry II, the land-tax still remained the main basis of English finance till the beginning of the eighteenth century. Its direct effects from the first in furnishing the crown with a large and continuous revenue gave a new strength to the monarchy, while its universal levy on every hide in the realm must have strengthened the national feeling.

"To these two main bases of the royal power, a permanent administration and a fixed revenue, Cnut added a third even more directly important engine of government in the institution of the hus-carls. Now for the first time the King had an armed force ready at his call."

In a speech in the House of Commons on December 17 1845, Richard Cobden, the famous free-trader, gives this historical Survey, "The only peculiar State burden borne by the land was the Land Tax: For a period of 150 years after the Norman Conquest the whole of the revenue of the country was derived from the land. During the next 150 years it yielded nineteen-twentieths of the revenue. For the next century down to the reign of Richard III it was nine-tenths. During the next seventy years to the time of Mary it fell to about three-fourths. From that time to the end of the Commonwealth, land appeared to have yielded one-half of the revenue. Down to the reign of Anne it was one-fourth."

We know very little about taxation matters in Denmark at the time of Canute. But the well-developed land-valuation and taxation systems which we see a century later in the laws of the Valdemar-Kings were, as far as we can tell, founded on ancient tradition and custom, and it was this ancient Danish system that had been taken across to England in the time of Regner Lodbrog's sons and later during the reigns of Svend and Canute.

Snorre Sturlason relates of Harald Fairhair in Norway, "Wherever King Harald conquered land for his kingdom he asserted his right to appropriate all Odel land and compelled the peasants, both wealthy and poor, to pay him land-tax."

Harald Fairhair was in close touch with the Danish Royal House. He himself was married to Ragnhild, a Danish princess, and his son Erik Bloodaxe to Gunhild, Gorm's daughter. Shetelig says of Harald, "He levied tax on those he had subjected by the right of conquest, just as the Danish King Gudfred had done at the beginning of the 9th century. Considering Vestfold's relations to Denmark it may well be that this served as a model for Harald's rule. At all events it forms one of the most important features in the union of the kingdom, and it can be said that a universal tax to the King was the first step in the creation of Norway as a State."

It seems justifiable to suppose that the foundation for King Gudfred's military system around 800 A.D., when with his powerful fleet he brought Charlemagne to a standstill, must have been a sound land-system. When one considers the land policy of the sons of Lodbrog in England, the traces of the assessment classification in the provinces east of Oslo Fjord, and the whole arrangement of the recruiting policy in Denmark as we later encounter it, it is obvious that all indications point the same way.

*

The two main factors in creative work are Nature and Man. The purpose af trade is to carry the raw materials from where they are found to where they can be worked, and to transport the finished goods from where they are produced to where they can be used. In Canute's day, commerce prospered and advanced greatly because of the peace and public security he guaranteed and the coalition of the great kingdoms which he endeavored to bind together with the common interests of trade and shipping.

Sir Charles Oman says, "Certainly he left behind him not the dilapidated realm that he had taken over from Edmund Ironside, but a flourishing and well-administered state. The rapidity with which the traces of the disasters of Ethelred's reign were removed is surprising. Probably no small part in the recovery was due to the fact that Cnut had given his English subjects the opportunity of peaceful trade with the whole of his broad dominions. Not only the North Sea but the Baltic was opened to them, while in his later years he was keeping good peace in both by his complete naval supremacy."

The north had held this supremacy for centuries. It was so absolute that we do not hear of an attack on the north being even contemplated by countries which were at odds with the Vikings. As long as Canute 'ruled the waves' the mastery of the seas was closely linked with the advancement of trade. He guarded the seas well and in 1018 smashed the Vikings in a major raid upon England—one of the last that occurred.

296

Canute the Great and Queen Emma presenting the golden cross to New Minster in Winchester in 1019 after the Queen's giving birth to Hardeknud, the heir to the throne, and before the King's expedition to Denmark to take over his father's kingdom after the death of his brother Harald.
The Winchester Manuscript.

"Commerce and trade were promoted by the justice and policy of the foreign kings", says Green "and with their advance rose the political importance of the trader. The boroughs of England, which at the opening of this period were for the most part mere villages, were rich enough at its close to buy liberty from the crown. Rights of self-government, of free speech, of common deliberation, which had passed from the people at large into the hands of its nobles, revived in the charters and councils of the towns. A moral revival followed hard on this political development. The old mental stagnation was broken up, and art and literature covered England with great buildings and busy schools. Time for this varied progress was gained by the long peace which England owed to the firm government of her Kings, while their political ability gave her

297

administrative order, and their judicial reforms built up the fabric of her law. In a word, it is to the stern discipline of these two hundred years that we owe not merely English wealth and English freedom, but England itself. The first of our foreign masters was the Dane."

Stenton says of Canute's efficient government that "it was so successful that contemporaries found little to say about it." Larson writes of him, "To England Canute brought the blessings of good government. For nearly twenty years England had peace. Furthermore, as the dominant ruler of the northern shores, as the ally of the Emperor and the friend of the Norman duke, he was able to close fairly effectually the Baltic, the North and the Irish Seas, together with the English Channel, to Viking fleets. So far as his dominions extended, Viking practices were outlawed. The check that the movement received in 1018 was the beginning of a rapid decline in its strength, and before the close of Canute's reign the profession of the sea-king was practically destroyed."

As Collingwood says of Canute, "He gave justice, peace and well-being such as England had not known for a generation."

Canute's grand political scheme was simply to control the trade-routes in northern Europe and cover both the Baltic and North Sea areas with Denmark as the center. That Canute spent most of his time in England was a political necessity, for he could not leave the recently conquered kingdom to others. No one but he could have tranquillized and won it over to himself. "Denmark was after all the central Kingdom," says Larson.

At that time England did not occupy the pivotal position in world commerce that she does now, trade-routes then following mainly along the coasts and rivers. Only after the invention of the compass, the opening of the Mediterranean to traffic, and Columbus' re-discovery of America, did England obtain that central position which the sea–going habits introduced to her culture by the Danes, permitted her to turn to account. When the hour came England was prepared.

Weinbaum says, "For a time there came into existence a Danish-English empire which controlled almost the whole of the North Sea and Baltic areas. Under Canute, England was a component part of a Nordic kingdom and was woven into the net of the greater Danish trade connections."

The improvement in trade increased the growth of English cities. Freeman says, "Some accounts tell us, doubtless with great exaggeration,

298

that London had now become almost a Danish city. But it is certain that the Danish element in the city was numerous and powerful." Trevelyan continues, "The accession of Canute, though so stoutly contested by the Londoners, was a blessing for them in disguise. Commerce between his English and Baltic dominions grew very large, when piracy was put down on the North Sea and the ports on both sides were opened to mutual trade. The Danish merchants became the leading citizens in London, as they had long been in York and the towns of the Danelaw. In the Eleventh Century the Danish 'lithsmen' and 'butsecarles' of London took the lead in transmarine trade, in the naval defence of the island, and in disputes over the succession to the Throne. Many of them at first were heathen but St. Clement Danes and dedications of City churches to St. Olaf tell the tale of their conversion. London regained the place she had first acquired under the Romans as the chief emporium of North European commerce."

"Wessex was no longer the chosen dominion, Winchester was no longer the chosen capital of an Emperor of the North, whose name was dreaded on the Baltic and revered on the Tiber" (Freeman).

"One of the most important results of the long peace under Cnut and the new connexion with the Scandinavian countries which was brought about by his rule, was the development of English trade and commerce." (Green).

The commodities traded were, as an old-English dialogue had it, "furs, silks, costly gems and gold, besides various garments, pigment, wine, oil and ivory with brass, and copper, and tin, silver and glass, and such like." In addition, according to Green, there were ropes and ship masts; and above all "the iron and steel that Scandinavian lands so long supplied to Britain."

It is strange to reflect that at that time the north exported considerable iron to England. It was the utilization of bog-ore in the marshes and streams that formed the basis for its production. Owing to the substantial amount of firewood that this necessitated, the north lost most of its forests and the denuded areas provided space for fresh cultivation. The forests of Jutland and west Norway were the most affected. Brøgger says of this, "The main reason for the extraction of iron-ore was the immense consumption of iron in the times of the Vikings and the petty kingdoms; we get an impression of it in the grave finds and isolated finds. These alone show that the use of iron between the 6th and 7th centuries and the late Middle Ages was on such a scale as to be quite fantastic."

In addition to all these commodities, Denmark exported to Italy the long, blonde braids of its young girls, it being a vogue among Venetian and Roman ladies to have fair hair.

Green says about London, "Under Cnut it became not only the commercial but the military center of the kingdom, and soon rose to be its political center as well.—London was no less fitted by position to become the center of the great Empire which Cnut was building up on either shore of the North Sea."

Sir Charles Oman says, "No doubt the bulk of this trade was conducted by Danes or Anglo-Danes; but it is not merely the carrier who is enriched by commerce; the merchant, the middle-man and the producer all make their profit, when trade develops and grows prosperous. The immense quantity of Cnut's silver pennies that survive bear witness to active trade; they are as common as those of Aethelred, though his reign was half as long." Ethelred's coins were struck for tribute, Canute's for trade.

The coins of Canute are exceedingly numerous. Actually, nearly 400 variations of the names of his mint-masters are known, and more places of mintage are mentioned than on the coins of any other English king. The question of exchange rates in the north caused no confusion in Canute's days; he unified the currency of all his countries on the basis of the mark, which had up to then been in use only in the Danelaw. He then stamped coins with a ratio of 240 pennies to the mark. And like Canute, the British still persistently and perhaps wisely refrain from adopting the decimal system of coinage and continue to use Canute's standard of 240 pence to the pound.

Worsaae wrote in his time, "Until well into the Middle Ages, Danish traders in England—probably as a relic of the time of Danish rule—continued to enjoy peculiar privileges in preference to Norwegian, German and other foreign merchants. In London, for instance, the Danes had not only the right to remain along with their merchandise at any time of the year, but they were also permitted to travel at will to markets all over England with the same freedom and privileges as the City's own citizens, whereas the German and Norwegian merchants were restricted to the actual City, without being able to sell in markets outside its walls." Green adds, "But Danes and Norwegians were traders over a yet wider

The London runic stone. About 1020-1040. Guildhall Museum.
"Ginne had this stone laid down tagether with Toke –"

field than the northern seas; their barks entered the Mediterranean while
the overland route through Russia brought the wares of Constantinople
and the East."

Nordic trade was widespread and Olrik says that at the close of the
Viking Period their market-towns had sprung up along all the coasts of
northern Europe from Novgorod to Bristol, Limerick and Dublin. The
Atlantic Ocean, the North Sea and the Baltic, which had previously lain
deserted, were drawn into world commerce. Down the ages, Nordic
merchant-families living in the harbor towns were among the first to lay
the foundations for England's future greatness on the seas.

301

A good insight into Nordic commercial morality is obtained in the following passage from 'Konongs skuggsja' (The Mirror of Kings), wherein the father says to his son, 'On returning to your lodgings, examine your wares lest they suffer damage after coming into your hands. If they are found to be injured and you are about to dispose of them, do not conceal the flaws from the purchaser; show him the defects and make whatever bargain you can; then you cannot be called a deceiver. Also, put a good price on your wares, though not too high, and yet near what you see can be obtained; then you cannot be called underhanded'. These are indeed good business ethics to this very day.

*

In the Knytlingesaga a sketch is given of Canute's appearance: "Canute was tall and very strong, a truly handsome man except for the fact that his nose was pinched, long and slightly crooked. He had beautiful long, fair hair, and eyes that were brighter and keener than those of most people. He was bountiful, a great warrior, valiant and triumphant, and a man of fortune in all that concerned might and power."

He possessed that combination of assurance and humility which is called dignity. Once in London, when the scaldic poet Thoraren Lovtunge wished to recite a lay for him, he found the King at table engrossed in discussion. He asked the King hesitantly if he wished to listen to his lay, saying, "It consists of only a few verses!" The King then turned to him and answered, "None before you has ventured to compose a mere ditty about me!"

When Canute died at Shaftesbury on the 12th of November 1035, he was still in his thirties. They died young in those days, and his children passed away at still earlier ages. His son Svend Alfifasøn in Norway died a few months later, in 1036. His daughter Gunhild died in Germany in 1038. King Harald Harefoot in 1040, and King Hardeknud in 1042. None of his sons could be compared to him in any way nor did they do honor to his name, and the Empire fell apart. In Norway, Magnus the Good, the son of Olav the Saint, became King, and in accordance with his agreement with Hardeknud, ascended the throne of Denmark after the latter's death, ruling from 1042 to 1045. In England, Edward the Confessor, the son of Ethelred, came to the throne after the death of Hardeknud in 1042. It was he who prepared the way for the Norman-

French Conquest in 1066, when the successors of the Danish Rollo invaded England.

Canute was a fortunate man. Sir Thomas Kendrick says, "In the twenty years that followed the crowning of Cnut, England, though sunk to the status of a mere province in an Anglo-Scandinavian kingdom, enjoyed a peace and prosperity such as she had not known since the days of mighty Æthelstan and Edward the Elder. For the Dane, suddenly altered from a young barbarian pirate into a dignified and benevolent monarch, loved much in the country that he had won, and, taking up his abode at royal Winchester, by his piety and statesmanship, by his careful and well-intentioned government, made of Danish tyranny a blessing in all respects preferable to a sickly independence under weakling Saxons such as Ethelred."

One cannot help wondering what would have happened if Denmark had not lost Canute and so England. The hand that held the kingdoms together was no more there. "Empires like those of Alexander, Charles or Cnut are in their own nature ephemeral. As united dominions, swayed by a single will, they last as long as there is an Alexander or a Charles at their head; they fall to pieces as soon as the sceptre of the great conqueror passes into weaker hands. So it was with the Anglo-Scandinavian Empire of the Great Cnut." (Freeman).

"The reign of Cnut, as far as the internal state of England is concerned, was a time of perfect peace. No foreign invasion, no revolt, no civil war, is recorded during the eighteen years of his government. We read of no district being ravaged either by rebels or by royal command; we read of no city undergoing or even being threatened with military chastisement. But a period of eighteen years in which we cannot see that a sword was drawn within the borders of England was something altogether unparalleled in those warlike ages, something which speaks volumes in favour of the King who bestowed such a blessing on our land. A great deal is proved by the absence of any recorded attempt on the part of any Englishman to get rid of the foreign King." (Freeman).

"Cnut's greatest gift to his people was that of peace. With him began the long internal tranquillity which was from this time to be the special note of our national history. During two hundred years, with the one terrible interval of the Norman Conquest, and the disturbance under Stephen, England, alone among the kingdoms of Europe, enjoyed unbroken repose. The absence of internal discontent under Cnut, perhaps too the exhaustion of the kingdom after the terrible Danish inroads, is proved by its quiet during his periods of absence. Everything witnesses to the growing wealth and prosperity of the country." (Green).

*

Canute's great Empire fell apart after his death, notwithstanding the grand political scheme which lay behind it, and despite the national and racial conditions that existed. The reason lay partly in the great distances of the outlying parts of the kingdom and the relative smallness of Denmark, partly in the fewness of the years left him in which to consolidate what he had conquered and train a successor, and also in the mediocrity and short lives of his heirs.

Trevelyan says as follows, "In the Eleventh Century it was difficult to hold together an Empire astride of the North Sea, as it was difficult in the Eighteenth Century to hold together an Empire astride of the Atlantic.

"Scandinavia and England, after being closely associated in hatred and in friendship for several centuries, drifted far apart, when England was drawn by the Normans into the orbit of France. Instead of remaining a maritime and Nordic State in touch with Scandinavia and only slightly connected with the main body of Europe, England became for many generations almost a part of French feudal civilization, engrossed either in her own island interests or in the continental ambitions of her French-speaking Kings. It is generally assumed that this change was quite inevitable and that on the whole more was gained than lost thereby. It may well be so. But the fact that Canute attempted a very different orientation for England is of profound interest, and though his Empire broke up, it was not without permanent effect, for it reinforced the Scandinavian and trading elements in the English nation.

"If he had lived till sixty instead of dying at forty, he might have left a more permanent mark on the world's affairs. He was a great ruler of men, and he was on the way to found a Nordic Empire astride of the North Sea, with Scandinavia for one pillar and England for the other. Sea-power would have been its cement and its master spirit. If he had succeeded he would have changed the history of the world."

God Almighty. Detail from the golden altar in Stadil Church.
Jutland. About 1225.

CONCLUSION

Denmark's external history reached its culmination in the Empire of Canute the Great. Since that time the frontiers of the kingdom have shrunk considerably and Denmark today is smaller than at the beginning of history. But the lasting effects of her history abroad are worthy of some consideration, even though it is impossible to deny that the influence of Denmark on world history after the days of Canute the Great is less apparent and more difficult to follow. The working day has been long, thousands of years spanning between the clinking blows of flint-chipping and the greased hum of modern dairy machinery. But the day is not yet at an end.

This book is intended as an account of Denmark's contribution to the world outside her borders. It is desirable that it should not be a panegyric, a one-sided self-glorification. If it appears in this light, it will be due in part to the possibly exaggerated high esteem of foreign scholars, and partly to the limitation of the task itself, which comprises what Denmark has given, not what she has received. The great contributions of the other Nordic peoples have thus lain outside this field; and the positive contributions have been given more attention than has the devastation brought about by the tribal migrations and the Viking wars.

It would be far from the truth to assert that everything which emanated from Denmark was good—or that all that was good came from Denmark. But all that Denmark has acquired from abroad and experienced at home has often been described by others. How much has she not received, learned, and brought home from the old civilizations of the Orient, from the classical Mediterranean cultures of antiquity, and the great European nations? But these things the Danes have tried to modify in their own fashion and infuse with some of their own spirit.

*

The basic and everlasting factors in trade: consumption, production and exchange, have today the same significance as in the Bronze Age. The fundamental importance of the relation between the people and the

306

soil of the fatherland, between man and nature, is unchanged. Internally it is of over all importance. Externally the relation between the people and the sea surrounding them is still of the same significance.

In two spheres Scandinavia has occupied a position of special importance in the history of European civilization: the evolution of freedom and of justice. With the exception of the Hellas and Palestine of antiquity there are few places where freedom and democracy have such deep roots as in the north. Denmark has contributed to these conceptions of freedom and justice.

It may well be said that other countries have skimmed off much of the cream of the Danish people. Considering all the emigrations which took place, it is almost remarkable that there is anything left, and no one can be surprised that after its immense exertions, the strength of the country failed for a time. The centrifugal movement of events diminished, even though it is still noticeable in shipping and trade, in the sciences and engineering.

Denmark's location, midway between the three seas in the north, gave her good protection as long as she controlled the seas, or was at least a strong sea-power, but on the other hand, it rendered any coherent extension of territory difficult. On all sides Denmark became gradually surrounded by countries the populations of which, to a greater or lesser degree, were blood of her blood and spirit of her spirit. The courses and conditions of world trade shifted, the character of commercial life changed, and with it, Denmark's position.

*

History is primarily an account of the politics of the past, while politics deals principally with the history of the future. It may be pleasant enough for Denmark to be an historic curiosity in Europe, but that is insufficient for a living people. One can assume responsibilities and derive inspiration from the past, but the past is not enough. The most important part of history lies in the future.

In the present state of the world much remains to be done, and the Danes are called upon to carry out a part of such work because they still have something to contribute. Of all the arts, the small, oft-unheeded one of cooperation is not the least. Had the Danes, the Scandinavians and the Europeans themselves mastered it at an earlier date and to a greater extent, many things would be different today. Just as the legends of the Skjoldungs echo with family feuds, so does the history of the tribal migrations resound with internecine warfare among the peoples who originated in the north. But in the great new formations of states and immense military undertakings during the Viking Period lay a great deal of cooperation which was not, however, sufficient to hold together the widely scattered territory that had been acquired. Even a united north was succesfully achieved for only a short period. It is as though the sense of independence was too strong, and wilfulness too great.

Is there anything the world needs more today than cooperation in a state of freedom and equality? In the Danish cooperative movement something of this is realized—small, free and independent landholders who, through cooperation, were able to capture a world market and compete successfully in the export of their products with great and powerful nations.

The developments in world trade and methods of transport make the art of cooperation more necessary to the life of the world than ever before, but the requisite for lasting collaboration is freedom and justice for all. The Vikings were hardly less realistic than we are, but it was not until the coming of Christianity that we find the ideal of equal rights of all men and nations.

The ancients' clear and realistic perception of the basic phenomenon of existence, the relation between the people and nature, is reflected in all the most important and significant periods in history. History also deals with the other basic condition of existence—the people's reciprocal dependence, by means of trade and shipping, with surrounding countries. The purpose of production is consumption. Trade serves both production and consumption. Therefore, our relationship with the environment which provides our working-place and our dwelling-place and the forces and raw materials we need, is one of the most important problems of history and politics.

In the middle of the vast universe the Earth hangs like a globe. If one slides one's hand down over it the highest mountain ranges can just be felt as a slight roughness on the palm of the hand, but one can neither feel nor see the human beings, the cities, the nations, and all that men have accomplished. This demonstrates the importance of the forces which affect our existence, and it shows us that mutual interdependence

308

The Valdemar Kings. Above: The Virgin Mary and Christ enthroned.
Below from left: King Valdemar the Victorious as Duke of Slesvig. King Knud VI.
King Valdemar the Great raising the crusader's cross. Knud Lavard,
Duke of Slesvig, canonized after his murder in 1131, holding the hand of Christ.
Relief above the cat-head door in the Cathedral of Ribe.

between peoples and nations is small and secondary, compared with the relation to the land. This applies to all nations and all ages in history.

*

Man does not live by bread alone, yet our daily bread is an important matter, for life itself depends upon it. The finest products of the most progressive industry are worth no more than the jewels in Aladdin's cave if food is lacking. Right from the time of the kitchen middens, food-policy has occupied an important place in the life of the Danes, though they have not laid their souls on the platter. An old proverb runs: 'Without his drink and food the hero is no good'. From ancient times the Danes have admired a hero, without despising food.

With common sense and productive efficiency, Denmark has taken

309

care to maintain the highest possible living standards ever since the days of the Stone Age. Indeed, few other nations have attained an average standard of living as high as theirs. The Dane is more of a realist than a materialist.

Throughout the whole of antiquity there was a high level of agricultural production in Denmark. The Dolmen People were able to feed a sizable population, and the peasant of the Iron Age survived a severe agricultural crisis. In the Valdemar Period Denmark was exporting corn, while later it carried on a considerable export of bullocks. But, in the days of autocracy, and during the palmy days of the landowning nobility, property rights and heavy taxation so affected the efficiency of the farmer that in the 18th century Danish agricultural products were quoted lowest of all on the London Exchange. Not until after the liberation of the peasants and the free-trade reforms at the close of the 18th century were conditions altered so radically that efficiency could again come into its own, and after a few generations the Danish agricultural products were quoted highest on the London Exchange.

Danish craftmanship during the Stone Age was admirable and in the Ages of Flint and Bronze a measure of home industry and export industry sprang up. In our own time Denmark has built up her exports, despite the fact that she lacks both minerals, metals and fuel. For this she can thank her geographical location, her freedom, her efficiency and her shipping.

*

In a short review of the last nine hundred years, one's attention is drawn particularly to the era of greatness during the Valdemar Period (1157-1241). Denmark was then a great power in Northern Europe, and in few periods have its people been so strong and contented. Strength and culture were characteristics of the age. It was a pious period during which Catholicism gave Denmark of its best. But it was an active piety, without self-centered asceticism. To serve one's country was the purest form of piety to the Valdemars, their statesmen and bishops. Erslev says, "They look upon themselves as being the living center of the whole people, but they are not weighed down by their great responsibilities. They have been installed in their places by God himself, and their first duty is to spread the sacred truths of Christianity among their people. They take religion in its widest sense; for them it is truth and justice – everything that furthers what is best for the kingdom and the people. The advancement of religion and the honor of the country were one and the same to the great Kings of those days."

It was in this period that the kings sought to control the Baltic and its trade. The conditions that made this possible were labor on the homeland soil by the free and independent peasant class, the strong organization of the military system and its connections with the internal administration of the Kingdom, and the rich herring fishery in the Sound–where the markets of Skaane were for nearly three centuries the great exchange mart between east and west in Northern Europe, and one of the few centers of world-trade existing in those days.

The conquests of the Valdemar Kings along the coasts of the Baltic: Rügen, Holstein, Lauenburg and Ratzeburg, parts of Mecklenburg and Pomerania and Esthonia toward the east–were not accompanied by any noteworthy colonization abroad. Even though the policy of the Valdemars may be regarded as a continuation of Denmark's Baltic policy from the days of Gudfred and the Jelling Dynasty, it had no lasting results.

Colonization took place within the kingdom. Between the years 1000 and 1300 as many as 3,500 new villages were built in Denmark, those whose names terminate in: -torp, -trup, and -strup. An immense amount of new land was cultivated, thus providing for the young generation and the increasing population. This brought in its train a density of population and in the time of the Valdemars the country has as many inhabitants as it did 150 years ago. The population remained static during the centuries of autocracy preceding the emancipation of the peasants in 1788, and it was only after those great social reforms that a considerable increase in numbers occurred. A nation's germinative force is closely tied in with the land question.

The upright good sense with which the Valdemars had developed the ancient Danish social structure formed the background for the strength of that period at home and abroad. The old valuation of land in 'bol' (hide) and the still older 'Fornskifte' were, in the opinion of scholars, originally kinds of military-levy districts in which each bol was obligated to provide a warrior for the battleship.

Military and land systems appear to have been originally linked together as expressions of the same idea, namely the people's duty to defend their soil and independence from external violence, and the

311

community's duty to protect the soil from dangers within. There is the possibility that the 'Herred' and the 'Lev' towns were old administrative land and military systems. Even though the words are those of the Viking Period, the old poem 'Bjarkemaal' perhaps contains a reminder of this in the words of the hero, Bjarke:

A foreigner,
with few friends,
once I came
to King's court.

Twelve demesnes
I gained to master,
realms to rule,
and red gold.

It was at the same time as the Skjoldung Period that the Eruli, and later the Goths, carried out great land reforms in Italy; these peoples had both retained their connections with the Nordic lands from which they originated, and their land reforms in the Roman empire–Agri Herulorum–were on a military basis. It is therefore possible that there is some connection with the Danish system whether it be the influence of the Roman land-laws dealing with the parcelling-out of land to soldiers, which we know from the time of Marius, or a continuation of an ancient Teutonic tradition which Caesar, who was himself interested in solving the land problem, had noted and referred to in his Commentaries on the Gallic Wars. He says (VI.22.):

"For agriculture they have no zeal, and the greater part of their food consists of milk, cheese, and flesh. No man has a definite quantity of land or estate of his own: the magistrates and chiefs every year assign to tribes and clans that have assembled together as much land and in such place as seems good to them, and compel the tenants after a year to pass on elsewhere. They adduce many reasons for that practice–the fear that they may be tempted by continuous association to substitute agriculture for their warrior zeal; that they may become zealous for the acquisition of broad territories, and so the more powerful may drive the lower sort from their holdings; that they may build with greater care to avoid the extremes of cold and heat; that some passion for money may

312

Archbishop Absalon, 1128-1201.
Portrait on his tomb-stone in
Sorø Conventual Church. Zealand.
Made in 1536 by
Master Morten Bussert to order of
Abbot Henrik Tornekrans.

arise to be the parent of parties and of quarrels. It is their aim to keep common people in contentment, when each man sees that his own wealth is equal to that of the most powerful."

In the Valdemar Period the old Danish land valuation in 'bol' was modernized. This usage must have existed in the military system of Gudfred, and was adopted in the 9th century during the colonization of England by the sons of Lodbrog, later forming the foundation for Canute the Great's assessment and taxation of English land through the Danegeld.

In Denmark itself no sources are preserved which provide material for an investigation of the land system previous to the time of the Valdemars, with the exception of such traces of earlier legislation as are contained in the provincial laws and the rent-rolls. Consequently, no definite proof can be produced that the land system of the sons of Lodbrog and of Canute the Great in England were fashioned on Danish models. And yet it is difficult to conceive of any other possibility when we see quite a new practice carried out in England simultaneously with the Danish colonization, a new practice, which Stenton calls a revolution.

313

The sons of Lodbrog seem to have built upon a fundament and continued a custom dating from the Denmark of King Gudfred. When this is compared with the traces of a similar system existing in the Danish-influenced Viken in southern Norway, and also with the fact that the 'bol'-appraisement and 'fornskifte'-division in Denmark must be presumed to date from the very period when Svend and Canute were carrying through the land-taxation system of the Danegeld in England, a line can be drawn which runs from Gudfred, through Canute to Valdemar.

Aakjær writes, "In Skaane they continued to use the old bol as the basis for taxation, but on the other hand, in the remainder of Denmark in the Valdemar Period, a new form of land valuation was instituted which is peculiar to our country—the gold-valuation."

In King Valdemar's "Jutish Law" the peasants war-levy was fixed on this basis. This Jutish gold-valuation—the earliest known application of which dates from 1180—was an assessment on the selling-price of the value of the land for trade and commerce—its capital value. Of the assessed land value, 1/24th—or more than 4 %—was paid in land-tax. In Zealand and Falster, Valdemar the Victorious had in 1213 introduced an assessment, the so-called 'Skyldvaluation'. This was more direct and rational, inasmuch as it did not first appraise the capital value of the land (which was merely an expression of the capitalized value of the land's potentialities to yield profit, the land rent) and then reckon back what amount of tax should be paid on the land value. In the Skyldvaluation the land-tax was assessed *directly* in proportion to the quantity of seed sown—but, it must be noted, not merely according to the amount of seed actually *used,* but to the measure a parcel of land *could* absorb.

Nørlund thinks that taxation of the land value mainly depended on assessment of the grain-rent, the manorial dues (landgilde) which were paid by the tenants to their lords, and that the number of leaseholders was greater than Erslev imagines. Valuation was certainly of importance both to the landowners' private collection and to the community's public collection of ground-rent in proportion to the value of the land. Examples from the period of conquest and colonization in England suggest that public interests were as great as, if not greater than that of the private landowners'.

In the Valdemar Period a very large proportion—no doubt the greater part—of the country's soil was cultivated by self-owning, independent

314

peasants. The large estates which later were copied from those in Germany were not known in Denmark during this time, even though wealthy families owned many scattered holdings. Erslev writes, "With the apportionment of the war-levy in mind, the lands were valued, the valuation determining the rent which the king could claim, instead of the actual war-levy. The valuation depended on an estimate of the amount of grain seed that could be sown on the land at the time of valuation. Thus from the valuation one can directly determine how much must be paid on the land in substitution for the war-levy. Indirectly, one can determine from the valuation how much grain seed could be sown on the land in question, and there are moreover, grounds for believing that the original grain-rent (landgilde) on the land was of the same amount as the 'leding'—the war-levy tax."

By his land, and recruiting-system, together with the older taxes, the complete land values of all the country were drawn into the King's iron-bound chest, and a firm foundation for the royal rule was thus created, while the profits from the labor of the people themselves were allowed to remain in their own hands. These measures constituted the main foundation of Denmark's strength and prosperity and simplified the colonization and cultivation inside the country. They created such favorable conditions that the youth of Denmark were able to remain in the country, and a rich culture developed.

In nearly every parish in Denmark there stands an ancient village church dating from that time—a witness to the people's spiritual strength. With dogged perseverance the stone-cutters of Jutland cut the hard granite into smooth squarestones or magnificent sculptured slaps for the outer walls, and inside many of the churches were adorned with the famous golden altars of Romanesque time. These churches point at the same time to the material prosperity which made such a capital investment possible. In the course of about 100 years, approximately 2,000 churches were built without public assistance or State support. Danish cathedrals were erected, the writing of history flourished, and folk-songs were composed. Few countries posses as rich a heritage of songs as Denmark. According to Goddard Leach, Svend Grundtvig's collection of Danish folk-songs and ballads is the world's most comprehensive body of national folk music.

In the same period ancient laws were incorporated into the great provincial laws. The spirit of these laws, their simple court rules, their clear

315

and forceful language, might well have served as models for those of later times. This ancient legal literature can hold its own with Roman Law.

The assessment and land-value-taxation of English lands by Canute the Great strengthened English national sentiment. Green says, "As a national tax levied by the Witan of all England, this land tax practically brought home the national idea as it had never been brought home before."

Harald Fairhair's land-tax in Norway had similar results. Shetelig calls it the first step toward making Norway a State. In Denmark it must have had the same effect, both in earlier days and in the Valdemar Period, as a realistic expression of the feeling of unity between the people and the soil of their country.

*

Abroad, the splendid era of the Valdemars was shattered on a light summer night in May of 1223 when the German Count Henry of Schwerin availed himself of the hospitality of Valdemar the Victorious to kidnap him and his young son. Lacking Valdemar's leadership, the Danish possessions along the south coast of the Baltic were lost, and Denmark itself experienced difficult times.

During the fighting with the Vendic pirates, it was the Zealander who had borne the chief burden. The Jutes, separated by some distance from the danger zone, were not so ready to obey a recruiting summons, so the king assembled a corps of armored soldiers and cavalry who pledged themselves to respond when called upon. In return they were granted exemption from land-taxation. They became the Lords men (Herremænd) and the tax-exemption they had secured enabled them, during times of peace, to purchase fresh land; thus the landowning squires and nobles grew in strength. This embryonic class of nobles had been of great importance in helping to save the Kingdom's independence from dangers abroad, but within the country it increased gradually in size and obtained an influence that was not proportionate to its value.

After the Valdemar Period, a movement was begun to compensate for the deficiency in land-taxes by the imposition of other forms of taxation. In the opinion of Arup, the plough-tax introduced by King Erik Plovpenning, c. 1230, was a duty imposed on every plough in Denmark, a tax which struck at the most important instrument of labor in the coun-

316

The Virgin Mary with the infant Saviour in celestial Jerusalem.
Central part of the golden altar from Lisbjerg Church.
About 1140-1150. Jutland.

try and consequently hampered enterprise. In Arup's view, ploughland was originally an indication of acreage, and not a technical designation for a tax-registration, which can be deduced from the fact that when the peasant could not pay his plough-tax, the sheriff impounded one ox from his team. Under later kings this process of shifting the tax from the ownership of land to the use of land was further speeded up, with villeinage, socage and bondage as consequence.

The independent peasants with occupying ownership rights disappeared in many parts of the country and the nobility gained possession of the major portion of the land in the Kingdom. When Valdemar the Victorious died in 1241, it is estimated that the number of independent peasants amounted to about 75 %. Less than 100 years later, on the death of King Erik Menved in 1319, they had dwindled to about 10 %, and in 1660 only about 5 % of the peasants had occupying ownership.

The nobles themselves numbered no more than a couple of thousand persons in all, divided into 500 families or about 100 clans, and within that class the higher nobility held the dominant position. These leading nobles came from no more than 40 clans which owned 85 % of the lands held by all orders of the nobility.

Aakjær says, "King Valdemar and his legislators would have turned in their graves if they could have seen how their sensible economic system had later been dealt with."

The principal causes for the undermining of the legal system of the Valdemars and the strength and commercial life of Denmark were the growing power of the great nobles, their exemption from land-tax, followed by depreciation in currency and money manipulations.

Next to the nobles, the Catholic Church was the largest landowner. The third was the King, but since the nobles filled most of the high offices of the Church, they had a land-political superiority over the Crown shown by the pledges extracted from the King at his coronation.

The Catholic Church had opened men's eyes to spiritual things of eternity, but in itself had not been blind to the things of this world. The Church very seldom gave away land, but there are numerous instances of its absorbing estates. The rent-roll of the Bishop of Roskilde alone shows that he owned 2,600 farms in Zealand, in addition to numerous building sites in Copenhagen and Roskilde. The Catholic Church owned about one-third of the land in Denmark, the mighty noble families owned roughly another third, so that only one-third was left to the king and the free peasants. As the important offices in the Church were as a rule filled by noblemen, these families obtained a domineering geopolitical power in the country.

It is true that the Church had encouraged art and architecture, and

318

that it assumed many social tasks of charity concerning the poor, sick and homeless, later taken over by the State. It is also true that many nobles performed the same services with patriarchal solicitude. But it is also true that the Church, the nobility and the State themselves had created the want and poverty which they afterward tried to alleviate, but not abolish. This was not merely a Danish phenomenon, but rather a universal one, and was consequently even more significant.

A gifted and reputable aristocracy is of great value to a nation and if it is based on outstanding qualities, high character, heroism and gifts of leadership, it may well stamp a period of culture. Heredity and spiritual obligations are the hallmarks of nobility, and in this respect the Danish aristocracy has an ancient title from the gifted ruling class of the Bronze Age to the men of noble birth in the Viking Period. Aristocracy and democracy are not incompatible if the task of both is to serve the people as a whole, but when aristocracy sinks into a privileged geocracy limiting its horizon to family and class, confining its interests to haughtiness, heraldry and genealogy, then it loses its link with the life of the people and thereby the justification for its continuance.

Their sense of class outweighed national responsibility, and while the Danish nobles closed ranks against the middle class and farmers, they welcomed the foreign nobleman—the only conditions imposed upon him being that he should take up permanent residence in Denmark and marry a Danish lady of noble birth, upon which he could become naturalized as a Danish nobleman whenever he desired. Depite its numerous eminent individual representatives, the aristocracy of Denmark lost its sense of national cohesion, and thereby its historic function, and finally its power.

The power of the nobles received its first blow during the Reformation, when the enormous estates of the Church passed to the King. Jørgensen calculates that the gross income of the Crown estates was thereby trebled. This gave the Crown a land-political superiority over the nobles which, after the Swedish War in 1660, led to the next step. With the support of citizens and peasants, the crown achieved hereditary rule and absolute monarchy. After the royal revolution in 1660, Count Hannibal Sehested re-established the land-policy on the foundation laid by the Valdemars by imposing a land-tax, the hartkorn-tax. These land-taxes restored Denmark to prosperity within a few years following the devastations of war.

Sehested also laid the foundation for the celebrated land valuations, later put into effect throughout the entire country by Dinesen and von Støcken during the reign of Christian V, while Ole Rømer, the astronomer, did the same thing in Copenhagen. No other European country had a valuation resembling it. The great registration and land-assessment, of which Count Reventlow (1748-1827) laid the groundwork under Frederik VI, was an important part of the great agricultural and free trade reforms carried through by the men responsible for the emancipation of the peasants in 1788. The latter reforms revitalized democracy in the nation and formed the basis for the outstanding improvements in Danish agriculture during the last century. It was principally the circle of gifted and upright noblemen around the Reventlows and Bernstoffs who deserve the credit for this.

Clearly and unmistakably, the history of Denmark, as well as its strength abroad, revolves around this ancient realistic understanding of the people's rapport with the soil of their country, the most enduring and vital problem in her history.

*

By its very nature, trade is a form of barter. Thus it was in the beginning and so it is still. That we later introduced money as a means of payment by a token standard does not alter that fact, even if we believe in the token and forget the reality, the commodities, which they represent.

Import is the beginning of trade. In his Commentaries on the Gallic War, Caesar says, "They give access to traders rather to secure purchasers for what they have captured in war than to satisfy any craving for imports." Caesar had seen the freedom of trade, but must have misunderstood its importance.

We know that in 873, Kings Halfdan and Sigfred made a commercial treaty with King Louis the German which set forth that merchants should travel unhindered between the nations. But, according to the Knytlingesaga, ever since the German Emperor Henry, in the twelfth century, whispered into the ear of the Danish Duke Knud Lavard, the words, 'It is now the custom among us here in Saxony, as also in other places far afield, to close the country's harbors and levy customs duties, and not permit anybody to bring ships into the harbor without paying

320

The Tirstrup crucifix.
About 1150-1175.
Djursland. Jutland.

fixed duties'—ever since that time, attempts have been made in various periods to restrict the free flow of trade. Poul Johs. Jørgensen says, "Customs duties were originally a personal payment made by foreigners in order to obtain protection and peace. The payment of customs duties on merchandise is a later conception. Perhaps such duties were first levied by Knud Lavard at Slesvig."

The trade of Hedeby-Slesvig declined, partly following repeated destructive attacks during wars, partly because of the silting-up of the channels, and partly because of high customs duties which forced the trade elsewhere. The German advance up through the Slavic lands to the Baltic created the opportunity for the foundation of the Hanseatic cities, and after Lübeck was founded in 1138, the Germans themselves built up a trade route between Hamburg and Lübeck which took over the erstwhile role of Hedeby, Sli and Eider. For this reason the trade route in the Baltic avoided previously frequented Danish harbors, the main route now running between the Hansa Cities and Visby on the island of Gotland. The Valdemars' policy of conquest was, to some extent, an attempt to counteract this development.

From the time of Canute the Great, trade flourished around the herring marts in the Sound where the great autumn markets prospered. Denmark was also a corn-exporting country in the Valdemar Period, and the Baltic ports with their hinterlands could import corn by ship from Denmark more cheaply than they could transport it overland. Low cost sea-transport, together with its location between the seas, remains one of Denmark's greatest assets, and its shipping and foreign trade are proof of this. It is at the same time one of the explanations why Denmark, lacking raw materials, metals and fuel, has been able to develop an export industry, because these things can be transported at less cost by sea than by land. From the days of antiquity, Denmark's favorable location has fitted her to be a mart for transit trade—one of Europe's free ports. That opportunity still exists.

During their trading period, the Hanseatic cities flourished while Denmark's trade diminished, and the customs dues of the Sound (Øresunds-told) which the Danish King Erik VII had introduced and later kings expanded, became a two-edged sword, leading the Danes into fateful conflicts with the great commercial nations, albeit for a while these dues brought vast sums of money into the Royal Exchequer. A blockade of trade routes is usually considered by other nations as an unfriendly act, and the resultant diplomatic estrangements necessitated considerable expenditure on naval and military preparations. In the long run, it was the Øresunds-told and the blockade policy that brought Denmark into conflict with Sweden, Holland, France and England, and finally caused the loss of the eastern third of ancient Denmark: Skaane, Halland and Blekinge. It is true that those provinces in a sense remained in the Nordic family, and one day perhaps will become the bridge linking the Nordic nations together. Denmark's power and prestige, however, have never been the same as before this loss.

Losing eastern Denmark because of customs duties can in some ways be compared to England's forfeiture of the American Colonies after the Stamp Act and the tariffs on tea, whereby the English-speaking nations were split.

Through all the long, lean period of mercantilism, when commerce was undermined by customs, import restrictions and prohibitions, trade did not thrive, despite all kinds of State support until, during the free trade policy of the Bernstorff's in the 18th century, life once again resumed its normal course despite all barriers and prohibitions. The effective liberation of trade under A. P. Bernstorff (1735-1797) was as vital a measure as the great land reforms of Reventlow. Together, they created the climate for Denmark s revival.

Bernstorff's Free Trade and Customs Law of 1797 has been called 'The Danish Customs Constitution'. By means of this legislation, Denmark assumed the lead among the nations of Europe–long before England adopted a free trade policy. It was not until fifty years later that England achieved the same standard of free trade, and more than a thousand parliamentary resolutions were required to attain what Bernstorff had effected in one single law. Sponneck, the Danish Director-General of Customs and Minister of Finance, in reference to this customs-law, wrote in 1840, "This law is not only one of the best examples of Danish legislation but also one of the finest memorials the history of European customs taxation can point to. One can state with confidence that no country in the world had a more perfect customs constitution than Denmark."

The optimistic tone of confidence and prosperity permeating the period of the peasants' emancipation appears doubly cheerful against the background of the mercantilistic period which preceded it and of the times of planned economy. Much of the spiritual restriction and economic crabbedness characteristic of the mercantilistic time reminds us of our own period, with its crushing taxation, enormous national debt, and public expenditures, the State's entry into commercial life with controls, customs prohibitions and restrictions, its agricultural crises, its periods of unemployment.

Denmark was a pioneer country in the spheres of trade policy and land legislation. The Encyclopædia Britannica says of slavery, "England had not been the first European power to abolish the slave trade; that honour belongs to Denmark." Canute the Great would have nodded in approval. At the same time, Reventlow abolished bondage, ended villeinage, founded the folk-schools, and established a rational system of forestry. Modern European forestry is founded on Reventlow's methods. Denmark's Golden Age of poetry and art, and Grundtvig's work among the people, church and schools, can only be appreciated against the background of the emancipation of peasant and trade. A remarkably large circle of eminent men of learning and letters lived in Denmark in the Golden Age of the last century.

In some ways, great men in Denmark have influenced the development of science. In astronomy it was Tycho Brahe who, by his exact description of the courses of the stars, assembled the material on which Kepler constructed his laws. Steno and Bartholin made epoch-making discoveries in anatomy, and Steno also founded two new sciences—Geology and Crystallography. Ole Rømer measured the speed of light, and Niels Finsen used its healing force in therapy. The Greek word for amber gave electricity its name, and in the homeland of amber H. C. Ørsted discovered electro-magnetism, thus laying the foundations of modern electro-techniques. His brother, Anders Sandøe Ørsted, created modern scientific jurisprudence, and Rasmus Rask, the science of comparative philology. L. A. Colding discovered the law of the conservation of energy, and Niels Bohr played an important part in explaining the construction and laws of the atom, and releasing the energy of atomic fission. Few countries have as many Nobel prize winners in proportion to their population as Denmark.

It is a proof of the importance of trade and commerce that up to the outbreak of World War II the Danes had the lowest tariffs, and the highest standard of living in Europe, and a larger import and export per head than any other country.

*

The ancient dwellers in the north were good lawmakers. They took their own customary laws out into the world with them from their homelands, and a sense of equality and fair play runs like a red thread through the best part of their history. It is, for instance, remarkable that the Vikings, who are usually described as pirates, when they first settled, established law, order, liberty and security. Very few pirates do that.

In his celebrated Roman Letter, Canute the Great promised "to administer just judgment to all." Bishop Gunner's preamble to the 'Jutish Law' of King Valdemar the Victorious states, not without influence from canon law, that "The law shall be fair, just, tolerable, in accordance with the customs of the country, convenient and practical, and intelligible so that all men can know and understand what the law says. It must not be composed or written for the especial benefit of any man, but to the advantage of all men who live in the land."

A Swedish contemporary says of Queen Margrete (1353-1412) who ruled the three Scandinavian countries, "She wanted to help everybody

Queen Margrete. 1353-1412.
From her sarcophagus in
the Cathedral of Roskilde.

to equal rights and law, to strengthen justice and to suppress all evil, for which God reward her."

In the Foreword to King Christian V's 'Danish Law' of 1683, it is written that the law shall be "equally fair and equally tolerable for all people, so that no one shall by law either enjoy any advantage or suffer more than others."

In the Danish Constitution of 1849 and the later constitutions, the freedom of religion, trade, the press, and of association, are secured. The rights of property and its inviolability is an important cornerstone in the social building of democracy, but the cutting of it is not yet completed, because it was not made clear where the limit is set between the property rights of the individual and those of the State. Hence an apparent weakness of democracy.

Nordic freedom has expanded in the shelter of the law. In other countries it has played a part in awakening the life of trade and culture. Nordic freedom is a precious golden heritage without which the Danes could not have achieved what they did in earlier days.

Freedom denotes not anarchy and violence, but the reverse. Freedom

325

is the mother of order. Despite their sense of freedom, the Danes are perhaps one of Europe's least hysterical peoples. Exaltation and ecstacy are emotions to which they seldom give way. They carried out the change of religion from heathendom to Catholicism and from Catholicism to Protestantism without bloodshed and conflicts. They brought about the Revolution in 1660 without civil war, and the emancipation of the peasants and of trade at the close of the 18th Century quietly and with dignity, while France was convulsed by the Reign of Terror. They achieved the June Constitution in 1849 without riots, while the cities of Europe resounded with street battles.

*

Following that dark period in the 14th century in which Count Geert of Holstein intervened in Denmark's history, King Valdemar Atterdag (re-dawns the day) (1340-1375) succeeded, by superlative statecraft, in re-establishing the Kingdom and laying the foundation for the great achievement which his daughter Queen Margrete (1375-1412) was to accomplish–the Nordic Union. Through her amazing political genius she united the three closely related Nordic countries and ruled with feminine tact and benign wisdom over a realm which was at that time the most extensive in Europe.

Arup says, "Queen Margrete, who accomplished the greatest of all known Nordic national achievements–the Union of the Three Kingdoms –towered above all petty and spiteful nationalistic conceptions. Margrete held the firm belief that more can be achieved along the paths of peace than those of dissension."

It was a misfortune both for the north and for Europe that the efforts to make the Union of the three nations firm and lasting did not succeed. However, the vitality inherent in the conception of union was not destroyed. When Queen Margrete's federative ideas once again become matters of practical policy, as in the Nordic Council, it will be necessary to avoid the errors which, in her day, led to the dissolution of the Kalmar Union. The mistakes were, first, the attempts of the Danes to dominate; secondly, the old tenacious sense of independence of the northern peoples; and thirdly, their neglect to solve the social questions which, in conjunction with the burdens of taxation which ensued, could, in the general unrest, be used to undermine the confidence and relations between the countries.

The peoples of the north have in the past wasted much of their vigor in grievous conflicts among themselves. After the Swedish wars, Count Hannibal Sehested made the wise proposal that the nations of the north conclude an alliance in which Sweden should represent land-power, and Denmark and Norway sea-power. This plan was not realized, but in the last centuries the Nordic countries have set an example of neighborliness to the world by settling all disputes through negotiation and arbitration instead of war and rape.

In their closely related diversity, the Nordic nations are in a position to compensate for each other's deficiencies, and the spirit of Queen Margrete is not dead. Abroad and within the Kingdom her policy was characterized by the will for peace. She created an atmosphere of peaceful and harmonious relations among people in all walks of life. As Arup says, "Her government secured for the Danish people a period in which peace and justice ruled in the land, and it was altogether a very fortunate era in the history of the Danish Nation. Margrete's government finally established the royal power in Denmark as the highest authority in the community to which the people should always have resort in order to obtain peace and justice. She once and for all accorded royal power its proper status and true purpose in Danish social life."

*

We who are familiar with air-raids, who have lived to see warfare with U-boats and atom-bombs, and have witnessed the grey human corpses in the concentration-camps, cannot but feel a strange recognition at the prophetic description of Ragnarok (the twilight of the gods) as drawn in the thousand years' old Edda.

It is stated in Vøluspá that one of the signs that Ragnarok is close at hand will be three successive severe winters during which blizzards will blow from all the corners of the world and the sun will have lost its power. Those winters will be preceded by three years of scarcity, during which the world will be filled with fighting. But these wars will not be the glorious combats of an earlier age, in which those who won the victory shared the honor equally with those who lost. For in the last days, men's souls will go astray so that they forget the decency and honor of former days in their raging lust. Then shall brother shed the blood of brother, and then shall father not spare son, nor son father. During this distress the giant wolf will gain strength to swallow the sun, so that

327

people will grope blindly in darkness and the wolf's brother will gulp down the moon, so that all the stars will plunge into the deeps. The Fenris wolf will escape and rush along with gaping mouth, his lower jaw sweeping the earth, his upper jaw the sky, and fire will flash from his nostrils and eyes. The Midgard sea-serpent will writhe so that the ocean will roll far inland. In the surf, the boat of the dead will break loose—this boat being built of fingernails of drowned men.

The sky will burst open and through the gap in the air will ride the sons of Muspel—the sons of fire—clothed in flames. The Tree of Life—tall ash Ygdrasil—will quiver, and horror will spread among all creatures above and below; even the dwarfs will stand outside their open stones gasping with fear. After the final struggle between the Gods and the Giants in which they all receive death-wounds, the giant Surt will stand alone on the battlefield. Then he will fling fire out over all the world so that the whole earth will blaze and burn.

When the fire has died down and the embers are out, all will be still. The earth will then rise up from the sea new-born, green and fair, and on its soil the corn will sway gently in the wind. Life will again move in the forest where two people have been hidden. They will breed a new race that shall replenish the earth.

Nidhug, the dragon shaped as an eagle, will rise from its piles of corpses and fly ponderously and low over the earth. Carcasses will hang on its wings, its feathers glittering blue-black as it sinks and disappears far out in the bottomless abyss at the edge of the world.

*

Are these old prophesies far from reality? In the light of the present day there is significance in this ancient vision from the prophesy of the sibyl, and it is natural to look at the facts of recent and coming days which are of current importance.

The warlike efficiency of the German people, their organizing ability, their "Wille zur Macht," their urge to break open new roads across other nations' frontiers, recall in some ways the reckless vitality of the tribes in the Migration Period. As Germany was in 1939, so were some of the Teutonic peoples 2,000 years ago. Despite superficial points of resemblance with the world of the Viking, the Nazis had nothing in common with them. Their system of non-aggression pacts, broken promises and violated pledges seems utterly foreign to the Nordic mind. Nazism

328

seized on the superficial, but not the inner, nature of the Vikings. The Nazis tried to deck themselves out in ancient words and signs, and stuffed themselves with symbols which had no substance. When soul and honor, freedom and righteousness disappear, only the rude, crude brute is left.

*

In olden days the organizing ability of the Danes was seldom rigid and dictatorial, but rather organic and alive and based on voluntary cooperation. The Danish Folk High Schools of Grundtvig and the farmers' Co-operatives are examples. In Denmark the technical schools train the young and give them the practical knowledge they need to live by, while the Folk High Schools, in the spirit of Grundtvig, teach them what they ought to live for. Grundtvig was a prophet with a keen perception of realities. In 1839 he wrote, "If one imagines all the heads which think and speak in German as being under one hat, that of a German Emperor Napoleon, the result would be a power which, from the point of view of humanity, would be more terrible than France in her most dangerous period. And to my mind, it necessarily follows that the Germans would be far more severe as masters owing to the fact that they are more serious and thorough."

In 1849, during the Danish-German war, he wrote, "The Germans have the immutable belief that Our Lord created the world all wrong and that it is the business of the Germans to re-create it according to their notions and ideas. The Englishman, however, takes the world as it is and strives to make it as useful for himself as possible. The German resembles a war-chariot rumbling over uneven cobbles. The Englishman is like a well-laden steamer of deep draught going at a steady speed, while the Dane is like a longboat with oars and sails, rising and falling with the waves, often far too tranquil but yet ever pretty, light, and mobile. If we imagine the boat to be either on the stones behind the chariot or on the sea abaft the ship, then we perceive the difference in our relationship with Germans or English."

The English-speaking peoples, who still use a language that takes its name from the ancient Danish Province of Angel have, in their democracy and sense of freedom, a heritage more closely related to the Vikings than to the tribes of the Migration Period, a heritage in which Denmark is not without a share. The three accomplishments which the English learned from the Vikings form a large part of the basic factors upon

329

which the British Empire was built—shipping, business and colonization. These three gifts, when combined with the toughness and endurance of the Anglo-Saxons, and inspired by the organizing abilities of the Franco-Danish Norman, enabled the English to succeed in solving the historic problem of reconciling qualities which other nations had found to be mutually exclusive: democracy, personal freedom and executive efficiency.

Wycliffe, who was born in 1324 near York, England, showed that a Nordic spirit breathed in him when he founded Protestantism. He translated the Bible into English and fought against the authority of the Pope, the worship of saints, the rule of the priests, and the doctrine of transubstantiation. Through his teaching, and the spiritual stimulus it effected, he exercised a strong influence upon the Lollard Movement which was occurring partly among the laymen and also among workers and trade-guild-members who claimed the land for the people. The Great Plague in the middle of the 14th century had so reduced the supply of manpower and left so many farms untenanted that wages had naturally tended to rise. This at length resulted in revolution because of the efforts of the king and barons to keep wages low. The revolution had its core in Kent, East Anglia, and the eastern towns of the Danelaw. Thorold Rogers has pointed out that despite persecutions and the fact that several of their leaders were hanged, the movement triumphed and, owing to the reforms which were carried through, laid the foundation for the Golden Age of England in the 15th and 16th centuries. The soil was again available to the people and wages and the standard of living rose to heights that had never been reached in the history of England. During these centuries the working-day was only eight hours long.

The later Lutheran Movement in Germany was also a child of the Nordic spirit, influenced as it was by Wycliffe, through John Huss in Bohemia. But Luther deserted the peasants, whereas Wycliffe and the Lollard Movement stood firm. In Germany, as in the north, the landed property of the Church passed over to the princes and nobles, just as had occurred in England under Henry VIII. This political transfer has been noticeable, both in German and English history, down to present times.

Wycliffe, Huss and Luther led Christianity back to the words of the Bible and opposed the authority of the Pope, the saints and the Virgin Mary. In Denmark the Nordic spirit was personified in Grundtvig's

Admiral Hans Pothorst who during the reign of King Christian I came to America twenty years before Columbus. Fresco in the vault of St. Marie Church. Elsinore, Zealand.

migthy figure when, in the last century, he once again led Christianity away from biblical phrases and back to the spirit behind the words. It was a continuation of the Reformation, and brought human beings face to face with God once again.

The Reformation abolished the Catholic idea of celibacy that is so contrary to the laws of nature. All the gifted people and religious geniuses in the service of the Catholic Church were forbidden to propagate and therefore could not transmit their faculties and talents to descendants. MacDougall considers that in this way celibacy played a large part in diminishing earnest and natural piety in the southern countries where it has been in operation for centuries. He thinks it is the reason why Italy and Spain have gradually become countries where superficial devotions veil the lack of genuine conviction. If, for example, we subtract from the history of civilization the contributions which the sons of the clergy in England, America and the north have made to the intellectual and political life of their countries, then we get an impression of the cost to a nation that celibacy incurs in its wake.

The free spirit of trade continued to operate in England through the ages, even though for a while it was suppressed, but not eradicated, by the Norman barons. Through most of the Middle Ages England was an agricultural community, but when the time came for trade to prosper once more the people were ready, and had Nordic initiative in reserve. In northern England the freedom-loving spirit was preserved, and it was in these districts that Richard Cobden found the greatest support in his battle for free trade and land-reform which led to the repeal of the Corn Laws and introduced England's resplendent era of free trade. The legends that surround the gallant bowman Robin Hood survived in the districts around the five Danish cities, Sherwood Forest and Nottingham. It was from East Anglia that Cromwell recruited his Ironsides.

*

The growth of modern North America and the expansion of its life have a strong Nordic element, introduced first and foremost by the migrants from Eastern England, but in later times also by Nordic emigrants.

The Puritan pilgrims came mainly from the eastern districts of England. Of the 25,000 colonists who settled in New England in 1640, at least 70 % came from Suffolk and Norfolk in East Anglia, from Lincolnshire, Nottingham, Yorkshire, Kent, Surrey, Sussex, Essex, Middlesex and Hertfordshire. Trevelyan writes, "This new world, so full of vigour, freedom and initiative, laid the foundations of the British Empire and of the United States. The migration of early Stuart times was a world-movement akin in its importance to the Anglo-Saxon and Norse settlement of England a thousand years before. The great majority of the first Anglo-Americans came from the south-east of England and represented her most pronounced Nordic stock. These original 25,000, to whom collectively may be extended the term 'Pilgrim Fathers', were a prolific stock and their descendants were the men who did most to set the political and social tone of the United States in its developments west of the Appalachian Mountains in later times, until about 1870."

The settlers, gold-miners and pioneers in America had many character traits in common with the northmen. According to Baker, the old Nordic and Anglo-Saxon type is probably more often found in some parts of the United States than in England itself.

The novel free Constitution drafted by William Penn for his new colony of Pennsylvania established the ancient ideal of equal rights for all, irrespective of race, religion or ideologies. It was, in the opinion of Graham, the example and spirit of William Penn's Constitution that became the model for Washington, Jefferson and the other Founding Fathers in framing the American Constitution. The Declaration of Independence inspired the Declaration of the Rights of Man during the French Revolution. From France it spread to the democracies of Europe and returned to the north along that road.

Abraham Lincoln, who saved the Union of the American People and effected the abolition of negro slavery, derives his descent from Norfolk and Lincoln in England, those districts where slavery was unknown in the days of Canute the Great. Henry George, the champion of economic liberty, derives his descent from Yorkshire, where exactly a thousand years before his time, Halfdan solved the land question.

The westward movement is characteristic of the English-speaking nations, having begun in Denmark 1500 years ago when the first Danish tribes crossed the North Sea to England. In the Viking Period, England became Denmark's greatest colony until it won its independence. In the last three centuries the movement continued across the Atlantic to the first colonies in North America, where the main stock of immigrants came from the old Danelaw in England. In this period America was

Commodore Vitus Bering (1681-1741) who discovered Alaska on July 16. 1741. After a painting in private possession.

England's greatest colony in the west until, in 1782, the first 13 states won their independence and founded the United States of America. In the last century the westward movement pushed on across the continent to the shores of the Pacific. Even though the United States has welcomed and absorbed immigrants from many other countries, English and Nordic blood and language and ideals have been of decisive importance.

In 1765, when the English Government tried to impose the Stamp Act upon them, the Americans answered, "If the King wanted money from a colony, he could ask for a grant." Compare this with the words of Asbjørn to the Norwegian king, "We will not bear taxes, but we will not object to giving the king grants." The spirit and the words are almost identical.

In the second Continental Congress in 1775, after the battles of Lexington and Concord and the Boston Tea Party, Thomas Jefferson declared that the Americans were "being with one mind resolved to die free men rather than live slaves." Compare this with the Danes' declaration in Northumberland to Toste Godwinson who tried to impose taxes on them contrary to Canute's laws, "We are born free and brought up

334

as free men. We will not bear with a proud and domineering chieftain, for our fathers have taught us to live free men or to die." The spirit and the words are almost the same.

The fourth of July is a festival day in the United States. It is so in Denmark, too. It is not a modern innovation, for Professor Henrik Steffens writes in his memories of the year 1782 in Copenhagen, "I still remember vividly the day when the conclusion of peace, the victory of struggling liberty, was celebrated. It was a fair day. In the harbor all the vessels were dressed over all, their mastheads adorned with long pennants, the most splendid were hoisted on the main flagstaffs, and there were others on the jackstaffs and strung between the masts. There was just wind enough to make flags and pennants fly free.–Father had invited a few guests and, contrary to the prevailing custom, we boys were bidden to table. Father explained the significance of this festival, our glasses were filled with punch, and as toasts were drunk to the success of the new republic, a Danish and a North American flag were hoisted in our garden."

The Battle of Copenhagen April 2. 1801 between the British Navy under Lord Nelson and the Danes under Admiral Olfert Fischer. Contemporary painting by C. A. Lorentzen. Frederiksborg Castle.

The driving force that propelled the Pilgrim Fathers, the immigrants and the pioneers westward, was not the mighty skyscrapers, the many automobiles, nor the American capital, for they did not exist. The immigrants found two things in America which they wanted and could use: land and liberty. With bare hands and strong determination they created all the other things and built up mighty, modern America from a wilderness.

*

The Saga says of Njal, 'He was peace-loving, and yet manly'. This expression can also be applied to the Danes of today.

Under pressure from abroad, and due to fatal errors from within, Denmark's military power dwindled away. In the 300 years since King Christian IV lost the battle of Lutter am Barenberg against Tilly, the military might of Denmark has been in retreat. And yet it is not very long ago that Denmark could defend herself powerfully.

The Battle of Copenhagen was fought on April 2, 1801. There Lord Nelson, the English naval hero, had the stiffest fight of his career. The Danish Admiral, Olfert Fischer, almost succeeded in defeating him and, from a military point of view, the battle was a draw. But by a diplomatic trick, Nelson forced the Danes to withdraw from the Baltic league of neutrality.

In memory of this battle the name of Copenhagen is carved on Nelson's sarcophagus, alongside those of Aboukir and Trafalgar. The gallant Lord Nelson, who was born in Norfolk and had the blue Nordic eyes, instinctively addressed the celebrated letter by which he rescued himself from his difficult position during the battle, 'To the Brothers of Englishmen, the Danes.' His admiration for the bravery and good sportmanship of the Danes was unreserved when, on his landing for negotiations with the Crown Prince during a brief truce, the people of Copenhagen greeted him with cheers. Those were pleasant times in which to fight.

But it was a misfortune for both Denmark and England when, six years later, in 1807, England attacked neutral Denmark because she feared that the large Danish fleet might be forced to join up with Napoleon's. This broke the commercial and naval power of Denmark and led to its separation from Norway. In the long run it was by no means advantageous to England that Denmark, which from a political and sentimental point of view was closely linked with England, was no

Admiral Olfert Fischer's
pocket powder-horn.
Cut in brier with the monogram:
O. F. in the ivory button.

longer a military factor in Northern Europe. This was one of the causes of Prussia's rise and of all that resulted therefrom.

Although Denmark's army was posted in the Duchies of Holstein and Slesvig for the very purpose of defending the country against Napoleon, despite the fact that the fleet was not equipped for war, despite the fact that 350 Danish merchant ships lay in English ports, and despite the fact that nobody in Denmark suspected England's intentions, the British fleet sailed past Kronborg with friendly salutes, anchored off Copenhagen, and demanded the surrender of the Danish fleet. Without its navy Denmark would have become an easy prey for Napoleon, but nevertheless the English insisted it be handed over until the conclusion of the war. They bombarded Copenhagen, destroyed 1,000 buildings, carried off the fleet, and in addition seized 1,400 Danish merchant ships on the high seas and in British ports.

It was cold comfort that Canning, planning the seizure, was condemned by a great part of the British public. 'Dishonorable as the expedition to Copenhagen', became in those days a common expression in England.

England is not justified in reproaching Denmark for not having been in a position since then to defend herself by means of that fleet which England herself destroyed. But, taking the long view, and recalling the Viking expeditions, England can justify the action by pointing out that it was the Danes who started such operations.

*

As recently as 1848-1850, Denmark was able to defeat the Germans in the battles of Fredericia and Isted. But in 1864, Denmark fought an unequal though honorable war alone against Germany and Austria—the same two powers that all the countries of the world had difficulty in defeating in the First World War. Denmark then stood almost more alone than did England in 1940-41. She was overcome by superior force and for a time lost Slesvig.

Trevelyan says of the situation, "A less fortunate episode in European affairs closed the epoch of Russell and Palmerston. A dispute lay between Denmark and her German neighbours, over the Slesvig-Holstein provinces, whence fourteen hundred years before a large part of the English people migrated to Britain. The merits of the case were divided, and there was room for the good offices of a judicious third party, friendly to all concerned. But Palmerston and Russell took up a position of bravado in encouraging 'little Denmark' which they could not make good when Bismarck called their bluff. Palmerston had declared that 'it would not be Denmark alone' with whom her assailants would have to contend. Yet when war came she found no ally, for our still unreformed army was in no condition to take the field against the united forces of Prussia, Austria, and indeed all Germany. And the famous Volunteer movement of the mid-Victorian epoch was as yet for home defence alone. Nor could we expect the help of France and Russia, whom our diplomacy had recently offended. The Palmerstonian era ended therefore with a humiliating rebuff. The importance of the case was even greater than men knew at the time, for the full meaning of the modern military monarchy of Prussia had yet to be revealed by the victories over Austria in 1866 and France in 1870."

When, after the first World War, Denmark regained loyal North Slesvig, the partly Germanized South Slesvig chose to remain under German rule. Sentimental and material interests may change, but race and origin stand fast in history. The German doctrine of 'blood and

338

soil' may have given the population of South Slesvig something to think about. They have been under German rule since 1864–but Danish in blood and tongue since the days of the Stone Age.

After the Second World War, the British army, by one of those strange accidents of history, was for a period master of Angel in South Slesvig, the only spot in Europe which, a millennium and a half ago, could rightly bear the name England.

*

In Denmark were united those roots that formed the Danish tree: a trunk not tall, but sturdy.

From the ancient Danish lands all the Teutonic peoples spread like strong, crooked branches, stretching in all directions.

How did this happen? What made Denmark this strange center of events?

I think it was the spirit, the peculiar blend of blood, the place where the seed was sown and the good soil in which the roots ran. Overarching it was the ever-changing sky with the keen, crisp air coming in from the sea. Running through the leafy cover was the restlessness of the wind from the west. All these gave nourishment and growth. And so the tree grew.

It spread its branches wide across the world. They now give shade to great stretches of sea and land, while the boughs beat and thresh in the fresh breeze, and drop their fruits for good and evil.

The tree still stands. A heart is carved in the bark.

Gold buckle from the Viking Age. Hornelund. Jutland.

BIBLIOGRAPHY

Åberg, Nils: *Striden mellan Rom och Germanien*, 1921. Svensk Hist. tidskr., 257-278.

Aakjær, Svend: *Det danske Sprogs Oprindelse og Udvikling*, 1927. Det danske Folks Historie I, 67-98. Chr. Erichsen, København. *D.S.*

− *Old Danish Thegns and Drengs*, 1927-28. Acta philolog. scand. II. *ODT.*

− *Bosættelse og Bebyggelsesformer i Danmark i ældre Tid*, 1933. Institutet for sammenlignende Kulturforskning. Serie A, XV. Bidrag til Bondesamfundets Historie II, 109-182. *B.B.*

− *Jarl, Aar og Lev-Mand*, 1934. Festskrift til Vilhelm Andersen, 320 pp. Gyldendal, København. *J.A.L.*

− *Gammeldansk Grundskyld og Grundrente*, 1934. Arbejdets og Samfundets Organisation, 27-30. *G.G.*

− *Maal og Vægt*, 1936. Nordisk Kultur. XXX. Schultz, København. *M.V.*

− *Om Navnet Vendsyssel*, 1938. Jydske Samlinger. 5 R. Bd. 4, 93-103. *N.V.*

− *Kong Valdemars Jordebog*, 1943. Indledning. Gyldendal, København. *V.J.*

− *Land Measurement and Land Valuation in Medieval Denmark*, 1960. The Scandinavian Economic History Review, vol. VII, no. 2, 115-149. *L.M.*

Almgren, Oscar: *Nordische Felszeichnungen als religiøse Urkunden*, 1934. Diesterweg, Frankfurt am Main.

Althin, Carl Axel: *Studien zu den bronzezeitlischen Felszeichnungen von Skaane*, LII, 1945. Gleerup, Lund.

Anderson, Ingvar: *Sveriges Historie gennem Tiderne*, 1941. Gad, København.

− *Skånes Historia*, 1947. Nordstedt, Stockholm. *Sk.*

Annales Quedlinburgenses, 1839. Monumenta Germaniae historica. Script. III.

Arbman, H. & M. Stenberger: *Vikinger i Västerled*, 1935. Bonniers, Stockholm.

− *Svear i Österviking*, 1955. Natur och Kultur, Stockholm.

− *The Vikings*, 1961. Ancient Peoples and Places. Thames and Hudson, London.

Arne, T. J.: *Østeuropas och Nordbalkans förhistoria*, 1927. Friis Johansen: De forhistoriske Tider i Europa I, 367-460. Koppel, København.

Arup, Erik: *Danmarks Historie I, II*, 1925, 1932. Hagerup, København.

Askeberg, Fritz: *Norden och Kontinenten i gammal tid*, 1944. Almqvist & Wiksell, Uppsala.

Baker, G. P.: *The Fighting Kings of Wessex*, 1931. Bell, London.

Bay, Sv. Aage: *Bonde og Viking*, 1954. Reitzel. København.

Becker, C. J.: *Skeletfundet fra Porsmose ved Næstved*, 1952. Fra Nationalmuseets Arbejdsmark, 25-30.

− *Smykkefundet fra Ørby. Et glimt fra Sjællands glemte Storhedstid*, 1955. Fra Nationalmuseets Arbejdsmark, 26-34.

− *Førromersk Jernalder i Syd- og Midtjylland*, 1961. Nationalmuseets Skrifter VI.

Beckman, Nathaniel: *Sverige i islandsk tradition*, 1922. Sv. Hist. tidskr., 152-167.

Belaiew, N. T.: *Rorik of Jutland and Rurik of the Russian Chronicles*, 1928. Saga-Book of the Viking Society X, 267-297.

Belloc, Hilaire: *A History of England* I, 1926. II' Ed. Methuen, London.

Bing, Just: *Fra trolldom til gudetro*, 1937. Oslo.

Birkeland, Harris: *Nordens historie i Middelalderen efter arabiske kilder.* Skrifter utgitt av Det Norke Videnskaps-Akademi i Oslo II, 2, 1-177.

Bjerrum, Anders: *Anglernes Hjemstavn*, 1951. Sønderjydske Årbøger II, 202-254.

Bjerrum, J. & Th. Ramskou: *Danmarks Sydgrænse*, 1948. Munksgaard, København.

Bjørkman, E.: *Beowulf*, 1917. Nordisk tidskrift, 174. *B.*

– *Engelska ortsnamn och deras betydelse som historiska minnesmärken*, 1919. Nordisk tidskrift, 553-570. *E.O.*

Blair, Peter Hunter: *An Introduction to Anglo-Saxon England*, 1956. Cambridge U.P.

Blinkenberg, Chr.: *Grækenlands forhistoriske Kultur*, 1927. Friis Johansen: De forhistoriske Tider i Europa I, 109-120. Koppel, København.

Bolin, Sture: *Skånelands historia* I-II, 1930-1933. Borelius. *S.*

– *Muhammed, Karl den Store och Rurik*, 1939. Scandia. XII, 181-222. *M.*

Bonjour, Adrien: *The Digressions in Beowulf*, 1950. Medium Ævum Monographs V. Basil Blackwell, Oxford.

Brate, Erik: *Pireus-lejonets runinskrift*, 1919. Antikvarisk tidskrift för Sverige, XX, 3.

Brix, Hans: *The Inscription on the older Jellingestone*, 1927-28. Acta philologica scandinavica II, 110.

Broholm, H. C.: *Danmarks Bronzealder* I, II, 1943, 1944. Nyt nordisk Forlag, København.

Brooke, George C.: *English Coins*, 1932. Methuen, London.

Bruce-Mitford, R. L. S.: *The Sutton Hoo Ship Burial*, 1947. British Museum, London.

Bryant, Sir Arthur: *The Story of England.* Makers of the Realm, I, 1960. Collins, London.

Brøgger, A. W.: *Osebergdronningen*, 1919. Nordisk tidskrift, 225 f. *O.*

– *Det norske folk i oldtiden*, 1925. Inst. for sammenlign. kulturforskning. Aschehoug, Oslo. *N.F.*

– *Bronsealderen i Central-, Vest- og Nordeuropa*, 1927. Friis Johansen: De forhist. Tider i Europa II, 169-275. Koppel, København. *Br.*

Brøndal, Viggo: *Danernes Navn*, 1920. Danske Studier, 17-41.

Brøndsted, Johs.: *Early English Ornament*, 1924. Levin & Munksgaard, København, London. *E.E.O.*

– *Vort Folks Oldtidsliv og forhistoriske Minder*, 1927. Det danske Folks Historie I, 103-260. Chr. Erichsen, København. *D.F.H.*

– *Handel og Samfærdsel i Oldtiden*, 1934. Nordisk Kultur, XVI, A, 3-26. *H.S.O.*

– *Danmarks Oldtid* I-III, 1938-1948. (2. Ed. 1957-1960). Gyldendal, København. *D.O.*

– & Poul Nørlund: Seks Tværsnit af Danmarkshistorien, 1941. Gyldendal, København. *Tv.*

– *Nordens første Bebyggelse*, 1950. Fra Nationalmuseets Arbejdsmark, 101-112. *N.*

– *The Vikings*, 1960. Penguin. *V.*

Bugge, Alexander: *Vikingerne* I-II, 1904-1906. Gyldendal, København. *Vik.*
– *Nordmændenes vikingefærder i det 9'de aarhundrede og grundlæggelsen av her-tugdømmet Normandiet,* 1911. Nordisk tidsskrift, 329-342. *N.*

Bull, Edv.: *Studier over Norges administrative inddeling i middelalderen,* 1917 No. Historisk tidskrift. V rk., bd. 4, 257-282. *St.*
– *Leding,* 1920. Steensen, Kristiania & København. *L.*

Bøggild-Andersen, C. O.: *Statsomvæltningen i 1660,* 1936. Munksgaard, København. *St.*
– *Norden i Verdenshistorien,* 1943. Hans Jensen: Det forenede Norden, 43-119, Arthur Jensen, København. *N.V.*

Chadwick, H. Munro: *The Origin of the English Nation,* 1907. Cambridge U.P.
– *The Heroic Age,* 1926. Cambridge U.P. *HA.*

Chadwick, Sonia E.: *The Anglo-Saxon Cemetery at Finglesham, Kent: a Reconsid-eration,* 1959. Medieval Archaeology, vol. 2, 1958, 1-71.

du Chaillu, Paul B.: *The Viking Age. The early History, Manners and Customs of the Ancestors of the English-speaking Nations* I-II, 1889. London.

Chambers, R. W.: *Widsith,* 1912. Cambridge U.P. *W.*
– *Beowulf,* 1932. Cambridge U.P. *B.*

Childe, V. Gordon: *The Relation between Greece and Prehistoric Europe,* 1958. Acta Congressus Madvigiani I, 293-316. Munksgaard, København.

Churchill, Sir Winston S.: *Københavns Universitets Promotionsfest den 10. Oktober 1950,* 1951. Bianco Luno, København. 19-22. *KU.*
– *A History of the English-speaking Peoples* I, 1956. Cassell, London. *HE.*

Clark, J. G. H.: *Prehistoric Europe. The Economic Basis,* 1952. Methuen, London.

Clausen, H. V.: *Studier over Danmarks Oldtidsbebyggelse,* 1916. Årbøger for nordisk Oldkyndighed og Historie III, R. 6 Bd., 1-226. *S.D.O.*
– *Kong Hugleik,* 1918. Danske Studier, 137-149. *K.H.*

Collingwood, R. G. & J. N. L. Myres: *Roman Britain and the English Settlements,* 1937. G. N. Clark: The Oxford History of England II, Ed.

Collingwood, W. G.: *Scandinavian Britain,* Early Britain, 1908. Society of Promot-ing Christian Knowledge, London.

Coon, C. S.: *The Races of Europe,* 1939. Macmillan, New York.

Corbett, William John: *The Foundation of the Kingdom of England,* 1922. The Cambridge Medieval History, vol. III. Ch. XIV, 340-370. Cambridge U.P. *F.*
– *England from A.D. 954 to the Death of Edward the Confessor,* 1922. The Cam-bridge Medieval History, vol. III, Ch. XV, 371-408. Cambridge U.P. *E.*

la Cour, Vilh.: *Geschichte des schleswigschen Volkes* I, 1923. Schleswigschen Ver-lag, Flensburg. *G.*
– *Sjællands ældste Bygder,* 1927. Aschehoug, København. *Sj.*
– *Kong Gorm og Dronning Tyre,* 1926-27. Historisk Tidsskrift, IX, rk. bd. 5, 189-252. *G.T.*
– *Vort Folks Oprindelse og ældste Historie,* 1927. Det danske Folks Historie I, 263-354. Chr. Erichsen, København. *V.F.O.*
– *Sønderjyllands Historie* I, 1931. Reitzel, København. *S.J.*

la Cour, Vilh.: *Kong Haralds tre Storværker.* 1934. Årbøger f. nord. Oldkynd. og Hist., 55-87. *H.St.*

– *Knud den Store,* 1937. Dansk biografisk Lexikon XII, 566. *K.St.*

– *Vort Folks Oprindelse,* 1941. Schultz Danmarkshistorie I. Schultz, København. *Sch.*

– *Danmarks ældste Konger,* 1944. Knud Fabricius: Danmarks Konger, 23-47. Jespersen og Pio, København. *D.K.*

– *Danevirkestudier,* 1952. Haase. *D.*

Danstrup, John: *A History of Denmark,* 1947. Wivel, København.

Dawson, John: *England and the Nordic Race,* 1924. Duckworth & Co., London. (Rec: W. G. Collingwood: Yearbook of the Viking Society, London, 1924, 120).

Depping, M.: *Histoire des expéditions maritimes des Normands,* 1844. Didier, Paris.

Douglas, David C.: *Rollo of Normandy,* 1942. The English Historical Review, vol. LXII, 417-436. *R.*

– *The Rise of Normandy,* 1947. Raleigh Lecture. Oxford U.P. *N.*

Erslev, Kr.: *Valdemarernes Storhedstid,* 1898. Jacob Erslev, København. *V.*

– *Dronning Tyre og Danevirke,* 1939. Historisk Tidsskr., IX rk. bd. 6, 1-53. *T.D.*

Estancelin, L.: *Recherches sur les voyages et découvertes des navigateurs Normands,* 1832. Delaunay, Paris.

Fabricius, A.: *Forbindelserne mellem Norden og den spanske Halvø i ældre Tider,* 1882. Gad, København. *N.S.*

– *Danske Minder i Normandiet,* 1897. Langhoff, København. *M.*

Fabricius, Knud: *Kongemagten gennem Tiderne,* 1944. Danmarks Konger, 7-22. Jespersen og Pio, København.

Fahlbeck, Pontus: *Den s. k. striden mellan Svear och Götar,* 1884. Sv. Hist. tidskrift, 105-154. *S.G.*

– *Beowulfsqvädet, 1891.* Antiqvarisk tidskrift för Sverige VIII, 2, 1884-1891, 1-87. *B.*

Feist, Sigmund: *Das Volkstum der Kimbrer und Teutonen,* 1929. Zeitschr f. schweizerische Geschichte, 129-160.

Fliche, Augustin: *L'Europe occidentale de 888 a 1125,* 1930. Gustave Glotz: Historie generaie. Tome II: Historie du moyen age. Les presses universitaires de France, Paris.

Foord, Edward: *The Last Age of Roman Britain,* 1925. Harrap, London.

Fossing, Poul: *Pytheas og Ravlandet Abalus,* 1943. Årbøger f. nord. Oldk. og Hist., 174-182.

Freeman, Edward A.: *The History of the Norman Conquest of England* I, 1867. Clarendon Press, Oxford.

Frets, G. P.: *Heredity of the Cephalic Index,* 1924. Martinus Nijhoff.s-Gravenhage.

Fridericia, I. A. *Danmarks Riges Historie* IIII, 1896-1907. Nordisk Forlag, København.

v. Friesen, Otto: *Herulernas bosättning i Skandinavien,* 1918. Studier tillegnade Esaias Tegnér, 485-495. Gleerup, Lund. *H.*

– *Rökstenen,* 1920. Jacob Bagges Söner, Stockholm. *Rök.*

v. Friesen, Otto: *Rö-Stenen i Bohuslän och runorna i Norden under folkvandrings-tiden*, 1924. Uppsala Universitets Årsskrift. *Rö.*

– *Runorna*, 1933. Nordisk Kultur VI. Schultz, København. Bonniers, Stockholm. *Ru.*

Funck-Brentano, Fr.: *Frankrigs Oprindelse*, 1926. Frankrigs Historie I. Koppel, København.

Fürst, Carl M.: *Stenålderskelett från Hvellinge i Skåne och något om våra forn-kranier*, 1910. Fornvännen, 13-29. *St.*

– *När de döda vittna*, 1920. Konst- och kulturhistoriskt bibliotek 2. Svenska Teknologföreningens Förlag, Stockholm. *D.*

Galster, Georg: *"Knud den Stores og Dronning Emmas billeder"*. Årbøger for nordisk Oldkyndighed og Historie. 1960. P: 96-117.

Gedde, Knud & C. F. S. Trock: *This is Denmark*, 1948. J. Gjellerup.

Gjessing, G.: *Fangstfolk*, 1941. Ascheoug, Oslo.

Glob, P. V.: *Den jydske Enkeltgravskultur*, 1945. Gyldendal, København.

Gosse, Sir Edmund W.: *The Ethical Condition of the Early Scandinavian Peoples*, 1874. Publ. of the Victoria Inst. or Phil. Soc. of Great Britain.

Graham, I. W.: *William Penn*, 1916. New York.

Gravlund, Thorkild: *Dansk Folkekarakter*, 1919. Gyldendal, København.

Gray, H. St. George: *On Danes' Skins*, 1906-07. Saga Book of the Viking Club, V, 218-229.

Green, John Richard: *The Conquest of England* I, II, 1906. Macmillan, London. *C.*

– *A Short History of the English People*, 1909. XXVII Ed. Macmillan, *HE.*

Grønbech, Vilh.: *Vor Folkeæt i Oldtiden* I-III, 1909-1912. Pio, København. *F.*

– *Religionsskiftet i Norden*, 1913. Gyldendal, København. *R.N.*

– *Nordiske Myter og Sagn*, 1927. Pio, København. *N.M.S.*

– *The Culture of the Teutons* I-III, 1932. Humphrey Milford. Oxford Univ. Press., London. Jespersen og Pio, Copenhagen. *T.*

Gudmundsson, Valtyr: *Island i Fristatstiden*, 1924. Gad, København.

Gudmundsson, Bardi: *Götalands politiske Stilling fra 950 til 1050,* 1927. Hist. Tids-skr., Oslo. V. rk. bd. 6, 533-572.

Gutenbrunner, S. & Jankuhn, H. & Laur, W.: *Völker und Stämme Südostschles-wigs im frühen Mittelalter,* 1952. Gottorfer Schriften I.

Günther, Hans F. K.: *Herkunft und Rassengechichte der Germanen,* 1935, München.

Haddon, A. C.: *The Wanderings of Peoples,* 1911. Cambridge Manuals of Science and Litt.

Haff, Karl: *Die dänischen Gemeinderechte* I-II, 1909. Deichert, Leipzig.

Hald, Kristian: *Vore Stednavne,* 1950. Gad, København.

Hamerik, Angul: *Dansk Musikhistorie til ca. 1700,* 1921. Gad, København.

Hatt, Gudmund: *Landbrug i Danmarks Oldtid,* 1937. Gad, København.

Hansson, Johan: *Arbejdslønnen og Jorden,* 1913. Rasmus Nielsen, Kolding.

Héricourt, J.: *Les Maladies des Societés,* 1918. Flammarion, Paris.

Heyne-Schucking: *Beowulf, 1946-49.* 16' Auflage. Else von Schaubert. Schöningh, Paderborn.

Hodgkin, R. H.: *A History of the Anglo-Saxons* I-II, 1935. Clarendon, Oxford.

345

Hodgkin, Thomas: *The History of England from the earliest Times to the Norman Conquest*, 1931. The Political History of England I. Longmans, London.

Holmberg, Åke: *Nordens Enhed*, 1941. Politikens Kronik: Dec. 5. 1941.

Hoops, Johannes: *Reallexicon der germanischen Altertumskunde* I-IIII. Karl J. Trübner, Strassburg, 1911-1919.

Hougen, Bjørn: *Handelsforbindelser i Norge indtil 600 e. Kr.*, 1934. Nordisk Kultur. XVI, 27-38. Schultz, København.

Hunt, William: *Canute*, 1887. Dictionary of National Biography, vol. IX, 1-8. Smith, Elder & Co., London.

Jacobsen, Lis: *Svenskevældets Fald*, 1929. Levin & Munksgaard, København. *Sv.*
– *Kong Haralds og Kong Gorms Jelling-Monumenter*, 1931. Scandia. IV, 234. *H.G.*
– & Erik Moltke: *Danmarks Runeinskrifter*, 1942. Munksgaard, København. *Ru.*

Jahn, Martin: *Der Wanderweg der Kimbern, Teutonen und Wandalen*, 1932. Mannus. Bd. 24, 150-157. *K.T.*
– *Die Heimat der Wandalen und Norwegen*, 1937. Acta archæologica, vol. VIII, 149-167. *W.N.*

Jankuhn, Herbert: *Haithabu*, 1938. Wachholtz, Neumünster. *H.*
– *Zur Frage nach der Urheimat der Angeln*. Zeitschr. d. Gesellschaft f. Schleswig-Holsteinische Geschichte, 1943. Bd. 70-71, 1-48. *A.*

Jespersen, Otto: *Growth and Structure of the English Language*, 1912. II' Ed. Leipzig, Teubner.

Jolliffe, J. E. A.: *Pre-Feudal England. The Jutes*, 1933. Oxford Historical Series. Oxford U.P. Milford, London. *J.*
– *The Constitutional History of Medieval England*, 1937. Adam & Charles Black, London. *C.*

Jordanes: *Getica*. Mon. Germaniae historica. Auctores antiquiss. Th. Mommsen. Tom. V. Weidmann, Berlin, 1882.

Jørgensen, Ellen: *Nyere Bidrag til de syditalienske Normanners Historie*, 1912-1913. Historisk Tidsskrift. VIII R. Bd. 4, 222-232.

Jørgensen, Poul Johs.: *Jordfællesskab*, 1922. Salmonsens Konversationslexikon, XIII, 179-184. *J.*
– *Dansk Retshistorie*, 1940. Gad, København. *R.*

Jørgensen, Peter: *Über die Herkunft der Nordfriesen*, 1946. Videnskabernes Selskabs Skrifter, København.

Karsten, T. E.: *Germanerna*, 1925. Natur och Kultur. Bd. 47.

Keary, C. F.: *The Vikings in Western Christendom*, 1891. Fischer Unwin, London.

Kendrick, Sir Thomas:*A History of the Vikings*, 1930. Methuen, London.
– *The Sutton Hoo Ship Burial*, 1947. British Museum, London. *S.*

Ker, W. P.: *Iceland and the Humanities*, 1906-07. Saga Book of the Viking Club. V, 341-353.

Kersten, Karl: *Zur älteren nordischen Bronzezeit*, 1935. Kiel.
– *Ein Moorleichenfund von Osterby bei Eckernförde*, 1949. Offa. 8, 1.

Klaatsch, Herman: *Menneskets og Kulturens Opstaaen og Udvikling*, 1924. Koppel, København.

Klindt-Jensen, Ole: *The Vikings in England*, 1948. Gyldendal, København. *V.*

Klindt-Jensen, Ole: *Bornholm i Folkevandringstiden,* 1957. Nationalmuseet. København. *B.*

– *Denmark Before the Vikings,* 1957. Ancient Peoples and Places. Thames and Hudson, London. *D.*

– *Gundestrupkedelen,* 1961. Nationalmuseet, København.

Knudsen, Gunnar: *De danske Stednavne,* 1939. Nordisk Kultur. Schultz.

Knorr, Fr.: *Bootkammergrab südlich der Oldenburg bei Schleswig,* 1911. Mitteilungen d. antropolog. Verein in Schl.-Holst. XIX, 68-77.

Koht, Halvdan: *Innhoog og utsyn i norsk historie,* 1921. Aschehoug, Kristania.

Kolding, Kr.: *Dansk Jord* I, II, 1942. Skandinavisk Bogforlag, Odense.

Kossinna, Gustav: *Ursprung und Verbreitung der Germanen in vor- und frühgeschichtlischer Zeit,* 1928. Mannus Bibliothek Nr. 6, Leipzig. *G.*

– *Wikinger und Wäringer.* Mannus, 1929, bd. 21, 84-112. *Wik.*

– *Die Wandalen in Nordjütland,* 1929. Mannus, bd. 21, 233-255. *W.N.*

Kretschmer, Ernst: *Körperbau und Character,* 1936. XI-XII Ed. Springer, Berlin.

– *Geniale Menschen,* 1948. 4. Aufl. Springer, Berlin.

Kroman, Erik: *Musikalsk Akcent i Dansk,* 1947. Munksgaard, København.

de Laet, Siegfried J.: *Wooden Animal Heads of Carolingian Times found in the River Scheldt,* 1936. Acta Archaeologica XXVII, 127-137.

Larsen, Henrik: *Nogle Oplysninger og Bemærkninger om danske Landsbyer,* 1918. Årbøger f. nord. Oldk. og Hist. III, 177-293.

Larsen, Martin: *Den ældre Edda og Eddica minora* I-II, 1943-1946. Munksgaard, København.

Larsen, Sofus: *Nordamerikas Opdagelse tyve Aar før Columbus,* 1925. Geografisk Tidskr., bd. 28, 88-110 (with English summary). *NO.*

– *Jomsborg,* 1927, 1928, 1931. Årbøger f. nord. Oldk. og Hist. III, R. bd. 17, 18, 21.

Larson, Laurence M.: *Canute the Great, and the Rise of Danish Imperialism during the Viking Age,* 1912. Heroes of the Nations. Putnam, New York and London.

Lauring, Palle: *Vikingerne,* 1956. Schønberg, København.

– *Danelagen,* 1957. Gyldendal, København.

– *A History of the Kingdom of Denmark,* 1960. Høst & Søn, København.

Leach, Henry Goddard: *A Pageant of Old Scandinavia,* 1946. The American-Scandinavian Foundation. New York. Princeton U.P., Princeton.

Leeds, E. Thurlow: *The Archaeology of the Anglo-Saxon Settlements,* 1913. Clarendon Press, Oxford.

Liebermann, F.: *Die Gesetze der Angelsachsen,* 1903 f. bd. I-III. Max Niemeyer, Halle.

Lindqvist, Sune: *Sveriges Handel och samfärdsel under forntiden,* 1934. Nordisk Kultur. XVI, 49-67. Schultz.

Lienhard-Egen, Ludwig: *Der Kimbrische Kernkreis,* 1940. Trilsch. Würtzburg-Aumühlen.

Ljungberg, Helge: *Den nordiska religionen och kristendommen,* 1938. Nordiska texter och undersøkninger. XI. Geber: Stockholm. Munksgaard, København.

Lukman, Niels Clausen: *Skjoldunge und Skilfinge. Hunnen- und Herulerkönige in ostnordischer Überlieferung,* 1943. Gyldendal, København.

347

Lundbye, J. T.: *Danmarks Veje i Oldtid og Middelalder*, 1934. Nordisk Kultur. XVI, 200-216. Schultz, København.

MacDougall, W.: *The Group Mind*, 1920. Cambridge Psychological Library.

Mackeprang, Mogens B.: *Danmarks Befolkning i Jernalderen*, 1936. Nordisk Kultur. Befolkning i Oldtiden, 11-32. Schultz, København.

Magoun, Francis P.: *The Sutton Hoo Ship-Burial: A Chronological Bibliography*, 1954. Speculum. XXIV, 116-126.

Matthiessen, Hugo: *Hærvejen*, 1934. Gyldendal, København.

Maurer, K.: *Die Bekehrung des norwegischen Stamme zum Christentum* I, II, 1855, 1856. München.

Mawer, Sir Allen: *Ragnar Lothbrok and his Sons*, 1908-1909. Saga Book of the Viking Club. VI, 68-89. *R.L.*
- *The Scandinavian Kingdom of Northumbria*, 1911. Saga Book of the Viking Club. VII, 38-64. *N.H.*
- *The Vikings*, 1913. Cambridge Manuals of Science and Litterature. *Vik.*
- *The Vikings*, 1921. The Cambridge Medieval History. Vol. III, Ch. XIII, 309-339. *C.*

Moberg, Ove: *Slaget på Fyrisvallerna och kampen vid Uppsala*, 1937. Scandia. X, 129-142. *F.*
- *Olav Haraldsson, Knut den Store och Sverige*, 1941. Glerup, Lund. Munksgaard, København. *O.*

Moltke, Erik: *Er Runeskriften opstået i Danmark?*, 1951. Fra Nationalmuseets Arbejdsmark, 47-58.

Montelius, Oscar: *Et i Sverige funnit fornitaliskt bronskärl*, 1902. Svenska fornminnesföreningens tidskrift XI, 1 f. *Sv.Br.*
- *Kulturgeschichte Schwedens*, 1906. Seeman, Leipzig. *K.S.*
- *Germanernes hem*, 1917. Nordisk tidskrift, 401 f. *G.H.*
- *Germanernes förfäder*, 1918. Geologiska föreningen i Stockholms förhandlingar, 749 f. *G.F.*
- *De ariska folkens hem*, 1921. Nordisk tidskrift, 401 f. *A. F.*

Much, M.: *Die Heimat der Indogermanen*, 1902. Costenoble, Wien.

Much, R.: *Hoop's Reallexicon*. Articles about Dänen, Heruler etc.

Müller, Sophus: *Vor Oldtid*, 1897. Nordisk Forlag, København.

Myres, I. L.: *Tidernes Morgen*, 1927. Haase, København. *T.M.*
- *The English Settlements*, 1937. II' Ed. Book V, 325-456, in: R. G. Collingwood & I. N. L. Myres: *Roman Britain and the English Settlements*. The Oxford History of England. Clarendon Press, Oxford. *E.S.*

Neergaard, Carl: *Guldfundene fra den efterromerske Jernalder*, 1915. Årbøger f. nord. Oldk. og Hist., 173-204.

Nerman, Birger: *Härstamma Danerna ifrån Svealand?*, 1922. Fornvännen, 129-140. *D.Sv.*
- *Goternas äldsta hem*, 1923. Fornvännen, 165-182. *G.H.*
- *Die Herkunft und die frühesten Auswanderungen der Germanen*, 1924. Kung. vitterhets historie och antikvitets akademiens handlingar, 5-63. *G.*
- *Det svenska rikets uppkomst*, 1925, Stockholm. *S.R.*

Nielsen, H. A.: *Bidrag til Danmarks Befolknings – særligt Stenalderfolkets – Antropologi*, 1906. Årbøger f. nord. Oldk. og Hist. II, rk. bd. 21, 237-318.

Noach, Ulrich: *Nordische Frühgeschichte und Wikingerzeit*, 1941. Geschichte der Völker und Staaten. R. Oldenburg, München, Berlin.

Nordenstreng, Rolf: *Vikingafärderna*, 1915. Norstedt, Stockholm.

Nordman, C. A.: *Den yngre stenålderen i Mellan-, Väst- och Nordeuropa*, 1927. Friis Johansen: De forhist. Tider i Europa II, 5-168. Koppel, København.

Norling-Christensen, Hans: *Gjølstrupfundet*, 1944. Fra Nationalmuseets Arbejdsmark, 99-104.

Nørlund, Poul: *De ældste Vidnesbyrd om Skyldtaxationen*, 1929. Historisk Tidskrift, 9. række, bd. 6, 54-95. *Sk.*

– *Trelleborg*, 1948. Gyldendal, København. *T.*

– *Gyldne Altre*. (Golden Altars. Danish Metal Work from the Romanesque Period). 1926. Society for Publication of Works on Danish Monuments. *G.*

Ohlhaver, H.: *Germanen erobern England*, 1937. Germanenerbe.

Olrik, Axel: *Den nordiske Nationalitetsforskel i sin tidligste Fremtræden*, 1898. Nordisk tidskrift, 601-616. Folkelige Afhandlinger, 1919, 52-69. Gyldendal, København. *N.N.*

– *Danerne ved deres Fremtræden i Historien*, 1903. Dansk Tidsskrift, 9-25. Folkelige Afhandlinger, 1919, 12 f. Gyldendal, København. *D.F.*

– *Danmarks Heltedigtning* I, II, 1903, 1910. Gad, København. *D.H.*

– *Eddamytologien*, 1917. Nordisk tidskrift, 81 f. *E.*

– *Nordisk Aandsliv i Vikingetid og tidlig Middelalder*, 1927. Gyldendal, København. *N.Aa.*

– & Hans Ellekilde: *Nordens Gudeverden*, 1926 f. Gad, København. *N.G.*

Olrik, Hans: *Konge og Præstestand i den danske Middelalder* I, 1892. Gad, København.

Olsen, Olaf & O. Crumlin Pedersen: *The Skuldelev Ships*. 1958. Acta Archaeologica. XXIX. 161-175.

– *Arkæologi under Vandet*, 1959. Fra Nationalmuseets Arbejdsmark, 1959, 5-20.

Oman, Sir Charles: *England before the Norman Conquest*, 1924. 6' Ed. Methuen, Oxford. *E.*

– *The Danish Kingdom of York*, 1934. The Archaeological Journal, XCI, 1-21. *Y.*

Sct. Omer, Munken fra: *Kong Knuts Liv og Gerninger* (Encomium Emmae. Gesta Cnutonis) oversat af M. Cl. Gertz. Selskabet for historiske Kildeskrifters Oversættelse, 1896. Schønberg, København.

Oxenstierna, Graf Eric: *Die Urheimat der Goten*, 1948. Uppsala. Johan Barth, Leipzig. Geber, Stockholm. *U.*

– *Die Goldhörner von Gallehus*, 1956. Selbstverlag, Lidingö. *G.*

– *Die Wikinger*, 1959. Kohlhammer, Stuttgart. *G.*

Paulsen, Peter: *Studien zur Wikinger-Kultur*, 1933. Veröffentlichungen der Schleswig-Holst. Univ. Gesellsch. R. II, nr. 1. Wachholtz, Neumünster.

Penka, Karl: *Die Herkunft der Arier*, 1886. Prochaska, Wien.

Petersen, Jan: *Handel i Norge i Vikingetiden*, 1934. Nordisk Kultur, XVI, 39-48. Schultz, København.

Philips, C. W.:*The Excavasion of the Sutton Hoo Ship-burial,* 1940. The Antiquaries Journal XX, 149-202.

Phillpotts, Bertha: *Edda and Saga,* 1931. Butterworth, London.

Pirenne, Henri: Mahomet et Charlemagne, 1937. 4' Ed. Alcan, Paris (Mohammed and Charlemagne, 1960. Meridian. New York).

Plettke, Alfred: *Ursprung und Ausbreitung der Angeln und Sachsen. Beiträge zur Siedlungsarchæologie der Ingväonen,* 1921. Die Urnenfriedhöfe in Niedersachsen, bd. III, heft I. Hildesheim & Leipzig.

Pollard, A. F.: *The History of England,* 1912. Home University Library. Williams & Norgate, London.

Powell, T. G. E.: *The Celts,* 1958. Ancient Peoples and Places. Thames and Hudson.

Prentout, Henri: *Essai sur les origines et la fondation du Duché de Normandie,* 1911. Honoré Champion, Paris. *N.*

– *Étude critique sur Dudon de Saint-Quentin et son histoire des premiers Ducs Normands,* 1916. Picard, Paris. *D.*

Ramsay, Sir James: *The Foundations of England* I, 1898. Swan Sonnenschein & Co., London.

Ramskou, Th.: *Lindholm Høje,* 1955. Acta Archaeologica XXVI, 177-185.

– *Hedeby,* 1962. Munksgaard, København.

Rason, Ernest: *Thyra, the Wife of Gorm the Old, Who was She, English or Danish?,* 1911-1914. Saga Book of the Viking Society VIII, 285-301.

v. Richthofen, Bolko: *Zur Herkunft der Wandalen,* 1931. Altschlesien, bd. 3, 21-36.

Rogers, Thorold: *Six Centuries of Work and Wages. The History of English Labour,* 10' Ed., 1909 (1884). Swan Sonnenschein & Co., London.

Ræder, A.: *Rom og kampen om jord,* 1929. Aschehoug, Oslo.

Schlabow, Karl: *Haartracht und Pelzschulterkragen der Moorleiche von Osterby,* 1949. Offa. 8, 3.

Scheel, Otto: *Die Wikinger. Aufbruch des Nordens,* 1938. Hohenstaufer Verlag, Stuttgart. *Wik.*

– *Die Heimat der Angeln,* 1939. Schriften des wissenschaftl. Akademie des N. S. D. Docentenbundes der Christian-August Univ., Kiel. *H.A.*

Schmidt, Ludwig: *Allgemeine Geschichte der germanischen Völker,* 1909. R. Oldenburg, München & Berlin.

Schreiner, Johan: *Viken og Norges samling,* 1927-29. No. Historisk tidskrift, V rk., bd. 7, 356-387.

Schuchhardt, Carl: *Arkona, Rethra, Vineta,* 1926. H. Schoetz & Co., Berlin.

Schück, Henrik: *Folknamnet Geatas i den fornengelske dikten Beowulf,* 1907. Alfquist & Wiksell, Uppsala.

Schück, Adolf: *Den äldsta gränsdragningen mellan Sverige och Danmark,* 1949. Lecture at the University of Copenhagen, December 16, 1949.

Schütte, Gudmund: *Altyske Annexionslærdomme,* 1909. Småskrifter udg. af Selskabet for germansk Filologi, nr. 15. Hagerup, København. *A.A.*

– *A Map of Denmark: 1900 Years old,* 1913-1914. Saga Book of the Viking Society. VIII, 53-84. *M.D.*

– *Hjemligt Hedenskab,* 1919. Gyldendal, København. *H.H.*

Schütte, Gudmund: *Vidsid og slægtssagnene om Hengest og Horsa,* 1920. Arkiv för nordisk filologi. 32, 1-32. *V.H.H.*
- *Our Forefathers the Gothonic Nations* I-II, 1929-1933. Cambridge. *F.G.N.*
- *Geaterspørgsmaalet,* 1930. Danske Studier, 70-81. *G.*
- *Anglerne, det evige Stridsemne,* 1952. Sønderjydske Årbøger, 204-237. *A.*
- *Kimbrerne,* 1941. Scandia. 277-283. *K.*
- *Anglernes Hjemstavn stadfæstet,* 1943. Årbøger f. nord. Oldk. og Historie, 207-211. *A.H.*
- *Gotthiod und Utgard* I, II, 1935, 1936. Aschehoug, Kjøbenhavn. Frommann. Jena. *Gu.*
- *Udvalgte Epistler,* 1947. Munksgaard, København. *Ep.*
Shetelig, Haakon: *Jernalderen i Central-, Vest- og Nordeuropa,* 1927. Friis Johansen: De forhist. Tider i Eur. II, 277-406. Koppel, København. *J.*
- *Det norske folks liv og historie gennem tiderne,* 1929. Aschehoug, Oslo. *N.F.*
- *Befolkning i Oldtiden,* 1936. Nordisk Kultur. Schultz, København. *B.*
- *Introduction to the Viking History of Western Europe,* Reprinted 1935 from: *Viking Antiquities of Great Britain and Ireland. Vik.*
- & Brøndsted, Johs. - Lindqvist, Sune & Skovmand, Roar: *Vikingetogene,* 1940. Omstridte Spørgsmaal i Nordens Historie. Gad, København. *O.Sp.*
Skautrup, Peter: *Det danske Sprogs Historie* I, 1944. Gyldendal, København.
Smith, A. H.: *The Sons of Regnar Lothbrok,* 1934. Saga Book of the Viking Society XI, 173-191.
Sponneck, W. C. E.: *Om Toldvæsen i Almindelighed og det danske Toldvæsen i Særdeleshed,* 1840. Gyldendal, København.
Starcke, C. N.: *The Primitive Family* II', Ed. 1896. The international Scientific Series, vol. LXVI. Kegan Paul, Trench, Trübner & Co., London. *F.*
- *Laws of social Evolution and social Ideals,* 1932, Munksgaard, København.
Starcke, Viggo, N. Bredkær, Abel Brink & J. L. Bjørner: *De store Landboreformer og Handelsfrihedens Tid,* 1936. Busck, København. *L*
- *Hannibal Sehested,* 1941. Økoteknisk Højskoles småskrifter, København. *H.S.*
- *The Viking Danes,* 1949. The National Travel Association. *V.*
- *Knud den Store,* 1949. Store Danske Personligheder I, Berlingske Forlag, København. *Kn.*
- *Hengest og Horsa,* 1949. Dagens Nyheder, København. *H.*
- *Kong Skjold,* 1955. Berlingske Tidende, København. *Sk.*
- *Kong Gudfred,* 1956. Berlingske Tidende, København. *G.*
- *Anglerne og Angel,* 1960. Vort Omstridte Land. *A.*
Steenstrup, Johannes: *Normannerne* I-IV, 1876-1882. Klein, København. *N.*
- *Nogle Bidrag til vore Landsbyers og Bebyggelsens Historie,* 1894-1895. Historisk Tidskrift. 6 r. bd. 5, 313-366. *L.*
- *Danmarks Sydgrænse,* 1900. Indbydelsesskrift til Københavns Universitets Årsfest. *D.S.*
- *Venderne og de Danske,* 1900. Indbydelsesskrift til Københavns Universitets Årsfest. *V.D.*
- *Jylland og Jyder,* 1910. Historisk Tidskrift. VIII rk. bd. 3, 1-49. *J.J.*

351

Steenstrup, Johannes: *Danmarks Riges Historie* I, 1901. Nordisk Forlag, København. *D.R.H.*

- *De danske Stednavne*, 1918. Gad, København. *St.*
- *Normandiets Historie 911-1066*, 1925. Videnskabernes Selsk. Skr. 7' Rk., V, 1. *N.H.*
- *Det danske Folk i Vikingetiden og Danevældens Tidsalder*, 1927. Det danske Folks Historie I, 355-439. Chr. Erichsen, København. *D.F.H.*

Stefánsson, Jón: *Western Influence on the earliest Viking Settlers*, 1906-1907. Saga Book of the Viking Club V, 288-296. *W.*

- *The Vikings in Spain*, 1909. Saga Book of the Viking Club VI, 31-46. *Sp.*

Stenton, Sir Frank. *Documents illustrative of the social and economic History of the Danelaw*, 1920. Records of social and economic History V. British Academy. Milford, London. *D.D.*

- *The Danes in England*, 1927. Raleigh Lecture. British Academy, London. *D.*
- *The free Peasantry of the Northern Danelaw*, 1926. Humanistiska Vetenskapssamfundet i Lund. Årsberättelse. 73-185. *P.*
- *Anglo-Saxon England*, 1943. The Oxford History of England. Ed. G. N. Clark. Clarendon Press, Oxford. *A.S.E.*
- *The Historical Bearing of Place-Name Studies: The Place of Women in Anglo-Saxon Society*, 1943. Transactions of the Royal Historical Society. Fourth Series, vol. XXV. London.
- *The Scandinavian Colonies in England and Normandy*, 1945. Transactions of the Royal Historical Society. Fourth Series, vol. XXVII. London.

Stille, Arthur: *Till frågan om Blekinges förbindelse med Sverige i äldre tid*, 1893. Skånske samlinger III, 2, 19-24.

Stjerna, Knut: *Svear och Götar under folkvandringstiden*, 1905. Svenska fornminnesföreningens tidskrift XII, 339-360.

Storm, Gustav: *Kritiske Bidrag til Vikingetidens Historie*, 1878. Den norske Forlagsforening, Kristiania.

Strasser, Karl Theodor: *Wikinger und Normannen*, 1928. Hanseatische Verlagsanstalt, Hamburg.

Strömberg, Märta: *Untersuchungen zur jüngeren Eisenzeit in Schonen*, 1961 Acta. Archaeologica Lundensia. Glecrup, Lund. Habelt, Bonn.

Thomsen, Vilhelm: *Det russiske Riges Grundlæggelse ved Nordboerne*, 1877, 1880. Samlede Afhandlinger: 1919, 233-444. Gyldendal, København. *R.R.G.*

- *Oldarisk Kultur*. Verdenskulturen I, 178-188. Samlede Afhandlinger, 1919, 213-230. Gyldendal, København. *O.K.*

Thorvildssen, Knud: *Grønhøj ved Horsens*, 1946. Årbøger for Nordisk Oldkyndighed og Historie I.

Toll, Hans: *Sigridis Storråda rediviva*, 1921. Sv. Hist. tidskrift, 216-224. *S.St.*

- *Erik Sejrsälls giften*, 1923. Sv. Hist. tidskrift, 282-286. *E.S.*
- *Kring Trekungarslaget vid Helgeå år 1025*, 1933. Stockholm. *T.*

Toynbee, Arnold J.: *A Study of History*, 1933 f. Oxford U.P.

Toyne, S. M.: *The Scandinavians in History*, (Foreword by George M. Trevelyan), 1948. Arnold, London.

Trevelyan, George Macaulay: *History of England*. II' Ed. 1942. Longmans, London.

Vinogradoff, Sir Paul: *The Growth of the Manor*. III' Ed. 1920. Allen & Unvin, London. *M.*

– *Feudalism*, 1922. The Cambridge Medieval History, vol. III. Ch. XVIII, 458-484. *F.*

Vogel, Walther: *Die Normannen und das Fränkische Reich*, 1906. Winter, Heidelberg. *N.*

– *Handelsverkehr, Städtewesen und Staatenbildung in Nordeuropa im früheren Mittelalter*, 1931. Zeitschr. d. Gesellsch. für Erdkunde zu Berlin. *H.*

de Vries, Jan: *Die historischen Grundlagen der Ragnarssaga Loðbrókar*, 1923. Arkiv för nordisk filologi. Ny följd. Bd. 35, 244-274. *R.L.*

– *Die Wikingersaga*, 1927. Germanisch-romanische Monatsschrift XV, 81-100. *W.*

– *Die ostnordische Überlieferung der Saga von Ragnar Lodbrok*, 1927-1928. Acta philologica scandinavica II, 115-149. *O.R.L.*

Wadstein, Elis: *Namnet Danmark*, 1918-19. Göteborgs Högskolas Årsskrift, XXIV-XXV. *D.*

– *Norden och Västeuropa i gammal tid*, 1925. Bonnier, Stockholm. *N.*

– *On the Origin of the English*, 1927. Skrifter utg. af Kungl. human. vetenskapssamfundet i Uppsala, bd. 24, 14. *O.E.*

Walberg, E.: *Om Rollo-Spörsmålet*, 1911. Nordisk tidskrift, 489-502.

Ward, Gordon: *The first Danes come to England*, 1949. 'Denmark.' Anglo-Danish Society. Strange Pronter Ltd, London. *D.*

– *Hengest*, 1949. Archaeologia Cantiana, vol. LXI, 77-97. *H.*

– *Hengest. An Historical Study of his Danish Origins and of his Campaigns in Frisia and South-East England*, 1949. Anglo-Danish Publ. Co. Ltd., London. *H.H.*

Weibull, Curt: *Om det svenska och det danska rikets uppkomst*, 1921. Hist. tidskr. f. Skåneland, 301-360. *SDR.*

– *Den älsta gränsdragningen mellan Sverige och Danmark*, 1921. Hist. tidskr. f. Skåneland, 1-18. *Gr.*

– *Sveriges och Danmarks älsta historia*, 1922. Gleerup, Lund. *SDH.*

Weibull, Lauritz: *Kritiska undersökningar i Nordens historia omkring år 1000*, 1911. Lybecker, København. *KU.*

– *Skandza und ihre Völker bei Jordanes*, 1925. Arkiv f. nordisk filologi. Ny följd. 37, 213-246. *Sk.*

– *Knut den Stores skånske krig*, 1910. Hist. Tidskr. f. Skåneland 4.

Weinbaum, Martin: *Alfred der Groze und Kanuth*, 1934. Menschen die Geschichte machten. I, 347-350.

Wessén, Elias: *De nordiska folkstammerna i Beowulf*, 1927. Kungl. vitterhets hist. och antikv. akad. handl. XXXVI, 5-86.

Wheeler, Sir Mortimer: *Rome beyond the Imperial Frontiers*, 1955. Penguin.

Whitelock, Dorothy: *The Beginnings of English Society*, 1959. Penguin.

Williams, Mary W.: *Social Scandinavia in the Viking Age*, 1920. Macmillan, New York.

Wilson, D. M.: *The Anglo-Saxons*, 1960. Ancient Peoples and Places. Thames and Hudson, London.

ADDITIONS TO THE BIBLIOGRAPHY

Bugge, Sophus & Olrik, Axel: *Röveren ved Graasten og Beowulf,* 1890. Dania I, 136 & 233.

Christensen, Aksel E.: *Birka uden Frisere,* 1966. Handels—og Söfartsmuseets Aarbog, 17-38. Kronborg, Helsingor.

Collinder, Björn: *Beowulf,* 1954. Natur och Kultur, Stockholm.

Grundtvig, N.F.S.: *Om Bjovulfs Drapa,* 1817. Danevirke II. 207-289.

Hansen, Adolf (& von Holstein Rathlou): *Bjovulf,* 1910. Gyldendal.

Kier, Christian: *Beowulf,* 1915. Thaning & Appel, Köbenhavn.

Klaeber, Fr.: *Beowulf,* 1924. Heath & Co., London.

Leake, Jane Acomb: *The Geatas of Beowulf,* 1966. University of Wisconsin Press.

Lindqvist, Sune: *Sutton Hoo och Beowulf,* 1948. Fornvännen.

Magoun, Francis P., Jr.: *Danes, North, South, East and West in Beowulf,* 1949. Malone Anniversary Studies. Baltimore.

– *Oral-Formulaic Character of Anglo-Saxon Narrative Poetry,* 1953. Speculum 28, 446-467. Cambridge, Massachusetts.

– *The Geography of Hygelac's Raid on the Lands of the West Frisians and the Hett-ware,* 1953. English Studies, 34. 160-163.

– *Beowulf and King Hygelac in the Netherlands,* 1954. English Studies, 35. 193.

Malone, Kemp: *The Identity of the Geatas,* 1929. Acta Phil. Scand. 84 f.

– *Healfdene,* 1935. Englische Studien LXX. 74-76.

Nerman, Birger: *Sutton Hoo—en svensk Kunga—eller Hövdinggrav ?,* 1948, Fornvännen. 65-93.

Oxenstierna, Eric: *The World of the Norsemen,* 1967. Weidenfeld & Nicolson, London.

Sawyer, P. H.: *The Age of the Vikings,* 1963. Edw. Arnold, London.

Schütte, Gudmund: *Dansk Landnam i Östjylland,* 1950. Randers Amts Aarbog.

Starcke, Viggo: *Centuries of Experience with Land Taxation in Denmark,* 1967. University of Hartford, Connecticut.

– *Jyder eller Göter? Hvem var Geaterne?,* 1968. Berlingske Tidende.

Thompson, E. A.: *The Early Germans,* 1965. Clarendon Press, Oxford.

Whitelock, Dorothy: *The Audience of Beowulf,* 1967. Clarendon Press, Oxford.

Woolf, Henry B.: *Hrothgar,* 1954. Louisiana State University Studics, 39-55. Baton Rouge.

LIST OF ILLUSTRATIONS

191. Dragon figure-head from a Danish Viking ship found in 1934 in the River Scheldt. British Museum. (Johs. Brøndsted & Poul Nørlund: Seks Tværsnit af Danmarks Historie, fig. 31.)

199. Halfdan's penny coined in London about 872 with the first London monogram. (Georg C. Brooke: English Coins, pl. IX.)

203. Silver brooch with the Anglian Beast in the Urnes Style. From a Viking grave in Lindholm Høje. Jutland. (Th. Ramskou: Acta Archaeologica XXVI, fig. 12.)

211. Europe in the Viking Period. (Herbert Jahnkuhn: Haithabu, fig. 9.)

215. The first English halfpenny. Coined by Halfdan in London about 872. (George C. Brooke: English Coins, pl. IX.)

223. English men and Norman horses crashing down in wild confusion in the Battle at Hasting on October 14, 1066. The Bayeux Tapestry.

233. King Gorm's runic stone. Jelling. Jutland. About 935. "Gorm the King made this monument to Tyre, his wife, the adornment of Denmark." (Lis Jacobsen & Erik Moltke: Danmarks Runeindskrifter, fig. 118. B.)

237. CNUT's coin from York about 880-890. (Det danske Folks Historie, I, p. 368.)

245. King Harald Bluetooth's runic stone. Jelling. Jutland. About 983. "Harald the King caused these monuments to be made to Gorm his father and Tyre his mother, the Harald who won all Denmark and Norway and made the Danes Christians." (Lis Jacobsen & Erik Molkte, "Danmarks Runeindskrifter« fig. 120.)

247. The Viking ship from Ladby on Fyn. Reconstruction in Ladby.

251. Diagram of the submerged Viking ships at Skuldelev blockading the original navigable channel of Roskilde Fjord, Zealand. The stone-filled ships are now being excavated (1962). The frame indicates sheet piling. (Olaf Olsen & Ole Crumlin Pedersen: Acta Archaeologica XXIX. 1958.)

255. King Harald Bluetooth baptized by Poppo about 960. Detail from the golden altar in Tamdrup Church. Jutland. (Knud Fabricius, "Danmarks Konger" p. 37.)

259. Viking sword. Bjørnsholm in Himmerland. Jutland. (Johs. Brøndsted: Danmarks Oldtid, III, fig. 307 a.)

265. The Viking fortress Trelleborg. West Zealand. (Aerial view.)

271. The Viking fortress Fyrkat. East Jutland. (Aerial view.)

273. Danish horse-collar from a Viking's grave from the days of Canute. Mammen. Jutland. (Johs. Brøndsted & Poul Nørlund: Seks Tværsnit af Danmarks Historie, fig. 41.)

277. Edmund Ironside and Canute the Great. (After Matthew of Paris.)

283. Stone-head of a King in the wall of the old grammar school at Slesvig just opposite the Cathedral. Supposed to be Canute the Great who around 1019 laid the foundation of the original Cathedral. (Poul Kürstein.)

285. Canute the Great's coin with the inscription: CNUT REX SV. Coined by THORMOD ON SIHT. – the mintmaster of the Swedish King Anund Jacob, at Sigtuna, Sweden. (The National Museum.)

291. Gilded bronze horse from a weather-vane on a Viking ship. Probably the only fragment that remains of the fleets from the time of Canute. (Chr. Axel Jensen: Fra Nationalmuseets Arbejdsmark, 1932, p. 53.)

297. Canute the Great and Queen Emma presenting the golden cross to New Minster in Winchester in 1019 after the Queen's giving birth to the heir to the throne, Hardeknud, and just before the King's expedition to Denmark to take over his father's kingdom after the death of his brother King Harald Svendsson in 1018. The Winchester Manuscript Liber Vitæ. British Museum. (Georg Galster: Årbøger for nordisk Oldkyndighed og Historie. 1960.)

301. The London runic stone. About 1020-1040. Found in 1852 on St. Paul's Churchyard. Guildhall Museum. "Ginne had this stone laid down together with Toke –" (Lis Jacobsen & Erik Moltke, "Danmarks Runeindskrifter" fig. 1019.)

305. God Almighty. Detail from the golden altar in Stadil Church. Jutland. About 1225. (Poul Nørlund: Gyldne Altre, fig. 157.)

309. The Valdemar Kings. Above: The Virgin Mary and Christ enthroned. Below: King Valdemar the Victorious as Duke of Slesvig († 1241). King Knud VI († 1202). King Valdemar the Great († 1182) raising the crusader's cross. Knud Lavard, Duke of Slesvig, canonized after his murder in 1131, holding the hand of Christ. Relief on the Cathedral of Ribe. The cat-head door.

313. Archbishop Absalon (1128-1201). Portrait on his tomb-stone in Sorø Conventual Church. Zealand. Made by Master Morten Bussert in 1536 to order of Abbot Henrik Tornekrans. (Johs Brøndsted & Poul Nørlund: Seks Tværsnit af Danmarks Historie, fig. 69.)

317. The Virgin Mary with the infant Saviour enthroned in celestial Jerusalem. Central part of the golden altar from Lisbjerg Church. About 1140-1150. Jutland. (Poul Nørlund: Gyldne Altre, pl. II).

321. The Tirstrup crucifix. About 1150-1175. Djursland. Jutland. (The National Museum).

325. Queen Margrete (1353-1412). From her sarcophagus in the Cathedral of Roskilde.

331. Admiral Hans Pothorst who during the reign of King Christian I came to America twenty years before Colombus. Fresco in the vault of St. Marie Church. Elsinore. Zealand. (The National Museum phot.)

334. Vitus Bering (1681-1741) who, as a Commodore in the Russian navy, on July 16. 1741 discovered Alaska. (After a painting in private possession.)

335. The Battle of Copenhagen April 2. 1801 between the British navy under Lord Nelson and the Danes under Admiral Olfert Fischer. Contemporary painting by C. A. Lorentzen. Frederiksborg Castle.

337. Admiral Olfert Fischer's pocket powder-horn. Cut in brier with the monogram: O. F. in the ivory button. (Egegården, Ørholm).

340. Gold buckle from the Viking Age. Hornelund. Jutland. (The National Museum.)

REFERENCES

In order to confine the number of figures and notes in the text to the least possible, the following system is employed:

The ARAB figure of the left column gives the number of the page in the present book (excepted is the chapter 'The Geatas', p. 99-107, which has been rewritten).

The ROMAN figure, followed by a colon indicates the passage, reckoned from the top of the page. Even if a passage is continued from the previous page, it is given the figure of I.

Wherever an author is represented by more than one of his works, an indexmark in ITALICS is added to the quotation which is also to be found in the bibliography. F.ex. Professor Johannes Brondsted's work, "Danmarks Oldtid" has the indexmark DO.

To sum up, a quotation on page 231 of the present work, passage six, deriving from Professor Johannes Steenstrup's work, "Danmark's Riges Historie", volume I, page 274, is indicated as follows:

231   VI: Steenstrup I 274 DRH.

and a quotation on page 116 of the present book, passage four, deriving from Dr. Gudmund Schütte's work, "Our Forefathers the Gothonic Nations", volume II, page 236, is indicated as follows:

116   IV: Schütte II 236 FGN.

✳

14   II: Green 72 HE. IV: Noach 4, 6, 18, 164.

15   I: Keary 21. Steenstrup 2 JJ. Hatt 76. II: C. Weibull 41 SDH. Much 295 f.

16   II: C. Weibull 348 SDR. V: Steenstrup 1 JJ.

18   I: C. Weibull 66 SDH. III: C. Weibull 42-43 SDH.

19   II: Nerman 21 SR.

20   I: Nordman 26. III: Haddon 16-26, 39. Montelius 749 GF. Brondsted I 123 DO. IV: Brondsted I 70 DO.

21   I: C. Weibull 22 SDH. II: Brogger 120 NF. III: Hatt 15. Brogger 126 NF. Klindt-Jensen 136 D. IV: C. Weibull 22 SDH.

22   II: Bolin I 47. Klaatsch 355. III: C. Beibull 23. SDH. IV: Penka 41, 57. Much 4. Arup I 45. V: Kossinna 283 G.

23   I: Haddon 16-26. Karsten 41-46. Brondsted I 319 DO. Montelius 749 GF. III: Brogger 13 NF. C. Weibull 24 SDH. Kossinna 155 G. Schütte II 339 FGN. Brondsted I 257, 310 DO. Nerman 5 SR. IV: Noach 17. C. Weibull 30 SDH.

24   II: Brondsted I 188 DO. III: Jankuhn 4 H. Lindqvist 49. IV: Coon 121.

25   I: Brondsted I 313 DO. V: Brondsted 7 HSO. Brogger 198 NF. Noach 18. C. Weibull 39 SDH.

26   II: Arup I 31. Brondsted I 311 DO.

27   I: Brogger 124 NF. III: Jankuhn 5 H. IV: Chadwick 344. Brondsted I 229, 230 DO. Glob 213, 236. Nordman 141.

28   I: Blinkenberg 21. Glob 238. Noach 7. Hatt 48.
29   II: Jankuhn 5 *H*. Kersten 107. Brøndsted I 311 *DO*. Hougen 29. III: Glob
     239. V: Arup I 44, 46.
31   III: Ax. Olrik 17 *N.Aa.* IV: Coon 123. V: Kretschmer 22. VI: Mac Dougall
     119.
32   II: Noach 18. Schwantes (Paulsen. Foreword.) III: Kersten 107. Schütte II
     338 *FGN*. Jankuhn 6 *H*. Schmidt 19.
33   I: Jankuhn 3 *H*. V: C. Weibull 54 *SDH*. VI: Müller 286. VII: Blinkenberg
     175. Much 119 f.
34   II: Montelius 97 *Sv.Br.* Müller 288. III: Montelius 97 *Sv.Br.*
35   III: Broholm II 9. IV: C. Weibull 54 *SDH*. V: Bolin I 72. Brøndsted II 28
     DO. Keary 23. VI: Brøgger 172 *Br.*
36   I: Kendrick 50. Clark.
37   I: Brøndsted 30 *Tv.* III: Lindqvist 55, 65. IV: Arup I 46.
38   II: Montelius 100, 103 *Sv.Br.* la Cour I 134 *SJ*. III: Jankuhn 10 *H*. Brønd-
     sted 31 *Tv.* Brøndsted II 93 *DO*. Broholm II 263.
40   I: Brøgger 195 *Br.* II: Brøgger 235, 236 *Br.* III: Strasser 12. Noach 12. IV:
     Brøgger 204 *NF*. V: Brøndsted 22 *Tv.*
42   II: Brøndsted 21 *Tv.* IV: C. Weibull 57 *SDH*. V: Brøgger 269 *Br.* Gjessing
     50. VI: Jankuhn 9 *H*. Gjessing 70, 89. Brøndsted II 150, 176, 228 *DO*.
     Lindqvist 49. Noach 23. Brøndsted 10 *Tv.*
46   II: Jankuhn 6, 9 *H*.
47   I: Tacitus Germ. 5, 2. II: Shetelig 303 *J*. Brøndsted III 11 *DO*. Haddon 41.
48   I: Brøndsted III 38 *DO*. Becker 279 *FJ*.
49   II: Hatt 35, 62, 101, 109, 135. III: Jankuhn 6 *H*. V: Grønbech I 1, 2 *F*.
50   II: Schütte I 139 *FGN*. la Cour 361 *Sch*.
51   I: la Cour 339 *Sch*. II: Much (Hoops III 42).
52   II: Brøndsted III 66 f. *DO*.
53   II: Funch-Brentano I 178.
54   III: Schütte II 321 *FGN*. Aakjær 77 *DS*. Arup I 49, 52. Brøndsted III 66, 99
     DO. Chadwick 208-215. la Cour I 273-275 *DFH*. la Cour I 347, 348
     Sch. Feist 129-166. Haddon 42. Lienhard-Egen 26. Schmidt 144. Schütte II
     299-301. 319-322 *FGN*. Schütte 277-283 *K*. Shetelig I 103 *NF*. Skautrup
     I 13.
55   I: Schütte 53-84 *MD*. V: Brøndsted III 67, 96 *DO*. Schmidt 146. VI:
     Shetelig 308 *J*.
57   II: Chadwick 215. IV: Schütte I 29 II 301, 320 *FGN*. Noach 45. V: Aakjær
     77 *DS*. Fossing 181.
58   III: la Cour I 273-280 *DFH*. IV: Schütte I 298, 318 *FGN*. la Cour I 275
     DFH. VI: A. Bugge II 20 *Vik*. Jankuhn 29 *H*. Noach 60, 74. Koht 14.
59   II: Jacobsen 37 *Sv*.
60   I: Chambers 200 *W*. Noach 44. Schmidt 144. Schütte II 224 *FGN*. III:
     Jordanes 60.
61   I: Jankuhn 10 *H*. II: Jankuhn 11 *H*. III: Chambers 417 *B*.
62   III: Arup I 63. IV: Penka 142, 159.

63 IV: Keary 23. Kendrick 63. Th. Hodgkin 79. Schütte I 51 II 15-20 *FGN*. Karsten 71. v. Friesen 108 f. *Rök*. Noach 41. Nerman 165 f. *GH*.

65 I: Arne 432. v. Friesen VII *Rök*. Schmidt 50. Åberg 260. Noach 72. Askeberg 40-44, 85. v. Friesen VIII *Rök*. Moltke 47 f.

66 II: Brøndsted III 204 *DO*. Schütte I 251 II 341, 346-353 *FGN*. Lukman 128. III: Chambers *W*. Koht 14.

67 II: v. Friesen 492 *H*. Lindqvist 60. Lukman 129. Åberg 260. v. Friesen 59 *Rö*. III: v. Friesen 51, 53 *Rö*. Chambers 437 *W*. IV: v. Friesen 51 *Rö*.

68 I: v. Friesen 46-56 *Rö*. Neergaard 186 f. II: Wessén 5-7. III: v. Friesen 15 *Ru*. v. Friesen 48 *Rö*. III: Wessén 61-79. Noach 70. Wessén 8, 10.

70 II: Schütte II 361 *FGN*. Brøndsted III 258 *DO*. Chambers 432, 434 *W*. Wadstein 9-11 *D*. III: Kendrick 56. Noach 68. Lukman 53.

71 I: Schütte II 347, 349 *FGN*. Nerman 53 *SR*. II: v. Friesen 485 f. *H*. III: v. Friesen 485 f. *H*.

72 I: la Cour I 310 *DFH*. Wessén 7. Karsten 144. v. Friesen 45, 74 *Rö*. Chadwick 109. A. Bugge I 17 II 32 *Vik*. Scheel 12 *W*. II: Wrenn 46, 184.

73 II: v. Friesen 15 *Ru*. Steenstrup I 407 *DFH*. IV: Pirenne 28. VI: Aakjær 102, 103 *NV*. Brøndsted III 44, 100 *DO*. VI: la Cour I 290 *DFH*. Kendrick 64. Kossinna 233 f. *WN*. Nerman 43 *G*. Schütte II 42-57 *FGN*. Skautrup 14.

74 III: Jahn 154-157 *KT*. Jahn 166 *WN*. v. Richtofen 21-36. IV: Haddon 43.

75 II: Schmidt 60.

76 III: Brøndsted III 99 *DO*. la Cour I 361, 372 *Sch*. Kendrick 64. Lindqvist 55. Nerman II *SR*. Schütte II 36-72 *FGN*. Penka 153.

77 I: Chadwick 148. Wessén 17. Günther 106. III: Steenstrup I 382 *DFH*. IV: Plettke 55. Kendrick 64. Schütte I 140 II 140-149 *FGN*. la Cour I 395 *Sch*. Nerman II *SR*. Hatt 76. Chadwick 274.

78 III: Karsten 72. IV: Lukman 46. Nerman 53 *G*. Mac Dougall 267. Madsen 71. Penka 107.

80 I: Brøndsted III 99 *DO*. Chadwick 219. la Cour I 361 *Sch*. Schütte II 46-47. *FGN*. Shetelig 336-340 *J*. Richtofen 23. Jahn 154, 166 *WN*. IV: la Cour I 280 *DFH*. Chadwick 208.

81 II: Schmidt 49, 50, 144. IV: Chadwick 110, 177. Schmidt 157. Schütte II 277, 293 *FGN*. Wadstein 36 *N*. Arup I 89 f. Askeberg 30, 34.

82 II: Collingwood & Myres 337. Arup I 88. Shetelig 9 *Vik*. Pirenne 239.

83 I: Grønbech III 64 *F*. Ermoldus Lib. 4. III: Chadwick 100, 177. Schütte II 157-190 *FGN*. V: Schütte 124 *A.A.* Åberg 263-268.

84 II: Schütte 116 *A.A.* III: Widsith 42-44. IV: Schütte II 92-138 *FGN*. Schmidt 168 f. VI: Chadwick 100. Chambers 90-94 *W*. la Cour I 302 *DFH*.

85 II: Kersten & Schlabow 1 f. III: Schütte II 118, 318 *FGN*.

86 III: Bede 1, 15. IV: Chadwick 92, 100, 177. Schütte II 221-276. *FGN*. Schmidt 152 f. Strasser 23.

87 I: Collingwood & Myres 340. Freeman I 13, 597. Schütte II 222, 236 *FGN*. Scheel 54 *Wik*. II: Schütte 111 *A.A.* V: A. Bugge I 6 *Vik*.

361

88   I: Schütte 107, 115. *A.A.* II: Schütte 118 *A.A.* III. Steenstrup 22 *DS*. IV: Green 7 *HE*. V: Trevelyan XXI.
89 III: Dawson (Cit. Collingwood 120). Trevelyan 28.
90   I: Trevelyan 28. VII: Trevelyan 29. IV: Green 9 *HE*. R. H. Hodgkin 78. Thomsen 362 *RRG*. Chadwick 97.
92   I: Brate 19. II: R. H. Hodgkin 90-100. Collingwood & Myres 332. Jolliffe 98 *J*. Ward 27 f. IV: Schütte 209 *H.H.* v. Friesen *Rök*. Scheel 46 *Wik*. Shetelig 352 *J*.
94   II: Plettke 57, 68. R. H. Hodgkin 91. Jolliffe 102-106 *J*. Arup I 52. Chadwick 67. III: Ward 27, 52, 54. Collingwood & Myres 345. Chambers 237-241 *W*. la Cour I 133-157 *SJ*. la Cour I 277 *DFH*. Schütte II 303, 324, 326 *FGN*. Schmidt 149.
95   I: Ward 53, 56. IV: Chadwick 52. Chambers 67 *W*. R. H. Hodgkin 78. Wessén 33. Blair 10.
96   II: Schütte II 311, 325 *FGN*. III: Collingwood & Myres 346. IV: Jolliffe 102-136. R. H. Hodgkin 94. Jankuhn 39, 41 *A*. Schütte II 324 *FGN*. Schütte 8 *VHH*. Chadwick 85.
97   I: Stenton 8-11 *ASE*. Wessén 33.
98 III: Karsten 152.
99   IV: Nerman 57, 78 *SR*. Schück 13. Stjerna 351. Wessén 18. V: Chadwick 278. Fahlbeck 74 *B*.
100   II: Chambers 2 *B*. Nerman 109 *SR*. Schück 16, 17. Wadstein 22, 161 *N*. C. Weibull 310 *SDR*. Wessén 52. III: Chambers 335, 407 *B*. Wadstein 21, 23 *N*. Noach 79. IV: Fahlbeck 5, 53 *B*.
101   I: Steenstrup I 78 *DRH*. Nerman 92 *SR*. Shetelig 2-4 *Vik*. Schück 29-31. II: Chambers 347 *B*.
102   II: Schütte 204, 208 *H.H.* Clausen 141, 144 *KH*. Schütte II 314 *FGN*. IV: Wadstein 10 *N*. Fahlbeck 26, 30 *B*. Wessén 51. Chambers 343 *B*. Schück 27.
103   I: C. Weibull 353 *SDR*. Schütte 71 *G*. Chambers 403, 404, 410-419 *B*. III: C. Weibull 320 *SDR*. IV: C. Weibull 319, 358 *SDR*.
104   II: Wadstein 23 *N*. C. Weibull 320 *SDR*. III: C. Weibull 310 *SDR*. IV: Stjerna 340. V: C. Weibull 326, 322 *SDR*. Fahlbeck 29 *B*. Bolin I 110.
105 III: Wadstein 29 *N*. Nerman 109 *SR*. Fahlbeck 28 *B*. Chadwick 278. Stjerna 352. Schütte 71 *G*.
106 III: Wadstein 31 *N*.
107   II: R. H. Hodgkin 1. III: Hodgkin 1.
108   I: Hodgkin 6. III: Chambers 69, 259 *W*.
109   II: Jankuhn 6 *A*. Wadstein 23 *OE*. III: Scheel 6 *A*. Scheel 46 *Wik*. IV: Jankuhn 8, 12 *A*.
110   I: Scheel 13 *A*. Scheel 49 *Wik*. Jankuhn 28, 38 *A*. Chambers 72, 74, 254 *W*. Schmidt 148. Oman 218. III: Chambers 243 *W*. Oman 217-218. Jankuhn 5 *A*. Schütte 78 *MD*. Schütte I 141 *FGN*. Annales Quedlinburgenses Scr. III 31.
111 III: Chambers 90-94 *W*. Chambers 31-40 *B*. Chadwick 132-135. Trevelyan

31. la Cour I 301 *DFH*. Schütte II 313, 314 *FGN*. Wadstein 64 *N*. V: Chadwick 133. Chambers 92 *W*. Chambers 34 *B*. la Cour 300 *DFH*. Schütte II 310 *FGN*. Schmidt 149. VI: Chambers 93, 149, 150 *W*. Olrik I 11 *DH*.

112 III: Chadwick 150. Chambers 203 *W*. Schütte II 307 *FGN*. Blair 9. Trevelyan 31.

113 I: Jankuhn 28, 32 *A*. Schütte 127, 129 *A.A.* Askeberg 24.

114 I: Gutenbrunner & Jankuhn 23. II: Plettke 55. Jankuhn 38, 41 *A*. Schütte 207-211 *AH*. III: Bjerrum 202 f. IV: Stenton 5 *ASE*.

115 III: Stenton 7 *ASE*. V: Oman 218. Chadwick 115, 117, 133.

116 II: Trevelyan 32, 33. Collingwood & Myres 359. III: Dawson 120. IV: Chadwick 184. Schütte II 236 *FGN*. Collingwood & Myres 350. V: Chadwick 91. la Cour 304-312 *DFH*. Collingwood & Myres 342.

118 I: Freeman I 13, 597. Chadwick 89, 57. Schütte II 222 *FGN*. II: Chadwick 144, 163. R. H. Hodgkin 31, 34. Schütte II 241 *FGN*. Scheel 54 *Wik*. III: Grundtvig 'Danskeren' 1849. IV: Pollard 12. Trevelyan 42.

119 I: Schütte 208 *AH*. Brøndsted III 101, 253 *DO*.

120 I: Bugge I 215 *Vik*. Chadwick 256-268. Chambers 71 *W*. Olrik & Ellekilde 404-407. Schütte 93 *H.H.* IV: Clausen 142, 173 *SDO*. Bugge I 215 *Vik*. Gravlund 24, 41.

121 III: S. Bugge (Cit. Brøndal 27). Bugge I 16 *Vik*. V: C. Weibull 328 *SDR*. VI: Schütte II 33, 371 *FGN*. Schütte II 73 *MD*. Wadstein 9 *D*. Nerman 171 *GH*.

122 II: Askeberg 88. Schütte 371 *FGN*. III: Skautrup I 19, 22. Jordanes (Mommsen) 59.

123 I: Karsten 71. Nerman 130 *D.Sv.* Chambers 432 *B*. III: v. Friesen 48 *Rö*.

124 I: Gutenbrunner 102. II. Wadstein 6, 20 *D*. Schütte II 360 *FGN*. L. Weibull 244 *Sk*. V: Jørgensen 165 *R*.

125 II: Schütte II 360 *FGN*. IV: Nerman 133 *D.Sv.* Wessén 25, 79. Kendrick 85. Chambers 433-445 *B*.

126 II: Brøndsted III 254 *DO*. Nielsen 237-318. Fürst 22, 27. Brøgger 178 *NF*. III: Frets 79, 80. IV: Mac Dougall 267, 268.

127 III: Chadwick 296.

128 I: Chadwick 150. Chambers 203 *W*. II: Schütte II 360 *FGN*. III: Schütte II 356-357 *FGN*. V: la Cour 419 *Sch*. Jørgensen 233-236 *R*. Bjørkman 568.

129: II: Steenstrup 353 *L*. Clausen 136 f. *SDO*. Aakjær 320 f. *JAL*. Hald 70 f. III: Schütte *128 A.A.* IV: Steenstrup 361 *L*. V: Schütte II 311 *FGN*.

130 I: Clausen 136 f. *SDO*. Schütte 191, 210 *H.H.* Kroman 185 f. III: Brøndsted III 257 *DO*. la Cour I 202 *SJ*. Kossinna 255 *W.N.* la Cour I 384 *Sch*. IV: Wheeler 114.

131 I: Chadwick 267. Jørgensen 269. Schütte II 362 *FGN*. II: Brøndsted III 257-259. *DO*. Bolin I 112. Nerman 129-140 *D.Sv.* Wessén 28. Chambers 430-445 *B*. III: Wrenn 46, 184.

132 III: Chambers 76-78 *W.* IV: la Cour I 312 *DFH.* Wessén 19. Schütte II 374
     FGN.
134 II: Brøndsted III 226, 245 *DO.* Norling-Christensen 99-104. III: Schütte II
     374 *FGN.*
135 I: la Cour I 320 *DFH.* Jørgensen 163. Schütte II 311 *FGN.* IV: Skautrup
     I 190. II: Wadstein 19-25 *D.* Schütte II 354 *FGN.* Wadstein 6, 158 *N.*
     II: Brøndal 41. III: Wadstein 40 *D.* Wessén 59. Chambers 76 *W.*
136 I: Coon 332. III: C. Weibull 65-67, 75 *SDH.* la Cour I 329 *DFH.*
137 I: Brøndsted I 236 *DFH.* Brøndsted III 173, 178 *D.O.* Kendrick 53. II:
     Shetelig 350 *J.* IV: Wessén 79.
138 I: Lukman ff. II: Askeberg 95-114. III: A. Olrik 60-61 *N.N.* IV: A. Olrik
     58 N.N.
139 I: A. Olrik 60 *N.N.* II: A. Olrik I 81 *E.* III: A. Olrik 58, 62 *N.N.* IV:
     A. Olrik 60, 58 *N.N.* A. Olrik I 321 *D.H.*
141 V: Brøndsted III 281, 288 *D.O.* VI: Brøndsted III 266 *D.O.*
142 I: Philpotts 8-10, Wessén 80. II: Scheel 201 *Wik.* Nerman 224-236 *S.R.*
     Kendrick 81, 87. Vogel 269 *H.* v. Friesen 128 *Rök.* III: Nerman 2, 36
     S.R. la Cour I 329 *DFH.* v. Friesen 128 *Rök.* IV: Chadwick 298. Ner-
     man 236 *S.R.* Schütte 45, 109 *H.H.* Grønbech 205-210 *NMS.*
143 II: Jankuhn 14 *H.* Nordman 15. Montelius 401 f. *G.H.* III: Pirenne 285.
     Haddon 47. Shetelig 347 *J.* IV: Haddon 48. Keary 21.
144 I: Askeberg 64, 92. Kossinna 127 *G.* Penka 42. II: Mac Dougall 148, 149.
     III: Aakjær I 71 *DFH.* Haddon 48.
145 I: Scheel 131 *Wik.* II: Matthiesen 9. Jankuhn 1 *H.* Lienhard-Egen 27.
146 II: Vogel 267 *H.* la Cour 240 *S.J.* III: Shetelig 5 *Vik.* IV: Wadstein 46
     *N.*S. Larsen 40.
147 IV: Scheel 118 *Wik.* IV: Scheel 120 *Wik.* Blair 290. Wilson 87. Pirenne 237,
     239. Oxenstierna 61-63 *Wik.* V: Steenstrup I 210-217 *DRH.* S. Larsen
     6, 7. Belaiew 281.
148 II: Paulsen 31. Vogel 18 *N.* Jørgensen 163 *R.* Askeberg 15. S. Larsen 6.
149 I: Storm 34 f. la Cour I 436 *Sch.* Koht 16, 52 f. Shetelig I 230 *N.F.H.*
     Scheel 234 *Wik.* II: Bull 262, 270, 273 *St.* Bull 55 *L.* Jørgensen 252,
     53 *R.*
150 II: Wadstein 64 *N.* III: Scheel 118-132 *H.A.* Noach 129-140. IV: Arbman
     & Stenberger 10-12. Arup I 97. S. Larsen 6. Vogel 266, 272 *H.* Arbman
     14 *Sv.*
151 II: Scheel 118-132 *Wik.* la Cour 28 *DK.* Erslev 26 *T.D.* Steenstrup 360
     DFH. IV: Vogel 54, 283 *N.*
152 II: Steenstrup I 214 *DRH.* H. Hodgkin 491. III: Brøndsted 32 *V.* IV: Baker
     92. V: Belloc I 241.
153 II: Scheel 132 *Wik. Jankuhn* (Einleitung) *H.* Wadstein 57, 108, 111 *N.*
     Gjessing 126. Birkeland 103. Shetelig etc. 19. *O.Sp.* Askeberg 11. Noach
     140. Gjessing 135. Vogel 270 *H.* III: Brøndsted 16, 43 *V.* Jankuhn 18
     H. Steenstrup 359 f. I *DFH.* Toynbee II 345.
154 III: Schreiner 358. Askeberg 172. V: Bull 273 *St.*

364

155 II: la Cour 30 *D.K.*
156 II: Arup I 101, 102. III: Wadstein 49 *N.* V: Collingwood 64.
157 I:–V: du Chaillu I Preface VII-VIII.
158 V: Williams IX. VI: Kendrick 12. Brøndsted 299 *V.* Belloc 13. Churchill I 74 *E.N.*
159 II: Trevelyan 73. III: Trevelyan 39, 69, 70. IV: Kendrick 21. Jørgensen 269 *R.* V: Steenstrup IV 206-217 *N.* Mawer 137 *Vik.* Trevelyan 82. Worsaae 208-212 *M.* VI: Trevelyan 82, 69.
160 II: Kendrick 15. Williams 215. III: Kossinna 90 *Wik.* Green 7 *H.E.* Trevelyan 72-77. IV: Trevelyan 39. IV: Collingwood 95.
161 III: Collingwood 95. IV: Trevelyan 39. V: Askeberg 34. VI: Trevelyan 70.
162 I: Th. Hodgkin 262. II: Green 98-100 *C.* Trevelyan 77. Vogel 43, 44 *N.* Stefánsson 288 *W.* Collingwood 104. IV: Gosse 9. Chambers 87 *W.* V: Kendric 18. VI: Keary 143-159.
163 I: R. H. Hodgkin 535. II: Collingwood 21. III: du Chaillu 3.
164 I: Larson 286. Askeberg 8. II: du Chaillu 3. III: R. H. Hodgkin 482. Askeberg 1. V: Collingwood 63, 64, 52, 53.
165 I: Trevelyan 81.
166 I: Shetelig 104 *Vik.* II: St. George Gray 218-224. III: Ramsay I 229. Kossinna 85-86 *Wik.* Shetelig 114 *Vik.* Askeberg 1.
167 IV: Grønbech I 7 *F.*
168 III: Larson 183. IV: Trevelyan 50. V: Mawer 94 *Vik.* Williams 18. Stefánsson 288 *W.*
169 II: Trevelyan 50. III: Ljungberg 11. IV: Steenstrup I 251 *DRH.* V: Ljungberg 141.
170 I: Ljungberg 146, 132. II: Ax. Olrik 59-61 *NN.* IV: Williams 17. V: Gosse 11-15. Grønbech I 115 *F.*
172 I: M. Larsen 26.
173 I: Keary 145, 147. III: Grønbech II 39 *F.* Steenstrup I 371 *N.* Mac Dougall 271. Hericourt 75 f. Arup I 90, 306. IV: Zinsser 153.
174 I: Gosse 6-17. III: Askeberg 38. IV: de Vries 116 *OR.*
175 I: Williams 333. Grönbech 25 *RN.* Ljungberg 255. Philpotts 12. Leach 16. II: Philpotts 12-14. III: Jespersen § 249. Schütte 273 *FGN.*
176 IV: St. Luke 22, 36. Olrik 81 *E.*
177 IV: C. N. Starcke 358 *L.*
178 I: Grønbech 16 *RN.* II: Trevelyan 51. IV: Ljungberg 210. V: Grønbech 15 *RN.* VI: Strasser 163.
179 II: Grønbech 28 *RN.* Jolliffe 43 *C.* III: Grønbech I 116 *F.* IV: Grønbech 17 *RN.*
180 IV: C. N. Starcke 118, 278 *F.* V: Olrik 16 *N.A.* Grønbech 37, 50 *RN.* VI: Grønbech 61 *RN.*
181 II: Grønbech 61 *RN.* III: Stefánsson 289 *W.* IV Grønbech I 10 *F.*
182 IV: Penka 170. V: Collingwood 61. Mawer 1, 2*Vik.* Jankuhn 16 *H.* Vogel 258 *H.*

183 II: Askeberg 114 f. Mawer 96 *Vik.* Paulsen 13.
184 V: Grønbech I 129 *F.*
185 II: Chadwick 313. Vogel 29-31 *N.* Steenstrup I 249 *N.* C. N. Starcke 107 *F.* R. H. Hodgkin 493-503. Green 63 *C.* III: Collingwood 57. Arbman 74 *V.* Oman 405 *E.*
186 II: Shetelig 10, 14, 109 *Vik.* Larson 3, 158. III: Shetelig 393 *J.* Steenstrup 224 *DRH.* Mawer 40 *Vik.*
187 III: Mawer 8 *Vik.* S. Larsen 39. Collingwood 58. IV: Freeman I 12. V: Baker 92.
188 III: de Vries 244 f. *RL.* Ramsay I 240. Mawer 88 *RL.*
189 I: Baker 109. III: Baker 108. IV: Baker 114. V: Vogel 409-412 *N.* de Vries 249 *RL.*
192 I: Vogel 294-297 *N.* III: Koht: 44. Shetelig etc. 18 *O.Sp.* V: Shetelig etc. 21 *O.Sp.*
193 II: Shetelig etc. 19 *O.Sp.* Shetelig 110 *Vik.* Steenstrup I 372 *DRH.* Vogel 261 *N.* Shetelig 123 *Vik.* Vogel 264 *N.* IV: R. H. Hodgkin I 520. Steenstrup I 373 *DFH.* Vogel 171-178 *N.*
194 III: Shetelig 134-139 *Vik.* Arbman & Stenberger 179-182. Noach 160. Scheel 143 *Wik.* Stefánsson 31-46 *Sp.*
195 I: Bjørkman 557. Arbman & Stenberger 90. IV: Trevelyan 71 V: Green 48 *HE.* Shetelig 194 *NF.* Bjørkman 564.
196 II: Collingwood 84. III: Collingwood 84.
197 I: Green I 97 *C.* II: Ramsay I 241, 242. Smith 180. Scheel 167 *Wik.* III: Mawer 58 *Vik.* Collingwood 81, 95. IV: Collingwood 86. Smith 181. Mawer 82 *RL.* Stenton 244-248 *ASE.*
198 I: Stenton 41 *D.* II: Mawer 25 *Vik.* Brooke 34. Arbman & Stenberger 64, 67, 80. Stenton 3 *D.* Shetelig I 195 *NF.* III: de Vries 263 f. *RL.* Oman 3-5 *Y.* V: Jespersen 76.
199 I: Shetelig 95 *Vik.* Bjørkman 569. Keary 353. Steenstrup I 412 *DRH.* Stenton 5, 9 *D.* II: Mawer 118 *Vik.* III: Bjørkman 566. IV: Stenton CXIV-CXVII *DD.* Stenton 29-33 *D.* Stenton 513 *ASE.*
200 I: Chadwick 64. Mawer 130, 131 *Vik.* Jespersen 16, 76-80. II: Mawer 139 *Vik.* III: Storm 84. Mawer 23 *Vik.* V: Askeberg 17 f. Arbman & Stenberger 94. Strasser 154, 155.
201 II: Trevelyan 81. III: Larson 281. IV: Mawer 136, 137 *Vik.*
202 I: Schütte 119 *HH.* II: Steenstrup I 812 *DRH.* Arup I 83. Jørgensen 15. III: Grønbech II 191 *F.* Grønbech I 10 *F.* V: Grønbech I: 33 *F.* Gosse 15.
203 I: Haff I 89-101. Bjørkman 568. Jørgensen 233-236 *R.* la Cour 419 *Sch.* Stenton 497 *ASE.* II: Vinogradoff 131 *M.*
204 II: Stenton 5 *D.* Vinogradoff 132 *M.* III: Worsaae 41, 206 *M.* Bugge II 245 *Vik.* Stenton 532 *ASE.* IV: Worsaae 207, 215 *M.* V: Trevelyan 81, 90. Rogers 256. Mawer 113 *Vik.* Vinogradoff 203 *M.* Bugge II 321 *Vik.* Stenton 499-505 *ASE.*
205 II: Vinogradoff 24, 25, 203 *M.* Jørgensen 198, 200. Bugge I 33 *Vik.* IV:

Lieberman 2, II, 466. Worsaae 212 *M*. Steenstrup IV 206-217 *N*. Steenstrup I 436 *DFH*. Trevelyan 82. Noach 255.

206 I: Stenton 503, 504, 643 *ASE*. Pollard 244. II: Stenton 34 *D*. III: Noach 255. IV: Mawer 143 *Vik*.

207 II: Ker 345, 346. III: Mawer 144 *Vik*. Philpotts 219.

208 III: V. Gudmundsson 154-160.

209 I: Mawer 145 *Vik*. II: Green 72 *HE*. III: Pollard 38. V: Churchill 20 *KU*.

210 II: Stenton CXXXVII *DD*. III: Stenton 5, 6, 10 *D*. Stenton 79 *P*. Aakjær 19-23 *ODT*. Stenton 517 *ASE*. IV: Stenton 487 *ASE*. Stenton CXXXI *D.D*. Stenton 14-17 *D*. Stenton 75, 84 *P*. Williams 47. Arbman & Stenberger 98, 99.

211 II: Arbman & Stenberger 99, 100. Lieberman II 655. Stenton 17 *D*. III: Jørgensen 236 *R*. Stenton 75, 80 *P*.

212 I: Pollard 38. II: Stenton 18 *D*. IV: Stenton 20 *D*. V: Trevelyan 81. Green 144 *C*. Kendrick 249. Stenton 3, 45 *D*. Collingwood 179. Stenton 27, 26, 40 *D*.

213 III: Vinogradoff 200, 266. H. Larsen 219. Aakjær 76 *VJ*. IV: Aakjær 222 *MV*. Hatt 148, 149. V: Stenton 39 *D*. VI: Vinogradoff 266 *M*. VII: Grønbech III 85 *F*.

214 II: Trevelyan 65. Nordenstreng 193. IV: Jørgensen 226 *R*.

215 I: Worsaae 221 *M*. II: Arbman & Stenberger 98. Vogel 271 *H*. III: Trevelyan 74, 54, 75, 80. Shetelig 386 *J*. IV: Larson 21.

216 II: Arbman & Stenberger 85. Stenton 36, 37, 41 *D*. III: Churchill 20 *KU*. VI: R. H. Hodgkin 693.

217 II: Mawer 141 *Vik*. III: Green 58 *C*.

218 III: A. Fabricius 143-161. Worsaae 176-177 *EN*. Worsaae 226 *M*. Trevelyan 102. IV: Mac Dougall 272, 273.

219 II: Steenstrup I 299 *N*. Steenstrup 75 *NH*. Worsaae 222 *M*. Mawer 140 *Vik*. Trevelyan 103-105. Arbman & Stenberger 169.

220 II: Steenstrup I 301 *DRH*. Worsaae 406 *EN*. III: Steenstrup I 305 *DRH*. Arbmann & Stenberger 177. IV: Arbman & Stenberger 169.

221 II: Trevelyan 104. III: Mawer 141 *Vik*. Worsaae 405 *EN*. Estancelin 67-83. IV: Depping 368. V: Mawer 141 *Vik*. Strasser 164. Steenstrup 35 *NH*. Th. Hodgkin 368 VI: Green 72 *HE*. VII: Trevelyan 102. VIII: Kossinna 88 *Wik*. Green 74 *HE*.

222 II: Bugge 335 *N*. Prentout 128. Steenstrup 279 *NH*. III: Walberg 498. Steenstrup 281 *NH*. Shetelig etc. 27 *O.Sp*. Prentout 141. Steenstrup 282, 283, 37 *NH*.

224 VI: Steenstrup 110 *NH*.

225 I: Worsaae 94 *M*. II: Shetelig 130 *Vik*. Noach 248. III: Steenstrup 389 *DFH*. IV: Steenstrup 122-126 *NH*. Shetelig 130-132 *Vik*. A. Fabricius 25. Noach 216. Mawer 139 *Vik*.

226 III: Walberg 497.

227 I: A. Bugge 339 *N*. Steenstrup 38 *NH*. Vogel 262, 384-402 *N*. II: Steen-

strup I 162 *N*. III: Walberg 498. Prentout 132. IV: Jacobsen 52 *Sv*. Walberg 500.

228   II: Walberg 491. III: Steenstrup 255-264 *NH*. IV: Worsaae 226 *M*.

229   I: Steenstrup 263 *NH*. Walberg 501. II: Worsaae 18 *EN*. IV: A. Fabricius 242. V: A. Fabricius 232. VI: A. Fabricius 32.

230   II: Kendrick 10. Vogel 20-24 *N*. Scheel 181 *Wik*. III: Green 72 *HE*. Trevelyan 101. IV: Green I 58 *C*.

231   I: Green 81 *HE*. II: Pollard 30. IV: Kendrick 100. VI: Steenstrup I 274 *DRH*. la Cour I 245 *SJ*. Paulsen 35. Lindqvist 64. Koht. 44. Strasser 70.

232   II: Thomsen 334, 343 *RRG*. Bolin 96-102. Oxenstierna 198 *W*. C. Weibull 70 *SDH*. Arup I 118. Ramskou 53. H.

234   III: Knorr 77. Kossinna 98 *Wik*. IV: Wadstein 70 *N*. la Cour I 458 *Sch*. Wessén 11. la Cour I 264 *SJ*. Jacobsen 45 *Sv*.

235   I: Jacobsen 57, 25 *Sv*. II: Steenstrup II 389 *N*. Jacobsen 52 *Sv*.

236   II: Jankuhn 20 *H*. Kendrick 106. Vogel 262 *H*. Askeberg 172. Bull 270 *St*. Erslev 7, 40 *TD*. III: Jacobsen 53 *Sv*. IV: Jacobsen 37 *Sv*. S. Larsen 53, 57. Lukman 164. Mawer 43-48 *NH*. Steenstrup II 93-103, 389-391 *N*. Arbman & Stenberger 81. Shetelig 95-103 *Vik*.

237   II: Jacobsen 81 *Sv*. Oman 1 *Y*. IV: Oman 5-10 *Y*.

238   II: Oman 13 *Y*. Brooke 34.

239   I: Erslev 6, 7 *TD*. II: Rason 285-301. Belloc 285. Green XXXIV *HE*. III: Oman 13 *Y*. Stenton 335 *ASE*. IV: Rason 292, 294. Erslev 10 *TD*.

240   II: Stenton 403 *ASE*. Steenstrup 387 *DFH*. Erslev 26-29 *TD*. V: Steenstrup III 67 *N*. Shetelig 101, 103 *Vik*. Noach 200. Worsaae 81-94 *M*.

241   I: Oman 10 *Y*. Rason 293. Brooke 35. Stenton 317, 318 *ASE*. II: Shetelig 101, 103 *Vik*. Stenton 356 *ASE*. III: Stenton 329 *ASE*. IV: Askeberg 18. Brøndsted 225 *EEO*. Paulsen 36, 75. Jacobsen & Moltke 72, 78, 779 *Ru*.

242   III: Jacobsen 82 *Sv*. Erslev 41 *TD*. Larson 4. IV: Brix 110. Brøndsted III 318-320 *DO*. Erslev 34 *TD*.

243   I: Mawer 70 *Vik*. II: L. Weibull 15 *KU*. IV: L. Weibull 12-15 *KU*. V: Arup I 123-125. Kn. Fabricius 9. S. Larsen 77, 78.

244   III: Schreiner 366. IV: Koht 46, 82. Noach 254. la Cour 77-87 *H.St*. Schreiner 369.

246   IV: Steenstrup I 328 *DRH*. L. Weibull 28-44 *KU*. la Cour 83-87 *H.St*.

247   I: L. Weibull 44 *KU*. II: Larson 30. L. Weibull 78-88 *KU*. Moberg 129 f. Noach 306. Jacobsen & Moltke 348-349 *Ru*.

248   IV: la Cour I 458 *Sch*. Schuckhardt 74 f. S. Larsen 75-78. V: Steenstrup I 322 *DRH*.

249   II: Steenstrup 9, 61 *VD*. III: Larson 153. Kendrick 181. IV: Kossinna 97, 101 *Wik*. Mawer 72 *Vik*. Steenstrup I 326 *DRH*. Steenstrup I 423 *DFH*. S. Larsen 14. Vogel 20 *N*.

250   II: L. Weibull 32 *KU*. la Cour 70 *H.St*. III: Jankuhn 19 *H*. la Cour I 279 *SJ*. C. Weibull 347 *SDR*. C. Weibull 4 *Gr*. Stenton 239 *ASE*.

252   IV: Arup I 123.

253 II: L. Weibull 37–43 *KU*. la Cour 86 *H.St*. Kendrick 102, 137. III: Steenstrup 59 *DS*. S. Larsen 78 f. IV: la Cour 65 *H.St*. Brøndal 32.
254 III: V. Gudmundsson 35. IV: Aakjær 156 *BB*. V: Hatt 145. VI: Vogel 261 *H*. Paulsen 13.
255 I: Steenstrup I 397 *DFH*. II: Arup I 124.
256 II: Lundbye 208. Arup I 124. III: S. Larsen 91. IV: H. Olrik I 23. V: Koht 80. VII: L. Weibull 45-49 *KU*.
257 II: Larson 40. IV: Stenton 379 *ASE*. V: Larson 15. VI: Freeman I 400.
258 I: H. Olrik I 108. II: Freeman I 392. la Cour I 279 *SJ*. Noach 280. IV: Steenstrup I 365 *DRH*. L. Weibull 58 *KU*. Steenstrup I 251 f. *N*. H. Olrik I 113. V: L. Weibull 93-97 *KU*. Steenstrup I 370 *DRH*. Jankuhn 22 *H*. la Cour 75 *H.St*.
260 II: Noach 283. L. Weibull 108 *KU*. Toll 216 *SS*. III: L. Weibull 110 *KU*. Toll 219-224 *SS*. Beckman 155.
261 V: Noach 301, 304. Shetelig I 381 *NF*. Larson 33. Shetelig 143 *Vik*.
262 I: Steenstrup I 407, 417 *DFH*. L. Weibull 111-122 *KU*. Arup I 133. S. Larsen 101.
263 II: Noach 303. Larson 38, 35. L. Weibull 141 *KU*. IV: Trevelyan 95. V: Green I 144 *C*. Green 59, 60 *HE*. Green II 65 *C*.
264 II: Whitelock 108, 110. III: Green 61 *HE*. Pollard 19-23. Stenton 463 *ASE*. Larson 84. IV: Arup I 128.
266 I: Freeman I 279, 331. II: Ramsay I 353. Larson 39. Green 62 *HE*. Freeman I 345. III: Larson 40. Shetelig 146 *Vik*. Scheel 303 *Wik*. IV: Kendrick 258, 262. Arup II 102.
267 II: Steenstrup I 377 *DRH*. III: Larson 42. IV: Larson 47.
268 II: Larson 49-53. III: Kendrick 266. L. Weibull 153-155 *KU*.
269 II: Freeman I 391, 417. III: Steenstrup I 381 *DRH*. Larson 54. IV: Kendrick 100. Steenstrup I 381 *DRH*.
270 I: Larson 55. II: Larson 56, 57. L. Weibull 155 *KU*. H. Olrik I 108. IV: Green 64 *HE*. VI: Bolin II 125, 128. Larson 55. H. Olrik 108, 109.
271 II: H. Larsen 219. Aakjær 76 *VJ*. Jørgensen 252 *R*.
272 I: Brøndsted 164, 166 *V*. Nørlund 149 *Tr*. II: Aakjær 209-245 *VJ*. Steenstrup I 407 *DFH*. Jacobsen & Moltke 384 *Ru*. IV: Larson 329. VI: Freeman I 504. Larson 259.
273 I: Trevelyan 98. Larson VIII. III: Larson 61. IV: Larson 64, 327.
274 IV: Steenstrup I 383 *DRH*. Larson 66 f. VI: Larson 72.
275 III: Rason 294.
276 II: Th. Hodgkin 400. Jørgensen 261 *R*. III: Freeman I 439. Larson 100. IV: Kendrick 270. V: Larson 102.
277 I: Green II 130 *C*. Freeman I 431. Larson 93, 102. Freeman I 391. II: Kendrick 118.
278 II: Larson 107. III: Trevelyan 113. IV: Larson 115-124. V: Larson 126-128.
279 II: Larson 30. Jørgensen 56-60 *R*. Trevelyan 99. III: Trevelyan 100. Freeman I 491. Green I 143 *C*. Lieberman 2, II, 500.
280 II: Larson 142. Lieberman 1, I, 273. IV: Larson 148. Freeman I 441.

281 I: Steenstrup III 410 N. II: Ramsay I 406. III: Freeman I 478. IV: Th. Hodgkin 416. V: Larson 252.
282 I: Steenstrup I 195-199 N. II. Steenstrup I 322-328 N. Brøndsted III 332 DO. Green II 68 C. Larson 157-160, 258.
283 I: Larson 162-179.
284 II: Larson 312. IV: Gjessing 135. Larson 235.
285 I: Steenstrup I 393 DRH. II: Worsaae 322-323 EN.
286 II: Arup I 133. la Cour I 495 Sch. Larson 216, 218. Worsaae 324 EN. V: Steenstrup III 327, 331 N. VI: Stille 20-22. L. Weibull 25, 77 KU.
287 II: Bolin I 134, 135. Bolin II 121, 122.
288 I: Larson 212, 223, 327. Steenstrup III 349, 350 N. Stenton 396-398 ASE. III: Larson 230. IV: Steenstrup I 425 DFH. Green II 148 C. Green 66 HE. Liebermann 1, I, 277.
289 II: Liebermann III 186. III: Th. Hodgkin 409. Larson 232-234. V: Steenstrup I 425 DFH. VI: Larson 237, 240.
290 I: Arup I 145. II: Freeman I 530, 504. III: Freeman I 504. IV: Larson 282, 328.
291 II: Larson 257.
292 II: Stenton 403 ASE. III: Larson 272.
293 I: Olrik & Ellekilde 159 NG. II: Larson 278, 279. Stenton 404 ASE. III: Th. Hodgkin 424. IV: Collingwood 161. Larson 281. Grønbech I 106 F. Freeman 479-481.
294 I: Larson 278. II: Trevelyan 98. III: Green II 143 C. Larson 282, 327. Stenton CXXXI DD. Stenton 14-17 D. IV: Trevelyan 96. Ramsay I 416. Vogel 274 H. Stenton 406 ASE. V: Green 114, 142, 143 C. Liebermann 2, II, 500.
295 VI: Shetelig I 230 NF.
296 IV: Oman 600 E.
297 I: Green 64 HE.
298 II: Stenton 393 ASE. Larson 329, 136. III: Collingwood 159. IV: Trevelyan XXI. Larson 260. VI: Weinbaum 349. VII: Freeman I 538. Liebermann 2, II, 344.
299 I: Trevelyan 98. II: Freeman I 560. III: Green II 148 C. IV: Green II 161 C. Green 66 HE. Vogel 259 H. V: Brøgger 145 NF.
300 II: Shetelig I 102 NF. III: Green II 182 C. IV: Oman 601 E. VI: Worsaae 414 EN. Stenton 533 ASE. Green 66 HE.
301 II: Olrik 73 N.Aa.
302 II: Williams 215.
303 II: Kendrick 270. III: Freeman I 532. IV: Freeman I 489.
304 I: Green 66 HE. III: Trevelyan 100. IV: Trevelyan 101. V: Trevelyan 100.
306 I: Trevelyan (Toyne. Foreword).
310 IV: Erslev 260 V.
311 II: Arup I 230. IV: Arup I 217. V: Jørgensen 195, 234 R.
313 III: Hatt 148, 149. H. Larsen 219. Jørgensen 252 f. R. Stenton 39 D. Nørlund 90.

370

314   II: Aakjær 27, 28 *GG*. Aakjær 74, 87 *VJ*. Aakjær 230 *MV*. Aakjær 139 *BB*.
      Erslev 21, 29, 30, 147, 268 *V*. III: Nørlund 88 f.
315   I: Erslev 33 *V*. III: Leach 292.
316   I: Arup I 272, 291. II: Green II 114, 143 *C*. III: Shetelig I 230 *NF*. V:
      Erslev 233 *V*. VI: Kn. Fabricius 7. Arup I 260, 285, 295.
318   II: Kolding 118, 236. Erslev 112 *V*. IV: Aakjær 30 *GG*. V: Arup I 246, 320.
      VI: Arup II 125, 226, 402.
319   II: Arup II 544. IV: Jørgensen 308 *R*. V. Starcke 15 *HS*. V. Starcke 9-36
      L. Fridericia IV 480.
320   V: Steenstrup I 279 *DRH*. Paulsen 12. Jørgensen 540 *R*.
321   II: Erslev 238-241 *V*.
322   I: Arup I 228, 280.
323   II: Bjørner 100 (Starcke etc. *L*.). III: V. Starcke 9 f. *L*.
324   V: Arup II 184.
326   III: Arup II 182. IV: Holmberg (5, XII, 1941). Arup II 204.
327   I: Bøggild-Andersen 91 *NV*. II: Arup II 184, 186. IV: Grønbech 81 f.
      NMS. M. Larsen I 70 f.
329   IV: Trevelyan XIX-XXI.
330   II: Rogers 247-268, 273, 326, 327. Hansson 5-12. Trevelyan 231, 240. III:
      Trevelyan 231, 240. III: Trevelyan 239.
331   I: Sofus Larsen 88 f. *NO*.
332   II: Mac Dougall 274-276. III: Trevelyan 121, 240, 411. Worsaae 227, 228 *M*.
333   I: Trevelyan 437-443. Green 787 *HE*.
338   III: Trevelyan 655.

INDEX

374

375

379